Praise for
Learning iOS Game

"An excellent introduction into the world of game development explaining every aspect of game design and implementation for the iPad, iPhone, and iPod touch devices. A great way for anyone interested in writing games to get started."
—Tom Bradley, Software Architect, Designer of TBXML

"A great developer and a great game. That's everything you can find in this book to learn how to write an awesome game for iPhone. Maybe you're the next AppStore hit!"
—Sebastien Cardoso

"With *Learning iOS Game Programming*, you'll be writing your own games in no time. The code included is well explained and will save you hours of looking up obscure stuff in the documentation and online forums."
—Pablo Gomez Basanta, Founder, Shifting Mind

"I always thought that to teach others one has to be an expert and a person with an established reputation in the field. Michael Daley proved me wrong. He is teaching others while studying himself. Michael's passion in teaching and studying, ease of solutions to problems, and a complete game as a resulting project makes this book one of the best I have ever read."

—Eugene Snyetilov

"If you're interested in 2D game programming with the iOS using OpenGL and OpenAL directly, this book walks you through creating a complete and fun game without getting bogged down in technical details."
—Scott D. Yelich

"Michael Daley brings clarity to the haze of iPhone application development. Concrete examples, thorough explanation, and timesaving tips make this book a must have for the up and coming iPhone game developer."
—Brandon Middleton, Creator of *Tic Tac Toe Ten*

"This is the A-Z guide to iOS game development; Michael's book takes you from the basics and terminology to using the techniques in practice on a fully working game. Before you know it, you will find yourself writing your own game, fueled by a firm grasp of the principles and techniques learned within. I could not ask for a better reference in developing our own games."

—Rod Strougo, Founder Prop Group

Learning iOS Game Programming

Learning iOS
Game
Programming

Michael Daley

✦✦Addison-Wesley

Upper Saddle River, NJ • Boston • Indianapolis • San Francisco
New York • Toronto • Montreal • London • Munich • Paris • Madrid
Cape Town • Sydney • Tokyo • Singapore • Mexico City

The publisher offers excellent discounts on this book when ordered in quantity for bulk purchases or special sales, which may include electronic versions and/or custom covers and content particular to your business, training goals, marketing focus, and branding interests. For more information, please contact:

U.S. Corporate and Government Sales
(800) 382-3419
corpsales@pearsontechgroup.com

For sales outside the United States, please contact:

International Sales
international@pearson.com

Visit us on the Web: informit.com/aw

Library of Congress cataloging-in-publication data is on file.

ISBN-13: 978-0-321-69942-8
ISBN-10: 0-321-69942-4
Text printed in the United States on recycled paper at R.R. Donnelley in Crawfordsville, Indiana.
First printing September 2010

Senior Acquisitions Editor
Chuck Toporek

Senior Development Editor
Chris Zahn

Managing Editor
Kristy Hart

Project Editors
Barbara Campbell and Jovana San Nicolas-Shirley

Copy Editor
Water Crest Publishing

Indexer
Lisa Stumpf

Proofreader
Sheri Cain

Publishing Coordinator
Romny French

Cover Designer
Chuti Prasertsith

❖

Dedicated to my mum, Jen

❖

Contents at a Glance

Table of Contents

Acknowledgments

Writing this book has been an amazing journey, and it's only through the efforts of many other people that you are reading this today. Without these people, I don't believe the book would have even been published, let alone become the valuable resource I believe it to be. For this reason, I would like to acknowledge those people who have supported me on this journey:

- First of all, I'd like to thank my editor at Addison-Wesley, Chuck Toporek, and his faithful sidekick/editorial assistant, Romny French. Chuck stumbled upon the video tutorials on my blog and encouraged me to write this book based on what he saw there. Along the way, Romny helped keep things moving, chased/supported me in getting my tax information in place so I could get paid, and helped us deliver the book to production. Without their support, guidance, and encouragement, I would never have been able to make the leap from game development blogger to author.

- John Bloomfield is a professional web designer and is responsible for the design and administration of the 71Squared.com blog. Without his great work on the blog, Chuck would never have seen my tutorials, and the opportunity to write this book may never have arisen. John is also my oldest and closest friend, and even though he is now living on the other side of the world in Australia, it didn't stop him from supporting and contributing to this project.

- Tom Bradley, a good friend, talented developer, and creator of TBXML,[1] spent many hours working with me, even into the early hours of the morning, helping me track down bugs and improve performance. Tom's support helped me through some sticky moments in the development of *Sir Lamorak's Quest* and was instrumental in getting the game finished on time.

- Ryan Sumo is a freelance video game artist residing in Manila, The Philippines. He created all the artwork used in *Sir Lamorak's Quest* that gives the game its retro look. He is a true professional and a pleasure to work with. His rapid delivery of art and great feedback and suggestions really helped give the game its great look. If you ever run into Ryan in Manila and show him a copy of this book, he is sure to buy you a drink. Examples of Ryan's work can be found at **ryansumo.carbonmade.com**.

- Vince Webb is an award-winning composer currently enrolled on an undergraduate music course in London and is the creator of the music and sound effects used in *Sir Lamorak's Quest*. His ability to create an atmosphere with his music really took *Sir Lamorak's Quest* to a new level. Vince is currently working on a number of

---

[1] TBXML: www.tbxml.co.uk

projects, and more information about him and his work can be found at www.vincewebb.com. Vince is a real talent, and I'm pleased to have had the opportunity to work with him.

- Games such as *Sir Lamorak's Quest* need a lot of testing, and through my **71Squared.co.uk** blog, I was able to get help from a great team of beta testers. These testers were all followers of the iPhone game development tutorials on the blog and provided fantastic feedback and suggestions. This feedback really helped polish the final product. Details of all those involved can be found in the credits in *Sir Lamorak's Quest: The Spell of Release* game.

- Saving the best for last, I want to thank my family. Developing *Sir Lamorak's Quest* and writing this book have taken a considerable amount of time. Throughout this period, my wife, Alison, and fantastic children, Caragh, Alex, and Matthew, have had to deal with me being locked away for hours and days at a time. Without their patience, love, and support, I would still be hunting for the game-development book of my dreams.

I certainly hope that you find this book to be the useful resource I believe it is, and I would appreciate any suggestions or feedback you have.

—Michael Daley
mike@71squared.com

About the Author

By day, **Michael Daley** works for the largest enterprise software company in the world supporting large corporate customers in communications. By night, Michael has taken on the task of learning how to build games for the iPhone. Michael started writing adventure games in BASIC on a Sinclair Spectrum 48k and progressed onto the Commodore 64 and the Amiga A500. Never having lost a passion for game programming, Michael got inspired to learn Objective-C when the iPhone came out, and he set out to learn how to build games for the iPhone.

Having written many games for his children over the years, the launch of the iPhone inspired him to create games for the platform that would be available to more than his children. Michael has a passion for learning new technologies and how to apply them. He's a true Apple fan, spending far too much time and money on the latest Apple equipment.

We Want to Hear from You!

As the reader of this book, you are our most important critic and commentator. We value your opinion and want to know what we're doing right, what we could do better, what areas you'd like to see us publish in, and any other words of wisdom you're willing to pass our way.

You can email or write me directly to let me know what you did or didn't like about this book—as well as what we can do to make our books stronger.

Please note that I cannot help you with technical problems related to the topic of this book, and that due to the high volume of mail I receive, I might not be able to reply to every message.

When you write, please be sure to include this book's title and author as well as your name and phone or email address. I will carefully review your comments and share them with the author and editors who worked on the book.

Email: chuck.toporek@pearson.com

Mail: Chuck Toporek
Senior Acquisitions Editor, Addison-Wesley
Pearson Education, Inc.
75 Arlington St., Ste. 300
Boston, MA 02116 USA

Reader Services

Visit our website and register this book at www.samspublishing.com/register for convenient access to any updates, downloads, or errata that might be available for this book.

Preface

Writing a game can be a daunting task. Even if you're an experienced programmer, the design patterns, terminology, and thought processes can seem strange and unusual. Having spent most of my working life creating business applications, writing games has been a hobby that has seen me create many games my children have played and enjoyed over the years. With the release of the iPhone and iPod touch, it was time to unleash one of my creations on the world.

My first task was to find a good book on developing games on the iPhone. After a lot of research, I decided that the book I wanted just didn't exist, and having had great feedback on a number of online tutorials I had created, I decided to write my own book. This was a perfect opportunity for me to create the game programming book I've always wanted myself.

Over the years, I've read many game development books and have been left wanting. Although they provide information on the individual components required to make a game and include small examples, they never go all the way to creating a complete game good enough to publish. I've always believed that a good book should both tell the reader what is required to make a game but also demonstrate how those components can be implemented inside a complete game project.

So, this book not only describes the components and technology needed to create a game on the iPhone, but it does so through the creation of a complete game: *Sir Lamorak's Quest: The Spell of Release*. This game is currently available for free download from the App Store, and is the game you learn how to build as you work your way through this book.

Download the Game!
You can download *Sir Lamorak's Quest* from the App Store: **http://itunes.apple.com/us/app/sir-lamoraks-quest-the-spell/id368507448?mt=8**. The game is freely available, so go ahead and download the game, start playing around with it, and help Sir Lamorak escape from the castle!

This book describes the key components needed to create this 2D game. It covers both the technology, such as OpenGL ES and OpenAL, as well as the key game engine components required, including sprite sheets, animation, touch input, and sound.

Each chapter describes in detail a specific component within the game, along with the technology required to support it, be it a tile map editor, or some effect we're trying to create with OpenGL ES. Once an introduction to the functionality and technology is complete, the chapter then provides details on how the component has been implemented within *Sir Lamorak's Quest*. This combination of theory and real-world implementation helps to fill the void left by other game development books.

About Sir Lamorak's Quest

My game-playing experiences started when I was given a Sinclair Spectrum 48k for Christmas in 1982. I was hooked from that moment, and I have had a close relationship with computers ever since.

While thinking about the game I wanted to develop for this book, my mind kept wandering back to the games I played in the 1980s. They may not have been visually stunning, although at the time I was impressed, but they were fun to play.

I spent some time working on the design of the game, which included not only the features I wanted in the game, but also how it should be implemented on the iPhone. One key aspect of the game is that it should be casual—that is, the concept of the game should be simple and easy to pick up, and players should be able to start and stop the game easily without losing their progress.

I also wanted the controls to be easily recognizable and therefore decided to implement an onscreen joypad to control the main character. It was important, though, to allow the player to swap the position of this joypad so that both left- and right-handed players found the game comfortable.

As for the game play itself, I decided to take a number of design ideas from games I played in the '80s and went with a top-down scroller, in which the player is trapped in a haunted castle and has to find a magic spell so that he can escape.

Organization of This Book

There are 16 chapters in the book, each of which deals with a specific area of creating Sir Lamorak's Quest, as follows:

- *Chapter 1, "Game Design"*—This chapter describes the design considerations I made while designing *Sir Lamorak's Quest*. It provides an insight into the kind of thought process required when sitting down to create a game. It doesn't cover *every* possible design decision needed for all genres of games, but it does cover the important ones.

- *Chapter 2, "The Three Ts: Terminology, Technology, and Tools"*—Even experienced programmers can become confused by the three Ts used within game development. This chapter runs through the common technology, terminology, and tools used to create *Sir Lamorak's Quest* and games in general. This chapter helps you understand the terms and technology covered throughout the book.

- *Chapter 3, "The Journey Begins"*—This is where we start to get our hands on some code and get the iPhone to render something to the screen. This chapter covers the process of creating our first project using the OpenGL ES template project within Xcode. The template is described in detail and sets the scene for the chapters that follow.

- *Chapter 4, "The Game Loop"*—The heartbeat of any game is the game loop. This loop is responsible for making sure that all the core elements of the game, such as AI and rendering, are done at the right time and in the right order. This may sound simple, but there are a number of different approaches to the game loop, and this chapter discusses them and details the approach taken *for Sir Lamorak's Quest.*

- *Chapter 5, "Image Rendering"*—Drawing images to the screen is a fundamental requirement for any game. This chapter provides an overview of OpenGL ES and runs through a number of classes created to simplify the creation and rendering of images to the screen.

- *Chapter 6, "Sprite Sheets"*—Sprite sheets are images that contain a number of smaller images. These sheets can be used to reduce the number of individual images held in memory and the number of different textures OpenGL ES needs to bind to improving performance. They are also commonly used when creating animated sprites. This chapter covers how to create sprite sheets that contain the images used in the game, regardless of whether they have fixed or variable dimensions.

- *Chapter 7, "Animation"*—Having created the means to store the different frames needed in an animation using sprite sheets, this chapter describes how separate images can be played in sequence to provide you with animation, such as the player character running.

- *Chapter 8, "Bitmap Fonts"*—The most common way to interact with your game's user is through the use of text. Being able to render instructions and information (such as the player's score or instructions on how to use the game) is important. This chapter describes how you can use open source tools to take any font and turn it into a bitmap font. Once the bitmap font is created, you'll see how to create a sprite sheet that contains all the images needed to render the characters in that font. It also details the `Bitmap` font class used in *Sir Lamorak's Quest*, which provides a simple API for rendering text to the screen.

- *Chapter 9, "Tile Maps"*—Tile maps allow large game worlds to be created from reusing a small number of tile images. This common approach has been used in the past to create large game worlds (think of the original *Super Mario Brothers* game for Nintendo) when memory is limited, back in the early days of home game systems. This technique is still popular today, and this chapter describes the use of an open source tile-editing tool to create tile maps, along with a class that can render these maps to the screen.

- *Chapter 10, "The Particle Emitter"*—Many games have impressive effects, such as fire, explosions, smoke, and sparks. These are created using a particle system. The particle system is responsible for creating and controlling a number of particles; each has its own properties, such as size, shape, direction, color, and lifespan. During a particle's life cycle, its position, speed, color, and size are changed based on the particle's configuration. This chapter details how to create a particle system that can be used to generate any number of organic effects.

- *Chapter 11, "Sound"*—Giving the player feedback using sound is important in today's modern games. This chapter describes how the media player functionality of the iPhone, along with OpenAL, can be used to play a cool soundtrack in the game, as well as 3D (surround) sound effects.

- *Chapter 12, "User Input"*—This chapter describes how to use the iPhone's unique touch and accelerometer capabilities to control your game. It details how to capture and process multiple touches at the same time and also how data from the accelerometer can be used within your own games.

- *Chapter 13, "The Game Interface"*—In this chapter, we start to look at how the game interface for *Sir Lamorak's Quest* was implemented. This includes how to deal rotation events to make sure that the user interface is always oriented correctly. It also describes how to mix both OpenGL ES and UIKit interface controls.

- *Chapter 14, "Game Objects and Entities"*—As the player runs around the castle in *Sir Lamorak's Quest*, we want him to be able to find objects, pick them up, and fight baddies. This chapter describes how objects and entities have been implemented within *Sir Lamorak's Quest*.

- *Chapter 15, "Collision Detection"*—Having the player and baddies run through walls and doors would really spoil the game, so it's important to be able to register collisions between either the player and the map or objects and entities within the castle. This chapter describes different types of collision detection and how this has been implemented within *Sir Lamorak's Quest*.

- *Chapter 16, "Pulling It All Together"*—At this point, a great deal of ground has been covered. There is, however, a number of things you can do to the game to add polish. This chapter covers how to save the player's game state for when he quits or leaves the game when he has an incoming call. Chapter 16 also covers performance tuning using instruments and tips for getting your game beta tested.

Audience for This Book

This book has been written for people who are already programmers but who have never written computer games before. Although it assumes that you already have some experience with Objective-C, each chapter provides enough information on both Objective-C and other technologies so you can follow the concepts and implementations.

By the time you complete this book, you will have an in-depth understanding of the game engine that was built for *Sir Lamorak's Quest* and the key capabilities and considerations are needed to create a 2D game engine. This enables you to take the same game engine developed in this book and use it in your own games, or simply use the knowledge you have gained about creating games in general and use one of the many game engines available for the iPhone, such as Cocos2D.

Who This Book Is For

If you are already developing applications for the iPhone for other platforms, but want to make a move from utility applications to games, this book is for you. It builds on the development knowledge you already have and leads you into game development by describing the terminology, technology, and tools required, as well as providing real-world implementation examples.

Who This Book Isn't For

If you already have a grasp of the workflow required to create a game or you have a firm game idea that you know requires OpenGL ES for 3D graphics, this is not the book for you.

It is expected that before you read this book, you are already familiar with Objective-C, C, Xcode, and Interface Builder. Although the implementations described in this book have been kept as simple as possible and the use of C is limited, a firm foundation in these languages is required.

The following titles can help provide you with the grounding you need to work through this book:

- *Cocoa Programming for Mac OS X, Third Edition*, by Aaron Hillegass (Addison-Wesley, 2008).
- *Learning Objective-C 2.0*, by Robert Clair (Addison-Wesley, 2011).
- *Programming in Objective-C 2.0*, by Stephen G. Kochan (Addison-Wesley, 2009).
- *Cocoa Design Patterns*, by Erik M. Buck and Donald A. Yacktman (Addison-Wesley, 2009).

- *The iPhone Developer's Cookbook, Second Edition*, by Erica Sadun (Addison-Wesley, 2010).
- *Core Animation: Simplified Animation Techniques for Mac and iPhone Development*, by Marcus Zarra and Matt Long (Addison-Wesley, 2010).
- *iPhone Programming: The Big Nerd Ranch Guide*, by Aaron Hillegass and Joe Conway (Big Nerd Ranch, Inc., 2010).

These books, along with other resources you'll find on the web, will help you learn more about how to program for the Mac and iPhone, giving you a deeper knowledge about the Objective-C language and the Cocoa frameworks.

Download the Source Code

Access to information is not only limited to the book. The complete, fully commented source code to *Sir Lamorak's Quest* is also available for download on InformIT.com.

There is plenty of code to review throughout this book, along with exercises for you to try out, so it is assumed you have access to the Apple developer tools, such as Xcode and the iPhone SDK. Both of these can be downloaded from the Apple iPhone Dev Center.[2]

---

[2] Apple's iPhone DevCenter: developer.apple.com/iphone.

1

Game Design

I love games. That's a fairly simple statement to make, but it really sums me up quite nicely. I've been playing games ever since I got my first computer back in 1982. That Sinclair Spectrum 48k (see Figure 1.1) was something I nagged my parents about for months! And there, among the torn wrapping paper on Christmas morning of 1982, was my first computer. It was black and shiny with little gray rubber keys, and as far as I was concerned, it was a thing of beauty and magic.

Figure 1.1   My original 1982 Sinclair ZX Spectrum.

I had no idea how or why it worked—it just did. As I sat and watched my first game *slowly* load and appear on my portable television and listened to the odd screaming noise coming from the cassette drive, I knew I was at the start of a long relationship with computers.

It wasn't long after getting that Spectrum that I started playing as many games as I could get. I wanted to know how the computer—and the games—actually worked. At the time, there were a number of magazines you could buy that gave you information on how to program in BASIC on the Sinclair. Those magazines, such as *Sinclair User* or *ZX Computing*, contained all the code for the programs, which also meant that you had to very carefully type in that code line by line before you could run the program. I spent many hours trying to get something to work, only to be disappointed.

What seemed like an exercise in futility also proved to be a valuable learning exercise. By typing all that code, I learned how things worked and what necessary building blocks were needed for a game. It also showed me that anyone—including me in my bedroom with a Spectrum—could write computer games without being part of some giant company.

The process of sitting down and working out how to create games on the iPhone has been very much a repeat of those early years. I've worked on plenty of ideas that have not worked and been disappointed, but this has been easily forgotten, as other ideas have proved to be successful. The feeling of achievement when something you have been working on actually does what you expect is fantastic. To this day, I still get the same excited feeling when I see something I've written actually working. I've had the same feeling when writing software at work, but to be honest, it's nothing like the feeling I get when I see something flying around the screen in a game. It's just so much more exciting.

Writing games for the iPhone, I feel like I'm 12 again, minus the complexion problems and homework. I think that many people are realizing that it is possible to create and share their own games. Although the technology has moved on considerably and the mechanism for sharing these games is much easier than reproducing tape cassettes, coming up with the ideas and working on bringing your very own game to life is very much the same.

This chapter covers the key design principles and game elements that I considered when designing and developing the game that we cover in this book, such as the following:

- High-level game design
- Storyline
- Game play components

It's important that we build a solid base from which the game will grow, and this chapter provides you with the information needed to start our journey into creating a game on the iPhone.

The Game That Started It All (For Me)

At the time, I was mostly inspired by Matthew Smith, the 17-year-old who created the hit title *Manic Miner*.[1] *Manic Miner* (see Figure 1.2) was a platform game with 20 levels, and it even had an in-game soundtrack, which was a first back then. Matthew created *Manic Miner* in just six weeks, and although he was obviously talented, it proved that anyone with some imagination and technical ability could create a game.

Figure 1.2   First level of *Manic Miner* on the ZX Spectrum.

Since then, computers have been a huge part of my life, and I've made my career out of them. Not designing best-selling computer games, but within the enterprise. Although this is something I have enjoyed, a big part of me has always wanted to create a game for others to play. I've created plenty of simple prototypes over the years in all sorts of languages (with Java being the latest), but none of them have seen the light of day. Until now.

I was already a huge fan of Apple long before the iPhone was launched, but of course, fell in love with the device as soon as I saw it. When Apple then released the SDK, I immediately downloaded it and started to play, as did thousands of others, and I watched as more and more games started to appear on the App Store.

It felt just like those early days with my Spectrum. It was obvious that people sat in their bedrooms, creating games for the iPhone and using Apple and the App Store as their

---

[1] See en.wikipedia.org/wiki/Manic_Miner to learn more about the game's history or search for "Maniac Miner" on YouTube to watch the game in action.

publisher *and* distributor. It wasn't long before I was hunting the Internet high and low for information that would help me start to develop a game, and that journey has ultimately lead to you reading this book.

So, What's the Big Idea?

Every game starts with a concept—an idea. When I started thinking about the game for this book, I went to the best source I could think of for ideas: my children. I must have sat there for about 30 minutes scribbling down notes as they described the most incredible world to me, how things should interact, what weapons you should have, and most importantly to them, how you die. When you have two boys, it's all about the gory details. I don't think I realized until then just how seriously they take their gaming, and once I explained that I would not be able to create Halo 10, they quickly scaled back their suggestions.

I have to admit that a number of ideas for this game have come from classic Spectrum games I played in the 1980s. I enjoyed them so much, I just could not resist using some of their classic game play within my first public iPhone game.

A Game That Fits *with* the iPhone

One of the big considerations while working on the concept for the game was how people actually use the iPhone. I love playing games on the iPhone, but I don't spend hours and hours playing those games like my boys do on their Xbox. Most people pick up their iPhone, launch a game, and play for a few minutes (often while in meetings), and then put them down again. This also seems to be an ever-increasing theme among games that I've seen on the App Store.

This is an important consideration and can impact the game design in different ways, including the following:

- Players should be able to quit and resume play where they left off (or at the beginning of the level from which they quit).
- The game controls need to be intuitive and easy to master, quickly. If your user is only expected to play in bits and spurts, having an easy-to-use set of controls is key. They also need to be designed specifically for the iPhone. Making use of the accelerometer and multi-touch are mechanisms that should be considered carefully.
- The storyline should not be so complex that time away from the game causes the players to lose the plot and feel lost when they play again.
- There needs to be a clear and easy-to-understand objective to the game. This could be a goal or simply score- or time-based.

These are just a few of the things I considered when designing the game. Given that I wanted the game to be casual, I decided that players would be allowed to carry on from where they left off at the last session. For the controls, the game makes use of an onscreen joypad that will be both familiar to most players and easy for them to use.

> **Note**
> I toyed around with a lot of options for the game controls, and discuss those options and the decision-making process later in Chapter 12, "User Input."

Based on the casual nature of the game (and that there's just no way I could build Halo 10), I ended up with a classic 2D game based in a haunted castle. The castle is inhabited by ghosts and ghouls, and it is a place where only the foolhardy dare to venture. With this in mind, I wrote a storyline to the game to help me build an image of how it was going to look and also give me something to refer back to as I programmed the game.

> **Tip**
> In the past, I've found it easy to wander off track when you get into the thick of the code for a game, so having something you can refer back to will help keep you on track.

The Storyline

You play the role of a young knight, Sir Lamorak, who seeks adventure—as well as fame, fortune, and the attention of the fair maidens in the local village—by proving that there is no such thing as ghosts in the long-abandoned Egremont Castle near the Forest of Ulpha.

As Sir Lamorak arrives at the old moss-covered castle, he starts to feel uneasy—as though a thousand eyes are watching him approach the main entrance. After jumping down from his trusty steed, Buttercup, his horse turns, snorts, and bolts back to town, leaving our brave Sir Lamorak all alone. With nothing but the wind pushing against him, Sir Lamorak is blown (or sucked, maybe) into the large wooden castle doors as they open with a loud creak, as the rusty hinges give way to years of neglect.

Slowly, Sir Lamorak moves forward into the main entrance of the castle and peers into the darkness before him. He sees nothing, but can hear the wind moaning through the castle and the dripping of water in the distance. Suddenly, a large gust of wind rips through the hallway with a howl, the main doors behind him slam shut, and Sir Lamorak jumps forward in panic. He turns and runs to the door, grabbing and pulling on the handles, but it will not open. He is trapped.

Standing in the darkness, wondering why on earth he decided to visit this place, Sir Lamorak hears an evil voice through the darkness:

"Only those who can cast the Spell of Release can leave this place, else, you are trapped here with us forever...mwahahahahaha!"

Shaking with fear, Sir Lamorak is now standing in a dark castle and has absolutely no idea what the Spell of Release is, where it can be found, or who the evil voice belonged to. One thing, however, is certain...he is not alone.

What's in a Name?

I love creepy stories, and this storyline sets us up nicely for the rest of the design. At this point, I also wanted to give the game a name. I can then refer to the game using this name going forward, and it helps build the game's identity.

You would not think that naming your game could cause problems, but you need to be aware of a couple of important issues when it comes to deploying your game to the App Store. At the time of writing, there are over 150,000 apps in the App Store. That's a lot of apps and a lot of names that have already been used up, and that is the tip. Before you spend time, and maybe money, on artwork for the game using its name, you need to make sure that no one else has used that name on the App Store. There is nothing more annoying than having everything done, only to find that someone else has used your cool name before you.

You also want to make sure you are not using a name that is copyrighted in some way, as it would also be a real pain to be asked to take down your game because of copyright issues. This goes for all content in your game, really. You are asked during the process of loading your app onto the App Store whether all the content is yours so as to make sure you are not infringing any copyrights. It's worth checking.

As for the name, all you can do is keep checking the App Store for the name you want to use and hope that someone else does not use it before you. For example, it is easier if you don't name your game something beginning with "i," as there are thousands of those being used.

You are also limited to the number of characters that are shown under app icons on the Springboard screen of the iPhone: It's around ten. For this reason, you either need a small catchy name or to use the initials of your full game name. If you use more than the max number of characters, the name will be shortened to fit under the icon.

The full name I'm using for this game is *Sir Lamorak's Quest: The Spell of Release*, and the shortened name for it is *SLQTSOR*.

The Game's Objective

Having created a gripping story for the game, I needed to come up with the game's objective. After all, once Sir Lamorak is in the castle, you've got to do something to get him out, and it appears the only way to do that is with the *Spell of Release*, whatever that is. Based on the game's storyline, I knew the objective was reasonably simple: The player would need to navigate Sir Lamorak around the castle looking for the Spell of Release. Building on the preceding storyline, I started to add some more detail. For example, the Spell of Release is written on an old parchment that has been torn onto three pieces by an evil wizard and is hidden throughout the castle.

Once all the pieces of the spell are found, the player needs to return to the entrance hall and escape through the main doors. Although that might sound simple, the evil wizard isn't going to make it so easy for Sir Lamorak to escape. The wizard placed nasty specters and obstacles to make the hunt for the spell harder. As Sir Lamorak moves throughout the castle, he accumulates a score based on the baddies he kills and is timed to see how quickly he completes the quest.

I was trying to think of a reason why someone would want to play this game over and over. I felt that by having the player complete the game as quickly as possible, while at the same time attempting to get a good high score (and not get killed by the baddies), it would make someone want to play the game again to better their high score as well as their time. That meant that the parchment pieces for the Spell of Release would have to be placed around the castle randomly, so that each time the game is played, the player would need to hunt for the parchment all over again, rather than memorizing the locations.

Game Play Components

With the storyline and objective in place, it was time to think about the mechanics of the game. I had to think of things like how the player would lose and regain health points and kill baddies and what things aside from the baddies could hinder Sir Lamorak's progress. To sort out these issues, I just started writing down my ideas. As part of the thought process, I wanted to make sure that the game play wasn't too hard or too easy. The game needed to require some thought and some skill. I also knew that it was going to take a lot of play testing to get it just right. From my previous experiences at developing games, even simple ones, balancing the difficulty of the game can be tough. The following sections present the game mechanics that I started with. And although I knew they could change as the game developed, it was important to lay down ideas and start plotting the course.

Time

Time can either be used to limit the amount of time a player has to carry out a task or used to measure how long something has taken. For this game, I decided to use time to record how long it takes the player to complete the game. Having both a score and a time gives players a couple of different measurements they can use when tracking both their progress and level of achievement within the game.

Another form of timer in the game is the player's health. The health of players will be constantly reducing, even when they are just standing still. This means they have to always be moving, looking for the food to make sure they don't run out of energy.

Lives

Games are supposed to be challenging, so it's inevitable that the player will die at some point. When this happens, we could slap them and make them start over again, or use up one of a predefined number lives and let them carry on. Although I have come across a number of games that make you start over from the beginning, I decided to give the player three lives.[2] This is just an arbitrary number, but most arcade games give you three lives at the start, so I thought I should, too. When it comes to adding the game content and then testing the game, the number of lives could change if we find that the game is too easy or too hard.

---

[2] For example, if the zombies kill you in *Zombieville USA*, that's it—you're done. You have to start over again at the very beginning. However, version 1.4 of the game released for the iPhone 3.0 SDK gives you the option of adding lives before you set out to save the town from the swarm of zombies. For more info on *Zombieville USA*, search for it on the iTunes App Store.

> **Note**
>
> It may seem odd to make a statement like that last one. However, experience has shown me that although I can have many killer ideas at the start of a project, and I want to set some in stone as they are core to the game play, some of them just don't end up in the game. They either were too complex to implement, they didn't work well with the game play, or play testing showed that they made the game either too easy or too hard. You should certainly keep track of these ideas, but recognize that some of them may need to be adapted or dropped later on.

Health

The health of players is critical to the game and is something they will need to manage as the game progresses. I didn't want to just have the player's health reduced when a baddie hits him, as I felt it reduced the player's involvement in the game. If he was quick to fire and move, then he could most likely move throughout the castle without too much effort. So, to add a little more depth to the game, I decided that the player's health would continually decrease, even when ghosts are not attacking the player. Just moving around uses up energy, and our hero is moving around the castle at a somewhat frenetic pace. Sir Lamorak certainly does not want to be in the castle longer than he needs to be, so the running around means that his energy levels within the game are continually reducing. When he does get slimed by a baddie, his health reduces even further.

To help our hero survive while in the castle, Sir Lamorak stumbles upon items to increase his health. By consuming these (done by simply moving Sir Lamorak over them), his health is increased. To further increase the thought required by the player, there are also a limited number of these items around the castle. Once they are used up, no others will be provided. This makes the game challenging and causes players to think carefully about how and when they use these items so that they don't run out of energy before completing the game. This also introduces an element of skill. Knowing when to find energy will be key to surviving while they hunt for the parchment pieces. Oh, and avoiding the baddies will be key to surviving, too.

Objects

All games have objects of one type or another. These could be weapons that are collected, energy packs, ammunition, extra lives, bonus points, and so on. What objects are needed within the game and how they should be used vary depending on the nature, storyline, and game mechanics that are going to be used. Although it would be cool to give Sir Lamorak an Uzi 9mm or the *Ghostbuster* backpacks, it doesn't really fit with the story. We also don't want him running around shouting "I'll be back...."

For this game, I decided that I would not go too far and settled on just three types of objects in the game: energy to restore health, keys to open locked doors, and the parchment pieces to allow the player to escape. As I mentioned earlier, it's good to get your ideas down, even if they may change later. Some of your ideas will be fundamental to the game story or plan and cannot change or be dropped, whereas others could be adapted based on how the game is progressing.

Keys

I decided that, to make things more challenging for the player, there are a couple of different door types. The first are normal doors that simply open and close randomly as the player is moving around the castle. The second type of door is a colored door. The idea is that these doors do not open unless the player is carrying the appropriately colored key with him. If he has the correctly colored key, the door opens as he approaches. If not, the door remains closed and blocks his way.

> **Game Hint**
>
> There is a second reason for allowing the player to carry and drop colored keys. Because the castle is like a maze, the keys could be dropped and used like breadcrumbs, enabling the player to identify rooms he has already visited and helping him to navigate his way around the castle.

Energy Items

A number of energy items can be found throughout the castle, each carrying a predefined amount of energy. As the player passes over these items, they are automatically collected and the player's health is increased accordingly. The player's health cannot increase beyond 100 percent, and once an item is absorbed, it's no longer available.

Parchment Pieces

There are only three of these items within the game. As you will remember from the game's storyline, the player has to guide Sir Lamorak around the castle to find these pieces of parchment. Once they have all been collected, our hero will be able to read the Spell of Release and exit the castle through the main doors. One further detail is that when picking up parchment pieces, they will be held within the player's inventory. This inventory will only be able to carry a maximum of three items, including keys, so the player needs to place all the parchment pieces into his inventory to be able to read them.

Doors

Doors within the castle will open and close on their own, with some assistance from the ghosts that inhabit the castle, of course. For example, the ghosts might close an open door that Sir Lamorak was just about to go through, forcing him to find another route and expend more energy. This type of obstacle can make game play more challenging, especially if the player was about to enter a room where an energy item is located. The way the doors open and close is completely random and not based on some fixed time that players could memorize after playing the game a few times. A door stays open or closed from between one and ten seconds. This is something that could change once we start playing the game to adjust the difficulty.

Weapons

Many games have a collection of weapons the player can use. Being a knight in a haunted castle, I've decided to give the knight just one weapon, a mighty axe, which Sir Lamorak flings at the baddies with great skill. Only a single axe should be thrown at a time, and it will bounce off walls, killing all the baddies it touches, and then disappear after a couple seconds.

Once it has vanished, the player can fire the axe again. Only being able to fire a single axe at a time is an idea I have seen used in some classic Spectrum games, and I'm hoping to introduce a little more skill into the game by using this technique rather than the player just shooting blindly to get past the baddies. It also answers the question of where Sir Lamorak keeps finding all of those axes. With a single axe, it is easy to believe that it acts sort of like Thor's Mighty Hammer, which boomerangs back after being thrown, and Sir Lamorak simply catches it on the rebound. Having a never-ending supply of axes is, well, just fantasy.

Entities

No game would be complete without entities. As Sir Lamorak runs around the castle looking for the Spell of Release, it would get rather boring if nothing happened but a few doors opening and closing on him. To really increase the challenge, we need to provide our hero with foes to battle. My idea here is to have a number of different entities that can appear and attack the player, such as the following:

- Ghost
- Pumpkin Head
- Witch
- Bat
- Zombie
- Frankenstein
- Vampires

These entities appear and hover around inside the castle and have two behaviors. First, they just move around randomly, changing direction and speed at will, with no defined path. This should stop the player from being able to get accustomed to their movement. The second behavior has them track and chase the player rather than just mill around. The entities may change some way to signify to the player which mode they are in, or stay the same and keep player guessing. These behaviors will also not be constant—that is, the ghost could change from wandering to chasing and back to wandering again at will, providing the player with further stress.

Player

This may be the last in the list of game components, but it is one of the most important. The player is the central character within the game around which the story has been built, and there are specific actions the player will need to be able to do. From the story-line created earlier, we know that the player is a knight trapped in a castle and that he carries an axe. Based on this and the game components we have already described, we can create a list of actions the player needs to be capable of, as follows:

- Move around the castle.
- Throw his axe in either the direction the player is facing or toward the player's touch on the screen.
- Collect energy items by walking over them.
- Collect keys. This also means he will need some kind of simple inventory in which to store the keys he is carrying. This is also true of the parchment pieces; he will need to be able to carry these as well.
- Walk through locked doors when he is carrying the correctly colored key.
- Be blocked from passing through closed doors or locked doors if he does not have the right key.
- Walk through the main castle door if all three pieces of parchment are held in the player's inventory.

These are the basic actions, based on our current game design, necessary to enable the player to interact with the game and achieve the objectives. How the player is to be actually implemented—his look and feel—will be covered through the rest of the book.

Summary

This has been a long, wordy chapter, but we have already covered a lot of ground. We have gone through what this book aims to provide and what to expect. We have also gone over the game idea that is going to be developed throughout this book. This led to us coming up with a storyline, the game's objective, and the components that are needed to implement the story and game objectives.

We have only briefly covered the components that we need to create within our game. We go into more detail on that later in this book.

Now that we have decided on the name, storyline, objectives, and components, we need to look at the technology we are going to need. By this, I mean, "How are we going to take those concepts and actually code them up for the game?" We start covering this in the next chapter, as we discuss the terminology that is often used within games, such as sprites, texture atlases, and so on. We also cover, at a high level, the technologies we will use to implement our game, including Objective-C, OpenGL ES, and OpenAL.

There are areas we did not discuss in this chapter, such as In-App purchases. Although *Sir Lamorak's Quest* isn't making use of this capability, it is worth considering how In-App purchasing could be used within your game. Allowing the player to purchase new content (levels, weapons, energy, and such) extends the life span of the game and can create a loyal fan base that can be approached when launching a new game.

The Three Ts: Terminology, Technology, and Tools

As you learned in the previous chapter, we covered the basic game design, storyline, and game components for Sir Lamorak's Quest. Although this is all-important information to have at the moment, it's no more than a story. What we now need to do is take a look at the three Ts: the terminology, technology, and tools we are going to use to turn this story into a fully functional (and entertaining) iPhone game.

> **Note**
>
> It is not intended that this book will teach you how to develop in Objective-C or C or teach you everything you need to know about the other technologies in their own right; there are many excellent books[1] and online resources that cover OpenGL and OpenAL in greater detail. We will, however, cover these topics in enough detail to allow you to understand why we are using them and how.

The *terminology* used when developing computer games can be very different from terminology you may have come across when creating other types of applications. The common terminology used in game development will be covered in this chapter, so you will more easily understand the concepts throughout the rest of this book.

The second area, *technology*, will discuss technologies such as Objective-C, which is Apple's programming language of choice on their platforms, including the iPhone, as well as game-specific technology, such as OpenGL ES (Open Graphics Language Embedded Systems) and OpenAL (Open Audio Language).

The third area covers the *tools* that are required to create *Sir Lamorak's Quest*. You will certainly have access to the development tools you need, but you may also have alternatives

---

[1] Books available for OpenGL include *OpenGL Programming Guide*, *OpenGL Shading Language*, and *OpenGL ES 2.0 Programming Guide*.

to some of the other tools I will use, such as Pixelmator (**www.pixelmator.com**). There is nothing to stop you from using your favorite graphics package.

By the time you finish this chapter, you will have a good understanding of the terminology you will see throughout this book, as well as having a high-level view of the technology and tools we are going to be using. Don't worry if you're unfamiliar with the technology mentioned so far; we will build up your knowledge of these areas as we run through this book. Google is a fantastic tool for getting more information on specific subjects you may become interested in as you read through the book. Knowing the technology and terminology that is going to be used will give you the ability to more easily find what you are looking for.

Terminology

First up is *terminology*. Whether you are an experienced programmer or novice, game development has a different terminology than what you've probably been accustomed to. This section covers the terms you will come across most frequently when reading this book.

Before deciding what technology you need to use for your game, such as how to render a sprite on the screen, you first need to know what a sprite is. If you think a sprite looks like a green fairy with wings, you *really* need to continue reading this chapter.

As you read through this section, you will find terms you see throughout this book. You may have an understanding of some of these terms already, such as *sprite* or *animation*, but I'll still cover them, specifically looking at how they are used within computer games.

Sprite

The term *sprite* refers to a 2D bitmap image that can be moved around the screen independently of everything else. Because early home computers, such as the Sinclair Spectrum or the Commodore 64 (or worse, the VIC-20), didn't have powerful CPUs and Graphics Processing Units (GPUs) to process and render graphics, sprites were used to render and move graphics around the screen.

> **Note**
>
> A GPU is a specialized processor that offloads graphics processing functions from the CPU. They are specially designed to support the mathematical calculations necessary when rendering 2D and 3D graphics.

On some of these early home computers, programmers assigned a bitmap image to a hardware sprite, which was then rendered on top of everything else drawn on screen. The sprite's position could then be changed by simply updating the location within a CPU register. No other drawing code was needed. These hardware-based sprites allowed early home computers to perform functions that would just not have been possible with the limited hardware resources of the day. Sprites were most often used in games to represent the player ship, missiles, bullets, and the enemies you were fighting. Figure 2.1 shows the sprite for Sir Lamorak.

Figure 2.1   Example of a sprite. This particular
sprite is the one used for Sir Lamorak.

The iPhone is many times more powerful than the home computers we had back in the 1980s. Its GPU, particularly in the iPhone 3GS, iPhone 4, and iPad, allows it to achieve some impressive visual effects, thanks to their support for OpenGL ES 2.0.

What Is OpenGL ES?

OpenGL ES is a subset of the OpenGL graphics language for mobile devices (ES stands for *Embedded Systems*). The first-generation iPhone and the second-generation iPhone 3G only supported OpenGL ES 1.1, and the iPhone 3GS, iPhone 4 and iPad support both OpenGL ES 1.1 and 2.0. The main benefit of OpenGL ES 2.0 is its support of shader language. This allows the programmer to define how the GPU should process data rather than only being able to use functions that have been predefined.

For *Sir Lamorak's Quest*, I'm going to simply refer to *sprites* as *images*. We will display more than our hero and bad guys in the game, so we will build a generic `Image` class that will be used to display sprites, backgrounds, buttons, and such.

How Do I Create a Sprite?

At this point, you may well be asking how you create the sprite images. This is something covered in more detail later on, but the quick answer is to open up your favorite graphics app—such as Photoshop or Pixelmator—and draw your sprite.

Once you have your sprite, export it in a supported format such as PNG. PNG is not the only format we can use to get graphics onto the iPhone. Other formats, such as GIF and BMP, can also be used. We will be using the PNG format throughout the book because it's the format recommended by Apple for use on the iPhone. In Chapter 5, "Image Rendering," when we have created the `Image` class, you will see how to load the PNG file into an OpenGL texture and render it to the screen.

One important point I haven't mentioned is that getting the sprite onto the screen is *much* easier (in my opinion) than actually *creating* the sprite. Of course, this could be because I seriously lack any artistic talent, but the code you'll use to display, animate, and move the sprite around the screen is actually pretty straightforward. If drawing isn't your strongest suit, there are plenty of freelance designers you can call upon to help make your dream game a reality.[2]

---

[2] Checking out game development forums, such as **www.idevgames.com** and **www.gamasutra.com,** is a good place to start looking for freelance graphical artists to help with your project.

Sprite Sheet

As described earlier, a sprite is a single image that is used (and reused) to represent an individual element onscreen, such as the player's character, an enemy, and so on. As you can imagine, having many individual sprites within a game—and having a separate file for each sprite, which is then loaded into the game—could be difficult to manage. To simplify sprite management and, more importantly, improve performance, it is common to store more than one sprite in a single image. Images that hold more than a single sprite are called *sprite sheets*.

The idea is that a single image contains a series of sprite images in the form of a grid. Each sprite can then accessed by using its column and row location within the larger image. Simple sprite sheets contain individual sprites, each with the same dimensions. This makes it easy to access a specific sprite on that sheet using its row and column location. For example, if we had a sprite sheet that contained sprites whose dimensions were all 40 pixels square, it would take a simple calculation to work out in pixels where a given sprite was using its row and column; for example:

```
x = column * 40
y = row * 40
```

Calculating these values for a sprite at column 3, row 2 would result in 120 for x and 80 for y. This calculation would give you the exact pixel location for the top-left corner of that sprite image. Figure 2.2 shows an example 4 × 4 sprite sheet with each sprite being 40 pixels square. The origin of this sprite sheet (that is, x = 0 and y = 0) is the top-left corner.

Figure 2.2   A simple 4 × 4 sprite sheet, containing 16 sprite images.

> **Note**
>
> Sprites don't have to be square; they just are in this example. A sprite could easily be a rectangle that does not have the same width and height, as long as each sprite has the same width and height.

More complex sprite sheets, or *packed sprite sheets* (like the one shown in Figure 2.3), are images that contain a number of smaller sub-images, each of which could be another sprite sheet or image. As you'll notice by looking at Figure 2.3, a packed sprite sheet can contain a number of different-sized sprites.

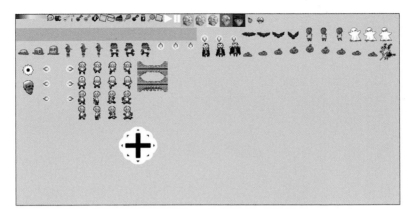

Figure 2.3   A packed sprite sheet can contain different-sized images; you'll
just need to be more careful when providing the coordinates for each image.

These more complex sprite sheets mean you cannot perform a fixed calculation as seen
already to work out where inside the sprite sheet a specific sprite may be. Instead, you
need to include a *control file*, which does two things:

- It defines the location of each sprite within the sprite sheet.
- It defines a key for each sprite in the sprite sheet (for example, the name of the
  sprite).

Control files can be either plain text or XML, and are often created when the sprite sheet
is created. The data contained in the control sheet can be populated manually (that is,
you sort out the coordinates for each sprite in the sprite sheet), or using a tool such as
Zwoptex[3], which can generate the sprite sheet and control file from separate images. When
your game launches, the control file is parsed so the game knows where the sprites are located within the sprite sheet.

> **Note**
>
> For the purposes of this game, we will be using both simple and complex sprite sheets. We
> look at how to use applications that help to create sprite sheets when we cover sprite
> sheets in Chapter 6, "Sprite Sheets."

---

[3] Zwoptex (http://zwoptexapp.com/flashversion/) is a flash-based sprite sheet generation tool that
allows you to perform complex arrangements of different sized images. A cocoa based version can be
found at (http://www.zwoptexapp.com/).

Just to make things interesting, you will likely see a different term used for sprite sheets when dealing with OpenGL ES as a sprite sheet is often referred to as a *texture atlas*. OpenGL ES and textures are covered later in this chapter, but for now, it is good to know that a texture is basically another term for an image that is mapped onto a shape drawn using OpenGL ES. Just as a sprite sheet contains many sprite images, a texture atlas is an image that contains many smaller texture images.

Creating a sprite sheet is basically the same as creating a sprite. You can use your favorite graphics package to place individual sprites into a larger image. Care must be taken to ensure that each sprite occupies the correct location within the sprite sheet. Because this can be a complex exercise, using tools to help with their creation is a recommended approach.

Sprite sheets are also useful when it comes to animation, which we review next, as well as tile images used within tile maps (again, something we cover later in this chapter).

Animation

I find it very hard to create animated sprites, but as I mentioned earlier, this could easily be because I have no skill when it comes to drawing. Animation is perhaps one of the most important elements of a game. Even with a simple game like Tetris, things move—they animate. Having your hero move around the screen in a fixed pose like some kind of statue is not much fun to watch. It's much more exciting to see your characters arms and legs moving as they walk around the screen. With most modern 3D games, the objects within the game (such as bad guys) are 3D models with many triangles used to represent a complex shape. Movement of these objects is achieved by applying mathematical transformations to the triangles making up the 3D object, causing them to move as required. Some games even employ a skeletal system allowing the animator to simply move the bones of a character and have their body follows as necessary.

Because *Sir Lamorak's Quest* is a simple 2D game, we won't need anything that complex. Instead, we'll use a simple form of animation that's very similar to stop-motion animation. This process shows one image (sprite) after another, with the new image (sprite) being in a slightly different position to the last. When pieced together (with code), the images appear to animate as one-image transitions to the next.

By now, you should start to see the benefits of having a sprite sheet. The sprite sheet defines the animation's different frames; then we use code to load each sprite (or frame) into the animation and display the animated sprites onscreen. Figure 2.4 shows a simple sprite sheet containing sprites that can be used within an animation. The first line shows the character running down, the next line running up, then right, and finally left.

> **Note**
>
> The ability to easily refer to each sprite on a sprite sheet when defining each frame of the animation makes the sprite sheet a very powerful tool, and one we will be using when we create the Animation class in Chapter 7, "Animation."

Figure 2.4   An animation sprite sheet.

We all want the best graphics available, but unless you or someone you know has the necessary graphics skills, you will need to use whatever you can find—legally, of course—to keep your project moving along. If you know you will be stuck with *developer art*, try to come up with a game that suits your drawing abilities. The game *Parachute Panic*[4] is a great example of what a developer can do with limited drawing skills; it's stick figure art at its best. Another great example is *Neon Tango* by Freeverse.[5] These two games are proof that you can use simple geometric shapes instead of complex art and still create a cool game that's fun to play.

Prototyping with Placeholders

Because I'm not the world's greatest graphic artist, one trick I've learned is to use images or animations I find on the Internet as a placeholder while prototyping a game. If you can find some graphics to stand in while you're developing the game, things can move ahead, and then you can swap out the graphics later. I've seen many projects stall and fail due to people getting hung up on the graphics.

Bitmap Fonts

All the graphics in *Sir Lamorak's Quest* will be rendered with OpenGL. In fact, the iPhone uses OpenGL ES (ES stands for *Embedded Systems*), which is a subset of OpenGL for mobile devices. We cover OpenGL ES in more detail in the section, "Technology."

Sadly, though, OpenGL ES doesn't support the ability to render fonts to the screen. As a result, we'll have to use bitmap fonts.

Bitmap fonts aren't too different from sprites and sprite sheets. In fact, we use sprites and sprite sheets to support bitmap fonts. This will be covered in Chapter 8, "Bitmap Fonts."

Because OpenGL ES lacks font support, you'll have to define a font as a series of images. To do this, you'll need to create a complex sprite sheet that contains an image for each character in the font. If we were doing this manually, it would be a real pain, but

---

[4] You can find *Parachute Panic* in the App Store by searching for Parachute Panic.

[5] *Neon Tango* (**www.freeverse.com/games/game/?id=7015**) by Freeverse is a great example of what can be done with simple geometric shapes. It helps that they have executed the game with extreme precision and some dazzling effects, but you get the idea.

luckily, tools such as Hiero[6] and bmfont[7] make the process of turning a font into a sprite sheet really easy. More detail on Hiero can be found in the section, "Tools."

AngelCode has created the bmfont tool, and it is this tool and its generated output that Hiero has been based. Although bmfont is much more feature-rich compared to Hiero, it is currently only available on the Windows platform. For this reason, I will be using the Java-based Hiero that will run on a Mac.

Tile Maps

Throughout this book, I have been referring to the 1980s, where my love of games and game programming started. Although technology has moved on greatly since then, those concepts are still valid to this day.

One of the issues with the old 8-bit (and even 16-bit) home computers and consoles was the availability of memory (RAM). When creating a platform-based game or role-playing game (RPG), it was not feasible to have large images of each level held in memory. It doesn't make sense to hold a huge image in memory either, especially when the player is only able to see the portion of the image that fits into their display. For the iPhone and iPod devices pre the iPhone 4 and iPad, the maximum display size in landscape mode is 480 × 320 pixels. The iPhone 4 has a display size of 960 x 640 pixels in landscape mode and the iPad has 1024 x 768.

To overcome this issue, tile maps were created. A tile map is usually a two-dimensional grid. Each grid cell contains information about that location within the tile map, such as the ID of the image that should be rendered when that tile location is displayed, as well as information on the type of tile in that location. For example, is this a solid tile that the player cannot move through, such as a wall, or is it an object that could hurt the player should they walk into it?

This method of storing and building environments greatly reduces the amount of memory needed to store images and provides benefits later on when you need to know where a player actually is within a map. Although the iPhone is many times more powerful than the old 8-bit machines, memory is still a limited resource, and anything that can reduce the amount of memory being used is a good thing.

Tile maps are usually made up of two elements, as follows:

- A sprite sheet that contains separate tile images that can be used to build the environment.
- A map file that specifies which tile should be used in specific tile locations in the map, and so on. This can be done manually, but it becomes complex very quickly as your map gets bigger.

---

[6] Hiero can be found at slick.cokeandcode.com/demos/hiero.jnlp. This link will run the application over the Internet rather than download it.

[7] bmfont can be found at **www.angelcode.com/products/bmfont/.**

In *Sir Lamorak's Quest*, our hero will be walking around inside a castle. Although we could create the necessary tile maps manually, it's much easier to draw the tile maps visually, and that is exactly what we are going to do. We cover the creation of tile maps in Chapter 9, "Tile Maps."

Most large games, such as Doom 3 or Quake Arena, have some kind of level editor, which allows the level designers to freely create new 3D levels. Although we don't need anything that complex, I still want to be able to easily create and change the map used in *Sir Lamorak's Quest*. Allowing your game to be data driven means that tuning and developing the game becomes a lot easier than when everything is hard coded.

One tool you can use for creating tile maps is Tiled.[8] More information on this free open-source application can be found in the section, "Tools."

Particle System

I'm sure you will have played many games where effects, such as smoke and fire, are used. There are two ways to create these effects. The first is to use sprite animation, and the second is to use a particle emitter. To use a sprite animation, you would need to create a number of frames for each phase of the effect and then play them back in sequence. This sprite animation technique was popularized by arcade games over 20 years ago and is still in use by game developers today.

However, today's desktops and console games pack powerful CPUs and GPUs that we could only dream of back then. Even the iPhone packs more processor and graphical punch than early arcade games. Rather than employing 20-year-old technology, we can create a *particle system* to animate effects in real-time.

Don't Panic

The particles we are talking about are not the same as those created within the Large Hadron Collider (LHC), which is rumored to be a harbinger of doom that will create a huge black hole that ends the world. We won't be creating exotic particles and hurling them around our iPhones.

The term "particle system" refers to a technique that enables you to simulate certain organic behaviors, such as fire, smoke, moving water, rain, and snow. A particle system enables you to configure the number of particles you want to generate and how you would like them to move, including the following:

- Their speed
- Their lifespan

Even with these simple settings, it is possible to create some impressive effects with a particle system.

---

[8] Tiled is a Java-based application and can be found at **mapeditor.org.**

> **What Is a Particle?**
>
> You may be wondering what we mean when we say *particle*. Don't think of it in terms of atoms or quarks like you would in a physics class. When it comes to game development, what we really mean when we say "particle" is "image". Each "particle" is in fact an image that is rendered to the screen at the particle's current location with the particle's size and color. The image could be a simple circle, a star, or whatever you want, just as long as it gives you the effect you are looking for.

A particle system normally has a *particle emitter*. The emitter is responsible for generating new particles and tracking their progress through their life before removing them when they die. When a particle is created, the particle emitter sets some parameters, including the following:

- **Speed:** The speed at which the particle moves.
- **Life span:** The amount of time a particle will live for. Each cycle through the game loop causes the particles lifespan to reduce until it reaches 0. The particle is then removed from the update list.
- **Direction:** The direction that particle will move. This direction could change over time based on other settings such as gravity.
- **Start color:** The color the particle will have when it is created.
- **End color:** The color the particle should have when it reaches the end of its life cycle.
- **Size:** The size of the particle.

Although the particle emitter will ask each particle to update itself, it is the particle's responsibility to track its own position, color, life span, and so on. This allows each particle to move independently of each other. Add to this a level of randomness, and it is possible to create very organic-looking effects, such as fog and smoke.

You'll see how to create a particle system in Chapter 10, "The Particle Emitter."

As with tile maps, it is possible to configure particle emitters manually, but this can take up a lot of time. It certainly speeds things up to use a visual editor for creating these effects, such as Particle Designer.[9]

Collision Detection

Collision detection is the ability to identify when one object collides with another. Sounds pretty simple, I know, but there's a bit more to it.

As Sir Lamorak walks around the castle, we don't really want him walking through walls or doors (well, not until he is dead and turns into yet another ghost who haunts the castle, which is not part of the game design). We also want to know when Sir Lamorak has been hit by a ghost or has walked over an energy item or that a ghost has been hit by Sir Lamorak's mighty axe.

---

[9] Particle Designer is an application I developed to allow particle emitters used within Sir Lamorak's Quest to be configured visually. It can be found at (http://particledesigner.71squared.com).

There are many ways to detect collisions. Some are simple and involve checks to see if the box inside which our player's sprite is drawn intersects the bounding box of another object, such as a ghost or wall. Other techniques are much more complex, especially when you start to work with physics engines, which is beyond the scope this book. These collisions are not just a binary *yes* or *no*; they can provide you with information on exactly where the two objects collided, and so on.

> **Note**
>
> We won't need a sophisticated collision detection system in *Sir Lamorak's Quest*; simple collision detection will do. What technique you use in your own game really depends on what is needed.

Collision detection is made up of two key elements:

- Detection of the collision
- How an object, such as the player, should react to that collision

For example, when the player walks into a wall, the only consequence will be that the player won't be able to move any further in the direction of the collision. However, if the player were to walk into a ghost, the reaction would be to remove the ghost from the game and reduce the player's health by a specified number of units.

Artificial Intelligence (AI)

Artificial intelligence (AI) is what makes your game "smart." The intent is not to create Skynet[10] and cause our iPhones to become sentient and take over the planet. And although they are in some sense, we want the enemies in our game to have some kind of artificial intelligence. We don't want our baddies to be so predictable that it's no challenge to fool them, so the AI in *Sir Lamorak's Quest* will control how the bad guys move around and how they decide to chase Sir Lamorak, as opposed to just moving around in some random way.

> **Note**
>
> AI really can make or break your game. Although we won't introduce or use more complex AI methods, such as A* path finding, you'll learn how to create a form of AI that makes the game more addictive to play.

Even when you're not using clever algorithms and decision graphs, the simple rules about how something should move or interact is still a form of AI. This basic entity control should give you a good start on your road to creating the next world-dominating game bent on the destruction of the human race—or maybe just a racing game—it's up to you.

---

[10] Skynet: **en.wikipedia.org/wiki/Skynet_%28Terminator%29**.

Game Loop

The last term I'm going to run through is the game loop. This is an important part of any game and is responsible for making sure that your game performs all the right functions at the right time and in the right order. There are a number of core activities that a game loop must do, such as the following:

- Take input from the user.
- Update the state of the player based on the user's input.
- Update the state of the other entities in the game, such as baddies.
- Check for collisions between entities.
- Render the game to the screen.

This is not all the items that need to be handled within a game loop, but it is an example of what needs to be done. The game loop is responsible for making sure that even when the player is not doing anything, the rest of the game is being updated. For example, the baddies are still moving around, ambient sounds still play, and so on.

> **Tip**
>
> You may read about game cycles, tick count, and so on, but they are all referring to the game loop or iteration through that loop.

At its most basic level, the game loop is exactly that—a loop—and functions are called within that loop for things that make the game tick. We will create our own game loop for *Sir Lamorak's Quest* in Chapter 4, "The Game Loop," but as we have been through so much and not seen a single line of code, I thought it might be helpful to put the basic game loop code here in Listing 2.1. The idea here is not for you to fully grasp what's going on within that loop. My intent is to show you that a simple game loop can actually be very small.

Listing 2.1 **The Game Loop**

```
#define MAXIMUM_FRAME_RATE 120
#define MINIMUM_FRAME_RATE 30
#define UPDATE_INTERVAL (1.0 / MAXIMUM_FRAME_RATE)
#define MAX_CYCLES_PER_FRAME (MAXIMUM_FRAME_RATE / MINIMUM_FRAME_RATE)

- (void)gameLoop {

    static double lastFrameTime = 0.0f;
    static double cyclesLeftOver = 0.0f;
    double currentTime;
    double updateIterations;

    // Apple advises to use CACurrentMediaTime() as CFAbsoluteTimeGetCurrent() is
    // synced with the mobile network time and so could change causing hiccups.
    currentTime = CACurrentMediaTime();
```

```
    updateIterations = ((currentTime - lastFrameTime) + cyclesLeftOver);

    if(updateIterations > (MAX_CYCLES_PER_FRAME * UPDATE_INTERVAL))
        updateIterations = (MAX_CYCLES_PER_FRAME * UPDATE_INTERVAL);

    while (updateIterations >= UPDATE_INTERVAL) {
        updateIterations -= UPDATE_INTERVAL;

        // Update the game logic passing in the fixed update interval as the delta
        [sharedGameController updateCurrentSceneWithDelta:UPDATE_INTERVAL];
    }

    cyclesLeftOver = updateIterations;
    lastFrameTime = currentTime;

    // Render the scene
    [self drawView:nil];
}
```

The loop shown in Listing 2.1 is an open loop, which means it runs at regular intervals using a timer external to the loop. The other type of game loop is called a *tight loop*. Once a tight loop starts, it continues to loop as fast as it can, running code within the loop over and over again. There are benefits and drawbacks to both methods, and the one you use will greatly depend on the type of game you are writing (more on this in Chapter 4).

The second function of the game loop is to make sure that the game runs at a constant speed. If you were to run a tight loop that just went as fast as it could, you would have a game in which objects would move around the screen faster on quick hardware and slower on slow hardware. This isn't something you want to happen. You want to give the players of the game a consistent experience regardless of the hardware the game is running on.

For the iPhone, it is a little easier, as we are dealing with a limited number of device types:

- iPhone (first generation, or Gen1)
- iPhone 3G
- iPhone 3GS
- iPhone 4
- iPod Touch (first generation, or Gen1)
- iPod Touch (second generation, or Gen2)
- iPad

Although similar, each device is different. For example, the iPhone 4 is faster than the iPhone 3GS, which is faster than the iPhone 3G, and the Gen2 iPod Touch is significantly faster than the iPhone 3G. The game loop is where we can handle these differences.

At its simplest, the game loop measures the amount of time, normally in milliseconds, that passes between each loop. The amount of time between each loop is called the *delta*.

This delta value is then passed to the functions that update the logic of the entities within the game and is used to calculate game elements, such as movement. For example, if you specify how far a ghost should move per millisecond, the ghost will only move that far regardless of the device's speed. Sure, the movement will appear smoother on faster devices than slower ones, but the amount of movement, as well as the game play, will be at a consistent speed.

Technology

So far, this chapter has gone through the basic terminology you will come across throughout this book and as a game developer. This section talks about the technologies you'll use to create the sample game, *Sir Lamorak's Quest.*

Objective-C

As the name implies, Objective-C is an object-oriented superset of the C programming language. Because Objective-C is a superset of C, it shouldn't take you long to learn Objective-C. If you have already have experience working with C or C++, you can continue to build iPhone games in those languages, but you'll need to know a bit of Objective-C to make use of the Cocoa Touch API. The key difference between Objective-C and C is that Objective-C fully supports object-oriented programming techniques, such as the use of classes and their instantiation.

The code throughout this book uses Objective-C 2.0 with a little C thrown in where necessary.

> **Note**
>
> C and C++ have historically been the most popular languages for writing games. Although you can use other languages, such as Java or Python, for game development, those languages are not supported on the iPhone. You'll have to stick to Objective-C, C, C++ or a mixture of these.

There are some great resources available for learning Objective-C. Apple itself has a number of great documents available that help you learn Objective-C such as "The Objective-C Language."[11] There are also great books available, such as the following:

- *Cocoa Programming for Mac OS X, Third Edition*, by Aaron Hillegass (Addison-Wesley, 2008).
- *Learning Objective-C 2.0*, by Robert Clair (Addison-Wesley, 2011).
- *Programming in Objective-C 2.0, Second Edition*, by Stephen G. Kochan (Addison-Wesley, 2008).
- *Cocoa Design Patterns*, by Erik M. Buck and Donald A. Yacktman (Addison-Wesley, 2009).

---

[11] *The Objective-C Language* can be downloaded in PDF format from **developer.apple.com/ documentation/Cocoa/Conceptual/ObjectiveC/ObjC.pdf**.

Cocoa Touch

Cocoa Touch is a set of object-oriented frameworks that provide a runtime environment for applications running on iOS. Cocoa Touch is an iPhone-specific framework that enables you to create touch-based user interface elements as well as access hardware-specific features of the iPhone, iPod touch and iPad, such as the accelerometer, gyroscope, camera, and the magnetometer.

You need to use Objective-C to access the Cocoa Touch API. This is why even if you want to develop your entire game in C or C++, there will also be small aspects of the game that are in Objective-C, so that you can gain access to Cocoa Touch-based functions, such as touch.

iOS 3.0 introduced some great features that provide access to the iPod functions on the iPhone, and these are all Cocoa Touch APIs. If you want to go deeper, though, and start to control the audio services at a lower level, you need to use C functions that the iOS SDK makes available to you, which can become a little trickier. We talk about this more in Chapter 11, "Sound."

OpenGL ES

OpenGL ES is a lightweight version of OpenGL for embedded systems (that's the ES), and is a software interface to the graphics hardware on your iOS device. OpenGL ES is a standard governed by the Khronos Group and implemented by graphics hardware manufacturers within their GPUs.

> **Note**
>
> There are currently two versions of OpenGL ES: 1.1 and 2.0. At the time of this writing, only the iPad, iPhone 3GS, iPhone 4 and iPod 3rd Gen support OpenGL ES 2.0; every other version of the iPhone and iPod Touch supports OpenGL ES 1.1. That said, the iPad, iPhone 4 and iPhone 3GS support both versions (1.1 and 2.0), so if you write your game on OpenGL ES 1.1, it will run on all the current iPhone, iPod Touch and iPad devices.

OpenGL has been around for a long time and has pretty much been the de-facto standard when it comes to software interfaces with graphics hardware. OpenGL is a huge API with around 700 different commands. On the other hand, OpenGL ES is a much smaller API that is really focused on performance. Within the full OpenGL standard, there are many ways of doing the same thing, but with OpenGL ES, they decided to only provide support for the fastest methods, which is important when you are running on a mobile device with limited memory, bandwidth, and CPU capabilities.

What OpenGL ES Can (And Can't) Do

OpenGL ES on the iPhone provides you with a great interface to access the features of the GPU. This interface enables you to create objects in both 2D and 3D space and apply color, texture, and transformations to these objects. Because OpenGL ES uses the GPU instead of the CPU, the graphics rendering is hardware accelerated, which means it's really fast. The GPU is capable of performing floating-point operations over 100 times faster than the CPU. It is a real number-crunching monster.

The objects themselves are made up of triangles. Mapping together different-sized triangles can make any shape you can think of, and this approach is taken by OpenGL ES. To define a shape, simply provide the points (known as *vertices*) for each point on the triangles, and then ask OpenGL ES to render those points to the screen. For example, you would use two triangles to create a square, as shown in Figure 2.5. There is, of course, more going on than meets the eye, but for the purposes of this book and our game, we'll keep OpenGL as simple as possible.

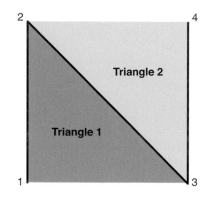

Figure 2.5   Two triangles making up a square.

Once you have defined your shape using vertices, you can optionally define the color (or colors) along with a texture (image) you want to be applied. Applying a texture (image) to the shape is a technique known as *texture mapping*. Texture mapping enables you to basically glue an image onto a geometric shape you have created. Doing so then allows OpenGL ES to make sure that the image is rendered correctly based on the position of the polygon onto which it has been placed. For example, if you are working in 3D and you are looking at your polygon in perspective with it turned away from the viewer, the image that has been texture mapped onto the polygon will be rendered correctly to appear in perspective (see Figure 2.6). OpenGL ES takes care of this, so it's not something you need to worry about.

Texture mapping is a large and complex subject with many different ways of doing things. When you start to create more complex games, it's worth delving further into texture mapping using sources, such as *OpenGL Programming Guide: The Official Guide to Learning OpenGL Versions 3.0 and 3.1, Seventh Edition* (Addison-Wesley, 2009).

We are not going to be working in 3D, which makes our lives easier for now as we start using OpenGL ES. We are going to be working in 2D, however, with our objects being flat polygons onto which we will place a texture (image) that will represent an entity within our game, such as the player or a ghost.

When we cover the creation of the `Image` class in Chapter 5, we cover in more detail how you create your polygon and how you apply a texture to it.

Figure 2.6   A textured polygon in perspective.

OpenGL ES 1.1 vs. 2.0

I've mentioned that there are two different versions of OpenGL ES currently, and it's worth going through the key difference between them. OpenGL ES 1.1 has what is called a *fixed pipeline* architecture, which means that the operations available are fixed. You provide data to OpenGL ES regarding vertex, color, material, lighting, and texture, and specific functions are then carried out using that data. You can change the data that is passed in, but you cannot change the functions themselves.

With OpenGL ES 2.0, you no longer have a fixed pipeline; instead, it has a *shader pipeline*. This means that instead of having the fixed functions into which you pass your data, you can write code to be executed inside OpenGL on the GPU in something called *shader language*. This code is compiled onto the GPU, and is then called whenever you need that function. This means you can pretty much do anything you like—you are not restricted to what is delivered out of the box with OpenGL ES, but perform any action you like on the data that you pass in.

On the up side, you are able to achieve some spectacular effects being able to control the functions that are performed on the GPU, and because these functions are being performed on the GPU, they are very quick. On the down side, it means there is more work to do because you have to create the functions you want to use. I expect to see more and more games taking advantage of OpenGL ES 2.0 now that it is supported on the iPhone 3GS, iPhone 4, and iPad, and over time, this will most likely be the way everyone goes. For our game and throughout this book, I will be using OpenGL ES 1.1, so as to get maximum compatibility with the currently available devices and also to keep things simple.

> **Note**
>
> Although a game written using OpenGL ES 1.1 will run on the iPad, iPhone 3GS and iPhone 4, a game written using OpenGL ES 2.0 will only work on the iPad, iPhone 3GS and iPhone 4. It is not possible to run these games on older hardware unless the game supports two rendering methods: one for OpenGL ES 1.1 and OpenGL ES 2.0. Creating different rendering methods within the same game and then deciding which should be used based on the hardware is a complex undertaking. Currently, most indie developers are sticking with a single OpenGL ES 1.1 render method.

> **iPhone GPUs**
>
> iPhones currently use two different Graphics Processing Units, as follows:
>
> - PowerVR MBX
> - PowerVR SGX
>
> All iPhone devices prior to the iPhone 3GS used the PowerVR MBX chip. From the iPhone 3GS, they use the PowerVR SGX chip. This is where the difference in OpenGL ES support comes from. The MBX chip only supports the OpenGL ES 1.1, whereas the SGX chip supports both OpenGL ES 2.0 and emulates OpenGL ES 1.1.
>
> A company called Imagination manufactures the PowerVR chips. Their website is a good source of technical information on their chips and they provide a number of resources for developers. The Imagination website for the PowerVR chips can be found at **www.imgtec.com/ powervr/powervr-technology.asp**.

OpenAL

OpenAL stands for Open Audio Library. It is a cross-platform 3D audio API that is well-suited for use with games.

The concept behind OpenAL is very similar to that of OpenGL ES. OpenAL is a software interface to the sound hardware that enables you to create audio sources that can be positioned within and moved through 3D space. In order to hear the sounds being generated, a listener is required. There is a single listener that can also be configured, which defines where in OpenAL 3D space the listener is located and also which way it is facing. The listener is normally located at the same location as the player.

Based on this information, OpenAL will then play the sound to the listener using the appropriate volume and pitch. This allows OpenAL to provide a real sense of 3D sound around the player. If the sound source or listener is moving, OpenAL will even apply the Doppler effect, much as you get when you hear an emergency siren coming toward you and then moving away from you. For *Sir Lamorak's Quest*, we are working in 2D, but that still allows us to play sounds around the player based in that 2D space. Having doors slam shut in the distance along with spooky sounds positioned around the player can add a lot of depth to the game.

There are many other items that can be configured within OpenAL, such as the distance model, which defines how quickly sound drops off as the listener moves away from the sound source among other things.

OpenAL enables us to play multiple sounds simultaneously. At a high level, you load audio data into a sound buffer and associate it with a sound source. Once that has been done, the sound in the sound buffer can then be played. The iPhone supports a total of 32 sound buffers, allowing you to play up to 32 sounds simultaneously.

OpenAL is covered in more detail in Chapter 11.

Tools

We have covered the terminology and technology, so now it's time to look at the tools we'll use to create *Sir Lamorak's Quest*.

From a developer point of view, everything you need to develop using the iPhone SDK can be downloaded from the iPhone Dev Center (**developer.apple.com/iphone**), as shown in Figure 2.7. This section also covers other tools that are useful when developing games. These are not available directly from the Apple Developer websites, but I have included their locations on the Internet with their descriptions so you know where to get them.

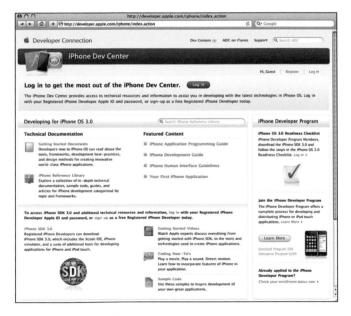

Figure 2.7   Apple's iPhone Dev Center.

The iPhone development center provides a huge amount of information about developing on the iPhone platform, including documents on getting started, a reference library, and other useful guides. It is also from this site that you can register as an iPhone developer. This is important, as you need to be a registered iPhone developer before you can download the tools necessary to develop on the iPhone. You can register for free, which gives you access to the development tools you will need as well as documentation, and this is where most people start. It also enables you to have a play with the iPhone SDK before parting with any money, which is always nice.

If you plan to submit iPhone games or applications to the App Store, you need to sign up to the iPhone Developer Program. For this, you pay $99 per year for the Standard Program.

Once you have signed up and registered, you will then be able to download all the tools and examples you need to start rocking and rolling on the iPhone.

The iPhone SDK

The iPhone SDK (available at **developer.apple.com/iphone**) includes everything you need to start developing on the iPhone. It includes the following:

- Xcode and Interface Builder
- The iPhone Simulator
- Additional tools for debugging and performance, such as Shark and Instruments

Once you have downloaded and installed the iPhone SDK, you will have a full development environment allowing you to develop for the iPhone.

Xcode

Xcode (shown in Figure 2.8) is Apple's integrated development environment (IDE) for developing Mac and iPhone applications. Xcode is a full-featured IDE and provides you with access to all the features you need to develop on the iPhone. These features include syntax highlighting, context-based access to documentation, and code sense, which automatically provides suggestions for the commands you are typing in. This can save you a significant amount of type when writing your code.

From within Xcode, you can create and manage your projects, debug your code, and also read Apple's developer documentation, without ever having to leave Xcode. Having access to all of these things in one place makes Xcode a great development environment.

Interface Builder

Interface Builder is an Apple tool that enables you to visually design views to be used on the iPhone. This application is used heavily when developing native view-based applications on the iPhone. As with most things, being able to visually design your views and then wire it up to the code you write greatly speeds up the development process. Figure 2.9 shows what Interface Builder looks like.

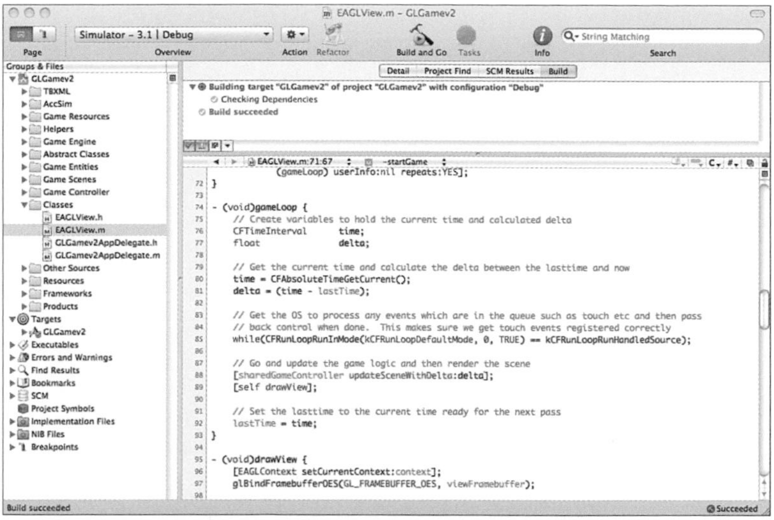

Figure 2.8   The Xcode IDE.

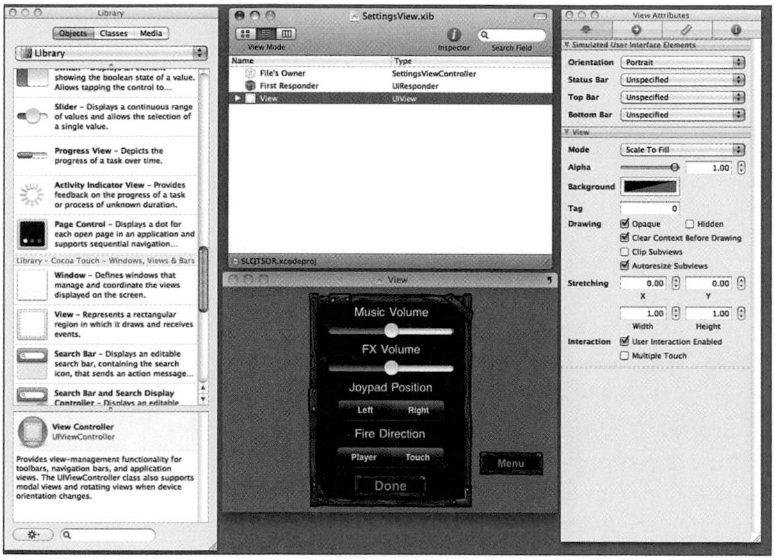

Figure 2.9   Using Interface Builder to create the Settings screen for Sir
Lamorak's Quest.

Although we will not be making much use of Interface Builder when building *Sir Lamorak's
Quest*, we will be using it to design items such as the settings screen, so it's important to know
that this tool exists.

The iPhone Simulator

The iPhone Simulator (shown in Figure 2.10) is a small application within Xcode that lets you to test your application on your desktop, without installing the app on your iPhone. Although the iPhone Simulator is a great tool for most applications, there is no substitute for testing your games on a real device.

Figure 2.10   The iPhone simulator running Sir Lamorak's Quest during testing.

Testing on the actual device is extremely important because the iPhone Simulator, which runs on your desktop, uses your Mac's CPU, memory, and graphics card, which are quite different from the iPhone's internal components. Let me reiterate that the differences between the iPhone Simulator and an actual device are substantial—game testing should really be done *only* on the device. Here's why:

- **Different CPUs**—Because the iPhone Simulator uses your Mac's CPU, the performance you see in the Simulator will be much different from what you experience on the device.
- **More (or Less) RAM**—Because you're using your Mac for development, design, and a host of other things, you probably have at least 2 GB of RAM on your development system. This provides you with a great deal of memory for textures. The iPhone device only lets you use 24 MB of memory for textures, sounds, and program code, so you have to watch how much texture data you are loading and remember to release what you don't need.
- **Different graphics capabilities**—Your Mac does not have the same graphics card as your iPhone, and the Simulator uses a software rasterizer for rendering to the screen.
- **Different OpenGL/OpenGL ES support**—Because the iPhone Simulator runs on your Mac, it supports the full implementation of OpenGL—not just OpenGL ES. Although this might sound like a good thing, it can be really problematic. You can

end up with something that works great in the iPhone Simulator, but just crashes or runs slowly on the iPhone. All your real testing should be on the real device.

- **Different device capabilities**—The iPhone and iPod Touch use technologies such as core location (a GPS/cellular location), Bluetooth, wireless, accelerometer, and with the iPhone 3GS, iPhone 4, and iPad, a magnetometer. Sure, your Mac has Bluetooth and wireless, but those can't be tested in the iPhone Simulator, nor can any game feature that relies on the accelerometer or magnetometer. If your game uses any device-specific technologies, you really should tether your iPhone and install and test the game there.

The bottom line here is that you should *always* test your game on a real device, and *only* rely on the iPhone Simulator for testing simple things, such as game preferences and prototyping your code. There really is nothing like the real thing.

Instruments

Instruments (shown in Figure 2.11) is great for tracking down things like memory leaks and identifying bottlenecks within your game. It is used to dynamically trace and profile your application when running on the iPhone Simulator or the iPhone device.

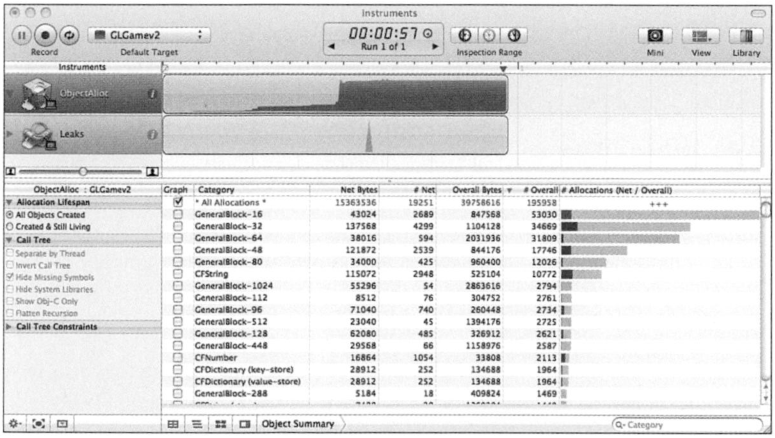

Figure 2.11   Instruments analyzes your application's code to help you find memory leaks and provide information that could help your game run faster and more efficiently.

Instruments has a graphical interface that is much easier to interpret than other debugging and performance tools, such as the command line-based GDB. It takes a little while to master the information it provides, but once you get the hang of using Instruments, you'll quickly wonder how you lived without it.

Shark

Shark is not some throwback to the *Jaws* movies, but it will attack your code in a good way. Shark is used to track down performance problems you may find in your code. Although you should always strive to get the best performance out of your applications, it is even more important with a game on a mobile device. You can be running a game quite happily, with everything working well, and then bang—suddenly the game starts chewing up a ton of memory or starts to act glitchy. The only way to really find out what's wrong with your code is to run Shark and profile the code at a low level.

Interpreting the information Shark provides (as shown in Figure 2.12) can be difficult, but it normally points you to the problematic code fairly quickly. Once Shark isolates the problem, it gives you clues on where to start focusing your attention.

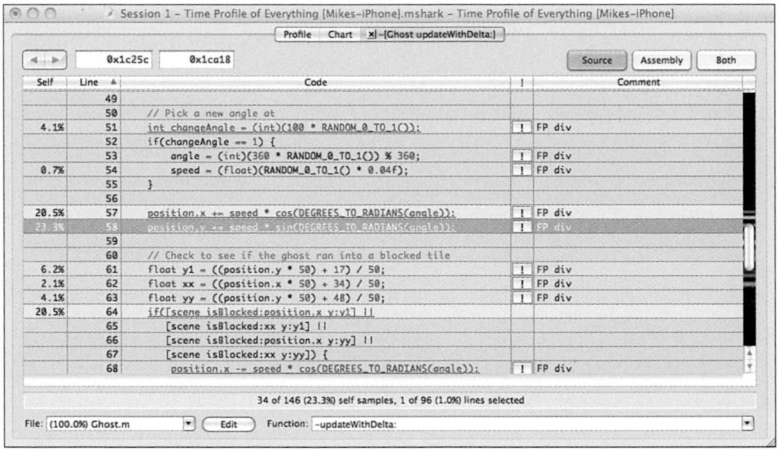

Figure 2.12   Shark, like Instruments, analyzes your application's code and helps you locate code that could be hindering performance.

Hiero

As each character of the font could be a different size, we cannot use the simple sprite sheet approach. In addition to creating a sprite sheet of font characters, Hiero (shown in Figure 2.13) also creates a control file that defines where each character image is within that sprite sheet. When we create our bitmap font class in Chapter 8, we will be using the control file produced by Hiero to get access to the characters within the bitmap font sprite sheet.

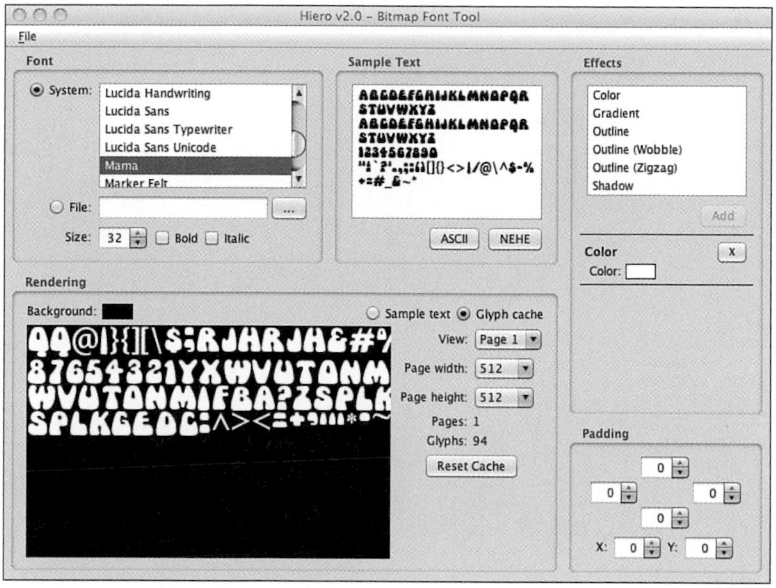

Figure 2.13   Hiero can be used to create sprite sheets for bitmap fonts
you want to use in your game.

Tiled

This is a free open source tile map editor. Tiled (shown in Figure 2.14) enables you to load tile images and then graphically draw your map. You can have multiple layers of tiles and multiple tile sets, and you can even define parameters associated with either the entire map, levels, or tile images.

Tiled will be covered in more detail in Chapter 9 when we build the tile map class to use as the output from the Tiled application for the game.

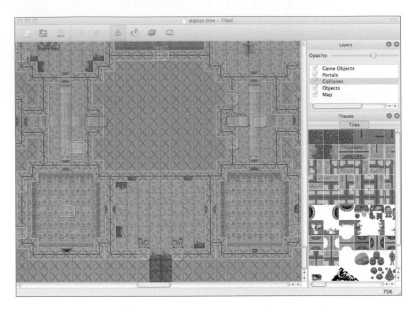

Figure 2.14   Tiled tile map editor.

Summary

This chapter covered a lot of material, but it was important to provide you with some insight into the terminology, technology, and tools we are going to use to build *Sir Lamorak's Quest*.

Before going any further, make sure you download and install the following applications on your system:

- The Xcode Tools (these get installed in a */Developer* directory at the root level of your hard drive). This includes Instruments and Shark automatically.
- Hiero, the bitmap font creation tool (**www.n4te.com/hiero/hiero.jnlp**).
- Tiled, the tile map editor (**mapeditor.org**).

What About Instruments and Shark?

After you've installed the Xcode Tools, you can find Instruments in */Developer/Applications*, and Shark in */Developer/Applications/Performance Tools*.

You might want to drag all of these applications to your dock so they're easier to get to during the development process.

With the information we have covered in this chapter, you will now be able to follow what is happening in the rest of this book. In the next chapter, we create a project in Xcode using the OpenGL ES project and take a detailed look at what the code does and why.

The Journey Begins

We have covered a lot in the first two chapters, and you should be starting to feel a little more comfortable with the terminology, technology, and tools we are going to use to create Sir Lamorak's Quest. Although the information we have covered has been important to understand before we start to dive into the code, diving into the code is fun and something I'm not going to keep you from any longer.

This chapter shows you how to create the Xcode project for *Sir Lamorak's Quest*, which you'll use throughout this book. We take a brief look at how you create things like projects in Xcode and take a walkthrough of the OpenGL ES template we will be using to get things started.

By the end of this chapter, you will have created a project and actually be rendering something to the screen. I think you will be surprised at how quickly you can get something rendered to the screen using the OpenGL ES Application template that is shipped with Xcode.

Creating the Project in Xcode

Before you go any further, you need to make sure that you have downloaded the iPhone SDK from the iPhone Dev Center. All the example projects in this book have been developed in the iPhone 3.1.3 SDK, using Xcode 3.2.3. All the code in this book has also been tested using the iPhone 4 SDK. After that has been done, you need to start the Xcode application, which can be found in */Developer/Applications*. I use Xcode a lot, so rather than having to hunt it down each time you want to use it, I recommend placing Xcode in your dock. Simply dragging the Xcode application icon to the dock will make it easily accessible from now on.

If this is the first time you have started Xcode, you will be shown a welcome screen, as shown in Figure 3.1.

Xcode's launch window (shown in Figure 3.1) gives you access to useful information such as the reference library and all the projects on which you are working. If you don't want this screen to appear when you start Xcode, simply uncheck *Show this window when Xcode launches* at the bottom of the window.

Figure 3.1   Xcode's welcome screen.

The next step is to create a new project. After closing the welcome window, go to *File >
New Project*. A window appears, asking you to choose a template for your new project
(see Figure 3.2).

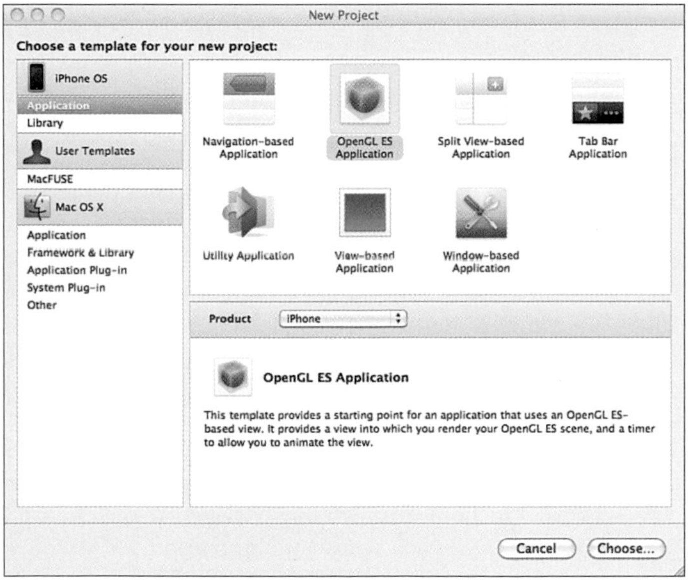

Figure 3.2   Xcode's New Project window.

Hint

Make sure that *Application* is selected under the iPhone OS section on the left side of the window, or you will not see the OpenGL ES Application template.

Once you have selected the OpenGL ES Application template and have made sure that the correct product is selected (that is, iPhone), click Choose. You will be presented with a panel in which you can choose where you want to create your project and what you want your project to be called.

Select a location and call the project **Chap03**. It is normal for project names to start with a capital letter. If there are a number of separate words in your title, mark the start of each word with a capital letter rather than a space.

Once you have pressed the Save button, you will be taken to the main Xcode window and presented with a number of files, as shown in Figure 3.3.

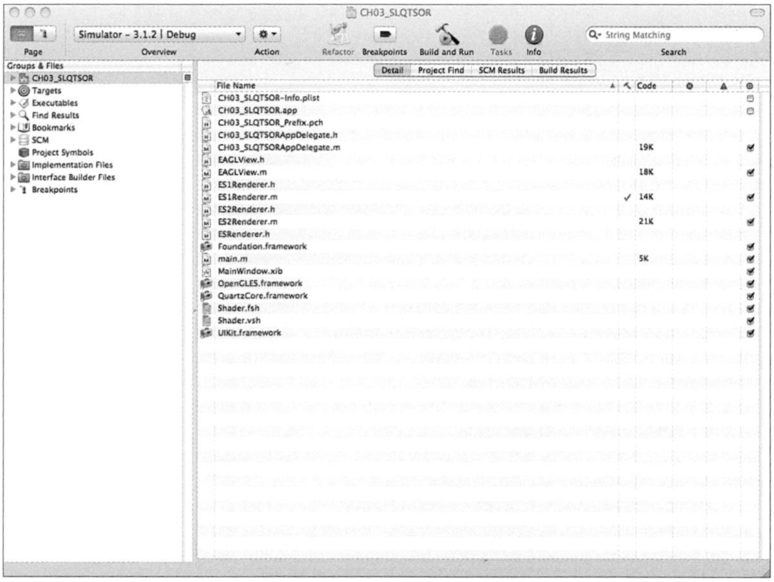

Figure 3.3   Xcode provides a detailed view of the files for your project.

Within the Xcode GUI, you will see a tree view on the left side. This is an outline of your project and enables you to see not only the groups and files you have created as part of your project, but also useful information such as errors and warnings that have been generated by the compiler, as well as breakpoints that have been set.

If not already selected, select the first entry in the tree view, called **Chap03** (if that is what you named your project). Once selected, you will notice that the large pane on the right side of the GUI shows you a number of files. This is the detail view and enables you to see all the files that currently exist within your project.

> **Note**
>
> To be honest, this is not a view that I use very much. I prefer to see the files in the tree view outline on the left and have the editor pane open on the right. Clicking a file in the detail pane causes the editor pane to open. This is personal preference, so find what works for you and go with it.

Running the Project

What we have created is a fully functional OpenGL ES application for the iPhone. We have not written a single line of code and yet we have a functioning application. To check out what it does, make sure that Simulator for the active iPhone SDK (for example, Simulator – 4.0) has been selected in the drop-down menu at the top left of the Xcode GUI (refer to Figure 3.3), and then hit the **_Build and Run_** button at the top of the GUI.

After a few seconds, the iPhone Simulator appears and the application we have just created runs. The application renders a multicolored square on the iPhone screen (as shown in Figure 3.4) that moves up and down. So there you have it—your first OpenGL ES application on the iPhone.

Figure 3.4   The iPhone Simulator running the
OpenGL ES template application.

Although we have not done anything yet other than create the project and give it a name, the application already contains the key elements needed to render to the screen using OpenGL, which is all that's needed to start working on the game.

Under the Hood

Now that we have our project created and running, let's look at the code that has been created. It's a good idea to understand what is there now before we start making changes. I will be covering the basics of Objective-C as we run through the code, but if there is anything you don't understand, it's worth checking out *The Objective-C Programming Language* from Apple.[1] In addition to the Objective-C documentation, the developer documentation available through Xcode is a valuable resource that provides a great deal of information on the SDK's APIs. This can also be accessed through **Help > Developer Documentation** within Xcode.

Application Delegate

The best place to start is the application delegate. This is an object to which the `UIApplication` class delegates some of its responsibilities. Using a delegate enables you to extend or customize the behavior of a class without needing to subclass it. For classes such as `UIApplication`, it is possible to specify a class that will receive notifications from the parent class (that is, `UIApplication`). The class that has been specified to receive these notifications is called a delegate.

Within `CH03_SLQTSORAppDelegate`, the following methods are delegate methods from `UIApplication`:

- **`applicationDidFinishLaunching`**: Sent by the default notification center after the application has been launched and initialized but before it has received its first event.

- **`applicationWillResignActive`**: Sent by the default notification center immediately before the application is deactivated. This occurs when an iPhone application is stopped when the user presses the Home button on his phone.

- **`applicationDidBecomeActive`**: Sent by the default notification center immediately after the application becomes active.

- **`applicationWillTerminate`**: Sent by the default notification center immediately before the application terminates.

---

[1] A PDF of *The Objective-C Programming Language* can be downloaded from Apple's developer site, at **developer.apple.com/documentation/Cocoa/Conceptual/ObjectiveC/ObjC.pdf**.

In Xcode, expand the tree view for *CH03_SLQTSOR* and then the Classes group. In here are the main files that have been created within our project in which we are interested. Select the *CH03_SLQTSORAppDelegate.h* file.

Once selected, you see an editor panel appear on the right side, containing the file's contents (also shown in Listing 3.1). Because the filename ends with *.h*, this particular file contains the interface definition for the class and is where you will find the following:

- Instance variable declarations
- Methods the class will respond to
- Properties that are going to be exposed by the class

Objective-C requires that you define the interface and implementation of a class in separate code blocks. Although it is perfectly fine to place both of these blocks in a single file, it is normal to create a *.h* (header) file for the interface definition, and a *.m* (method) file for the implementation definition.

Listing 3.1   **CH03_SLQTSORAppDelegate.h**

```
#import <UIKit/UIKit.h>

@class EAGLView;

@interface CH03_SLQTSORAppDelegate : NSObject <UIApplicationDelegate> {
    UIWindow *window;
    EAGLView *glView;
}

@property (nonatomic, retain) IBOutlet UIWindow *window;
@property (nonatomic, retain) IBOutlet EAGLView *glView;

@end
```

Examining the Header File

Let's take a closer look at what is inside the *CH03_SLQTSORAppDelegate.h* file:

```
#import <UIKit/UIKit.h>
```

First, the header file is importing the headers for all the classes found in the UIKit framework. This UIKit framework provides you with the classes you need to create and manage your application's user interface on the iPhone. UIKit includes all the objects, event handling, windows, views, and controls specifically designed for the touch interface. The classes include the UIView class, which we see later:

```
@class EAGLView;
```

@class defines a forward declaration in the header file. It tells the compiler that even though we are not importing the header for a class called EAGLView, it exists, and we will be importing it later. It's good practice to use a forward declaration like this in the header files and then do the actual import in the implementation file. It reduces the chances of circular references, which can become a real headache when you have a lot of source files all referring to one another.

> **Note**
>
> If you are wondering what the `EAGL` prefix to `EAGLView` stands for, it is "Embedded Apple OpenGL".

```
@interface CH03_SLQTSORAppDelegate : NSObject <UIApplicationDelegate> {
    UIWindow *window;
    EAGLView *glView;
}
```

This interface declaration is where the actual interface for the class is defined. The first line of the declaration provides the name of the class, `CH03_SLQTSORAppDelegate`, and links it to its superclass, `NSObject` (that is, it is going to inherit from `NSObject`). It also tells the class that it must adhere to the `UIApplicationDelegate` protocol.

A *protocol* is a great way to define a list of method declarations that are not attached to a specific class definition. By placing `<UIApplicationDelegate>` as part of the interface declaration, you are indicating to your class that it must implement the methods defined within the protocol so that the class can react correctly when it is sent delegate messages.

Having named the class and declared its parent along with any protocols, instance variables (ivars) are then defined in between the curly brackets (`{...}`).

The header file has two *instance variables* (or ivars), as follows:

```
UIWindow *window;
  EAGLView *glView;
```

This defines an ivar called `window` that is going to hold a pointer to an instance of the `UIWindow` class and `glView` that is going to hold a pointer to an instance of the `EAGLView` class. The `*` in front of the ivar names specifies that the instance variable is a pointer.

Outside the curly brackets, you'll see the property definitions followed by the `@end` class keyword:

```
@property (nonatomic, retain) IBOutlet UIWindow *window;
@property (nonatomic, retain) IBOutlet EAGLView *glView;

@end
```

`@property` is a convenient way of declaring the getter and setter accessor methods that are normally used to provide encapsulation (that is, you can tightly control the behavior of the getter and setter code and underlying management, while hiding that complexity from clients using your API). Although getter and setter accessor methods are really useful, they can also be a real pain to keep writing.

Objective-C helps us by giving us the `@property` declaration. By declaring a property in this way and then using the `@synthesize` declaration in the implementation code block, you don't have to write any code—the compiler will do the coding for you. If you declare a property in this way and don't use @synthesize in the implementation, you are still responsible for creating the getter and setter methods yourself. If you don't create those methods, you will be given a compiler error.

Examining the Implementation File

Now that we have covered the header file, we can look at the implementation file where the actual methods for this class are defined. Back in Xcode, select the *CH03_SLQTSORAppDelegate.m* file from the tree view. The contents of the file (also shown in Listing 3.2) appear in the editor screen on the right.

Listing 3.2   **CH03_SLQTSORAppDelegate.m**

```
#import "CH03_SLQTSORAppDelegate.h"
#import "EAGLView.h"

@implementation CH03_SLQTSORAppDelegate

@synthesize window;
@synthesize glView;

- (void) applicationDidFinishLaunching:(UIApplication *)application
{
    [glView startAnimation];
}

- (void) applicationWillResignActive:(UIApplication *)application
{
    [glView stopAnimation];
}

- (void) applicationDidBecomeActive:(UIApplication *)application
{
    [glView startAnimation];
}

- (void)applicationWillTerminate:(UIApplication *)application
{
    [glView stopAnimation];
}

- (void) dealloc
{
    [window release];
    [glView release];
    [super dealloc];
```

```
}
```

```
@end
```

To start, we import the header file (*CH03_SLQTSORAppDelegate.h*), along with *EAGLView.h*:

```
#import "CH03_SLQTSORAppDelegate.h"
#import "EAGLView.h"
```

These two lines notify the compiler to load the definition from the class's header file along with the definition of the EAGLView class. If you recall, there was a forward declaration of EAGLView earlier in the header file. This means that we were interested in using this class, but didn't require the class's definition. As we are accessing the class's properties and methods, we now have to notify the compiler to actually load the definition from the header file.

```
@synthesize window;
@synthesize glView;
```

Next, we synthesize the properties that were defined in the header file. This is really just telling the compiler that we want to have the getter and setter methods written for us rather than do it ourselves. As we saw earlier, if you define properties in the header but do not synthesize them or create your own getter and setter methods, you will get compilation errors.

```
- (void) applicationDidFinishLaunching:(UIApplication *)application
{
    [glView startAnimation];
}
```

We are now defining the methods within our class. The method declaration syntax is different from C or Java, but it is close enough to make it familiar very quickly. On the first line, we are declaring that the return type for this method is void, which means nothing is returned. This is followed by the name of the method and then any arguments that are required.

It is normal practice for method names to start with a lowercase letter, with each subsequent word being capitalized.[2] This is known as CamelCase. Following the name are any arguments that the method requires. This is an aspect of Objective-C that I really like. For example, rather than the method just telling you it needs three parameters and that one is an int, the next is a float, and the last is a double, you actually define names for the arguments, which are then displayed to you when you use this method in your code.

---

[2] Apple's *Introduction to Coding Guidelines* can be found at **developer.apple.com/mac/library/ documentation/Cocoa/Conceptual/CodingGuidelines/CodingGuidelines.html**.

Inside the preceding method, we are then sending a message to (calling a method on) the `glView` instance variable. You will remember from the header file that `glView` was declared with a type of `EAGLView`, so `glView` is a pointer to an instance of `EAGLView`. You may be wondering where we are actually creating the instance of `EAGLView` and linking it with `glView`. That's a good question, and I'll cover that in a moment.

The next sends a message to `glView`, telling it to run the method called `startAnimation`. Message expressions are enclosed in square brackets, with the object specified first and then followed by the name of the method to be run:

```
[glView startAnimation];
```

Why don't we see `glView` being allocated and initialized inside `CH03_SLQTSORAppDelegate`? Declaring an object of type `EAGLView` is not enough to actually create the new object to which `glView` will point. To allocate the memory needed to store an instance of `EAGLView`, it is necessary to send the class the `alloc` message. This causes the class to create the storage space necessary in memory to hold an instance of the class; for example:

```
glView = [EAGLView alloc];
```

If a class requires some kind of initialization, as most classes do, it is also necessary to make sure that the object created is initialized correctly. This is achieved by calling `init` on the object. `init` is by default the method name used to initialize an object, but it does not stop you from creating your own initializer method that could be called when creating an instance of your own classes (for example, `initWithMyName`). It is common practice to have `init` at the start of your initializer method name and to clearly mark your designated initializer method in the header file using comments. To initialize `glView`, you would use the following:

```
[glView init];
```

Rather than perform these operations separately, they are normally placed together:

```
glView = [[EAGLView alloc] init];
```

> **Note**
>
> Message nesting, as shown in the previous example, is valid because the `alloc` method returns the instance it just created, and the `init` method is sent to whatever was returned by `[EAGLView alloc]`. It should also be noted that `alloc` is a class method and not an instance method.

Knowing this, you are most likely wondering why this command cannot be seen in the application delegate methods we have been looking at. The reason is because the application's `window` and `glView` objects have been linked to objects inside an Interface Builder file. These files have the *.xib* extension, and are created using Interface Builder.

Interface Builder enables you to create GUI's for the iPhone and Mac. By default, the OpenGL ES template application has one of these files that contains the configuration of the applications `window` and `glView` objects. We will not need to touch this file to create the game, so for now it's enough to know this file exists and can be seen in the **Resource** group in the project outline. The file that contains your app's user interface is called *MainWindow.xib*. If you want to have a look at this file, simply double-click the *MainWindow.xib* file to open it in Interface Builder.

Inside this file, a UIWindow object has been linked to the window ivar in our application delegate, and a UIView object has been given a class identify of EAGLView and linked to the glView ivar in the app delegate. This means that when the *MainWindow.xib* file is unarchived, it creates a new instance of EAGLView to which glView points. When *MainWindow.xib* is unarchived, EAGLView is sent the initWithCoder message. This method inside EAGLView performs the necessary initialization, and therefore no code is necessary for this object to be allocated and initialized in the application delegate.

EAGLView

Having covered the app delegate, we should move onto EAGLView. This has been mentioned a lot in the previous section, and it contains the core of our current application. EAGLView is responsible for creating the OpenGL context that the application will be using to render to the screen. Select *EAGLView.h* in Xcode, and let's work through the code.

EAGLView.h

The header starts by importing the UIKit and QuartzCore[3] headers and also the *ESRenderer.h* header that defines a protocol.

```
#import <UIKit/UIKit.h>
#import <QuartzCore/QuartzCore.h>
#import "ESRenderer.h"
```

Next is the interface that specifies the name of the class, EAGLView, and inherits from a superclass of UIView. This means that EAGLView will have all the same abilities as UIView, plus whatever is added to EAGLView's implementation:

```
@interface EAGLView : UIView
```

Instance variables are defined next, within the interface definition code block, as shown here:

```
id <ESRenderer> renderer;
BOOL animating;
BOOL displayLinkSupported;
NSInteger animationFrameInterval;
```

---

[3] The QuartzCore framework provides access to Core Animation and other effects that are rendered in hardware for optimal performance. Core Animation provides the layer onto which OpenGL commands are rendered.

```
id displayLink;
NSTimer *animationTimer;
```

Although we have already discussed the creation of ivars in an interface, it is worth running through the `id` type used previously for the `renderer` ivar.

The `id` type can point to any Objective-C object. It provides no information about an object other than it is an object. This allows Objective-C to support dynamic typing, which allows a program to identify information about an object at runtime rather than compile time. The preceding declaration basically states that `renderer` will be an object of some type, as yet unknown, but that the object will support the `ESRenderer` protocol.

After the interface code block, two properties are defined. The first property is exposing the `animating` ivar that is a `BOOL`, which holds the current animating state of `EAGLView`. This property is defined as read only, and the getter accessor method that is created is given the name `isAnimating`. Notice in the following line of code that the name of the getter is specified using the `getter=` property attribute:

```
@property (readonly, nonatomic, getter=isAnimating) BOOL animating;
```

The `nonatomic` property causes the getter/setter code generated to simply return the value and does not generate robust access to properties in a multi-threaded environment. If you are not using multiple threads, the `nonatomic` property is the best and fastest option.

`animating` in the context of the `EAGLView` class is when the class is regularly rendering to the screen (that is, `animating` = `YES`). If the class is not currently rendering to the screen, `animating` = `NO`.

The next property is exposing the `animationFrameInterval` ivar. This is used within the calculation that defines how many times (that is, frames) per second the screen should be rendered:

```
@property (nonatomic) NSInteger animationFrameInterval;
```

The header file is completed with the declaration of the following three methods:

```
- (void) startAnimation;
- (void) stopAnimation;
- (void) drawView:(id)sender;
```

Notice the hyphen (–) at the beginning of each method declaration. This defines the methods to be instance methods so they can be used by instances of the class. If the method declaration began with a plus sign (+), that method can be used only by class objects.

EAGLView.m

Now let's look at the *EAGLView.m* file to see what it's doing.

The implementation starts off by importing the `EAGLView` header and two header files, called `ES1Renderer` and `ES2Renderer`:

```
#import "EAGLView.h"
#import "ES1Renderer.h"
#import "ES2Renderer.h"
```

`ES1Renderer` and `ES2Renderer` are classes that have been created by the OpenGL ES template and are used to provide access to OpenGL rendering based on the version of OpenGL ES that the device supports. These classes will be covered later in more detail.

Next is the declaration of a class method called `layerClass`. This method is overriding the `layerClass` method within the `UIView` class that `EAGLView` inherits from. This enables us to return the class we want to use as the backing layer for our view. Because we want to render using OpenGL, we need to return the `CAEAGLLayer` class that is a wrapper for a Core Animation surface, which is fully compatible with OpenGL ES functional calls:

```
+ (Class) layerClass
{
    return [CAEAGLLayer class];
}
```

Following the `layerClass` method declaration is the designated initializer for the `EAGLView` class. As described earlier, Interface Builder's configuration was used to associate a `UIWindow` with the app delegate's `window` ivar and also to associate a `View` with the `EAGLView` class and the `glView` ivar. Because `glView` was linked in the `xib` file, and it was using the `EAGLView` class, when the application runs and the `MainWindow.xib` file is unarchived, the `initWithCoder` method will be called within `EAGLView`:

```
- (id) initWithCoder:(NSCoder*)coder
```

This initializer first calls the parent class `initWithCoder` method. If a matching object is returned, it's then assigned to the "self" property and processing continues grabbing a pointer to the object's `CAEAGLLayer`. This is where we call the class method, `layerClass`, which we just defined.

```
if ((self = [super initWithCoder:coder]))⁴        {
        // Get the layer
        CAEAGLLayer *eaglLayer = (CAEAGLLayer *)self.layer;
```

The `eaglLayer` pointer is then used to set properties on `CAEAGLLayer`:

```
eaglLayer.opaque = TRUE;
```

This defines if the `CAEAGLLayer` to which we will be rendering should be transparent or not. In some applications, being able to see through the `CAEAGLLayer` could be useful, but it has a huge impact on performance. It's not a good idea to allow this within a game. Instead, the layer should be set to opaque.

---

⁴ This is one of the most confusing lines in Objective-C, and a great explanation of what it means can be found at **cocoawithlove.com/2009/04/what-does-it-mean-when-you-assign-super.html**.

> **Note**
>
> Allowing a `CAEAGLLayer` to be transparent requires a great deal of blending to the content behind the layer to show through. Blending is an expensive process that is likely to result in performance problems.

```
eaglLayer.drawableProperties = [NSDictionary dictionaryWithObjectsAndKeys:
                                [NSNumber numberWithBool:FALSE],
                                kEAGLDrawablePropertyRetainedBacking,
                                kEAGLColorFormatRGBA8,
                                kEAGLDrawablePropertyColorFormat,
                                nil];
```

After the opaque property has been set, it defines the `drawableProperties`. `drawableProperties` enables you to provide a dictionary of objects and keys that specify if the drawable surface retains its contents after displaying them, and also the internal color buffer format to be used for the drawable surface.

By default, the backing is not retained, which is good for games. Retaining the backing means that the contents of the render buffer that was used to render the screen are kept intact in case you want to reference that information before the next screen is rendered. This has a big impact on performance, and best practice states that it should be set to `FALSE` for games; `FALSE` is its default setting.

The color format `RGBA8` specifies a 32-bit format that corresponds to the OpenGL ES `GL_RGBA8888` format. Although using a 32-bit color format for your images gives you the maximum number of colors to use when rendering to the screen, it also takes up more memory and bandwidth on the iPhone. To maximize on performance, it is good practice to use the 16-bit format, `RGB565`, instead. This can have a positive impact on performance and should be used if the restrictions of using a 16-bit color format do not affect the quality of your images.

Once the layer properties have been set, the class then creates an instance of `ES2Renderer`:

```
renderer = [[ES2Renderer alloc] init];
```

`ES2Renderer` is a class that creates an `EAGLContext` to be used when rendering in OpenGL. It also creates and binds a `framebuffer`, `renderbuffer` and contains the actual OpenGL ES rendering commands. When `renderer` has been allocated and initialized, a check is performed to see if an instance of `ES2Renderer` was successfully created:

```
if (!renderer)
{
    renderer = [[ES1Renderer alloc] init];

    if (!renderer)
    {
        [self release];
```

```
        return nil;
    }
}
```

If renderer was not successfully created, an instance if `ES1Renderer` is created and again checked for success. If `renderer` is still `nil`, `EAGLView` is released and `nil` is returned to the calling class. If the creation of either an `ES1Renderer` or `ES2Renderer` instance was successful, the initialization continues.

As mentioned in Chapter 2, "The Three Ts: Terminology, Technology, and Tools," there are currently two versions of OpenGL ES: 1.1 and 2.0. Although all iPhones support version OpenGL ES 1.1, only the iPhone 3GS, iPhone 4, iPod Touch 3ʳᵈ Gen and iPad support OpenGL ES 2.0. The default behavior of the `EAGLView` class, created by the OpenGL ES template, is to configure an OpenGL ES 2.0 context using the `ES2Renderer` class—thus, the "2" in the class name. If that fails, it then attempts to create an instance of the `ES1Renderer` that creates a context using the 1.1 API—thus, the "1" in the class name. How logical is that?

If you are planning to develop your game to support both OpenGL ES 1.1 and 2.0, this is the approach to use. Having two distinct classes that handle either OpenGL ES 1.1 or 2.0 keeps the code clean and easy to maintain.

So, continuing with the initialization of the `EAGLView` class, once `renderer` has been assigned to an instance of either `ES1Renderer` or `ES2Renderer`, the ivars of the class are given default values, as follows:

```
animating = FALSE;
displayLinkSupported = FALSE;
animationFrameInterval = 1;
displayLink = nil;
animationTimer = nil;
```

Because we have not started to animate yet, animating is set to `FALSE`. `displayLinkSupported` is also set to `FALSE`. A check is performed last to set the final value for this ivar.

Version 3.1 of iPhone OS introduced a new API, `CADisplayLink`. When writing a game, it is often desirable to be notified of the vsync[5] state of the screen. `CADisplayLink` does this and enables you to call a method when the screen has physically finished being drawn. On the iPhone, the screen is physically redrawn 60 times per second, which means our game can render a maximum of 60 frames per second (FPS). Knowing when the screen has been rendered allows you to synchronize graphics rendering with the screen's refresh rate, which makes the game graphics render smoothly.

---

[5] Vertical synchronization, or vsync, refers to the synchronization of frame changes with the vertical blank interval of the screen.

> **Note**
>
> Because `CADisplayLink` was added to iPhone OS version 3.1, it won't be available on iPhones that run an older version of the OS. Although it would be great if everyone could upgrade to the latest version of the iOS so we only had to worry about the latest version, that never happens. There will always be someone who is running the previous or even the previous, previous, previous version of iOS, Unless something critical in your game is not available on those older versions, it's always a good idea to make sure your game will run on an older version of the OS to get maximum reach.

Other factors can impact how smooth a game renders, and we discuss this in more detail when we create the game loop in Chapter 4, "The Game Loop."

That is exactly what the next check in the code is doing:

```
NSString *reqSysVer = @"3.1";
NSString *currSysVer = [[UIDevice currentDevice] systemVersion];
if ([currSysVer compare:reqSysVer options:NSNumericSearch] !=
    NSOrderedAscending)
    displayLinkSupported = TRUE;
```

This code retrieves the current version of the system running on the device and compares that against the `reqSysVer` string. If the current version is less than `"3.1"`, `displayLinkSupported` stays at `FALSE`; otherwise, it is set to `TRUE`. This value is used later in the class when the animation is started.

The `return self` command in the initializer then marks the end of this method. At this stage, we now have an allocated and initialized instance of `EAGLView` to which `glView` is pointing.

The next method is used to draw the contents of the view to the screen:

```
- (void) drawView:(id)sender
{
    [renderer render];
}
```

When this class was initialized, `renderer` became a pointer to an instance of either `ES1Renderer` or `ES2Renderer`. Remember that this class imports the *ESRenderer.h* header file that defines a protocol. This protocol defines `render` as a method that must be supported by any class that uses that protocol. As you will see, both the `ES1Renderer` and `ES2Renderer` classes use that protocol, which means that `renderer` will respond to the `render` method. We will see what the `render` method does when we review the `ES1Renderer` class.

Straight after the `drawView` method is the `layoutSubviews` method, as follows:

```
- (void) layoutSubviews
{
    [renderer resizeFromLayer:(CAEAGLLayer*)self.layer];
    [self drawView:nil];
}
```

This method overrides a method inside UIView. The default implementation of the method inside UIView does nothing. The method inside the EAGLView calls the resize-FromLayer method inside the renderer object passing in the CAEAGLLayer, which is used for this view. The resizeFromLayer method inside the renderer object then binds a render-Buffer to the EAGLContext and gets the width and height of that buffer. Don't worry if this is not making much sense at the moment—this will be covered in more detail when we run through the `ES1Renderer` class.

The next two methods are defining the getters and setters necessary for the `animationTimeInterval` ivar:

```
- (NSInteger) animationFrameInterval
{
    return animationFrameInterval;
}


- (void) setAnimationFrameInterval:(NSInteger)frameInterval
{
    if (frameInterval >= 1)
    {
        animationFrameInterval = frameInterval;

        if (animating)
        {
            [self stopAnimation];
            [self startAnimation];
        }
    }
}
```

The first method, `animationFrameInterval`, is a getter and basically returns the current value of the `animationFrameInterval` ivar as an `NSInteger`. The second method is the setter and takes an `NSInteger` as the first argument. If the `frameInterval` value passed in is greater than or equal to 1, `animationFrameInterval` is updated. If the value of `frameInterval` were to be less than 1, nothing would be changed.

When the `animationFrameInterval` has been changed, the method then checks the state of the `animating` ivar. If it is `YES` (that is, the class is rendering to the screen a defined number of times per second), the animation is stopped and then started again. This is necessary because the method that starts the animation uses the `animationFrameInterval` value to calculate how many times per second the screen should be drawn. If the `animationTimeInterval` value changes, the FPS needs to be changed as well.

We are almost done reviewing `EAGLView`, with just three more methods to run through. We have just been discussing the `stopAnimation` and `startAnimation` methods that are called when setting the `animationFrameInterval` ivar, and these are the next two methods in the class:

```
- (void) startAnimation
{
    if (!animating)
    {
        if (displayLinkSupported)
        {
            displayLink = [NSClassFromString(@"CADisplayLink")
                displayLinkWithTarget:self selector:@selector(drawView:)];
            [displayLink setFrameInterval:animationFrameInterval];
            [displayLink addToRunLoop:[NSRunLoop currentRunLoop]
                forMode:NSDefaultRunLoopMode];
        }
```

`startAnimation` is called when you want to start rendering to the screen. Nothing will be drawn to the screen until this method is called; until then, the app is going to be a little plain. When this method is called, it first checks to see if the class is already animating by checking the `animating` ivar. If it isn't, it checks the `displayLinkSupported` ivar. Remember that this is set within the initializer of this class and is set to TRUE if the OS version on the iPhone is "3.1" or greater.

If the app is running on an iPhone with iPhone OS 3.1 or greater, it moves on to configure the `CADisplayLink` class. It does this by pointing the `displayLink` ivar at an instance of the `CADisplayLink` class and also specifying that the target for the display link is `self` and that the method (selector) that should be run is `drawView`.

Setting the target to `self` means that the `drawView` selector,[6] which is called when `CADisplayLink` fires, will run inside this class. You could have a method run inside another class instance if you want; in that case, you would specify that class instance as the target rather than `self`.

Once an instance of `CADisplayLink` has been created, its `frameInterval` is set to the `animationFrameInterval`, and it is added to the current run loop (thread). As mentioned earlier, the iPhone draws its screen 60 times per second. With a `frameInterval` of 1, the `drawView` method will be called 60 times per second. If you set the `frameInterval` to 2, the `drawView` method would be called just 30 times per second.

If `CADisplayLink` is not supported in the current version of iPhone OS, the method configures an `NSTimer` to call the `drawView` method:

```
        else
            animationTimer = [NSTimer scheduledTimerWithTimeInterval:
                (NSTimeInterval)((1.0 / 60.0) * animationFrameInterval)
                target:self
                selector:@selector(drawView:)
```

---

[6] In Objective-C, methods are referred to as selectors.

```
                userInfo:nil
                repeats:TRUE];

        animating = TRUE;
    }
}
```

This code shows an instance of `NSTimer` being created: `animationTimer`. This timer fires on a scheduled basis calculated by dividing `1.0` by `60.0`, which is the maximum number of frames the iPhone can display per second, and multiplying that by the `animationFrameInterval`. As with `drawView`, this causes the `animationTimer` to fire 60 times per second if the `animationFrameInterval` is 1, and 30 times per second if it's 2. This is basically mimicking the behavior of the `CADisplayLink`.

The key difference here is that `animationTimer` has no idea what the state of the screen refresh is, so it fires even if the screen is only halfway through being redrawn. This isn't normally a problem for simple 2D games, but when the complexity of the game increases, and the game updates and renders start to take longer, game play will become choppy.

Note

There are other factors to consider in terms of timing with game rendering and updates. These are covered in Chapter 4 when we talk about the game loop.

The final action of the `startAnimation` method is to set the `animating` ivar to `YES`.

`stopAnimation` is a simple method that reverses what has been performed in the `startAnimation` method:

```
- (void)stopAnimation
{
    if (animating)
    {
        if (displayLinkSupported)
        {
            [displayLink invalidate];
            displayLink = nil;
        }
        else
        {
            [animationTimer invalidate];
            animationTimer = nil;
        }

        animating = FALSE;
    }
}
```

The method checks to see if the class is animating, and if so, it then checks to see if `displayLinkSupported` is set. If it is supported, `displayLink` is invalidated, which stops it from firing and also removes it from the run loop, and the `displayLink` ivar is set to `nil`. In Objective-C, it is valid to send messages to `nil`. Sending a message to `nil` simply has no effect at runtime.

If `displayLinkSupported` is `FALSE`, the `animationTimer` is invalidated, which again stops it from firing and removes it from the run loop. `animationTimer` is also set to `nil` and the `animating` ivar is set to `FALSE`, as we have stopped animating the view.

The very last method that is defined is `dealloc`. This standard method is called when a class is no longer needed and its retain count has reached zero. The contents of this method should release all objects that the class created and basically clean up after itself:

```
- (void) dealloc
{
    [renderer release];

    [super dealloc];
}
```

`dealloc` is actually overriding the `dealloc` method inside `UIView`, which in turn is overriding the `dealloc` method inside `NSObject`. `NSObject` is the root class of almost all Objective-C class hierarchies through which objects inherit a basic interface to the runtime system and the ability to behave as Objective-C objects (for example, allocation and initialization).

One thing that should be remembered is that as you are overriding the `dealloc` method, you need to call your superclass's `dealloc` method as well, allowing the superclass to perform its own cleanup and move up the class hierarchy as necessary.

ES1Renderer

We have now been through the `EAGLView` class and covered in some detail what is happening. You will also remember that we mentioned the `ES1Renderer` and `ES2Renderer` classes, as instances of these were being created and used inside the `EAGLView` class.

As described earlier in this chapter, `ES1Renderer` deals with creating an OpenGL ES context that supports the OpenGL ES 1.1 API, and `ES2Renderer` deals with the 2.0 version of the API. Because we are only using OpenGL ES 1.1 in this book, and because OpenGL ES 2.0 is very different, I will only review the `ES1Renderer` class, and not `ES2Renderer`. OpenGL ES 2.0 is beyond the scope of this book.

Examining ES1Renderer.h

In Xcode, select the ES1Renderer.h file. Let's take a closer look.

First, we have the usual imports, and in this class, we are importing the header files we need when dealing with OpenGL:

```
#import "ESRenderer.h"
#import <OpenGLES/ES1/gl.h>
#import <OpenGLES/ES1/glext.h>
```

Importing these headers enables us to use the OpenGL ES commands available as part of OpenGL ES 1.1—thus, the `ES1` in the path of the header files.

Next, the interface is declared that is inheriting from `NSObject` and implementing the `ESRenderer` protocol. This is important—it makes sure that the `ES1Renderer` class is going to contain the methods defined in the protocol, such as `render`. Remember from earlier that we call the `render` method from inside the `EAGLView` class.

Next, the interface is declared with a number of ivars:

```
@interface ES1Renderer : NSObject <ESRenderer>


    EAGLContext *context;
    GLint backingWidth;
    GLint backingHeight;
    GLuint defaultFramebuffer, colorRenderbuffer;
```

The most important ivar being declared is `context`. This is an instance of `EAGLContext`, and it's that context into which all drawing will be done. The context is responsible for managing state information, commands, and resources needed to draw using OpenGL ES. Before drawing to the context, a complete framebuffer needs to be bound to the context. That may not make any sense at the moment, and I'll cover framebuffers later, but basically, the framebuffer is a chunk of memory that needs to be associated to the context.

The `backingWidth` and `backingHeight` ivars are going to hold the pixel dimensions of the `CAEAGLLayer` that is being used within `EAGLView`. Notice that the types being used are not just `int` or `uint` as you would normally use in Objective-C or C. Although you could easily just use Objective-C or C types, when dealing with the OpenGL API, it is standard practice to use the OpenGL types. This is because it makes porting OpenGL code to other platforms much easier since the OpenGL types are designed to be consistent between platforms, as opposed to programming language types.

Having defined the necessary ivars, the class then declares two public methods, as follows:

```
- (void) render;
- (BOOL) resizeFromLayer:(CAEAGLLayer *)layer;
```

The `render` method is used to render to the screen, as the name would imply. The `resizeFromLayer`, as described earlier, binds a render buffer to the `context` and gets the width and height of the layer that is passed in.

Examining ES1Renderer.m

Now let's look at the implementation of the `ES1Renderer` class, so open up the *ES1Renderer.m* file in Xcode.

The `ES1Renderer` class has a standard initializer that doesn't take any arguments:

```
- (id) init
{
    if (self = [super init])
    {
```

The first action of the initializer is to assign the value of [super init] to self and is a standard pattern when initializing a class.

Now that self is correctly assigned to our instance of the class, we assign a new instance of the EAGLContext: the context:

```
context = [[EAGLContext alloc] initWithAPI:kEAGLRenderingAPIOpenGLES1];
```

As we saw earlier, EAGLContext is responsible for managing the state information, commands, and resources when drawing with OpenGL ES. You'll notice that, when initializing the context using initWithAPI, we are passing in kEAGLRenderingAPIOpenGLES1 that tells the context that it needs to support the OpenGL ES 1.1 API. If we were setting up a context to support the 2.0 version, you would use the kEAGLRenderingAPIOpenGLES2 constant instead.

Next, check to make sure that the context has been created correctly:

```
if (!context || ![EAGLContext setCurrentContext:context])
   {
       [self release];
       return nil;
   }
```

If context is nil or NO when setting the context, self is released, which is important because it has been allocated and is taking up memory. Second, nil is returned to the calling class, signifying that the class instantiation has failed. This tells the calling class, EAGLView in our case, that there was a problem creating and setting the OpenGL ES context and the necessary action can be taken.

Creating the Framebuffer and Renderbuffer

The initializer has now created and set the context for our view to an EAGLContext that supports OpenGL ES 1.1, so it's now time to create and bind the *framebuffer* and *renderbuffer* that are going to be used with our context. Remember from earlier that a context cannot be used without a framebuffer.

The terms *framebuffer* and *renderbuffer* are new, so it's worth running through what they are and how they are used at a high level before we look at the code to create them.

When using OpenGL ES, the platform on which you are developing needs to provide a platform-specific library that provides functions to create and manipulate a rendering context. It is the rendering context that maintains a copy of all the OpenGL ES state variables and executes the OpenGL ES commands. On the iPhone, the EAGLContext class provides this by executing the OpenGL ES commands and interacting with Core Animation that ultimately presents the final image to the user via the CAEAGLLayer.

Although the context we have created processes OpenGL commands, it is not the final destination for those commands. On the iPhone, all images are rendered into framebuffer objects. Framebuffer objects are able to very precisely control the creation of color, depth, and stencil targets. These targets are commonly known as renderbuffers and are where pixels are finally created. Renderbuffers are normally 2D images with a height, width, and color format.

As part of the initialization of OpenGL ES, it is necessary to create the framebuffer and renderbuffer and assign the renderbuffer to the context we have as storage for the final image that is going to be rendered to the screen.

Now that you know what framebuffers and renderbuffers are, let's look at how they are generated.

All OpenGL commands start with a `gl` prefix (such as `glRotate`), which makes them easy to spot in your code. You will also notice some OpenGL ES commands that end in OES. These commands are specific to OpenGL ES and are not found in the full OpenGL API:[7]

```
glGenFramebuffersOES(1, &defaultFramebuffer);
glGenRenderbuffersOES(1, &colorRenderbuffer);
```

These commands are actually reasonably easy to identify. You can see that we are creating a framebuffer (using `glGenFramebufferOES`) and a renderbuffer (using `glGenRenderbufferOES`). In OpenGL, everything you generate has a name. This name is normally a `GLuint` value that can be used to reference that object later.

The `glGenFramebufferOES` command places the `GLuint` name for the framebuffer that is created into the `defaultFramebuffer` ivar. The same is done for the `colorRenderBuffer`.

It is possible to generate more than one buffer at a time. Replacing the number `1` in the current commands with a larger number will cause OpenGL ES to generate the specified number of buffers. If more than one buffer is required, the second argument would need to be an array able to hold all the buffer names returned. For now, only one renderbuffer and framebuffer is required, so `1` is specified:

```
glBindFramebufferOES(GL_FRAMEBUFFER_OES, defaultFramebuffer);
glBindRenderbufferOES(GL_RENDERBUFFER_OES, colorRenderbuffer);
```

Having created the buffers, they are then bound to `GL_FRAMEBUFFER_OES` and `GL_RENDERBUFFER_OES`. Because it is possible to generate a number of framebuffers or renderbuffers, it's important to make sure you bind to the ones you want to use, which is what the previous commands are doing:

```
glFramebufferRenderbufferOES(GL_FRAMEBUFFER_OES,
    GL_COLOR_ATTACHMENT0_OES, GL_RENDERBUFFER_OES, colorRenderbuffer);
```

Finally, the renderbuffer is attached to the framebuffer as `GL_COLOR_ATTACHMENT0_OES`. It is possible to have multiple renderbuffers associated to a single framebuffer. Here, `glFramebufferRenderbufferOES` is used to attach the render buffer to the framebuffer as a specific attachment.

---

[7] Information on the OpenGL ES API can be found at **www.khronos.org/opengles/1_X/**.

That's it for the initializer. All that is left is to return the object to the caller:

```
return self;
```

What we have just reviewed is the tip of the iceberg with regard to the initialization of OpenGL ES. To gain a deeper understanding of how to work with OpenGL ES on the iPhone, you should review Apple's documentation, *OpenGL ES Programming Guide for iPhone OS*.[8] The next method in the source file is `render`, but I'm going to come back to that method in a moment and actually look at the `resizeFromLayer` method next. This method is important because it completes the setup of OpenGL ES. Once an instance of `ES1Renderer` has been created, the `resizeFromLayer` method is called, and it carries out some important steps:

```
- (BOOL) resizeFromLayer:(CAEAGLLayer *)layer {
```

The actual method declaration specifies that the method returns a `BOOL`. This is used to see if the methods actions were successful or not. The only argument is an `CAEAGLLayer` object. The layer is passed in from the calling method—`EAGLView`, in this case—and is the `CAEAGLLayer` that has been associated with the `EAGLView` instance.

To make sure that the correct renderbuffer is currently bound, this method uses the `colorRenderbuffer` ivar that has been populated with the renderbuffer name generated earlier:

```
glBindRenderbufferOES(GL_RENDERBUFFER_OES, colorRenderbuffer);
```

When the renderbuffer has been bound, it's then time to allocate storage to the `EAGLContext` that was created earlier. The context receives OpenGL ES commands, but it's not the final destination for those commands. The Core Animation layer that was defined within `EAGLView` will ultimately place pixels onto the screen, and it needs somewhere to store these pixels. That storage location is the renderbuffer, previously created during the class initialization. The following command binds the `layer` drawable object to the OpenGL ES renderbuffer that has just been bound:

```
[context renderbufferStorage:GL_RENDERBUFFER_OES fromDrawable:layer];
```

Now that the necessary storage has been assigned for our CAEAGLLayer, the dimensions are taken from the renderbuffer. These dimensions are used later when setting up the glViewport:

```
glGetRenderbufferParameterivOES(GL_RENDERBUFFER_OES,
    GL_RENDERBUFFER_WIDTH_OES, &backingWidth);
glGetRenderbufferParameterivOES(GL_RENDERBUFFER_OES,
    GL_RENDERBUFFER_HEIGHT_OES, &backingHeight);
```

---

[8] The *OpenGL ES Programming Guide for iPhone OS* can be found at **developer.apple.com/iphone/ library/documentation/3DDrawing/Conceptual/OpenGLES_ProgrammingGuide/**.

The dimensions of the renderbuffer are placed in the `backingWidth` and `backingHeight` ivars ready for use later; then the framebuffer is checked to make sure all components have been set up correctly:

```
if (glCheckFramebufferStatusOES(GL_FRAMEBUFFER_OES) !=
      GL_FRAMEBUFFER_COMPLETE_OES) {
    NSLog(@"Failed to make complete framebuffer object %x",
    glCheckFramebufferStatusOES(GL_FRAMEBUFFER_OES));
    return NO;
}

return YES;
```

If the check fails, a message is logged and `NO` is returned; otherwise, `YES` is returned.

The render method

Now it's time to tackle the most interesting method in this class: the `render` method. The `render` method is called on a regular basis from the `EAGLView` class, and is responsible for rendering the multi-colored box on the iPhone screen and moving it up and down, as shown earlier in Figure 3.4. It's where we actually start to create some pixels after all the setup has been done.

Because we are going to be rendering something to the screen, a number of new concepts around OpenGL need to be covered. I cover them briefly in this chapter and then go into more detail when we start to create our own class for rendering sprites to the screen.

To start off, the `render` method is very simple, and it takes no arguments:

```
- (void) render {
```

The next line, which is a comment, tells us that this is the place for us to insert our own rendering code. As mentioned earlier, the template has created a full application, and there is nothing to stop us from changing the code in the render method and rendering something other than the colored square shown in Figure 3.4. We could drop in some code that rendered an entire 2D scene, but we're not quite there yet.

After the comment, you will see a couple of arrays:

```
static const GLfloat squareVertices[] = {
      -0.5f,  -0.33f,
       0.5f,  -0.33f,
      -0.5f,   0.33f,
       0.5f,   0.33f,
};
```

The first array, `squareVertices`, is used to store the vertices to draw a square. Each corner of the square is defined using a vertex, which is a point in three-dimensional space. In OpenGL, a vertex normally has three elements: x, y, and z values. Although a vertex can have three elements, that doesn't mean it *has* to have all three. As you can see in this example, there are only the x and y values, since the square is in 2D. Each line represents just the x and y coordinates of each vertex.

Figure 3.5 shows how the *x*-, *y*-, and *z*-axis are arranged in OpenGL.

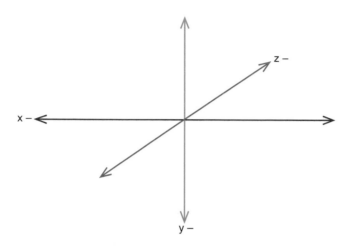

Figure 3.5   OpenGL axis configuration.

By default, the origin (that is, the point at `0, 0, 0`) in OpenGL ES on the iPhone is in the middle of the screen. OpenGL ES also uses it own units (that is, each unit in OpenGL does not represent a single pixel on the screen by default). It is up to you to define what an OpenGL unit represents, such as a pixel, a meter, a mile, and so on.

Figure 3.6 provides you with a template for the default OpenGL units used, which is why the values defining the vertices of the square may look a bit odd. If you were expecting the units to be in pixels, we would be defining vertices that create a square that is only fractions of a pixel wide, which is not so useful. As you saw when you ran the application earlier, the square is bigger than the values shown in the earlier code. The reason for this is because, *by default, an OpenGL unit is half the width and height of the iPhone screen.*

To get a better understanding of this, let's make a change to the application and see what happens.

If you are running the application through the iPhone Simulator, iPhone 3GS, iPhone 4, or iPad, you can make changes to the *ES2Renderer.m* file. If you are running the application on an earlier iPhone model, make your changes in the *ES1Renderer.m* file. The changes needed are the same in both files.

Open up the appropriate file and locate the `render` method. Replace the current definition of the `squareVertices` with the following:

```
static const GLfloat squareVertices[] = {
        -1.0f,  -1.0f,
         1.0f,  -1.0f,
        -1.0f,   1.0f,
         1.0f,   1.0f,
};
```

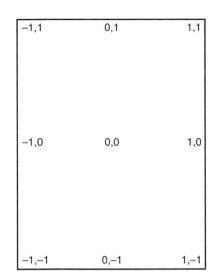

Figure 3.6   Mapping the iPhone's default
OpenGL coordinates.

Now run the application by pressing Build and Run. The application should run and
show a colored square moving up and down the screen as before, but this time, the rectangle will be the full size of the iPhone screen, as shown in Figure 3.7.

> **Note**
>
> The gray bar you see at the bottom of Figure 3.7 is due to the fact that the colored square
> was moving when the screenshot was taken. The colored rectangle really does fill the entire
> screen, and OpenGL ES moves this block up and down, as with the earlier example (thus,
> the gray bar shown here).

This demonstrates that the x and y dimensions of the screen in OpenGL units are -1.0 to
1.0, even though the x and y aspect ratios are different. If you change those values, you
see that you can make it draw shapes other than a square just by changing the vertices. You
also notice that the colors displayed within the shape you draw also change.

Figure 3.7   Chap03 application with changed
vertices.

Defining the Color Values

Now let's look at the next array, which defines the colors used within the shape being drawn:

```
static const GLubyte squareColors[] = {
      255, 255,   0, 255,
      0,   255, 255, 255,
      0,     0,   0,   0,
      255,   0, 255, 255,
};
```

By defining a separate color for each individual vertex, OpenGL will blend the color from that vertex into the colors from the other vertices in the shape. If the color were the same for each vertex, you would then end up with a shape being filled with only one color. If any of the vertices have different colors, the shape will be filled with the colors blending into each other.

Each vertex color in the `squareColors` array is represented by four values. Looking at the array, you'll notice that the numbers are grouped into fours. Each group of four represents values for Red, Green, Blue, and Alpha, respectively. There are four groups in total, defining a separate color for each vertex in the shape. Most colors in OpenGL are defined using these four elements.

Positioning

The next variable created is going to be used when calculating the position to render the square:

```
static float transY = 0.0f;
```

The following method makes sure that the current `EAGLContext` is the context that was created earlier:

```
[EAGLContext setCurrentContext:context];
```

We have actually already set this in the `init` method, and because we only have one context, this line is redundant. It does no harm being included and would be necessary if you were using more than one context. The same goes for the next line of code:

```
glBindFramebufferOES(GL_FRAMEBUFFER_OES, defaultFramebuffer);
```

As with the context, we have already bound `defaultFramebuffer`. If you had more than one frame buffer, you would be able to select and bind the required one at this point.

Now that we have things set up as we need, it's time to define the `glViewport`. The point of computer graphics is to be able to take a 3D image and project it onto a 2D surface (i.e., the screen) and still have it look three-dimensional. Within OpenGL, converting a 2D or 3D object coordinates into pixels on a screen is performed through three operations, as follows:

- Transformations
- Clipping
- Viewport

Transformation is the process of rotating, scaling, and translating a model, view, or projection. Transformations are represented by matrices, which can be multiplied together to perform a number of transformations on a single vertex for example. Although you don't need to be completely up to speed on your matrix mathematics, it is worth just refreshing a little so that the terminology being used is at least familiar. I ended up looking through my children's school textbooks to refresh my knowledge of matrix math.

Clipping is the process of discarding those pixels that lie outside of a defined clipping plane (rectangular window).

Viewport is the final stage where our transformed 3D models are rendered onto a 2D screen. This is also known as the viewport transformation.

Based on this short explanation, you can see that you will need to define the size of the viewport onto which the rendered scene is displayed. This is really simple for *Sir Lamorak's Quest*, since we are defining a viewport that matches the full size of the iPhone's screen. This is exactly the setup used within the OpenGL ES template:

```
glViewport(0, 0, backingWidth, backingHeight);
```

Remember that the `backingHeight` and `backingWidth` were set from reading the dimensions of the renderbuffer associated with the context. Here, we are defining the `Viewport` to match the dimensions of the iPhone's screen.

Now that you have defined the viewport, you need to make sure that the matrices associated with `GL_PROJECTION` and `GL_MODELVIEW` are reset. Within OpenGL, there are different matrix modes: `GL_PROJECTION` and `GL_MODELVIEW,` for example. Each mode has its own 4×4 matrix that can be transformed.

The `GL_PROJECTION` mode is used while rendering the 2D representation of the rendered scene within the viewport. Most of the time, especially in a 2D game, the matrix for this mode does not need to be changed. The more useful matrix mode to use is `GL_MODELVIEW`. This mode is used to apply transformations to the vertices (that is, translation, rotation, and scaling):

```
glMatrixMode(GL_PROJECTION);
glLoadIdentity();
glMatrixMode(GL_MODELVIEW);
glLoadIdentity();
```

These commands are used to reset the matrix being used by each of the matrix modes. An *identity matrix*, shown in Figure 3.8, is a square matrix of any dimension whose elements are 1 from the top-left to bottom-right of the matrix, with zeros everywhere else. Any other square matrix that is multiplied by this matrix will equal itself (that is, no transformation will be made).

$$\begin{bmatrix} 1 & 0 & 0 \\ 0 & 1 & 0 \\ 0 & 0 & 1 \end{bmatrix}$$

Figure 3.8   An identity matrix.

The `glLoadIdentity()` command loads this default matrix and resets any transformations that have occurred on the current active matrix mode.

How OpenGL Works

Now is a good time to talk about how OpenGL works. OpenGL is literally a state machine. You put OpenGL into various states, and it stays that way until you change it. The commands that were just discussed, such as `glMatrixMode`, are *state commands*. This means that the last `glMatrixMode` command we used took `GL_MODELVIEW` as its parameter, and that the current matrix mode is now `GL_MODELVIEW`.

Any OpenGL transformation we perform now will effect how the vertices (model) are represented in 2D space. There are many other state commands in OpenGL, and we will see a couple of them shortly.

Applying Transformations on the Model

Now that we know that the matrix mode is `GL_MODELVIEW` and the identity matrix has been loaded, we can start to perform some transformations on the model. If you think back to when we ran the application, you'll remember that the colored square box was moving up and down on the screen. Given that the vertices defining the shape are fixed in an array, you may be wondering how the square is able to move. This is accomplished using the following OpenGL command:

```
glTranslatef(0.0f, (GLfloat)(sinf(transY)/2.0f), 0.0f);
```

`glTranslatef` multiplies the current matrix by a matrix that moves (that is, translates) the local coordinate system by the x, y, and z amount provided. In the previous command, the x and z values are always `0.0f`, which makes it so no translation happens along these axis. For the y-axis, a simple calculation is performed using the `transY` value, as defined earlier. Each time this method is called, the command translates the origin along the y-axis and draws the shape. This is how the shape moves along the vertices without changing the shape of the object.

This is a simple way of changing where rendering should take place within a scene. As you see in later chapters, it is sometimes necessary to actually perform matrix calculations on the models vertices themselves rather than use the built-in OpenGL transformations.

After the translation takes place, the `transY` variable is incremented, which causes the shape to continuously move as each frame is rendered:

```
transY += 0.075f;
```

As part of this transformation, the application needs to clear the screen between each frame. To accomplish this task, the application requires the two following commands:

```
glClearColor(0.5f, 0.5f, 0.5f, 1.0f);
glClear(GL_COLOR_BUFFER_BIT);
```

The first command, `glClearColor`, sets the color to be used when clearing the screen, and the second, `glClear`, actually does the clearing.

The clear color is defined with the standard four elements for a color (red, green, blue, and alpha). One difference you will notice from the colors defined in the `squareColors` array (described earlier in the section, "Defining the Color Values") is that the numbers are all floats. It is normal in OpenGL to use floats in the range of 0.0 and 1.0 for things like colors and even texture coordinates, which we will see later. When defining the clear color, each element can only have a value between 0.0 and 1.0, which is zero (0.0 = 0%) to full intensity (1.0 = 100%).

The `glClear` command takes a bitwise OR of masks that indicate the buffers that are to be cleared. The possible options are as follows:

- `GL_COLOR_BUFFER_BIT`
- `GL_DEPTH_BUFFER_BIT`

These commands are used only for clearing the color buffer; however, if you wanted to clear both the color buffer and the depth buffer, you would structure the command as follows:

```
glClear(GL_COLOR_BUFFER_BIT || GL_DEPTH_BUFFER_BIT);
```

Rendering to the Screen

Once the screen is cleared, you can get down to the business of actually getting something rendered to the screen.

So far, we have an array of vertices and an array of colors for each vertex. Now we want to feed that data into OpenGL, which renders the information to the screen. To do this, we make use of OpenGL pointers: namely, the `glVertexPointer` and `ColorPointer`:

```
glVertexPointer(2, GL_FLOAT, 0, squareVertices);
```

`glVertexPointer` enables you to specify the location and size of an array of vertex coordinates to use when rendering. `glVertextPointer` takes the following four parameters:

- **Size:** The number of coordinates per vertex—in this case, 2, as we are only using x and y coordinates.
- **Type:** The data type of the coordinates in the array—in this case, the data type is `GL_FLOAT`.
- **Stride:** The number of bytes to stride (jump) between each vertex.
- **Data:** The first coordinate element of the data array to read.

We will go into these in more detail in Chapter 5, "Image Rendering," but for now, we are telling OpenGL that we have an array called `squareVertices` that contains vertex coordinates made up of two `GL_FLOATS` (that is, x and y), and that there is no stride (or jump) between them.

Having told OpenGL what data we want to use for our vertices, we need to tell OpenGL to actually use this data. This is accomplished using the following OpenGL ES command:

```
glEnableClientState(GL_VERTEX_ARRAY);
```

`glEnableClientState` enables individual client-side capabilities, such as `GL_VERTEX_ARRAY`, which tells OpenGL that we will use an array of vertices defined by `glVertexPointer`.

> **Note**
>
> All client-side capabilities are disabled by default, so you need to switch them on and off as necessary. To disable a client-side capability, use `glDisableClientState`.

Having defined the vertices, we can now do the same for the colors array using almost identical commands, as follows:

```
glColorPointer(4, GL_UNSIGNED_BYTE, 0, squareColors);
glEnableClientState(GL_COLOR_ARRAY);
```

After setting all this up, the following command is used to have OpenGL render to the screen:

```
glDrawArrays(GL_TRIANGLE_STRIP, 0, 4);
```

That's it—just one command (sort of anticlimactic, really). Having set up the arrays to hold the vertices and colors, and then configured OpenGL to use those arrays, we basically just issue the `glDrawArrays` command, and off it goes.

The `glDrawArrays` command uses just three parameters. The first parameter is the mode used to draw the vertices; possible values are as follows:

- `GL_POINTS`
- `GL_LINE_STRIP`
- `GL_LINE_LOOP`
- `GL_LINES`
- `GL_TRIANGLE_STRIP`
- `GL_TRIANGLE_FAN`
- `GL_TRIANGLES`

Each of these constants defines the primitives OpenGL should render with the given vertices. For our purposes, we are using `GL_TRIANGLE_STRIP`, which enables us to define two triangles using just four vertices. Whereas OpenGL supports quads, OpenGL ES does not; it only renders triangles (see the section, "What OpenGL ES Can (And Can't) Do," in Chapter 2). Because almost everything we will render is going to be a quad (rectangle) with an image attached, we need to use two triangles to define that quad.

The second parameter defines the start index within the array of vertices that has been passed in, and the third parameter defines how many vertices are to be read from the array.

As you can imagine, this means we could load an array of vertices and then pick and choose where we start within that array and how many vertices we use. With `glDrawArrays`, one limitation is that the vertices must be sequential once you start rendering them. `glDrawElements` is the command to use if you want to jump around inside an array without using sequential vertices.

Having issued the `glDrawArrays` command, we now have an image in the render-buffer that is ready to be displayed. All that is left is to present that image to the screen. The final two commands in this method responsible for doing this are the following:

```
glBindRenderbufferOES(GL_RENDERBUFFER_OES, colorRenderbuffer);
[context presentRenderbuffer:GL_RENDERBUFFER_OES];
```

The first command that binds the renderbuffer isn't necessary in this example. As you saw earlier, the renderbuffer has already been bound, so you don't need to bind it here, but the template includes it for completeness.

The second command actually does all the work by asking the context to present the renderbuffer to the screen. You may remember from earlier that it's actually the context using Core Animation that finally places the pixels in the renderbuffer onto the screen. However, it is the `presentRenderbuffer` command that actually makes it happen.

> **Note**
>
> Something we discuss in later chapters is performance. It's worth noting that we should re-duce the number of these draw commands as much as possible throughout the code. There is CPU overhead when you call the OpenGL draw commands because data is moved to the GPU and so forth. If you have hundreds of draw commands per frame, you quickly run into performance problems. We cover how to overcome this performance issue when we create the `Image` class in Chapter 5.

Summary

This has been a long journey into the code of the OpenGL ES template. Although I'm not attempting to teach you in detail about the technologies that are necessary to write a game in OpenGL on the iPhone, I think it was important to explain in some depth how the OpenGL ES template works.

You have seen how to set up an OpenGL ES view capable of rendering using a frame-buffer and renderbuffer, and how to decide which version of OpenGL ES you want to use. You have walked through the steps to configure OpenGL ES before you actually render something to screen (such as the matrix mode). You have also seen how you can perform transformations, such as translations on the models you are rendering.

Finally, you saw how you take the data that defines your model and, along with color information, feed it into OpenGL ES so it renders those elements to the renderbuffer before it can render the image to the screen.

If there is anything you didn't understand, you might want to go back and re-read this chapter. There are also some excellent resources on the Internet that you can refer to if you need to refresh your memory about things, such as matrix mathematics and OpenGL.

The next chapter deals specifically with the game loop. In Chapter 4, you take the OpenGL ES template app created in this chapter and make changes so that it is better-suited to handling a game. After that's set up, we run through the concept of a *game loop* in more detail.

The Game Loop

One of the most important elements of a game is the game loop. It is the heartbeat that keeps the game ticking. Every game has a series of tasks it must perform on a regular basis, as follows:

- Update the game state
- Update the position of game entities
- Update the AI of game entities
- Process user input, such as touches or the accelerometer
- Play background music and sounds

This may sound like a lot, especially for a complex game that has many game elements, and it can take some time to process each of these stages. For this reason, the game loop not only makes sure that these steps take place, but it also ensures that the game runs at a constant speed.

This chapter shows you how to build the game loop for *Sir Lamorak's Quest*. We take the OpenGL ES template app created in Chapter 3, "The Journey Begins," and make changes that implement the game loop and the general structure needed to easily extend the game in later chapters.

Timing Is Everything

Let's start out by looking at some pseudocode for a simple game loop, as shown in Listing 4.1.

Listing 4.1   **A Simple Game Loop**

```
BOOL gameRunning = true;
while(gameRunning) {
    updateGame;
    renderGame;
}
```

This example game loop will continuously update the game and render to the screen until `gameRunning` is `false`.

Although this code does work, it has a serious flaw: It does not take time into account. On slower hardware, the game runs slowly, and on fast hardware, the game runs faster. If a game runs too fast on fast hardware and too slow on slow hardware, your user's experience with the game will be disappointing. There will either be too much lag in the game play, or the user won't be able to keep up with what's going on in the game.

This is why timing needs to be handled within your game loop. This was not such a problem for games written back in the 1980s, because the speed of the hardware on which games were written was known, and games would only run on specific hardware for which they were designed. Today, it is possible to run a game on many different types of hardware, as is the case with the iPhone. For example, the following list sorts the devices (from slowest to fastest) that run the iOS:

- iPhone (first generation)
- iPod Touch 1G
- iPhone 3G
- iPod Touch 2G
- iPhone 3GS/iPod Touch 3G
- iPad/iPhone 4

As a game developer, you need to make sure that the speed of your game is consistent. It's not a good idea to have a game on the iPhone 3GS running so fast that the player can't keep up with the action, or so slow on an iPhone 3G that the player can make a cup of tea before the next game frame is rendered.

There are two common components used to measure a game loop's speed, as follows:

- **Frames Per Second (FPS):** FPS relates to how many times a game scene is rendered to the screen per second. The maximum for the iPhone is 60 FPS, as that is the screen's maximum refresh rate. In Listing 4.1, this relates to how many times the `renderGame` method is called.

- **Update speed:** This is the frequency at which the game entities are updated. In Listing 4.1, this relates to how many times the `updateGame` method is called.

Collision Detection

Timing is important for a number of reasons—not only the overall game experience, but, maybe more importantly, for functions such as collision detection. Identifying when objects in your game collide with each other is really important and is a basic game mechanic we need to use. In *Sir Lamorak's Quest*, having the player able to walk through walls is not a great idea, and having the player's sword pass through baddies with no effect is going to frustrate the player and keep them from playing the game.

Collision detection is normally done as part of the game's update function. Each entity has their AI and position updated as play progresses. Those positions are checked to see if it has collided with anything. For example, Sir Lamorak could walk into (or collide with) a wall, or a ghost could collide with an axe. As you can imagine, the distance a game entity moves between each of these checks is important. If the entity moves too far during each game update, it may pass through another object before the next check for a collision.

Having entities move at a constant speed during each game update can help to reduce the chances of a collision being missed. There is, however, always a chance that a small, fast-moving entity could pass through another object or entity unless collision checks are implemented that don't rely solely on an entities current position, but also its projected path. Collision detection is discussed in greater detail in Chapter 15, "Collision Detection," which is where we implement it into the game.

The Game Loop

The game loop is a key, if not *the* key, element in a game. I spent considerable time tweaking the game loop for *Sir Lamorak's Quest*, and it was something that I revisited a number of times, even after I thought I had what was needed.

There are so many different approaches to game loops. These range from the extremely simple closed loops you saw earlier in Listing 4.1, up to multithreaded loops that handle things such as path finding and complex AI on different threads. I found that I actually started off with the very simple approach that then became more complex as the game developed (and as I ran into issues).

We will not review some of the different game loops that I tried through the development of *Sir Lamorak's Quest*. Instead, we'll focus on the game loop used in the game, rather than diving down some rabbit hole we'll never end up using.

Frame-Based

The easiest type of game loop is called a frame-based loop. This is where the game is updated and rendered once per game cycle, and is the result of the simple game loop shown in Listing 4.1. It is quick and easy to implement, which was great when I first started the game, but it does have issues.

The first of these issues is that the speed of the game is directly linked to the frame rate of the device on which the game is running—the faster the hardware, the faster the game; the slower the hardware, the slower the game. Although we are writing a game for a very small family of devices, there are differences in speed between them that this approach would highlight.

Figure 4.1 shows how frames are rendered more quickly on fast hardware and more slowly on slower hardware. I suppose that could be obvious, but it can often be overlooked when you start writing games, leaving the player open to a variable playing experience. Also remember that each of these frames is performing a single render and update cycle.

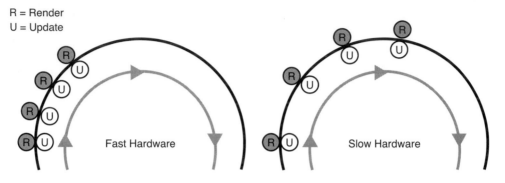

Figure 4.1   Entity following a curved path on slow and fast hardware.

A time-based variable interval loop is similar to the frame-based approach, but it also calculates the elapsed time. This calculation is used to work out the milliseconds (*delta*) that have passed since the last game cycle (frame). This delta value is used during the update element of the game loop, allowing entities to move at a consistent speed regardless of the hardware's speed.

For example, if you wanted an entity to move at 1 unit per second, you would use the following calculation:

```
position.x += 1.0f * delta;
```

Although this gets over the problem of the game running at different speeds based on the speed of the hardware (and therefore the frame rate), it introduces other problems. While most of the time the delta could be relatively small and constant, it doesn't take much to upset things, causing the delta value to increase with some very unwanted side effects. For example, if a text message arrived on the iPhone while the user was playing, it could cause the game's frame rate to slow down. You could also see significantly larger delta values causing problems with elements, such as collision detection.

Each game cycle causes an entity in Figure 4.2 to move around the arc. As you can see in the diagram, with small deltas, the entity eventually hits the object and the necessary action can be taken.

However, if the delta value were increased, the situation shown in Figure 4.3 could arise. Here, the entity is moving at a constant distance, but the reduced frame rates (and, therefore, **increased** delta) has caused what should have been a collision with the object to be missed.

Don't worry—there is a reasonably easy solution, and that is to use a time-based, fixed interval system.

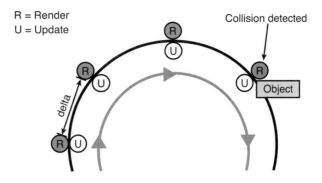

Figure 4.2   Frames using a small delta value.

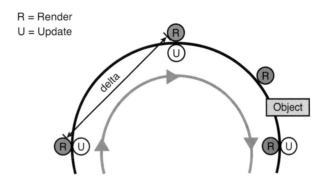

Figure 4.3   Frames using a large delta.

Time-Based, Fixed Interval

The key to this method is that the game's state is updated a variable number of times per game cycle using a fixed interval. This provides a constant game speed, as did the time-based variable interval method, but it removes issues such as the collision problem described in the previous section.

You'll remember that the previous methods tied the game's update to the number of frames. This time, the game's state could be updated more times than it is rendered, as shown in Figure 4.4. We are still passing a delta value to the game entities, but it's a fixed value that is pre-calculated rather than the variable delta that was being used before (thus, the term *fixed interval*).

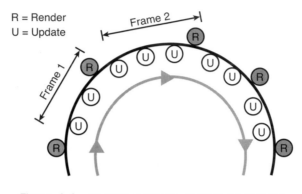

Figure 4.4   Variable numbers of updates per frame with a single render.

This system causes the number of game updates to be fewer when the frame rate is high, but it also increases the number of game updates when the frame rate is low. This increase in the number of game updates when the game slows down means that the distance each frame travels is constant. The benefit is that you are not losing the chance to spot a collision by jumping a large amount in a single frame.

Getting Started

The project that accompanies this chapter already contains the game loop and other changes we are going to run through in the remainder of this chapter. You should now open the project *CH04_SLQTSOR*. We run through the changes and additions to the project since Chapter 3.

> **Note**
>
> This project should be compiled against version 3.1 or higher of the iPhone SDK. The `CADisplayLink` function used in this example is only available in version 3.1 of the iPhone SDK. If you compile this project using iPhone SDK 3.0 or less, it still works, but you will

need to use `NSTimer` rather than `CADisplayLink`. Using iPhone SDK 3.0 or less will also generate warnings, as shown in Figure 4.5.

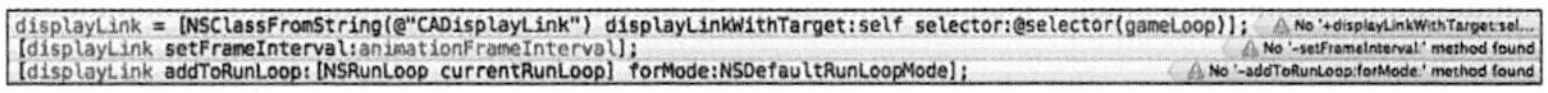

Figure 4.5   Errors generated in EAGLView.m when compiling against iPhone SDK version 3.0 or lower.

When you open the *CH04_SLQTSOR* project in Xcode, you see a number of new groups and classes in the **Groups & Files** pane on the left that have been added to the project since Chapter 3, including the following:

- **Group Headers:** This group holds global header files that are used throughout the project.
- **Abstract Classes:** Any abstract classes that are created are kept in this group. In *CH04_SLQTSOR,* it contains the **AbstractScene** class.
- **Game Controller:** The game controller is a singleton class used to control the state of the game. We will see how this class is used and built later in this chapter.
- **Game Scenes:** Each game scene we create (for example, the main menu or main game) will have its own class. These classes are kept together in this group.

Let's start with the changes made to the `EAGLView` class.

Inside the EAGLView Class

The first change to *EAGLView.h,* inside the Classes group, is the addition of a forward declaration for the `GameController` class. This class does not exist yet, but we will create it soon:

```
@class GameController;
```

Inside the interface declaration, the following ivars have been added:

```
CFTimeInterval lastTime;
GameController *sharedGameController;
```

These instance variables will be used to store the last time the game loop ran and point to an instance of the GameController class, which we create later. No more changes are needed to the header file. Save your changes, and let's move on to the implementation file.

Inside the EAGLView.m File

In Xcode, select *EAGLView.m* and move to the `initWithCoder:` method. The changes in here center around the creation of the `renderer` instance. In the previous version, an instance of `ES2Renderer` was created. If this failed, an instance of `ES1Renderer` was created instead. We are only going to use OpenGL ES 1.1 in *Sir Lamorak's Quest*, so we don't need to bother with `ES2Renderer`.

Because we are not using ES2Renderer, the *ES2Renderer.h* and *.m* files have been removed from the project. The Shaders group and its contents have also been removed.

There is also an extra line that has been added to the end of the initWithCoder method, as shown here:

```
sharedGameController = [GameController sharedGameController];
```

The next change is the actual code for the game loop. We are going to have EAGLView running the game loop and delegating the rendering and state updates to the ES1Renderer instance called renderer. Just beneath the initWithCoder: method, you can see the game loop[1] code, as shown in Listing 4.2.

Listing 4.2   **EAGLView gameLoop: Method**

```
#define MAXIMUM_FRAME_RATE 45
#define MINIMUM_FRAME_RATE 15
#define UPDATE_INTERVAL (1.0 / MAXIMUM_FRAME_RATE)
#define MAX_CYCLES_PER_FRAME (MAXIMUM_FRAME_RATE / MINIMUM_FRAME_RATE)

- (void)gameLoop {

    static double lastFrameTime = 0.0f;
    static double cyclesLeftOver = 0.0f;
    double currentTime;
    double updateIterations;

    currentTime = CACurrentMediaTime();
    updateIterations = ((currentTime - lastFrameTime) + cyclesLeftOver);

    if(updateIterations > (MAX_CYCLES_PER_FRAME * UPDATE_INTERVAL))
        updateIterations = (MAX_CYCLES_PER_FRAME * UPDATE_INTERVAL);

        while (updateIterations >= UPDATE_INTERVAL) {
        updateIterations -= UPDATE_INTERVAL;

        [sharedGameController updateCurrentSceneWithDelta:UPDATE_INTERVAL];
    }

    cyclesLeftOver = updateIterations;
    lastFrameTime = currentTime;

    [self drawView:nil];
}
```

[1] The game loop code used is based on a tutorial by Alex Diener at http://sacredsoftware.net/tutorials/Animation/TimeBasedAnimation.xhtml.

When the game loop is called from either CADisplayLink or NSTimer, it first obtains the current time using CACurrentMediaTime(). This should be used instead of CFAbsoluteTimeGetCurrent() because CACurrentMediaTime() is synced with the time on the mobile network if you are using an iPhone. Changes to the time on the network would cause hiccups in game play, so Apple recommends that you use CACurrentMediaTime().

Next, we calculate the number of updates that should be carried out during this frame and then cap the number of update cycles so we can meet the minimum frame rate.

The MAXIMUM_FRAME_RATE constant determines the frequency of update cycles, and MINIMUM_FRAME_RATE is used to constrain the number of update cycles per frame.

Capping the number of updates per frame causes the game to slow down should the hardware slow down while running a background task. When the background task has finished running, the game returns to normal speed.

Using a variable time-based approach in this situation would cause the game to skip updates with a larger delta value. The approach to use depends on the game being implemented, but skipping a large number of updates while the player has no ability to provide input can cause issues, such as the player walking into a baddie without the chance of walking around or attacking them.

I tried to come up with a scientific approach to calculating the maximum and minimum frame rate values, but in the end, it really was simple trial and error. As *Sir Lamorak's Quest* developed and the scenes became more complex, I ended up tweaking these values to get the responsiveness I wanted while making sure the CPU wasn't overloaded.

The next while loop then performs as many updates as are necessary based on updateIterations calculated earlier. updateIterations is not an actual count of the updates to be done, but an interval value that we use later:

```
while (updateIterations >= UPDATE_INTERVAL) {
    updateIterations -= UPDATE_INTERVAL;

    [sharedGameController
        updateCurrentSceneWithDelta:UPDATE_INTERVAL];
}
```

This loops around reducing the interval in updateIterations by the fixed UPDATE_INTERVAL value and updates the games state. Once updateIterations is less than the UPDATE_INTERVAL, the loop finishes, and we load any fractions of an update left in updateIterations into cyclesLeftOver. This means we don't lose fractions of an update cycle that we can accumulate and use later.

With all the updates completed, we then render the scene:

```
[self drawView:nil];
```

The CADisplayLink or NSTimer now calls the game loop until the player quits or the battery runs out (which it could do, given how much they will be enjoying the game!).

This is not a complex game loop, although it may take a while to get your head around the calculations being done. I found that moving to this game loop reduced the CPU usage on *Sir Lamorak's Quest* quite significantly and really smoothed out the game.

The final changes to EAGLView are within the startAnimation method. To get things ready for the first time we run through the gameLoop, we need to set the lastTime ivar. Because the gameLoop will not be called until the animation has started, we need to add the following line to the startAnimation method beneath the animating = TRUE statement:

```
lastTime = CFAbsoluteTimeGetCurrent();
```

The selectors used when setting up the CADisplayLink and NSTimer also need to be changed. The new selector name should be gameLoop instead of drawView.

Having finished with the changes inside EAGLView, we need to check out the changes to ES1Renderer. This class is responsible for setting up the OpenGL ES context and buffers, as noted in Chapter 3. However, we are going to extend ES1Renderer slightly so it sets up the OpenGL ES state we need for the game and renders the currently active scene.

ES1Renderer Class

When you look inside the ES1Renderer.h file, you see a forward declaration to the GameController class, which is in the next section, and an ivar that points to the GameController instance. The rest of the header file is unchanged.

In Xcode, open the *ES1Renderer.m* file. The *GameController.h* file is imported, followed by an interface declaration, as shown here:

```
@interface ES1Renderer (Private)
    // Initialize OpenGL
    - (void)initOpenGL;
@end
```

This interface declaration specifies a category of Private and is being used to define a method that is internal to this implementation. (I normally create an interface declaration such as this inside my implementations so I can then declare ivars and methods that are going to be private to this class.) There is only one method declared, initOpenGL, which is responsible for setting up the OpenGL ES states when an instance of this class is created.

Although Objective-C doesn't officially support private methods or ivars, this is a common approach used to define methods and ivars that should be treated as private.

The next change comes at the end of the init method:

```
sharedGameController = [GameController sharedGameController];
```

This is pointing the sharedGameController ivar to an instance of the GameController class. GameController is implemented as a singleton. This is a design pattern, meaning there can be only one instance of the class. It exposes a class method called sharedGameController that returns a reference to an instance of GameController.

You don't have to worry if an instance has already been created or not because that is all taken care of inside the `GameController` class itself.

The next change is within the `render` method, shown in Listing 4.3. This is where the template initially inserted drawing code for moving the colored square. We will see the code used to draw the square again, but it's not going to be in this method. If you recall, this method is called by the game loop and needs to call the render code for the currently active scene.

Listing 4.3   **EAGLView render Method**

```
- (void) render {

    glClear(GL_COLOR_BUFFER_BIT);

    [sharedGameController renderCurrentScene];

    [context presentRenderbuffer:GL_RENDERBUFFER_OES];
}
```

First of all, `glClear(GL_COLOR_BUFFER_BIT)` clears the color buffer and then clears the screen, making it ready for the next scene to be rendered. For the rendering, the game controller is asked to render the currently active scene. This is how the `render` message is passed from the game loop to `ES1Renderer`, and then onto the game controller and eventually the `render` method inside the currently active game scene. Figure 4.6 shows how a game scene fits into the other classes we are reviewing.

The last line in this method presents the render buffer to the screen. If you remember, this is where the image that has been built in the render buffer by the OpenGL ES drawing commands is actually displayed on the screen.

Having looked at the changes to the `render` method, we'll move on to the `resizeFromLayer:` method. If you recall, the `resizeFromLayer:` method was responsible for completing the OpenGL ES configuration by assigning the renderbuffer created to the context (`EAGLContext`) for storage of the rendered image. It also populated the `backingWidth` and `backingHeight` ivars with the dimensions of the renderbuffer.

The following line of code has been added to this method that calls the `initOpenGL` method:

```
[self initOpenGL];
```

If this looks familiar, that's because this method was placed inside the interface declaration (described earlier) as a private category. As the `resizeFromLayer` method assigns the render buffer to the context and finishes up the core setup of OpenGL ES, it makes sense to place this OpenGL ES configuration activity in this method so we can set up the different OpenGL ES states needed for the game.

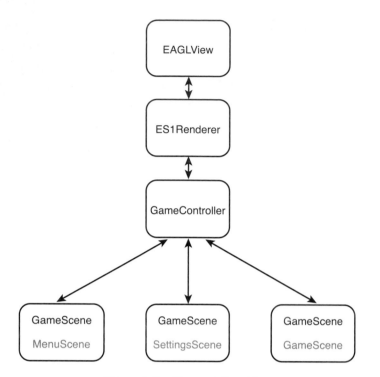

Figure 4.6   Class relationships.

Now move to the bottom of the implementation and look at the initOpenGL method. This method sets up a number of key OpenGL ES states that we will be using throughout the game.

If you move to the bottom of the implementation, you can see the following implementation declaration:

```
@implementation ES1Renderer (Private)
```

You can tell this is related to the interface declaration at the top of the file because it's using the same category name in brackets. There is only one method declared in this implementation: initOpenGL.

At the start of the method, a message is output to the log using the SLQLOG macro defined in the *Global.h* header file. The next two lines should be familiar, as they were covered in Chapter 3. We are switching to the GL_PROJECTION matrix and then loading the identity matrix, which resets any transformations that have been made to that matrix.

The next line is new and something we have not seen before:

```
glOrthof(0, backingWidth, 0, backingHeight, -1, 1);
```

This command describes a transformation that produces an orthographic or parallel projection. We have set the matrix mode to GL_PROJECTION, so this command will perform a transformation on the projection matrix. The previous function sets up an orthographic projection—in other words, a projection that does not involve perspective (it's just a flat image).

> **Note**
>
> I could go on now about orthographic and perspective projection, but I won't. It's enough to know for our purposes that glOrthof is defining the clipping planes for width, height, and depth. This has the effect of making a single OpenGL ES unit equal to a single pixel in this implementation because we are using the width and height of the screen as the parameters.

As mentioned earlier, OpenGL ES uses its own units (that is, a single OpenGL ES unit by default does not equal a single pixel). This gives you a great deal of flexibility, as you can define how things scale as they're rendered to the screen. For *Sir Lamorak's Quest*, we don't need anything that complex, so the previous function—which results in a unit equal to a pixel—is all we need.

Configuring the View Port

It is not common to make many changes to the GL_PROJECTION matrix apart from when initially setting up the projection.

As we are setting up the projection side of things, this is a good place to also configure the view port:

```
glViewport(0, 0, backingWidth , backingHeight);
```

The Viewport function specifies the dimensions and the orientation of the 2D window into which we are rendering. The first two parameters specify the coordinates of the bottom-left corner, followed by the width and height of the window in pixels. For the width and height, we are using the dimensions from the renderbuffer.

With the projections side set up, we then move onto setting up the GL_MODELVIEW matrix. This is the matrix that normally gets the most attention as it handles the transformations applied to the game's models or sprites, such as rotation, scaling, and translation. As noted in Chapter 3, once the matrix mode has been switched to GL_MODELVIEW, the identity matrix is loaded so it can apply the transformations.

```
glMatrixMode(GL_MODELVIEW);
glLoadIdentity();
```

Next, we set the color to be used when we clear the screen and also disable depth testing. Because we are working in 2D and not using the concept of depth (that is, the *z*-axis), we don't need OpenGL ES to apply any tests to pixels to see if they are in front of or behind other pixels. Disabling depth testing in 2D games can really help improve performance on the iPhone.

Not using the depth buffer means that we have to manage z-indexing ourselves (that is, the scene needs to be rendered from back to front so objects at the back of the scene appear behind those at the front):

```
glClearColor(0.0f, 0.0f, 0.0f, 1.0f);
glDisable(GL_DEPTH_TEST);
```

We finish up the OpenGL ES configuration by enabling more OpenGL ES functions. You may remember that OpenGL ES is a state machine. You enable or disable a specific state, and it stays that way until you change it back. We have done exactly that when disabling depth testing, which now stays disabled until we explicitly enable it again:

```
glEnableClientState(GL_VERTEX_ARRAY);
glEnableClientState(GL_COLOR_ARRAY);
```

The preceding states are used to tell OpenGL ES that we are going to be providing an array of vertices and an array of colors to be used when rendering to the screen. Other client states will be described and used later in Chapter 5, "Image Rendering."

That's it for the configuration of OpenGL ES. A lot of the OpenGL ES configuration should have looked familiar to you. A number of the functions in there were present in the render code from the OpenGL ES template. In the template, the states were set each time we rendered. Although this is fine, it isn't necessary to do that unless you are using state changes to achieve specific effects.

> **Tip**
>
> Keep the number of state changes being made within the game loop to a minimum, as some, such as switching textures, can be expensive in terms of performance. Is really is worth creating your own state machine that stores the states set in OpenGL ES. These can then be checked locally to see if they need to change i.e. there is no point in setting them if the values are the same.

That completes all the changes that have been made to the ES1Renderer class. We have added a pointer to the game controller, so rendering can be delegated to an instance of that class. We have also added some core OpenGL ES configuration to the class as well, making it responsible for all OpenGL ES setup that gives us a single place to go when we need to change that setup.

Game Scenes and the Game Controller

Having looked at the changes that were needed within EAGLView and ES1Renderer, we need to now look at the game controller and game scenes. Because we have the game loop in place, we need to introduce new classes that will handle the introduction of other game elements. The game elements I'm talking about are the different scenes used in *Sir Lamorak's Quest*, such as the following:

- **The main menu:** This is where players are taken when they first launch *Sir Lamorak's Quest*. The main menu provides the player with options to change the game settings, view credits, or start the game.
- **The game itself:** This is where the (game) action takes place.

The idea is that a game scene is responsible for its own rendering and game logic updates. This helps to break up the game into manageable chunks. I've seen entire games containing multiple scenes coded in a single class. For me, this is just too confusing, and creating a separate class for each scene just seemed logical.

In addition to the game scenes, we need to create a game controller. We have already seen the game controller mentioned in the `EAGLView` and `ES1Renderer` classes, so let's run through what it does.

Creating the Game Controller

Figure 4.6 shows the relationship between the classes (that is, `EAGLView`, `ES1Renderer`, and `GameController`), and the game scene classes.

The GameController Class

If we are going to have a number of scenes, and each scene is going to be responsible for its rendering and logic, we are going to need a simple way of managing these scenes and identifying which scene is active. Inside the game loop, we will be calling the game update and render methods on a regular basis. And because there will be multiple scenes, we need to know which of those scenes is currently active so the update and render methods are called on the right one. Remember from looking at `EAGLView` that inside the game loop, we were using the following code to update the game:

```
[sharedGameController updateCurrentSceneWithDelta:UPDATE_INTERVAL];
```

This line calls a method inside an instance of `GameController`. We are not telling the game controller anything about the scene that should be rendered as are expecting the `GameController` to already know.

> **Note**
>
> One important aspect of the game controller is that it is a singleton class. We don't want to have multiple game controllers within a single game, each with their own view of the game's state, current scene, and so forth.

Inside the *Game Controller* group, you find the *GameController.h* and *GameController.m* files. Open *GameController.h* and we'll run through it.

Although it may sound complicated to make a class a singleton, it is well-documented within Apple's Objective-C documentation. To make this even easier, we use the

SynthesizeSingleton macro created by Matt Gallagher.[2] Matt's macro enables you to turn a class into a singleton class simply by adding a line of code to your header and another to your implementation.

At the top of the *GameController.h* file, add the following `import` statement to bring in this macro:

```
#import "SynthesizeSingleton.h"
```

> **Note**
>
> I won't run through how the macro works, because all you need can be found on Matt's website. For now, just download the macro from his site and import the *SynthesizeSingleton.h* file into the project.

Next is another forward declaration to `AbstractScene`, which is a class we will be looking at very shortly. This is followed by an interface declaration that shows this class is inheriting from `NSObject` and implements the `UIAccelerometerDelegate` protocol:

```
@interface GameController : NSObject <UIAccelerometerDelegate>
```

`UIAccelerometerDelegate` is used to define this class as the delegate for accelerometer events, and it supports the methods necessary to handle events from the accelerometer.

Within the interface declaration, we have just a couple of ivars to add. The first is as follows:

```
NSDictionary *gameScenes;
```

This dictionary will hold all the game scenes in *Sir Lamorak's Quest*. I decided to use a dictionary because it allows me to associate a key to each scene, making it easier to retrieve a particular scene:

```
AbstractScene *currentScene;
```

As you will see later, `AbstractScene` is an abstract class used to store the ivars and methods common between the different game scenes. Abstract classes don't get used to create class instances themselves. Instead, they are inherited by other classes that override methods which provide class-specific logic.

> **Note**
>
> Objective-C does not enforce abstract classes in the same way as Java or C++. It's really up to the developer to understand that the class is meant to be abstract, and therefore subclassed—thus placing `Abstract` at the beginning of the class name.

---

[2] SynthesizeSingleton; see **cocoawithlove.com/2008/11/singletons-appdelegates-and-top-level. html**.

This works well for our game scenes, as each scene will have its own logic and rendering code, but it will have ivars and methods, such as `updateSceneWithDelta` and `renderScene`, that all scenes need to have. We run through the `AbstractScene` class in a moment.

After the interface declaration, the next step is to create a single property for the `currentScene` ivar. This makes it so `currentScene` can be both read and updated from other classes.

Creating the Singleton

So far, this looks just like any other class. Now let's add two extra lines of code to make this a singleton class:

```
+ (GameController *)sharedGameController;
```

This is a class method identified by the + at the beginning of the method declaration. Because this is going to be a singleton class, this is important. We use this method to get a pointer to the one and only instance of this class that will exist in the code, which is why the return type from this method is `GameController`.

Next, we have two more method declarations; the first is as follows:

```
- (void)updateCurrentSceneWithDelta:(float)aDelta;
```

This method is responsible for asking the current scene to update its logic passing in the delta calculated within the game loop. The next method is responsible for asking the current scene to render:

```
- (void)renderCurrentScene;
```

Now that the header is complete, open *GameController.m* so we can examine the implementation.

Inside GameController.m

To start, you can see that the implementation is importing a number of header files:

```
#import "GameController.h"
#import "GameScene.h"
#import "Common.h"
```

`GameScene` is a new class; it inherits from the `AbstractScene` class. Because we will be initializing the scenes for our game in this class, each scene we created will need to be imported. *Common.h* just contains the DEBUG constant at the moment, but more will be added later.

Next, an interface is declared with a category of `Private`. This just notes that the methods defined in this interface are private and should not be called externally to the class. Objective-C does not enforce this, although there really is no concept of a private method or ivar in Objective-C:

```
@interface GameController (Private)
```

```
    - (void)initGame;
@end
```

As you can see from this code, we are using `initGame` to initialize game scenes.

Next is the implementation declaration for `GameController`. This is a standard declaration followed by a synthesize statement for `currentScene`, so the necessary getters and setters are created. The next line is added to turn this class into a singleton class:

```
SYNTHESIZE_SINGLETON_FOR_CLASS(GameController);
```

The macro defined within the *SynthesizeSingleton.h* file adds all the code necessary to convert a class into a singleton. If you look inside the *SynthesizeSingleton.h* file, you see the code that gets inserted into the class when the project is compiled.

Notice that this class also has an `init` method. The `init` is used when the initial instance of this class is created. The formal approach to getting an instance of this class is to call the method `sharedGameController`, as we defined in the header file. This returns a pointer to an instance of the class. If it's the first time that method has been called, it creates a new instance of this class and the `init` method is called.

> **Tip**
>
> The name of the class method defined in the header is important; it should be `shared`, followed by the name of the class (for example, `sharedClassName`). The class name is passed to the macro in the implementation, and it is used to create the `sharedClassName` method.

If an instance already exists, a pointer to that current instance will be returned instead, thus only ever allowing a single instance of this class to exist. If you tried to create an instance of this class using `alloc` and `init`, you will again be given a pointer to the class that already exists. The code introduced by the synthesize macro will stop a second instance from being created.

`initGame` is called within the `init` method and sets up the dictionary of scenes, as well as the `currentScene`.

If you move to the bottom of the file, you see the implementation for the private methods.

Inside the `initGame` method, we are writing a message to the console, before moving on to set up the dictionary. It's good practice to make sure that all these debug messages are removed from your code before you create a release version. The next line creates a new instance of one of the game scenes, called `GameScene`:

```
AbstractScene *scene = [[GameScene alloc] init];
```

As you can see, `GameScene` inherits from `AbstractScene`. This means we can define `*scene` as that type. This enables you to treat all game scenes as an `AbstractScene`. If a game scene implements its own methods or properties that we need to access, we can cast from `AbstractScene` to the actual class the scene is an instance of, as you will see later.

Now that we have an instance of `GameScene`, we can add it to the dictionary:

```
[gameScenes setValue:scene forKey:@"game"];
```

This creates an entry in the dictionary that points to the scene instance and gives it a key of game. Notice that the next line releases scene:

```
[scene release];
```

Adding scene to the dictionary increases its retain count by one, so releasing it now reduces its retain count from two to one. When the dictionary is released or the object is asked to release again, the retain count on the object will drop to zero and the object's dealloc method will be called. If we didn't ask scene to release after adding it to the dictionary, it would not be released from memory when dictionary was released without another release call, which we may not realize we need to do. This is a standard approach for managing memory in Objective-C.

The last action of the method is to set the currentScene. This is a simple lookup in the gameScenes dictionary for the key game, which we used when adding the game scene to the dictionary. As additional game scenes are added later, we will add them to the dictionary with the following method:

```
currentScene = [gameScenes objectForKey:@"game"];
```

We only have a few more methods left to run through in the GameController class. Next up is the updateCurrentSceneWithDelta: method, shown here:

```
- (void)updateCurrentSceneWithDelta:(float)aDelta {
    [currentScene updateSceneWithDelta:aDelta];
}
```

This takes the delta value calculated within the game loop and calls the updateSceneWithDelta method inside the currentScene. Remember that we have set the currentScene to point to an object in the gameScene dictionary. These objects should all inherit from AbstractScene and therefore support the update method.

The same approach is taken with the render method, shown here:

```
-(void)renderCurrentScene {
    [currentScene renderScene];
}
```

The final method to review is accelerometer:didAccelerate, shown here:

```
- (void)accelerometer:(UIAccelerometer *)accelerometer didAcceler-
ate:(UIAcceleration *)acceleration {

}
```

This delegate method needs to be implemented because the class uses the UIAccelerometerDelegate protocol. When the accelerometer is switched on, this method is passed UIAcceleration objects that can be used to find out how the iPhone is being moved. This can then be used to perform actions or control the player inside the game. We aren't using this method in *Sir Lamorak's Quest*, but it's useful to understand how this information could be obtained. More information on user input can be found in Chapter 12, "User Input."

AbstractScene Class

`AbstractScene` was mentioned earlier, and as the name implies, it is an abstract class. All the game scenes we need to create will inherit from this class.

Open *AbstractScene.h* in the Abstract Classes group, and we'll take a look.

The header starts off by importing the OpenGL ES header files. This allows any class that inherits from *AbstractScene.h* to access those headers as well. The class itself inherits from `NSObject`, which means it can support operations such as `alloc` and `init`.

A number of ivars are defined within the interface declaration. Again, the ivars will be available to all classes that inherit from this class. The idea is to place useful and reusable ivars in this abstract class so they can be used by other game scenes. The ivars you will find here include the following:

- `screenBounds`: Stores the dimensions of the screen as a `CGRect`.
- `sceneState`: Stores the state of the scene. Later, we create a number of different scene states that can be used to track what a scene is doing (for example, transitioning in, transitioning out, idle, and running).
- `sceneAlpha`: Stores the alpha value to be used when rendering to the screen. Being able to fade everything in and out would be cool, so storing an overall `sceneAlpha` value that we can use when rendering enables us to do this.
- `nextSceneKey`: A string that holds the key to the next scene. If the `GameController` receives a request to transition out, the next scene specified in this ivar will become the current scene.
- `sceneFadeSpeed`: Stores the speed at which the scene fades in and out.

After the interface declaration, two more properties are defined, as follows:

```
@property (nonatomic, assign) uint sceneState;
@property (nonatomic, assign) GLfloat sceneAlpha;
```

These simply provide getter and setter access to the `sceneState` and `sceneAlpha` ivars.

Next, a number of methods are defined to support the game scenes, including the `update` and `render` methods we have already discussed:

```
- (void)updateSceneWithDelta:(float)aDelta;
```

```
- (void)renderScene;
```

There are also a few new methods, too. The first relates to touch events. The `EAGLView` class responds to touch events as it inherits from `UIView`, and these need to be passed to the currently active game scene. The active scene uses this touch information to work out what the player is doing. The following touch methods are used to accept the touch information from `EAGLView` and allow the game scene to act upon it:

```
- (void)touchesBegan:(NSSet*)touches withEvent:(UIEvent*)event
view:(UIView*)aView;
```

```
- (void)touchesMoved:(NSSet*)touches withEvent:(UIEvent*)event
  view:(UIView*)aView;
- (void)touchesEnded:(NSSet*)touches withEvent:(UIEvent*)event
  view:(UIView*)aView;
- (void)touchesCancelled:(NSSet*)touches withEvent:(UIEvent*)event
  view:(UIView*)aView;
```

The next method declared is similar to the touch methods. Just as touches are fed to each game scene, accelerometer events also need to be fed down in the same way. We have already seen that `GameController` is the target for accelerometer events; therefore, `GameController` needs to pass down accelerometer event information to the current game scene:

```
- (void)updateWithAccelerometer:(UIAcceleration*)aAcceleration;
```

That's it for the header file. Now let's move to the implementation file by opening *AbstractScene.m*.

You may be surprised by what you find in the implementation file. When I said earlier that the abstract class doesn't do anything, I really meant it. Apart from setting up the synthesizers for the two properties we declared, it just contains empty methods.

The idea is that the game scene that inherits from this class will override these methods to provide the real functionality.

That being the case, let's jump straight to the final class to review in this chapter: the `GameScene` class.

GameScene Class

The `GameScene` class is responsible for implementing the game logic and rendering code for the scene. As described earlier, a game scene can be anything from the main menu to the actual game. Each scene is responsible for how it reacts to user input and what it displays onscreen.

For the moment, we have created a single game scene that we will use for testing the structure of *Sir Lamorak's Quest*. You find the *GameScene.h* file inside the Game Scenes group in Xcode. When you open this file, you see that all we have defined is an ivar, called `transY`. We have no need to define anything else at the moment because the methods were defined within the `AbstractScene` class we are inheriting from.

> **Tip**
>
> When you inherit in this way, you need to make sure the header of the class you are inheriting from is imported in the interface declaration file (the *.h* file).

Because there is not much happening in the header file, open the *GameScene.m* file. This is where the magic takes place. All the logic for rendering something to the screen can be found in the *GameScene.m* file.

To keep things simple at this stage, we are simply implementing a moving box, just like you saw in Chapter 3 (refer to Figure 3.4). You may recall from the previous chapter that the logic to move the box, and the box rendering code itself, were all held within the render method. This has now been split up inside GameScene.

The updateSceneWithDelta method is called a variable number of times within the game loop. Within that method, we have defined the transY ivar, which increases within the updateSceneWithDelta method:

```
- (void)updateSceneWithDelta:(float)aDelta {
        transY += 0.075f;
}
```

When the updating has finished, the game loop will render the scene. This render request is passed to the GameController, which then asks the currently active scene to render. That request ends with the next method, renderScene.

The renderScene method is where the code to actually render something to the screen is held. As mentioned earlier, we are just mimicking the moving box example from the previous chapter, so the first declaration within this method is to set up the vertices for the box:

```
static const GLfloat squareVertices[] = {
    50, 50,
    250, 50,
    50, 250,
    250, 250,
};
```

> **Note**
>
> Do you notice anything different between the data used in this declaration and the one used in the previous project? Don't worry if you can't spot it; it's not immediately obvious.
>
> The vertex positions in the previous example were defined using values that ranged from -1.0 to 1.0. This time, the values are much bigger.

This behavior uses the OpenGL ES configuration we defined earlier in the initOpenGL method (located inside the ES1Renderer class). We configured the orthographic projection and view port. This now causes OpenGL ES to render using pixel coordinates, rather than defining the vertices for the square.

Going forward, this will make our lives much easier, as we can more easily position items on the screen and work out how large they will be.

Having defined the vertices for the square, we can define the colors to be used within the square. This is exactly the same as in the previous example.

Next, we perform a translation that moves the point at which the square is rendered. As before, we are not changing the vertices of the square, but instead moving the drawing origin in relation to where the rendering takes place:

```
glTranslatef(0.0f, (GLfloat)(sinf(transY)/0.15f), 0.0f);
```

Once the translation has finished, we point the OpenGL ES vertex pointer to the `squareVertices` array and the color pointer to the `squareColors` array:

```
glVertexPointer(2, GL_FLOAT, 0, squareVertices);
glColorPointer(4, GL_UNSIGNED_BYTE, 0, squareColors);
```

If you have a photographic memory, you may notice that there are a couple of lines missing from this section of code that were present in the previous example. When we last configured the vertex and color pointers, we enabled a couple of client states in OpenGL ES, which told OpenGL ES that we wanted it to use vertex and color arrays. There is no need to do that this time because we have already enabled those client states inside `ES1Renderer` when we performed the `initOpenGL` method. Remember that OpenGL ES is a state machine, and it remembers those settings until they have been explicitly changed.

Having pointed OpenGL ES at the vertices and colors, it's now time to render to the screen:

```
glDrawArrays(GL_TRIANGLE_STRIP, 0, 4);
```

At this point, our lovely colored box is rendered, but it isn't on the screen just yet. When this method is finished, it passes control back to the `GameController` and then up to the render method in `EAGLView`, whose next task is to present the renderbuffer to the screen. It is at that point that you actually see the square in the display.

Summary

We have created a number of new classes that give us a structure on which we can build going forward. We now have the ability to create any number of different game scenes, each of which will perform its own logic and rendering, all being controlled by the `GameController` class.

We use this structure throughout this book and build upon it to create *Sir Lamorak's Quest*.

In the next chapter, we go more in-depth on how to render images to the screen. This involves looking at OpenGL ES in greater detail and creating a number of classes that make the creation, configuration, and rendering of images in *Sir Lamorak's Quest* much easier.

Exercises

If you run the project for this chapter, you see the colored box moving up and down the screen. If you want the project to do more, try making some changes to the project, such as the following:

1. Create a new game scene called `TriangleScene` and change the rendering code so that it draws a triangle rather than a square.

   Hint

   Rather than drawing two triangles that make a square, which `GL_TRIANGLE_STRIP` is for, you only need a single triangle; `GL_TRIANGLES` is great for that. Remember, a triangle only has three points, not four.

2. After you create your new class, initialize it in the `GameController initGame` method and add it to the dictionary with a key.

Hint

Don't forget to make your new scene the current scene.

If you get stuck, you can open the *CH04_SLQTSOR_EXERCISE* project file to see what you need to do.

Image Rendering

One of the key elements of *Sir Lamorak's Quest*—and, in fact, all games, unless you're thinking about the old text-based adventures—is the ability to render images (sprites) to the screen. Without graphics, the game would be pretty dull.

In this chapter, we run through the key concepts needed to render images to the screen using OpenGL ES. We cover the basics of rendering triangles, texture mapping, loading textures from image files, and improving performance.

We won't cover all aspects of these items (doing so would require a book about double the size of the one you hold in your hands), but we cover enough so you understand how to use OpenGL ES within the following classes:

- `Image`
- `Texture2D`
- `TextureManager`
- `ImageRenderManager`

Together, these classes enable us to render any image we want to the screen quickly, both in terms of the code needed within the game as well as the game's performance.

Introduction to Rendering

A good place for us to start this chapter is looking at how we render something to the screen using OpenGL ES. If you tried the example at the end of the last chapter, you saw how a square and a triangle are configured and rendered to the screen.

The first point to note is that with OpenGL ES, there is no concept of a *quad* (that is, a primitive shape that can be defined using four vertices). Although quads are supported in OpenGL, OpenGL ES can only render shapes using triangles to the screen.

Although you may think this is a limitation, it really isn't. Every imaginable shape can be rendered to the screen by joining triangles together. Computer animation has been doing it this way for years. For example, you can render a quad using two triangles, as shown in Figure 5.1.

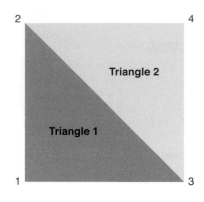

Figure 5.1   Creating a quad using the GL_TRIAN-
GLE_STRIP mode.

For *Sir Lamorak's Quest*, we will be rendering a lot of images on the screen, including the following:

- The player/character, Sir Lamorak himself.
- The baddies (that is, ghosts, monsters, a bat, and so on)
- Doors
- Tiles for the tile map
- Letters for fonts

Each of these items requires us to define a quad and then fill it with the necessary image (texture). We cover how to map a texture to a quad (or any shape, for that matter) later. For now, let's focus on how to define and render a quad.

Rendering a Quad

To render a quad, you need to define two triangles and then "stick" them together. If you tried the exercise at the end of Chapter 4, "The Game Loop," you may have spotted the hint I gave you. This hint suggested you try using a different drawing mode when asking OpenGL ES to render the contents of the vertices array we had set up. In Chapter 4, we used the `glDrawArrays` command and one of the following modes:

- `GL_TRIANGLES`
- `GL_TRIANGLE_STRIP`

These are not the only modes available to use, however. You can also use the following:

- `GL_POINTS`
- `GL_LINE_STRIP`
- `GL_LINE_LOOP`

- `GL_LINES`
- `GL_TRIANGLE_FAN`

For our needs, we'll work with `GL_TRIANGLES` and `GL_TRIANGLE_STRIP`.

The difference between these is in how OpenGL ES uses the vertices we provide and how many vertices we actually need. We used the following command in Chapter 4's example to render our quad (square):

```
glDrawArrays(GL_TRIANGLE_STRIP, 0, 4);
```

The first parameter defines the mode we want to use when rendering, and is set to `GL_TRIANGLE_STRIP`. The second parameter defines the stride, `0` (which we cover later), and the third parameter, `4`, defines how many vertices we wanted OpenGL ES to render.

So, what does using the `GL_TRIANGLE_STRIP` mode tell OpenGL ES to do? The clue is in the name. OpenGL ES creates a *strip of triangles* using the last two vertices from the previous triangle, plus an additional vertex to create a new triangle. This new triangle shares two of its vertices with the previously defined triangle. As you can see in Figure 5.1, a triangle will be drawn using vertices 1, 2, and 3 when OpenGL ES renders the vertices, and a second triangle will be drawn using vertices 3, 2, and 4.

It is also possible to turn the square into a house, giving the square a pointed roof by using just one more vertex; `GL_TRIANGLE_STRIP` makes this very simple. To create the triangle for the roof, simply add one more vertex to the four we have already defined. OpenGL ES then joins that vertex to the previous two to form another triangle. Figure 5.2 shows you the result of adding this extra vertex.

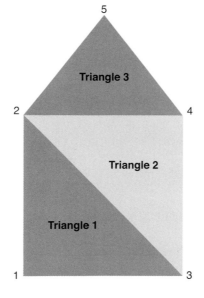

Figure 5.2   This house was created by adding a
fifth vertex.

Here, we've created three triangles using only five vertices. The triangles shown in Figure 5.2 are defined using the following vertices:

```
Triangle 1 = 1, 2, 3
Triangle 2 = 3, 2, 4
Triangle 3 = 4, 2, 5
```

The order in which the vertices are passed to OpenGL ES when using `GL_TRIANGLE_STRIP` is important so that it renders the triangles you are expecting. For example, if you provided the vertices in a different order than the preceding—say 1, 2, 4, and 3—you would get the result shown in Figure 5.3.

> **Tip**
>
> Having the vertices out of order is a common problem and certainly something I had to sort out a number of times. If you see an image such as that shown in Figure 5.3, there's a good chance that your vertices aren't in the correct order. The order of vertices should be kept the same to reduce confusion and rendering issues that are hard to trace.

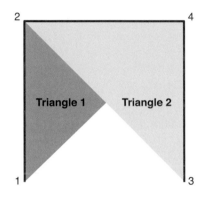

Figure 5.3   Result of using vertices in the order 1, 2, 4, and 3.

When using `GL_TRIANGLES`, OpenGL ES renders a single triangle for each set of three vertices in the array. To create the same quad shown in Figure 5.1, the vertices defined within the vertices array passed to OpenGL ES would need to be `1, 2, 3, 3, 2, 4`. When using `GL_TRIANGLES`, you need to define each triangle with all three of its vertices. If you don't, `GL_TRIANGLES` won't link from one triangle to the next, as is done when using `GL_TRIANGLE_STRIP`.

It is important that you understand the difference between these two modes. If you need to render a number of triangles that are all linked together, use `GL_TRIANGLE_STRIP`. However, if you want to render a bunch of triangles that aren't linked and are randomly placed, `GL_TRIANGLES` is the mode to use.

> **Note**
>
> Although I have said that you can use `GL_TRIANGLES` to render triangles in different loca-
> tions that are not linked, it is actually possible to achieve the same result using a
> `GL_TRIANGLE_STRIP`. If you define degenerate (zero-area) triangles in your vertex array, you
> can instruct OpenGL ES to move to a new vertex location without actually rendering the de-
> generate triangle. This enables you to introduce discontinuities, or "jumps," in the strip.
> `GL_TRIANGLE_STRIP` can also improve performance when rendering complex meshes
> (shapes).

Notice that you need four vertices to render a quad using `GL_TRIANGLE_STRIP` but six
vertices to render a quad when using `GL_TRIANGLES`. If you were rendering only a single
quad at a time, it would make sense to use `GL_TRIANGLE_STRIP` because it reduces the
number of vertices you need. There are, however, reasons why you don't want to draw
every item on the screen using separate OpenGL calls to `glDrawArrays`. We cover those
reasons later in this chapter.

Texture Mapping

Texture mapping is the process of applying an image (texture) to a primitive (for example, a
point, line, or polygon). This technique is useful because it enables you to add more real-
ism to a scene than using primitives alone. For example, if you wanted to render a wall
made of stone, you could render each stone on its own, providing all the vertices needed
to define the points for each stone, and then color the stone as necessary.

This would work but would be very hard to manage and could easily cause performance problems given the number of polygons required. An easier approach is to define a
polygon that is the size of your wall and then fill it with an image of a real stone wall. This
will look much more realistic and gives you the effect you need with a single polygon
rather than thousands.

The basic concept of texture mapping is that for each vertex defining a point in a
polygon, you also provide a vertex to a point in a texture. You then supply this information to OpenGL ES, which renders the texture inside the polygon while performing all
the complicated work involved to make the texture fit.

Texture Coordinates

Texture coordinates are used to define a location inside a texture. The vertices that define
a polygon can (in theory) be any number you want within an OpenGL ES 3D space. The
coordinates that define a texture are constrained by default, though, from 0 to 1 along
both the *t* and *s* axis, as shown in Figure 5.4.

The same coordinate system is used no matter how big or small the size of the texture
(that is, the maximum width or height of a texture is specified as `1.0`, regardless of the actual texture size). If you go beyond `1.0`, the results depend on how you have configured
parameters for clamping and tiling.

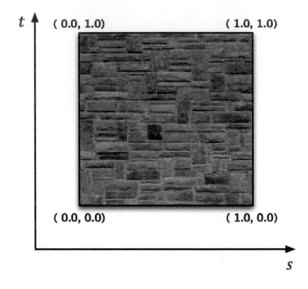

Figure 5.4   Texture coordinates and axis names.

Although the axis used when defining a polygon is normally called (x, y), it is common for the same axis when defining texture coordinates to be referred to as (s, t), as shown in Figure 5.4. Just to make things even more confusing, it is also common to see the polygon axis referred to as (u, v) rather than (x, y). This leads to the term *UV mapping*, which is used in many 3D applications (that is, the mapping of the (s, t) coordinates onto the (u, v) coordinates).

Figure 5.5 shows how we can map the texture coordinates to the polygon coordinates.

In looking at Figure 5.5, you can see that the following mapping coordinates are used to map the full texture to the polygon vertices:

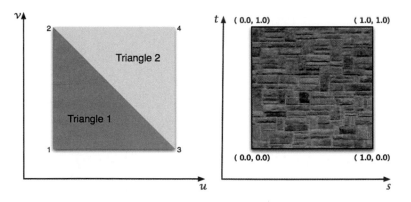

Figure 5.5   Polygon and texture coordinates.

```
Vertex 1 = (0.0, 0.0)
Vertex 2 = (1.0, 0.0)
Vertex 3 = (0.0, 1.0)
Vertex 4 = (1.0, 1.0)
```

If you just wanted to map a portion of the full texture to the polygon, we can adjust the texture coordinates as necessary. Figure 5.6 shows the texture coordinates for mapping just a quarter of the texture to the polygon.

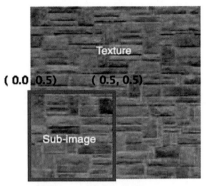

Figure 5.6   Texture coordinates defining one quarter of the texture.

This time, the mapping from the polygon vertices to the texture coordinates would be as follows:

```
Vertex 1 = (0.0, 0.0)
Vertex 2 = (0.5, 0.0)
Vertex 3 = (0.5, 0.5)
Vertex 4 = (0.0, 0.5)
```

If the polygon dimensions are larger or smaller than the texture defined by the texture coordinates, the texture is scaled up or down by OpenGL ES to fit the polygon dimensions. This is a useful technique for scaling images. By simply changing the dimensions of the polygon but keeping the mapping between the polygon vertices and the texture coordinates the same, the image can be scaled up or down as necessary. Two parameters control how OpenGL ES handles scaling:

```
glTexParameteri(GL_TEXTURE_2D, GL_TEXTURE_MIN_FILTER, GL_NEAREST);
glTexParameteri(GL_TEXTURE_2D, GL_TEXTURE_MAG_FILTER, GL_NEAREST);
```

We show you how to use these parameters later in this chapter.

Now that we have covered the basics on texture coordinates and how they can be mapped to polygon coordinates, we can move onto looking at the code we need to create a texture, load image data associated with that texture, and render that texture to the screen.

Interleaved Vertex Arrays

Before we push into the `ImageRenderManager` class, it's worth discussing *Interleaved Vertex Arrays* (IVA), which are used in the `ImageRenderManager`.

We have seen the term *vertex array* already, but we have not talked about it in much detail. From the code we have already seen, you may remember that we have been using vertex arrays to define the vertex data we have been passing to OpenGL ES:

```
static const GLfloat squareVertices[] = {
      50,  50,
     250,  50,
      50,  25,
     250, 250
};
```

This code shows how to define the square's vertices used in the `CH04_SLQTSOR` project in Chapter 4. This is known as a *vertex array*. At the moment, it contains nothing but vertex information for the square's geometry. We also define an array to store color information in `CH04_SLQTSOR`. This array contained the definition of a color for each vertex in the `squareVertices` array.

With an IVA, you create a single array that contains all the information in one contiguous block (for example, vertex and color), as illustrated in Figure 5.7. There is also other data that is also normally stored in arrays and passed to OpenGL ES, such as texture coordinates.

Figure 5.7 shows individual vertex and color arrays that have then been merged into a single IVA. Reducing the number of arrays that we need to pass to OpenGL ES improves performance; this is key to what `ImageRenderManager` was designed for.

Vertex Array

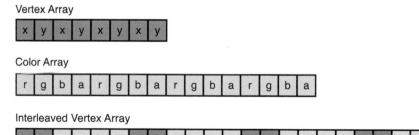

Color Array

Interleaved Vertex Array

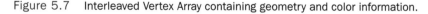

Figure 5.7   Interleaved Vertex Array containing geometry and color information.

When telling OpenGL ES about which vertex array to use when rendering, we have been using `glVertexPointer` and `glColorPointer`, as shown here:

```
glVertexPointer(2, GL_FLOAT, 0, vertexArray);
glColorPointer(4, GL_FLOAT, 0, colorArray);
```

Although the commands are different, the parameters they take and their meaning are very similar. When using `glColorPointer`, the first parameter defines the number of components per color. Under OpenGL ES, this parameter must be `4`, as a color is made up of red, green, blue, and alpha. When using `glVertexPointer` or `glTexCoordPointer`, the first parameter defines the number of coordinates per vertex.

The third parameter is the *stride*, which specifies the number of bytes between consecutive vertices or colors. Until now, we have been using `0` for this value, which means that the color and vertices arrays have been tightly packed. In a vertex array, one vertex pair follows immediately after the previous vertex pair, as can be seen in the vertex and color arrays in Figure 5.7.

When using IVAs, we need to set the stride to the distance in bytes between the start of one vertex pair and the start of the next vertex pair. Using the IVA in Figure 5.8 as an example, the `glVertexPointer` stride would need to be `24` and the `glColorPointer` stride would also need to be `24`.

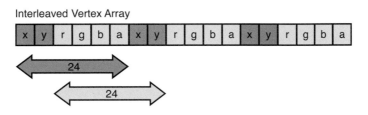

Figure 5.8   Color and vertex stride.

In case you're wondering how those figures were calculated, the answer is that vertices are stored using two `GLFloats`, each of which requires 4 bytes of storage. Because we need to advance six elements within the IVA (*x, y, r, g, b, a*) to reach the next vertex pair, simply multiply 4 (the size of the float) by 6 (the number of elements in the IVA). This gives you 24, the number of bytes OpenGL ES needs to advance to find the next vertex pair. The same applies to the `glColorPointer`.

> You may have to read through that again to clearly understand what is being done, but once you understand the concept of stride, it will become much easier.

In this example, we calculated the number of bytes manually; however, you will be pleased to know that it is possible to have the compiler calculate this value for you by using the `sizeof` statement. If you have not seen the `sizeof` statement before, it returns the number of bytes needed to store the type that has been passed to it. We could have used the following instead:

```
glVertexPointer(2, GL_FLOAT, sizeof(GLFloat) * 6, &iva[0].geometryVertex);
glColorPointer(4, GL_FLOAT,sizeof(GLFloat) * 6, &iva[0].colorVertex);
```

> **Note**
>
> This example uses the `&iva` array to specify the start element in the array along with the structure element (for example, `geometryVertex`). This tells OpenGL ES where to get the necessary data from within the array.

This would have given OpenGL ES the same numbers we calculated manually, and you would not have had to worry about how much storage a `GLFloat` actually needs.

Even with this approach, we still had to specify how many elements we needed to stride over. To make things even easier, we could have used a structure to store the vertex and color information and simply retrieved the size of that structure or element within the structure. We are going to cover structures next.

Structures

Now that we have seen what an IVA looks like, how do we actually create one? For this, we need to use structures. A *structure* is a collection of variables grouped together under a single name. The variables can be of different types, and each has a unique name used to identify it within the structure. What is also handy is that a structure can be embedded within a structure, which is perfect for our needs.

We need a number of structures in which to store our image data. You will find the structures we are going to run through inside the *CH05_SLQTSOR* project. In this project is a group called *Global Headers*, inside which you'll find the *Structures.h* header file. If you open this file, you see all the structures that are needed by the `ImageRenderManager` and `Image` classes.

When rendering images in *Sir Lamorak's Quest,* we need to define the quad in which the image will be rendered, the texture coordinates, and a color that we can use to apply transparency or a color filter to our image. Because each vertex of the quad will be made up of three pieces of information—namely, vertices, texture coordinates, and color—it makes sense to use a structure that stores this information. The `Color4f` structure will be covered later in the chapter when we examine the `Image` class.

The structure we are going to use is called `TexturedColoredVertex`, as shown in Listing 5.1. This structure has two other structures within it: `CGPoint` and `Color4f`. `CGPoint` is itself a structure included within the Core Graphics API. If you wanted to make sure your game engine was portable, it would be a good idea to actually create your own structure to store points rather than using a structure that is specific to the iPhone. The second structure is Color4f which we will cover later in this chapter.

Listing 5.1 The TexturedColoredVertex Structure

```
typedef struct {
    CGPoint geometryVertex;
    Color4f vertexColor;
    CGPoint textureVertex;
} TexturedColoredVertex;
```

Having a vertex on its own is not much use unless you are rendering points, so we need a structure that enables us to define a quad (that is, four `TexturedColoredVertex` structures). This structure, `TexturedColoredQuad`, is shown in Listing 5.2.

Listing 5.2   **The TexturedColoredQuad Structure**

```
typedef struct {
    TexturedColoredVertex vertex1;
    TexturedColoredVertex vertex2;
    TexturedColoredVertex vertex3;
    TexturedColoredVertex vertex4;
} TexturedColoredQuad;
```

The final structure needed to support the rendering manager and `Image` class is the `ImageDetails` structure, shown in Listing 5.3.

Listing 5.3   **The ImageDetails Structure**

```
typedef struct {
    TexturedColoredQuad *texturedColoredQuad;
    TexturedColoredQuad *texturedColoredQuadIVA;
    GLuint textureName;
} ImageDetails;
```

The structure shown in Listing 5.3 stores information about the image's quad, texture coordinates, and color. The structure also stores the OpenGL ES texture name used by the image, and where inside the `ImageRenderManager` IVA `texturedColoredQuadIVA` is held.

Image Rendering Classes

Inside the Chapter 5 example project (*CH05_SLQTSOR*), you see a new group called *Game Engine*. This is where the core classes for the game are stored. This group also contains two additional groups: `Image` and `Managers`.

Inside the `Image` group, you find the `Image` class files and a further group called `Texture2D` that contains the `Texture2D` class. The `Texture2D` class is responsible for actually creating an OpenGL ES texture and associating it with image data loaded from an image file. The `Image` class is used to wrap instances of the `Texture2D` class, providing a simple API allowing us to rotate, scale, translate, and render the texture to the screen.

Inside the `Managers` group, you see two further groups called `Texture Manager` and `Image Render Manager`.

Inside the `Texture Manager` group is the `TextureManager` class. This class enables us to cache textures that have been created and share them between `Image` class instances.

Inside the `Image Render Manager` group is the `ImageRenderManager` class. This class is responsible for batching up images that need to be rendered and then rendering them using the least number of OpenGL ES API calls necessary. This is important so that we can reduce the number of OpenGL ES API calls when rendering a large number of images to the screen.

We now run through the steps needed to create and render an image to the screen and, at the same time, take a look at the classes we use in *Sir Lamorak's Quest* to carry out these functions.

Although the steps needed to actually create and render an image to the screen are not complex and can be achieved in just a few lines of code, we need something slightly more complex. This extra complexity is required to manage our resources more efficiently and maintain performance when we have a large number of images to render.

> **Note**
>
> From this project onward, the *Common.h* file has been renamed to *Global.h* in the *Global Headers* group.

Texture2D Class

As described earlier, the actual loading of image data and generation of an OpenGL ES texture is performed within the `Texture2D` class. By now, you should be getting the idea of how the class header files are created and used, so I won't run through the headers of the class files we are going to be looking at, unless there is something specific I want to point out.

Now, open the *Texture2D.m* file, and let's run through the functions it performs.

Initialization

The `Texture2D` class does not actually provide any functionality outside of its initialization. After the object has been initialized with an image, its only job is to store information about the OpenGL ES texture that was generated from the image data. Other classes such as the `Image` class then use this information. For this reason, `initWithImage:filter:` is the only method in this class.

Loading the Image

To create a texture in OpenGL ES, we need to have some image data that is going to be used for our texture. `Texture2D` uses the `UIImage` class to load an image and then extract the image data needed by OpenGL ES. This is useful because `UIImage` is able to load a variety of different image formats, such as PNG, BMP, GIF, and so on.

If you look inside the `initWithImage` method inside `Texture2D`, you see that a `UIImage` instance is passed in from which the underlying bitmap image data is referenced:

```
CGImageRef image;
image = [aImage CGImage];
```

`CGImage` gives us the underlying bitmap image data that has been loaded by `UIImage`, and we are placing it inside a `CGImageRef` structure. This enables us to read data from that structure when we look for the image format, size, and so forth.

The class then checks to make sure that image data has been found. If not, an error is raised.

Using `image`, we can now retrieve information about the image's alpha and color space. Because we now have access to the `CGImage` information using `CGImageRef`, we can easily get to the information we need using the following commands:

```
CGImageGetAlphaInfo(image)
    CGImageGetColorSpace(image)
```

With this information, we are able to detect if the image has an alpha component and its color space. We will need this later when getting the image data ready for OpenGL ES.

Sizing the Image

Let's run over a couple of important points about OpenGL ES textures.

The first is that the size of all textures in OpenGL ES has to be power-of-two. This means that your image needs to have a width and height equal to one of the following values:

```
2, 4, 8, 16, 32, 64, 128, 256, 512, 1024
```

The width and height don't need to be the same (that is, 128×128), as you could have a texture that is 512×64, but they do need to use a value from the previous list.

The second point is the reason why I stopped listing numbers at 1024. The largest single texture that can be loaded into OpenGL ES on the iPhone is 1024×1024 pixels. If you need to display a larger image, you would need to chop it up into separate images, each no larger than 1024×1024. Using smaller images to create much larger images is a common trick used in game development, and we will be covering this when we look at tile maps in Chapter 9, "Tile Maps."

> **Note**
>
> The iPhone 3GS, iPhone 4 and iPad support texture sizes of 2048×2048.

Now that we have captured information about the image that has been loaded, we need to make sure that the size of the image is both a power-of-two and not above 1024. You could just make sure that all images you create are already the right size before you use them, but that can become a pain, and you may have images that cannot have a size that is power-of-two.

To make things easy, `Texture2D` is going to handle the sizing for us. All we need to do is get the current size of the image we have loaded and then check to make sure that the dimensions are both power-of-two and no larger than the 1024×1024 limit.

Getting the content size is easy enough, as follows:

```
contentSize = CGSizeMake(CGImageGetWidth(image),
    CGImageGetHeight(image));
```

Having obtained the image size, we now need to make sure that it's power-of-two. There is no magic in this—just a couple of loops for width and height. The loops to calculate the width and height of the image, making sure they are a power-of-two, is shown in Listing 5.4.

Listing 5.4   **Setting the Image Size in Texture2D to a Power-of-Two**

```
width = contentSize.width;
    if((width != 1) && (width & (width - 1))) {
        pot = 1;
        while( pot < width)
            pot *= 2;
        width = pot;
    }
height = contentSize.height;
    if((height != 1) && (height & (height - 1))) {
        pot = 1;
        while( pot < height)
            pot *= 2;
        height = pot;
    }
```

If the width of the image is greater than 1 and it's not already a power-of-two, we start at 1 and keep multiplying by 2 until the new width is greater than the current width. This gives us a width that encompasses the image and is power-of-two. We then do the same for the height. The width and height variables are used when creating the OpenGL ES texture and will not affect the actual image we have loaded.

Having calculated the dimensions of the image to be power-of-two, we need to make sure that it does not exceed the maximum texture size.

For this, we use Core Graphics functions and create a CGAffineTransform loading in the identity matrix. The identify matrix we are loading in performs the same function in Core Graphics as the identify matrix we covered back in Chapter 3, "The Journey Begins:"

```
CGAffineTransform transform = CGAffineTransformIdentity;
```

Having loaded this matrix, we check to see if the width or height is greater than the maximum allowed. If it is, the CGAffineTransformScale command is used to halve the size of the image, as shown in Listing 5.5.

Listing 5.5   **Adjusting the Image Size to 1024×1024**

```
while((width > kMaxTextureSize) || (height > kMaxTextureSize)) {
    width /= 2;
    height /= 2;
    transform = CGAffineTransformScale(transform, 0.5, 0.5);
    contentSize.width *= 0.5;
    contentSize.height *= 0.5;
}
```

We now have a `width` and `height` that contains the power-of-two dimensions of the image and that are no larger than the maximum texture size allowed.

Generating Image Data

Having calculated a width and height that are power-of-two and are large enough to encompass our image, we need to get this data into OpenGL ES. Unfortunately, it's not as simple as just feeding a few parameters into OpenGL ES. What we need to do is actually generate a new bitmap image of the dimensions that we have just calculated and render the image we have just loaded into this newly created image.

To do this, we are going to create a new `CGContextRef` called `context` and it will be into this context that we render this new image.

Based on the `pixelFormat` that we identified when loading the image, we set up a color space, storage for our bitmap data, and the context into which we are going to render the image.

The `Texture2D` class is using a switch statement to identify the correct configuration to use based on the `pixelFormat`. Listing 5.6 shows the configuration code for the `kTexture2DPixelFormat_RGBA8888` pixel format.

Listing 5.6   **Configure the Bitmap Context for Rendering the Texture**

```
colorSpace = CGColorSpaceCreateDeviceRGB();
data = malloc(height * width * 4);
context = CGBitmapContextCreate(data, width, height, 8, 4 * width, colorSpace,
    kCGImageAlphaPremultipliedLast | kCGBitmapByteOrder32Big);
CGColorSpaceRelease(colorSpace);
```

This is setting up our color space, as well as a container to hold the bitmap data of the image we are going to render called `data`. These are then used to set up our context.

Having configured a context into which we are going to render our image with its new OpenGL ES compatible size, we are now ready to render our image, shown in Listing 5.7.

Listing 5.7   **Rendering the Texture Image**

```
CGContextClearRect(context, CGRectMake(0, 0, width, height));
CGContextTranslateCTM(context, 0, height - contentSize.height);
if(!CGAffineTransformIsIdentity(transform))
    CGContextConcatCTM(context, transform);
    CGContextDrawImage(context, CGRectMake(0, 0, CGImageGetWidth(image),
        CGImageGetHeight(image)), image);
```

As you can see, we are clearing the context we have created and then moving the origin within that context so that the image we render is in the right place. If we have resized the image because it was larger than the maximum allowed, we then apply the scale transform created earlier.

Finally, we actually draw the bitmap image data we have loaded into the new context.

> **Tip**
>
> The coordinate system used in Core Animation and Quartz is different than that used in OpenGL ES. In OpenGL ES, the *y*-axis runs from 0 starting at the bottom of the screen and works its way up, but Core Animation is in reverse. Core Animation's *y*-axis starts with 0 at the top of the screen and works its way down. This means that images loaded into OpenGL ES textures appear upside down. This is a simple issue to fix, and is covered when we examine the `Image` class, later in this chapter.

There is one more check to perform before creating the OpenGL ES texture. If the pixel format of the image was identified as `kTexture2DPixelFormat_RGB565`, we need to convert the data from 32- to 16-bits using the code in Listing 5.8. This code is taken directly from Apple's example `Texture2D` class, and is found in a number of code samples.

Listing 5.8   **Code Used to Convert RGP565 Image Data from 32- to 16-Bits**

```
if(pixelFormat == kTexture2DPixelFormat_RGB565) {
    void* tempData = malloc(height * width * 2);
    unsigned int *inPixel32 = (unsigned int*)data
    unsigned short *outPixel16 = (unsigned short*)tempData;
    for(int i = 0; i < width * height; ++i, ++inPixel32)
        *outPixel16++ = (((((*inPixel32 >> 0) & 0xFF) >> 3) << 11) |
            (((((*inPixel32 >> 8) & 0xFF) >> 2) << 5) |
            (((((*inPixel32 >> 16) & 0xFF) >> 3) << 0);
        free(data);
        data = tempData;
}
```

At the end of this section, we have a variable called `data` that contains the bitmap image data of our newly drawn image, and we know that this image has dimensions that are power-of-two, and are within the maximum size allowed. This may have seemed like a lot of code, but having `Texture2D` deal with these issues saves us from needing to do it manually for each new image.

Generating a Texture Name

A key step in creating an OpenGL ES texture is generating a texture name. This is an important step because the texture name enables us to tell OpenGL ES which texture we are referencing. One area of confusion is the texture name itself. From the terminology used, it sounds like you should be able to assign a descriptive name to a texture, such as "Bob" or "Shirley." However, that's not the case—not just because Bob and Shirley are silly names to give a texture, but because a texture name in OpenGL ES is actually a unique number, specifically a `GLuint`.

Now that we know that the name of a texture is actually a number, we can get OpenGL ES to generate a name for us using the following command:

```
glGenTextures(1, &name);
```

The `name` ivar has been defined in the header file as a `GLuint` and is then used within the `glGenTextures` command to request a new texture name from OpenGL ES. You may have noticed that the command is plural and not singular (that is, *textures*). This is because you can ask OpenGL ES to generate more than one texture name at a time. The first parameter taken by the `glGenTextures` command specifies how many textures you want OpenGL ES to generate.

If you were generating more than one texture name at a time, the second parameter would point to an array of `GLuint`'s rather than a single `GLuint`.

It's good practice to generate your textures at the start of the game rather than during game play. There's an overhead involved in generating a texture name, not to mention the overhead of actually loading image data and associating it with a texture. To stop this from impacting performance, it is therefore normally done upfront before the game play starts.

Binding the Texture and Setting Parameters

Remember that OpenGL ES is a state engine, so before any operations can be carried out on a texture, OpenGL ES needs to know what texture the operations should be directed to. Binding the texture we want to use does this. This is the next command you see after we have generated the texture in the `Texture2D` class:

```
glBindTexture(GL_TEXTURE_2D, name);
```

The first parameter is the *target*. When using OpenGL ES, this must be `GL_TEXTURE_2D`. This is because OpenGL ES only supports the `GL_TEXTURE_2D` target, and we will be using a two-dimensional image to create our texture. Although OpenGL supports other targets, OpenGL ES only currently supports `GL_TEXTURE_2D`. The second parameter is the *texture name* that we want to bind to, and so we provide the texture name that was previously generated.

> **Tip**
>
> Binding to a texture does incur an overhead, and it is therefore good practice to reduce the number of bindings you make per frame as much as possible. One way of doing this is to use a sprite sheet (texture atlas) that enables you to store many different images within a single texture. This is covered in Chapter 6, "Sprite Sheets."

After we have told OpenGL ES which texture we want to use, we can then start to set parameters associated with that texture. When creating a new OpenGL ES texture, there are two key parameters that must to be set, as follows:

```
glTexParameteri(GL_TEXTURE_2D, GL_TEXTURE_MIN_FILTER, aFilter);
glTexParameteri(GL_TEXTURE_2D, GL_TEXTURE_MAG_FILTER, aFilter);
```

The first parameter is the *target*, which is the same target that we used when binding our texture. The second parameter specifies the *parameter name* (that is, the parameter we want to configure), and the third parameter is the actual *parameter value*.

The parameters we are configuring are used to define how OpenGL ES should handle images when they are being shrunk (`GL_TEXTURE_MIN_FILTER`) or enlarged (`GL_TEXTURE_MAG_FILTER`).

Other parameters can be configured, but these are the only two we need to worry about. By default, the preceding parameters are set to use something called a *mipmap*. A mipmap is a pre-calculated and optimized collection of images that are used with a texture. They are basically different sizes of the same image that can be used based on the size of the texture being rendered. Rather than shrinking images up and down in real time, OpenGL ES can work out which image size, from those available in the mipmap, is closest to what it needs and use that.

We are not going to be using mipmaps in our game, as the iPhone is pretty good at interpolating images on the fly using its graphics chip and FPU.

The values that can be used for these parameters are as follows:

- **`GL_NEAREST`**: Returns the value of the texture element that is nearest to the center of the pixel being textured.
- **`GL_LINEAR`**: Returns the weighted average of the four texture elements that are closest to the center of the pixel being textured. This filter should be used if you want to have your image perform sub-pixel rendering. This is important if you want your images to move smoothly at slow speeds and not only be rendered at exact pixel locations.

Put simply, `GL_NEAREST` gives a pixilated look to images that are scaled up or down, whereas `GL_LINEAR` gives you a smoother anti-aliased look.

In `Texture2D`, the value to be used for these parameters is taken from the filter that has been passed into the initializer method. This enables us to change the filter from one image to the next.

> **Tip**
>
> The value for both the minification and magnification parameters within a texture level should match. This is a restriction of the PowerVR MBX chip found on all devices prior to the iPhone 3GS, iPhone 4, and iPad. The iPhone 3GS, iPhone 4 and iPad use the PowerVR SGX chip, which does not have this restriction—nor does the iPhone Simulator.

Loading Image Data into the OpenGL Texture

We can now finish creating our OpenGL ES texture by loading the bitmap image data we generated earlier into the OpenGL ES texture to which we are currently bound.

Inside the `Texture2D` class, you see that we are again using a switch statement based on the `pixelFormat` to identify which command to use. The following OpenGL ES command loads image data into the texture for the `kTexture2DPixelForm_RGBA8888` pixel format:

```
glTexImage2D(GL_TEXTURE_2D, 0, GL_RGBA, width, height, 0, GL_RGBA,
    GL_UNSIGNED_BYTE, data);
```

The parameters used in this command are as follows:

- **Target:** The target texture. Must *be GL_TEXTURE_2D.*
- **Level:** The level-of-detail number. Level 0 is the base image level. Level n is the nth mipmap reduction image and must be greater than or equal to zero.
- **Internal format:** The color components in the texture. This must be the same as the format parameter later.
- **Width:** The width of the texture image.
- **Height:** The height of the texture image.
- **Border:** The width of the border. Must be zero.
- **Format:** The format of the pixel data.
- **Type:** The data type used within the pixel data.
- **Pixels:** A pointer to the image data in memory.

On issuing the preceding command, the image data held in the `data` ivar is loaded into OpenGL ES and associated with the currently bound texture.

The last few actions of the `Texture2D` class are to set up some parameters that make it easier to manage texturing mapping.

When we looked at texture mapping earlier in this chapter, you saw that the axis names within a texture are (s, t). To finish off the creation of our texture, we are going to define our texture's maximum s and t values. This is important, as the actual image we have loaded may be smaller than the dimensions of the texture we have created. We are therefore going to calculate the `maxS` and `maxT` values for our image within our texture.

Figure 5.9 shows an image that is 56×48 pixels inside an OpenGL ES-compatible texture of 64×64 pixels. The texture size is the smallest power-of-two size that can encompass the image we have loaded. This means that the image's right-hand edge has an s texture coordinate of 0.875 and the top edge has a t texture coordinate of 0.75.

The last few lines of code in the `Texture2D` class are used to set the `maxS` and `maxT` values that give us the maximum value for the s and t. We also calculate the texture ratio for each axis. This is useful when we have a pixel location within the image, and we want to convert that to a texture coordinate. Multiplying the pixel value by the appropriate axis ratio value gives us the texture coordinate. Listing 5.9 shows these calculations in the `Texture2D` class.

Listing 5.9   **Texture and Ratio Calculations**

```
maxS = contentSize.width / (float)width;
maxT = contentSize.height / (float)height;
textureRatio.width = 1.0f / (float)width;
textureRatio.height = 1.0f / (float)height;
```

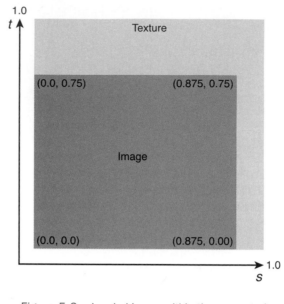

Figure 5.9   Loaded image within the generated
OpenGL ES texture.

The last step is to release both the drawing context we created and also the bitmap data that was generated. This has been handed to OpenGL ES when we loaded the texture image data, so we can safely get rid of our copy:

```
CGContextRelease(context);
free(data);
```

That completes the `Texture2D` class. We are now going to move onto the `TextureManager` class, which enables us to have a single `Texture2D` instance shared between multiple `Image` instances. This helps to reduce the amount of memory consumed if multiple images require the same texture. This normally occurs when you use a sprite sheet. The sprite sheet is a single texture containing multiple smaller images. We can create many `Image` class instances that use the same texture, but only reference a small area of the texture by setting the appropriate texture coordinates.

Rather than having multiple instances of `Texture2D`, the `TextureManager` enables us to use a single `Texture2D` instance for all images taken from a sprite sheet.

TextureManager Class

The design of our rendering classes means that every texture we load will involve the creation of a `Texture2D` instance. `Texture2D` is responsible for actually loading the image we provide into an OpenGL ES compatible texture and storing the texture name, along with information such as the maximum *s* and *t* texture coordinates for later use.

The main class used when rendering images will be the Image class. When you create a new Image instance, the Image class handles the creation of the OpenGL ES texture using Texture2D. Because of the close relationship between an Image instance and Texture2D instance, there could be situations where many Image instances share the same texture.

An easy way to solve this is to create a texture manager. This singleton class will be responsible for taking requests for new textures and checking to see if a texture has already been loaded. The check will be performed on the name of the image to be loaded.

If a match is found, a reference will be returned to the texture that already exists. If no match is found, a new texture is created, cached, and passed back.

Let's look at the TextureManager class to see how this is being done. You find the TextureManager class inside the *CH05_SLQTSOR* project inside the Game Engine > Managers > Texture Manager group.

Initialization

The first thing to note is that this is a singleton class. Singleton classes were covered in Chapter 4 when we looked at the GameController class. We want only a single instance of this class; making it a singleton makes sense.

Apart from setting up the class as a singleton and initializing the cachedTextures dictionary, there are no other special activities carried out during initialization.

Retrieving and Creating a Texture

TextureManager only has three methods, excluding the class method used to get the shared instance of the class.

The first method is textureWithFileName:filter:. This method is used to request a texture from the texture manager. The method accepts two parameters. The first is the file name of the image file we want to create a texture from and the second is the filter we want the texture to use. Remember from the previous section on the Texture2D class that when a texture is created, you configure the minification and magnification filters to be used. The filter we pass into this method is used to define those parameters when a texture is created. Listing 5.10 shows the textureWithFileName:filter: method.

Listing 5.10   **TextureManager textureWithFileName:filter: Method**

```
- (Texture2D*)textureWithFileName:(NSString*)aName filter:(GLenum)aFilter {

    Texture2D *cachedTexture;

    NSString *key = [NSString stringWithFormat:@"%@.%

    if(cachedTexture = [cachedTextures objectForKey:key]) {
        return cachedTexture;
    }

    NSString *filename = [aName stringByDeletingPathExtension];
    NSString *filetype = [aName pathExtension];
```

```
    NSString *path = [[NSBundle mainBundle] pathForResource:filename
        ofType:filetype];
    cachedTexture = [[Texture2D alloc] initWithImage:[UIImage
        imageWithContentsOfFile:path] filter:aFilter];
    [cachedTextures setObject:cachedTexture forKey:aName];
    return [cachedTexture autorelease];
}
```

Once inside the method, the first check is to see if we can find a texture that has been created for the same image name. This is an easy check because an `NSMutableDictionary`, `cachedTextures`, was defined within the header file and allocated and initialized in the `init` method. All we need to do, therefore, is look for an object in the `cachedTextures` dictionary with a matching key.

If a match could not be found, it means we have not yet created a texture for an image with this name, and one should be created using `Texture2D` and adding it to the `cachedTextures` dictionary.

> **Tip**
>
> You may notice that in the preceding code, we are creating an instance of UIImage using the `imageWithContentsOfFile` rather than a more commonly used `imageNamed`. This is because when using `imageNamed`, iOS caches a copy of the image in memory in case it needs it later. We actually throw away the image eventually once the image data has been given to OpenGL ES, so we don't need the image kept in memory. Using `imageWithContentsOfFile` does not cause this caching to happen.

That's it for the `textureWithFileName:filter:` method. It's really simple, but effective in keeping the number of textures we load in memory to a minimum.

Releasing One or All Textures

To finish off the `TextureManager` class, we need a couple of housekeeping methods. The first is a method that enables us to remove a texture from the cache. When we are done with a texture, it's good to be able to remove it from the cache and free up memory. If you are using a large number of textures in your game, you may need to load a different set of textures as you transition between each scene.

With that in mind, we have the `releaseTextureWithName:` method. This, like the `textureWithFileName:` method, takes a filename and type and then looks it up in the `cachedTextures` dictionary. If a match is found, the object is removed from the dictionary, thereby decrementing its retain count by one. If the dictionary was the only object retaining the texture, its retain count will now be zero. Consequently, the texture will not be de-allocated and removed from memory.

The last method is `releaseAllTextures`. This is a simple method that just removes all objects from the `cachedTextures` dictionary, short and sweet.

ImageRenderManager Class

So far, we have seen the classes that turn an image into an OpenGL ES texture and manage those textures to help reduce the amount of memory we are using. The next class we discuss is `ImageRenderManager`, which is responsible for actually rendering images to the screen.

I mentioned at the start of this chapter that we were going to be looking at how to improve performance when using OpenGL ES. The `ImageRenderManager` class is fundamental to improving the performance of our game engine for *Sir Lamorak's Quest*.

I've also mentioned already that there is an API overhead associated with using OpenGL ES commands, such as `glDrawArrays` and `glDrawElements`. There is nothing stopping us from placing the actual rendering code into our image class, making each image responsible for its own rendering. However, if you display a large number of images on the screen, you start to see performance problems due to the high volume of API calls.

A common approach to overcoming this problem is to reduce the number of these API calls. This is the purpose of the `ImageRenderManager` class.

Although the `ImageRenderManager` class is not that big, it does introduce some new concepts such as IVAs, memory structures for storing data, and the allocation of memory using functions such as `calloc`.

It's also worth pointing out that this class is linked very closely to the last class we will be looking at in this chapter: the `Image` class. The `Image` class will be responsible for managing information about an image, such as its scale, rotation, location, and memory structure, that will be used by the `ImageRenderManager`.

The `ImageRenderManager` is also a singleton class. You've probably started to notice a singleton pattern here. We have a number of classes ending in `Manager`, all of which have been set up as singletons, and `ImageRenderManager` is no different. We need only one instance of `ImageRenderManager` that will be responsible for batching up and rendering our images.

Initialization

Having covered the theory behind IVAs and structures, it's time to look at the code within the `ImageRenderManager` class, which uses those concepts.

If you open the *ImageRenderManager.m* file (found inside the *Game Engine > Managers > Image Render Manager* group), let's look at how it has been implemented and the functions it provides.

As stated earlier, we are implementing the class as a singleton class. This is important, as we only want to have a single instance of this class controlling the rendering in the game. Listing 5.11 shows the `init` method within the `ImageRenderManager` class.

Listing 5.11   **ImageRenderManager init Method**

```
- (id)init {
  if(self = [super init]) {

    iva = malloc(kMax_Images * sizeof(TexturedColoredQuad));

    ivaIndices = calloc(kMax_Images * 6, sizeof(GLushort));

    ivaIndex = 0;

    renderTextureCount = 0;
  }
  return self;
}
```

Within the `init` method, we allocate the memory needed to store the IVA array we are going to use. The maximum number of images the IVA can hold is defined in the header file as `kMax_Images`. If we needed to handle more images, we would need to increase this number to compensate. Keeping this number as small as possible will help to save memory.

You can see that we are making use of the `sizeof` command. When allocating the `iva` array, we are asking iOS to allocate enough memory to store `kMax_Images` multiplied by the size in bytes of the `TextureColoredQuad` structure. We don't need to worry about what is in that structure and how much space it uses up; the `sizeof` command does that for us. In case you are interested, the `TexturedColoredQuad` structure actually uses 128 bytes.

The `iva` array is an array of `TexturedColoredVertex` structures and is used to store the geometry, color, and texture coordinates for each image to be rendered by the `ImageRenderManager`. It is this array that is used to provide OpenGL ES with the information it needs to render.

The `ivaIndices` array stores the indices to be used inside the `iva` array. As the `Image` class renders an image, it's allocated the next available slot in the `iva`.

`ivaIndex` stores the next available index into the `iva` array, and `renderTextureCount` stores the number of unique textures used when rendering images. This is reset each time the `ImageRenderManager` renders all the images in its `iva` and is done when the `renderImages` method is called.

Adding an Image to the Render Queue

When we ask an image to render, it won't actually be rendering anything directly to the screen. Instead, it calls the `addImageDetailsToRenderQueue:` method, passing in its `ImageDetails` structure, as shown in Listing 5.12.

Listing 5.12   **ImageRenderManager addImageDetailsToRenderQueue: Method**

```
- (void)addImageDetailsToRenderQueue:(ImageDetails*)aImageDetails {

    [self copyImageDetails:aImageDetails];

    [self addToTextureList:aImageDetails->textureName];

    ivaIndex++;
}
```

First, the `copyImageDetails` method is called. This method copies the image's `TextureColoredQuad` structure into the `iva` at the next available slot. It also points the image's `TexturedColoredQuadIVA` structure to this new entry. As we see when reviewing the `Image` class, once this copy has been done, the `Image` class transforms the information in the `iva` based on the image's configuration. This means that the image's `TexturedColoredQuad` structure holds only a clean un-transformed version of the image, and all transformations are performed on the copy within the IVA.

Figure 5.10 shows how each image's `TexturedColoredQuad` structure is held within the `iva`.

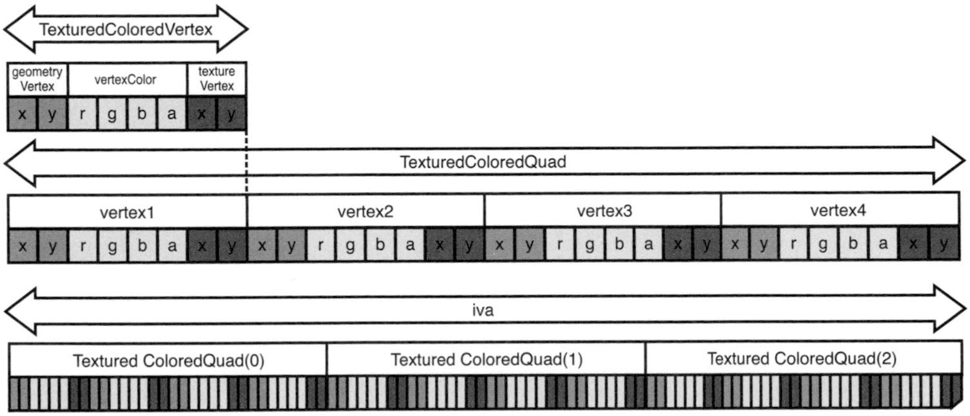

Figure 5.10   Example of an iva array containing TexturedColoredQuads.

With the image copied to the IVA, call the `addToTextureList:` method, shown in Listing 5.13, and increment the `ivaIndex`.

Listing 5.13   ImageRenderManager addToTextureList: Method

```
- (void)addToTextureList:(uint)aTextureName {

    BOOL textureFound = NO;
    for(int index=0; index<renderTextureCount; index++) {
        if(texturesToRender[index] == aTextureName) {
            textureFound = YES;
            break;
        }
    }

    if(!textureFound)
        texturesToRender[renderTextureCount++] = aTextureName;

    textureIndices[aTextureName][imageCountForTexture[aTextureName]] =
        ivaIndex;
    imageCountForTexture[aTextureName] += 1;
}
```

Listing 5.13 checks to see if the texture name of the image being added to the render queue has already been added to the queue by another image. The texture name is taken from the `ImageDetails` structure, and a loop is run over the `texturesToRender` array.

The `texturesToRender` array is used to store a list of all the texture names that are used by the images that have been added to the render queue. This is a unique array of texture names, meaning that even if the same texture is used in many images, it will be added to this array only once. If a matching texture name is found in the loop, the `textureFound` flag is set to `YES`.

When we ask the `ImageRenderManager` to render, we move through the textures in this array, binding to them once and then rendering all images that use that texture before moving to the next. After all images in the queue have been rendered, the queue is then cleared, ready for any images that need to be rendered in the next frame.

If the texture was not found, the texture name is added to the `texturesToRender` array.

With the texture added if necessary, we then add the image's `ivaIndex` to the `textureIndices` array and increment the image count for that texture.

The `textureIndices` ivar is a two-dimensional array that is indexed using the texture name and image count for that texture. For example, if you are processing an image using texture name `1`, and it is the fifth image in the render queue that uses that texture, the image's `ivaIndex` are added to the `textureIndices` array at `[1][5]`.

You can see from the code that we are using another array, called `imageCountForTexture`, to store the number of images that have been added to the render queue for a specific texture name, with the texture name being used as the index into this array.

The `textureIndices` array holds all indices into the `iva` for images that share the same texture name. When rendering, we loop through the `textureIndices` array, retrieving the IVA index for each image using the current texture. These IVA indices will then be used to tell OpenGL ES which entry in the IVA should be used to render each image. This enables us to render all the images for a given texture in one go and reduce the number of texture bindings needed.

Although this method is not large, it is complex, so it's worth re-reading this section if you are not clear on how to add images to the render queue.

Rendering Images

The last method to cover in the `ImageRenderManager` is `renderImages:` (shown in Listing 5.14), which is responsible for actually rendering images to the screen.

Listing 5.14   **ImageRenderManager renderImages Method**

```
- (void)renderImages {

    glVertexPointer(2, GL_FLOAT, sizeof(TexturedColoredVertex),
        &iva[0].geometryVertex);
    glTexCoordPointer(2, GL_FLOAT, sizeof(TexturedColoredVertex),
        &iva[0].textureVertex);
    glColorPointer(4,GL_FLOAT,sizeof(TexturedColoredVertex),
        &iva[0].vertexColor);

    for(NSInteger textureIndex=0; textureIndex<renderTextureCount;
        textureIndex++) {

        glBindTexture(GL_TEXTURE_2D, texturesToRender[textureIndex]);

        int vertexCounter=0;

        for(NSInteger imageIndex=0;
            imageIndex<imageCountForTexture
                [texturesToRender[textureIndex]];
            imageIndex++) {
        NSUInteger index =
            textureIndices[texturesToRender[textureIndex]][imageIndex]
            * 4;
        ivaIndices[vertexCounter++] = index;     // Bottom left
        ivaIndices[vertexCounter++] = index+2;   // Top Left
        ivaIndices[vertexCounter++] = index+1;   // Bottom right
        ivaIndices[vertexCounter++] = index+1;   // Bottom right
        ivaIndices[vertexCounter++] = index+2;   // Top left
        ivaIndices[vertexCounter++] = index+3;   // Top right
    }
```

```
    glDrawElements(GL_TRIANGLES, vertexCounter, GL_UNSIGNED_SHORT,
        ivaIndices);

    imageCountForTexture[texturesToRender[textureIndex]] = 0;
}

renderTextureCount = 0;

ivaIndex = 0;
}
```

The first step in this method is to configure OpenGL ES to use the `iva` array for its data. These commands take a number of parameters. The first two parameters tell OpenGL ES the size of each element and the number of elements to use for describing a single item. For example, we tell OpenGL ES to use two `GLFloats` to describe a single vertex.

The third parameter is the stride for which we are passing the size of the `TextureColoredVertex` structure. The fourth parameter is a pointer to a specific member of the `TexturedColoredVertex` structure of the first element of the `iva` array—for example:

```
iva[0].geometryVertex
iva[0].textureVertex
iva[0].vertexColor
```

This notifies OpenGL ES where to start reading data from within the structure. This also means that the stride for each pointer is always the same (that is, the size of a `TexturedColorVertex`), as shown in Figure 5.11.

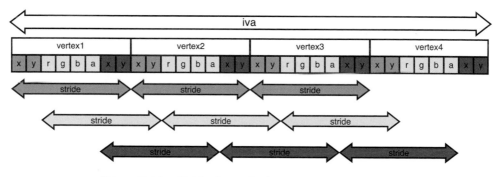

Figure 5.11   Strides for each element inside the iva array.

With the pointers set up so that OpenGL ES knows from where it's reading the data, we then start to loop through the textures we have in our `texturesToRender` array.

The number of textures to loop through is defined by the `renderTextureCount` that we mentioned earlier.

Inside the loop, we bind to the current texture and set the `vertexCount` to zero. For each texture, the `vertexCount` is going to keep track of how many vertices we actually need OpenGL ES to render, which will be passed to the `glDrawElements` command.

Next, we perform another loop. This loop iterates through all the images that have been added to the render queue for the current texture and populating the `ivaIndices` array. Each time we run through this loop, we retrieve the IVA `index` from the `textureIndices` array for the currently bound texture and image we are processing. Remember that this is the index within the `iva` for the first `TexturedColoredVertex` of the image's `TexturedColoredQuad` structure.

The `ivaIndices` array holds a pointer to each vertex required for rendering each image. You may remember that each image we render is made up of two triangles defining a quad. This means that we need six vertices for each quad that is going to be rendered.

Having obtained the index to the first vertex in the `iva` array for the image we are currently processing, we add six `ivaIndices` entries, incrementing the index into the `iva` as necessary.

Because the pointers were already set up to the `iva` at the start of the method, all that is left is to ask OpenGL ES to draw the indices we have defined:

```
glDrawElements(GL_TRIANGLES, vertexCounter, GL_UNSIGNED_SHORT, ivaIndices);
```

This is different from what we have done before. Until now, we have used `glDrawArrays`. The difference is that with `glDrawArrays`, OpenGL ES just runs sequentially through the data that has been provided from a defined start location and for a defined number of elements.

This time, we need to jump around the data that has been passed to OpenGL ES (that is, rendering the images within the IVA that share the same texture). If a large number of images are being rendered in one go, it is worth sorting the contents of the IVA array, so reducing the amount of jumping around is done for optimal performance.

The `glDrawElements` command does this for us. We are telling it to draw `GL_TRIANGLES`, which is why we need six vertices to define each quad, three vertices for each triangle. Second, we pass the `vertexCounter` that holds the number of vertices that are inside the `ivaIndices` array; finally, we tell OpenGL ES that the `ivaIndices` array is made up of `GLUint`'s and finally pass the `ivaIndices` array itself.

This causes OpenGL ES to render all the images for the currently bound texture, after which we clear the image count for that texture and move onto the next texture to be rendered.

Once we have finished looping through all the textures on the render queue, we then reset the `renderTextureCount` so the `ImageRenderManager` is ready to start queuing the next batch of images.

That is an awful lot to take in. The number of arrays and how we are storing our vertex data make this and the `addImageDetailsToRenderQueue:` method complex and a little difficult to follow.

> **Note**
>
> Although you don't need to fully understand how the `ImageRenderManager` works to make use of it, I do recommend that you re-read this section if things are still not clear. Understanding how we are manipulating the image data inside the `ImageRenderManager` will be very useful, and grasping these concepts is essential to our journey into the more advanced areas of OpenGL ES.

The Image Class

We have covered a lot already in this chapter, but we have one final push before we are finished. Having built the underlying functions that enable us to create OpenGL ES textures, manage them, and render them to the screen, we now come to a key class in rendering within our game engine.

The `Image` class provides a wrapper around the OpenGL ES texture that has been created and stores information, such as the following:

- Position
- Scale
- Rotation
- Rotation Point
- Color
- Flip Horizontal
- Flip Vertical
- Texture Coordinates

The `Image` class also provides us with the API we will be using when changing these properties and asking the image to render.

If you now open the *Image.m* file, we'll run through the `Image` class implementation.

Initialization

You'll notice that there are two initializers for this class. The first, `initWithImageNamed:filter:`, is used when you are creating an image that uses the full texture provided.

The second initializer, `initWithImageNamed:filter:subTexture:`, is called when creating an image that is going to use a sub-region of the texture—for example, when the `SpriteSheet` class provides an image for a sprite.

When looking at the first initializer, you'll see that the first task is to call a private method, `initializeImage:filter:`. This method is responsible for obtaining the texture for the image filename that has been passed in. This filename is passed over to the texture manager instance, which decides if either a new `Texture2D` object or a cached `Texture2D` object is passed back.

Next, we set up the base properties for the image. This involves taking information from the texture object created and storing it in local ivars, as well as setting the default values for properties, such as `rotation`, `scale`, `flipHorizontal`, and `flipVertical`. I've done this to reduce the amount of messaging that is needed between class instances to retrieve this info. It's the kind of information that could be requested a lot, so reducing the amount of chatter between classes is not a bad thing.

> **Note**
>
> Although Apple has done a lot of work to minimize the time needed to call a method or property, there is still a small performance hit. Reducing the class messaging as much as possible in the core sections of your game will really pay off!

One item we have not covered yet is the `Color4fMake` function. Inside the *Global.h* file found in the *Global Headers* group are a number of macros and functions. Their use should be easy to see from the names they have been given.

When defining these functions, I am using `static inline` to improve performance. By making these functions `inline`, we are hinting to the compiler that it should put effort into calling the function faster than it would otherwise, generally by substituting the code of the function into its caller. This would remove the need for a call and return sequence and may allow the compiler to perform other optimizations between the bodies of both functions. You will see more functions added to this file as we implement other classes, such as the `ParticleEmitter`, later in this book.

The functions defined currently enable us to easily create new structures with a given set of values. The structures themselves are defined within the *Structures.h* file, which can be found in the same group as *Global.h*.

To store the scale of our image, we have a new type called `Scale2f`, with the `2f` part of the name denoting that the type contains two `floats`. Inside `Scale2f` is one element called `x` and one called `y`. They store the scale to be used for each of those axes.

For storing the color of the image, we have a type called `Color4f`. As with `Scale2f`, the `4f` tells us that this type contains four `floats`. Each `float` represents an element of the color being red, green, blue, and alpha, and their values can range from `0.0` to `1.0`. It is also possible to store this information using `GLUint`'s, causing the possible values for each element to range from `0` to `255`.

Getting back to the *Image.m* file, when the `initializeImage` method is complete, and having associated a texture to the image and set up the base ivars, the `initWithImageNamed:filter:` method sets the `imageSize` and `textureSize`.

The `imageSize` is the width and height in pixels of the full image inside the texture that has been created, and `textureSize` stores the `texture.maxS` and `texture.maxT` values that we discussed earlier in this chapter when looking at the `Texture2D` class.

We also set the `textureOffset` to zero; this initializer assumes that we want the full size of the image within the texture rather than a sub-image.

The final stage of initializing the image is to call another private method, `initializeImageDetails`. If the name looks familiar, it's because it is responsible for setting up the `ImageDetails` structure we covered in detail earlier in this chapter. It is shown in Listing 5.15.

Listing 5.15   ImageRenderManager initializeImageDetails Method

```
- (void)initializeImageDetails {

    if (!imageDetails) {
        imageDetails = calloc(1, sizeof(ImageDetails));
        imageDetails->texturedColoredQuad = calloc(1,
            sizeof(TexturedColoredQuad));
    }

    imageDetails->texturedColoredQuad->vertex1.geometryVertex =
        CGPointMake(0.0f, 0.0f);
    imageDetails->texturedColoredQuad->vertex2.geometryVertex =
        CGPointMake(imageSize.width, 0.0f);
    imageDetails->texturedColoredQuad->vertex3.geometryVertex =
        CGPointMake(0.0f,
        imageSize.height);
    imageDetails->texturedColoredQuad->vertex4.geometryVertex =
        CGPointMake(imageSize.width, imageSize.height);

    imageDetails->texturedColoredQuad->vertex1.textureVertex =
        CGPointMake(textureOffset.x, textureSize.height);
    imageDetails->texturedColoredQuad->vertex2.textureVertex =
        CGPointMake(textureSize.width, textureSize.height);
    imageDetails->texturedColoredQuad->vertex3.textureVertex =
        CGPointMake(textureOffset.x, textureOffset.y);
    imageDetails->texturedColoredQuad->vertex4.textureVertex =
        CGPointMake(textureSize.width, textureOffset.y);

    imageDetails->texturedColoredQuad->vertex1.vertexColor =
    imageDetails->texturedColoredQuad->vertex2.vertexColor =
    imageDetails->texturedColoredQuad->vertex3.vertexColor =
    imageDetails->texturedColoredQuad->vertex4.vertexColor = color;

    imageDetails->textureName = textureName;

    dirty = YES;
}
```

`initializeImageDetails` allocates memory for the `ImageDetails` structure. It then points the `imageDetails->textureColoredQuad` element to memory allocated to store the `TexturedColoredQuad`.

With the `ImageDetails` structure in place, we then set up the geometry, texture, and color details inside `imageDetails->TexturedColoredQuad`.

> **Note**
>
> You may remember from when we covered the `Texture2D` class that all images loaded into an OpenGL ES texture are upside down. While loading the texture coordinates into the `ImageDetails` structure in Listing 5.15, you can reverse the *y*-axis coordinates so the images appear correctly onscreen.

You can see from the code that we are using the image's instance properties for setting up the data inside the `imageDetails` structure. This allows the same method to be called when creating an image using the full texture size or an image that defines a sub-image within a larger image.

The final steps in this method set the `imageDetails->textureName` to the texture name and the dirty flag is set to `YES`. This flag tells the image that certain properties have been changed (that is, rotation, scale, position, and so on). This causes the image to recalculate the vertices held within the `ImageRenderManager` IVA using matrix transformation functions, which we look at shortly.

You'll remember that there were two initializers for the `Image` class. The second of those is `initWithImageNamed:filter:subTexture:`. This performs the same basic functions as the previous initializer. The key difference is that an extra parameter is passed into the method called `subTexture`. This parameter takes a `CGRect` that defines an area in pixels inside the image's texture. This enables us to create an image that has dimensions of the rectangle specified. Only the area within these dimensions will be displayed when the image is rendered.

This provides us with the base functions needed to support new classes, such as the `SpriteSheet` class, where we need to be able to create an image that only represents a small area of the original texture.

In this method, rather than set the `textureOffset` to zero and the `textureSize` to the maximum, the dimensions of the `CGRect` are used instead.

Notice that we are using the texture's `textureRatio` value to calculate the texture coordinates for the sub-image by multiplying the `textureRatio` with the specified pixel values.

Retrieving a Sub-Image

We have mentioned the `SpriteSheet` class a number of times, along with the need to be able to create an image using a sub-region within a large texture. The `Image` class can help us do this because it contains all the information we need to generate such an image.

The `subImageInRect:` method, shown in Listing 5.16, accepts a `CGRect` that is used to define a region within the texture of the image. A new `Image` is created that is configured to only render the region specified.

Listing 5.16   **ImageRenderManager subImageInRect: Method**

```
- (Image*)subImageInRect:(CGRect)aRect {
    Image *subImage = [[Image alloc] initWithImageNamed:imageFileName
        filter:minMagFilter subTexture:aRect];
    subImage.scale = scale;
    subImage.color = color;
    subImage.flipVertically = flipVertically;
    subImage.flipHorizontally = flipHorizontally;
    subImage.rotation = rotation;
    subImage.rotationPoint = rotationPoint;
    return [subImage autorelease];
}
```

The method itself is pretty basic. It creates a new `Image` instance called `subImage` using the `initWithImageNamed:filter:subTexture:` method. This enables us to pass in the `CGRect`, and we end up with a new `Image` instance that represents just that region of the texture.

Next, we set the properties of that new image to match those of the parent image and then return the `subImage` and `autorelease` it.

Auto-releasing `subImage` is important. It is not the responsibility of the `Image` class but of the requester to retain `subImage`. For this reason, the `Image` class should release the image at some point, whereas the requester should retain it.

Duplicate an Image

Another useful function is the ability to duplicate an image, as shown in Listing 5.17.

Listing 5.17   **The imageDuplicate Method**

```
- (Image*)imageDuplicate {
    Image *imageCopy = [[self subImageInRect:subImageRectangle] retain];
    return [imageCopy autorelease];
}
```

This is a convenience method, as it needs to perform the same actions that the `subImageInRect:` method does but without taking a `CGRect` as a parameter. Instead, it uses the `subImageRectangle` property of the `Image` class to call the `subImageInRect:` method. The image returned needs to be retained, as it could be auto-released before being passed onto the caller. When `imageCopy` is returned, the `autorelease` reduces the retain count as necessary.

Rendering an Image

Now that we have covered how an `Image` instance is created, it's time to look at how we actually render an image. You'll see from the *Image.h* file that a number of methods can be used to render an image, as follows:

- render
- renderAtPoint:
- renderAtPoint:scale:rotation:
- renderCentered:
- renderCenteredAtPoint:
- renderCenteredAtPoint:scale:rotation:

These are convenience methods, used to make the process of rendering an image to the screen easier. The majority of these methods are simply setting the properties of the image before it is rendered. Listing 5.18 shows the renderCenteredAtPoint:scale:rotation: as an example.

Listing 5.18   **The renderCenteredAtPoint:scale:rotation: Method**

```
- (void)renderCenteredAtPoint:(CGPoint)aPoint scale:(Scale2f)aScale
        rotation:(float)aRotation {
    scale = aScale;
    rotation = aRotation;
    point.x = aPoint.x - ((imageSize.width * scale.x) / 2);
    point.y = aPoint.y - ((imageSize.height * scale.y) / 2);
    dirty = YES;
    [self render];
}
```

This method takes in a CGPoint, defining the pixel location the image should be rendered to, as well as a Scale2f value and a rotation value that specifies the number of degrees the image should be rotated.

The image's scale and rotation are set to the values passed in and then the image's point is calculated to make sure that the image will be rendered with its center at the point provided. This calculation also takes into account the scale to be used so that the correct center point is still calculated.

You see that all the rendering methods follow the same pattern, except for the render method. This method actually calculates the rotation, scaling, and translation necessary on the image's vertices and then adds the image to the ImageRenderManager render queue. The render method is shown in Listing 5.19.

Listing 5.19   **The render Method**

```
(void)render {

    imageDetails->texturedColoredQuad->vertex1.vertexColor =
    imageDetails->texturedColoredQuad->vertex2.vertexColor =
    imageDetails->texturedColoredQuad->vertex3.vertexColor =
    imageDetails->texturedColoredQuad->vertex4.vertexColor = color;
```

```
    [sharedImageRenderManager addImageDetailsToRenderQueue:imageDetails];

if (dirty) {
    loadIdentityMatrix(matrix);

    translateMatrix(matrix, point);

    if(flipVertically) {
        scaleMatrix(matrix, Scale2fMake(1, -1));
        translateMatrix(matrix, CGPointMake(0, (-imageSize.height *
            scale.y)));
    }

    if(flipHorizontally) {
        scaleMatrix(matrix, Scale2fMake(-1, 1));
        translateMatrix(matrix, CGPointMake((-imageSize.width *
            scale.x), 0));
    if(rotation != 0)
        rotateMatrix(matrix, rotationPoint, rotation);

    if(scale.x != 1.0f || scale.y != 1.0f)
        scaleMatrix(matrix, scale);

    transformMatrix(matrix, imageDetails->texturedColoredQuad,
        ImageDetails
        ->texturedColoredQuadIVA);

    dirty = NO;
    }
}
```

The first task of the method is to set the `TextureColoredQuad` color to the current color of the image. When this is done, the image is added to the `ImageRenderManagers` render queue.

The next check is to see if the image is marked as `dirty`. Remember from earlier that when we change something like the image's `scale` or `rotation`, the `dirty` flag is set to YES. This enables us to perform transforms only on the image's vertices if they have changed. If there is no change, we can simply use the values from the last render and move on.

If, however, the image has been marked as `dirty`, we calculate the transformations that need to be done.

These transformations are calculated using our own transformation functions. OpenGL ES has its own transform and matrix functions, such as `glLoadIdentity`, `glScale` and `glRotate`, but these can only be set once before a `glDrawElements` is called. As we have seen, when we covered the `ImageRenderManager`, we are rendering all the images for a texture using just a single `glDrawElements` command, so there is no possibility to call the OpenGL ES transforms between each image.

The solution to this is to actually transform the vertices information for the image directly, and it is for this reason that we have two `TexturedColoredQuads` inside the image's `ImageDetails` structure.

As you may remember from earlier, `imageDetails->texturedColoredQuad` holds the base information for the image (that is, its origin is `0,0`, and it is not scaled or rotated). The second `TexturedColoredQuad` inside `ImageDetails` called `texturedColoredQuadIVA` points to an entry in the `ImageRenderManager`'s IVA. Having these two copies enables us to transform the vertice's information inside the `imageDetails->TexturedColoredQuad` and place the results inside `imageDetails->texturedColoredQuadIVA`.

When the `ImageRenderManager` then renders, it will be rendering the image with any scale, rotation, or translation applied without the need to use the OpenGL ES transform functions.

There are a few things needed to make this magic happen. The first is that each image has to have its own matrix, which is used to perform the transform calculations. This is defined within the *Image.h* file and is an array of nine `floats` called `matrix`.

The next requirement is the actual transform functions themselves. If you look inside the *Transform2D.h* file inside the *Global Headers* group, you see the transform functions we are using. I'm not going to run through these functions in detail or try to describe the matrix math.[1] They are not doing anything special apart from applying matrix calculations to the data that is passed in. These functions are also `inline`, as were the functions in the *Global.h* file. This again is to improve performance, as described earlier.

So, knowing that we have the necessary functions to transform the vertices, we can go back to the *Image.m* file and finish off looking at the render method.

Inside the render method we have just performed a check to see whether an image is `dirty`; now we'll perform the transform calculations.

First, the images matrix is reset by loading the identity matrix. Then, a translation is performed on the matrix using the image's point information. Next, a check is carried out to see if the image has been flipped horizontally or vertically. If so, a simple scale transform is done using –1 on the axis being flipped. A translation is also performed to make sure that the images position is updated to match its new orientation.

If the image has been rotated, the rotation transform is calculated followed by the scale transform if necessary. After these have all been done, the resulting matrix is multiplied against the vertices inside `imageDetails->texturedColoredQuad`, with the results being loaded into `imageDetails->texturedColoredQuadIVA`. Finally, the `dirty` flag is set to `NO`.

---

[1] More information on matrix math can be found at www.gamedev.net/reference/articles/article1832.asp.

Getters and Setters

The last few methods we need to cover in the `Image` class are some getters and setters. We could have just used those generated by `@synthesize`, but we need to not change only the value of the property but also set the `dirty` flag. Because we need to set this flag, we need to create our own getters and setters, as shown in Listing 5.20.

Listing 5.20   **Getters and Setters**

```
- (void)setPoint:(CGPoint)aPoint {
        point = aPoint;
        dirty = YES;
}

- (void)setRotation:(float)aRotation {
        rotation = aRotation;
        dirty = YES;
}

- (void)setScale:(Scale2f)aScale {
    scale = aScale;
        dirty = YES;
}

- (void)setFlipVertically:(BOOL)aFlip {
        flipVertically = aFlip;
        dirty = YES;
}

- (void)setFlipHorizontally:(BOOL)aFlip {
        flipHorizontally = aFlip;
        dirty = YES;
}
```

These simple methods are setting the image's properties to the values passed in. The only extra piece that gets added is setting of the `dirty` flag.

Summary

This is a large chapter, and the concepts and code we have run through have been complex in places. Although the actual task of rendering something to the screen using OpenGL can be done in just a few commands, it's the infrastructure we have built around those commands that is going to make our lives easier as we implement the game logic.

Although it can take a great deal of time to get your game engine working as you would like, without having implemented any of your actual game logic, it is time well spent. Putting in the time now to make your core classes functional and clean to use will save you plenty of time in the long run.

This chapter is a milestone on our journey to creating *Sir Lamorak's Quest*. Being able to load any image and render it to the screen, applying scale, rotation, and transparency, is the backbone of any game engine. Now that we have the game's spine, we can start to hook up the other bones that form the game engine and eventually become *Sir Lamorak's Quest*.

Exercise

If you run the project that accompanies this chapter, you see that you are presented with a still image and a rotating scaling image. All the logic needed to make this happen is inside the `GameScene` class, introduced in Chapter 4.

Having a spinning, scaling image is pretty cool, but how about making it *do* something different?

As a suggestion, how about making the spinning image bounce around the screen so that when the center of the image reaches the edge of the screen, it bounces off. You already have all you need to render the image; you just need to add some more logic to handle the movement and bouncing.

You could also try changing the image being used in the project as well, or load more images and have them render to the screen.

> **Tip**
>
> When adding any files to your project, make sure you right-click within Xcode's *Groups & Files* section and select *Add Existing File*. This ensures that the file is registered with the project, or else your code will not be able to see your file, even if it is where you expect it to be.

If you get stuck trying to make your image bounce, check out the project called *CH05_SLQTSOR_EXERCISE* to see how it can be done.

6

Sprite Sheets

Chapter 5, "Image Rendering," was large and covered a number of complex concepts. Having done all that hard work, and with the classes in place for representing and rendering images, we can move on to the other components needed in the game engine for Sir Lamorak's Quest.

As the title suggests, this chapter is all about sprite sheets. If you remember from Chapter 2, "The Three Ts: Terminology, Technology, and Tools," a *sprite sheet* is a large image that contains a number of smaller images.

There are two key benefits to using sprite sheet, as follows:

- You reduce the number of times you need to ask OpenGL ES to bind to a new texture, which helps with performance.
- You gain the ability to easily define and reuse image elements of the game, even in animations.

This chapter reviews the `SpriteSheet` and `PackedSpriteSheet` classes and shows how to extract specific images from within a larger image sprite sheet.

Introduction to Sprite Sheets

As mentioned in Chapter 2, there are two different types of sprite sheets, as follows:

- Basic, where all the images in the sprite sheet have the same dimensions.
- Complex, where the images in the sprite sheet could all have different dimensions.

For *Sir Lamorak's Quest*, we are going to be using both kinds of sprite sheets. Although it is possible to merge both the simple and complex sprite sheet functionality into a single class, I have split them into two different classes to make things easier to understand. Basic sprite sheets are handled in a class called `SpriteSheet`, whereas the `PackedSpriteSheet` class handles complex sprite sheets.

> **Note**
> I use the term *packed* because you can place smaller sprite sheets within this larger sprite sheet, thus reducing the number of separate sprite sheets used in the game.

Another term for a sprite sheet is a *texture atlas*, but I will continue to use the old-school term of "sprite sheet" throughout this book.

Simple Sprite Sheet

The `SpriteSheet` class takes the image provided and chops it up into equally sized sub-images (sprites). The dimensions to be used when dividing up the sprite sheet will be provided when a new sprite sheet is instantiated. Information is also provided about any spacing that has been used within the provided sprite sheet image. Spacing is an important property within a sprite sheet. Without going into detail, when defining texture coordinates within an image for OpenGL ES, it is possible to sample a pixel beyond the edge of the texture you are defining. This can cause your textures to have an unwanted border that is made up of pixels from the image around the image defined with your texture coordinates. This is known as *texture bleeding*.

To reduce the risk of this happening, you can place a transparent border around each image within a sprite sheet. If OpenGL ES then goes beyond the edge of your texture, it will only sample a transparent pixel, and this should not interfere with the sprite you have defined. Zwoptex[1] enable you to specify the number of pixels you would like to use as a border around your sprites. Figure 6.1 shows a simple sprite sheet image with single pixel border between each sub-image. If you are drawing non-square triangles, the spacing may need to be more than one pixel to help eliminate texture bleeding.

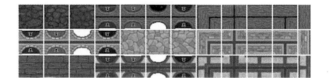

Figure 6.1   Sprite sheet with spacing between each sprite.

In terms of how we are going to access the sprites on a simple sprite sheet, we're going to use its grid location. A simple sprite sheet makes a nice grid because all the images are the

---

[1] Zwoptex (**www.zwoptexapp.com/flashversion/**) is a Flash-based sprite sheet builder. There is also a Cocoa-based version of this tool available. This Cocoa version generates output the same as the flash version, but was not available during the writing of this book.

same size. This makes it easy to retrieve a sprite by providing its row and column number. Figure 6.2 shows a sprite sheet of twelve columns and three rows with the sprite at location {5, 1} highlighted.

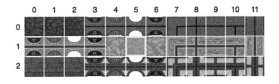

Figure 6.2   Sprite sheet grid with location {5, 1} highlighted.

Complex Sprite Sheets

The PackedSpriteSheet class takes an image and the name of the control file. The control file is parsed to obtain the location and size of every sprite within the sprite sheet image.

The control file is the key difference between a basic (SpriteSheet) and complex (PackedSpriteSheet) sprite sheet. With the basic sprite sheet, you can work out where each sprite is by performing a simple calculation using its grid position. This is harder to do with a complex sprite sheet because the sprites can be different sizes and are often placed randomly throughout the image to make the best use of space.

To help identify the coordinates of the sprites in a complex sprite sheet, the control file provides information on where each sprite is located inside the sprite sheet, along with its dimensions. The control file also gives each image a *key*, usually the name of the image file of the original sub-image, which then allows the PackedSpriteSheet class to reference each sprite. Figure 6.3 shows the complex sprite sheet that we use in *Sir Lamorak's Quest*.

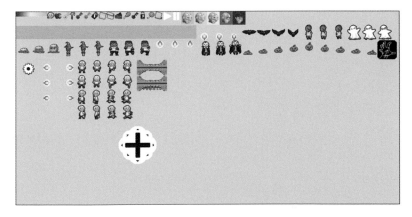

Figure 6.3   Complex sprite sheet from *Sir Lamorak's Quest*.

As you can see from Figure 6.3, a complex sprite sheet has many images that are all different sizes and shapes—thus the need for a control file to make sense of it all.

You could create your own control file for these files, providing the information on the pixel locations within the image and its dimensions, but to be honest, that is a really tedious job. Luckily for us, there are tools that can help.

The Zwoptex tool (mentioned earlier, and discussed in Chapter 2) is one such tool. It not only produces a PNG image of the generated sprite sheet, but it also creates the control file you need to identify the individual images within.

Zwoptex has a number of different algorithms that can help pack images, but it also enables you to move the images around, making it possible for you to pack as many images as possible into a single sheet. There are some good algorithms out there for optimizing the packing of variably sized images, but you'll always get the best results doing this manually.

Figure 6.4 shows the flash version of Zwoptex editing the complex sprite sheet.

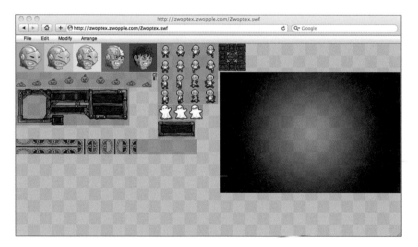

Figure 6.4   The Flash-based Zwoptex tool, used for editing a complex sprite sheet.

Zwoptex has three different outputs, as follows:

- A project file that stores your settings and images for a particular sprite sheet
- A PNG image of the sprite sheet
- A *plist* control file, which you can add to your game

The thing I like the most about Zwoptex is that it gave me the control file as a *plist* file. Although you can obviously handle raw XML if needed (or any other format, for that matter), having a *plist* file makes things so much easier (and I like to take the easy route whenever possible).

Now that you know what Zwoptex is, let's show you how to use it.

Using Zwoptex

Using Zwoptex is really easy. Just point your browser to **www.zwoptexapp.com/ flashversion/**. Once there, Zwoptex opens, and you can start creating your sprite sheet.

The first step is to import images. Start by going to the menu **File > Import Images** (see Figure 6.5), and you see an **Open File** panel for you to navigate to the file(s) you want to import.

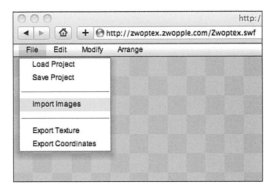

Figure 6.5   Import images into the sprite sheet.

After you select your images, hit the **Select** button to load the images into Zwoptex. All the images you've selected will be placed at the top-left corner of the screen, as shown in Figure 6.6.

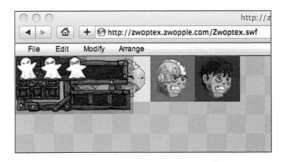

Figure 6.6   Zwoptex imports the images in the top-left corner of the canvas.

Now that you've placed the images in Zwoptex, there are a number of ways to arrange the sprites on the canvas. Under the **Arrange** menu, you will find different options for laying out the sprites. Figure 6.7 shows the sprites having been laid out using the **Complex By Width (no spacing)** option.

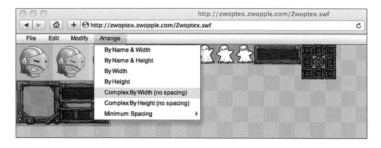

Figure 6.7   Sprite options menu and arranged sprites.

You can do this manually by clicking any sprite and moving it to the position you want. You can also use the **Modify** menu to change the size of the canvas to fit your needs.

By default, Zwoptex trims transparent edges from the imported images. This can be a problem, however, if the image you imported will be used as a simple sprite sheet. These images need to retain their original dimensions or the calculations used to define the position of each sprite will be incorrect.

Within the **Modify** menu is the option to **Untrim Selected Images**. This should be used to ensure that the images are returned to their original size. This is not necessary if the image won't be used as a sprite sheet.

Having arranged your sprites, you can then export both the image (texture) and the control file (coordinates). There are two options within the **File** menu that let you do this: **Export Texture** and **Export Coordinates**. Both options enable you to select the location where you would like the file(s) saved.

That's it! You now have a sprite sheet image file and its accompanying control file.

The SpriteSheet Class

Having looked at the basics of a sprite sheet, we can now look at our implementation of the SpriteSheet class. In Xcode, open the *CH06_SLQTSOR* project and look inside the Game Engine group. You will see a new group called *Sprite Sheet*, inside of which are the SpriteSheet classes header and implementation files.

Initialization

Inside the *SpriteSheet.m* file, you find the following class methods:

- `spriteSheetForImageNamed:spriteSize:spacing:margin: imageFilter`
- `spriteSheetForImage:sheetKey:spriteSize:spacing:margin:`

These methods are used to create new sprite sheets either from an image file or from an `Image` instance that has already been created. Notice that both of these are class methods. This means you don't need an instance of the `SpriteSheet` class to access them. Having also defined a static `NSDictionary` within the class, you can use these class methods to access the dictionary information that only has a single instance.

The idea is that a sprite sheet is cached when it is created. Whenever a new sprite sheet that either uses the same image file or key is requested, a reference to the sprite sheet already created is returned. This helps with performance when you have a large number of entities that share the same sprite sheet (for example, the `Door` class, which you will see soon).

These class methods still make use of the standard initializer methods; they just cache the sprite sheet returned by these methods for later use. Listing 6.1 shows the `spriteSheetForImageNamed:spriteSize:spacing:margin:imageFilter:` method.

Listing 6.1   **The spriteSheetForImageNamed:spriteSize:spacing:margin:imageFilter: Method**

```
static NSMutableDictionary *cachedSpriteSheets = nil;

+ (SpriteSheet*)spriteSheetForImageNamed:(NSString*)aImageName
     spriteSize:(CGSize)aSpriteSize spacing:(NSUInteger)aSpacing
     margin:(NSUInteger)aMargin imageFilter:(GLenum)aFilter {

  SpriteSheet *cachedSpriteSheet;

  if (!cachedSpriteSheets)
     cachedSpriteSheets = [[NSMutableDictionary alloc] init];

  if(cachedSpriteSheet = [cachedSpriteSheets objectForKey:aImageName])
     return cachedSpriteSheet;

  cachedSpriteSheet = [[SpriteSheet alloc]
     initWithImageNamed:aImageName spriteSize:aSpriteSize
     spacing:aSpacing margin:aMargin imageFilter:aFilter];
  [cachedSpriteSheets setObject:cachedSpriteSheet forKey:aImageName];
  [cachedSpriteSheet release];

  return cachedSpriteSheet;
}
```

The first line in Listing 6.1 defines a static `NSMutableDictionary`. This creates a single instance of `NSMutableDictionary` that the class methods use to cache the sprite sheets. This dictionary has been defined at the class level, which means that only a single copy of this dictionary will exist, regardless of how many `SpriteSheet` instances are created. This provides us with a single cache of the sprite sheets.

The rest of the class simply checks to see if an entry already exists in the dictionary for an image name passed in (using `spriteSheetForImageNamed`). If the other method passes in a ready-made image, the `sheetKey` provided is used.

If no match is found, a new sprite sheet is created and added to the dictionary. Otherwise, the matching entry from the dictionary is passed back to the caller.

The initializer used when an image name is provided is shown in Listing 6.2.

Listing 6.2   **SpriteSheet initWithImageNamed:spriteSize:spacing:margin:imageFilter Method**

```
- (id)initWithImageNamed:(NSString*)aImageFileName
    spriteSize:(CGSize)aSpriteSize spacing:(NSUInteger)aSpacing
    margin:(NSUInteger)aMargin imageFilter:(GLenum)aFilter {

    if (self = [super init]) {
        NSString *fileName = [[aImageFileName lastPathComponent]
            stringByDeletingPathExtension];

            self.image = [[Image alloc]
                initWithImageNamed:filename filter:aFilter];

            spriteSize = aSpriteSize;
            spacing = aSpacing;
            margin = 0;

            [self cacheSprites];
    }
    return self;
}
```

The start of the initializer method is standard, and we have seen it many times already. The first interesting action comes when we create an image instance of the image used as the sprite sheet.

We are using the `Image` class that we created in the last chapter, passing in the image name that has been provided along with the image filter.

Next, the sprite's size, spacing, and margin are defined. At this point, we branch off and call a private method, called `cacheSprites`, which caches the information for each sprite in this sprite sheet. Calculating this information only once is important to help performance. This information should never change during the lifetime of a sprite sheet, so there is no need to calculate each time we request a particular sprite.

We examine the `cacheSprites` method in a moment; first, there is another initializer method to look at, as shown in Listing 6.3.

Listing 6.3   SpriteSheet initWithImage:spriteSize:spacing:margin Method

```
- (id)initWithImage:(Image*)aImage spriteSize:(CGSize)aSpriteSize
      spacing:(NSUInteger)aSpacing margin:(NSUInteger)aMargin{
   if (self = [super init]) {
      self.image = aImage;

      spriteSize = aSpriteSize;
      spacing = aSpacing;
      margin = aMargin;

      [self cacheSprites];
   }
   return self;
}
```

The previous initializer took the name of an image file and created the image as part of creating the sprite sheet. This second initializer takes an image that's already been created. Not only is it useful to create a sprite sheet using an image instance that already exists, but it is also the method that's used when we create a sprite sheet from an image held in a complex (or packed) sprite sheet.

The only difference in this initializer from the last is that we set the sprite sheet's image to reference the `Image` instance that has been passed in. This method still calls the `cacheSprites` method, and that's the next method we discuss.

The `cacheSprites` method (shown in Listing 6.4) is a private method, as we only use it internally in the `SpriteSheet` class.

Listing 6.4   SpriteSheet cacheSprites Method

```
- (void)cacheSprites {

   horizSpriteCount = ((image.imageSize.width + spacing) + margin) /
      ((spriteSize.width + spacing) + margin);
   vertSpriteCount = ((image.imageSize.height + spacing) + margin) /
      ((spriteSize.height + spacing) + margin);

   cachedSprites = [[NSMutableArray alloc] init];
   CGPoint textureOffset;

   for(uint row=0; row < vertSpriteCount; row++) {
      for(uint column=0; column < horizSpriteCount; column++) {

         CGPoint texturePoint = CGPointMake((column *
```

```
            (spriteSize.width + spacing) + margin),
            (row * (spriteSize.height + spacing) + margin));

        textureOffset.x = image.textureOffset.x *
            image.fullTextureSize.width + texturePoint.x;
        textureOffset.y = image.textureOffset.y *
            image.fullTextureSize.height + texturePoint.y;
        CGRect tileImageRect = CGRectMake(textureOffset.x,
            textureOffset.y, spriteSize.width, spriteSize.height);

        Image *tileImage = [[image subImageInRect:tileImageRect]
            retain];

        [cachedSprites addObject:tileImage];

        [tileImage release];
    }
  }
}
```

The first two calculations work out how many sprites there are in the sprite image, and a new NSMutableArray is created. This array holds Image instances created for each image in the sprite sheet. Again, creating the images at this stage and caching them improves performance. This is not an activity you want to be performing in the middle of game play.

With the array created, we then loop through each row and column, creating a new image for each sprite. We use the information we have about the sprite sheet, such as size, spacing, and margin, to calculate where within the sprite sheet image each sprite will be. With this information, we are now able to use the subImageInRect method of the Image class to create a new image that represents just the sub-image defined.

Retrieving Sprites

Having set up the sprites on the sprite sheet, the next key activity is to retrieve sprites. We have already discussed that one of the key tasks of the SpriteSheet class is to return an Image class instance configured to render a single sprite from the sprite sheet, based on the grid location of the sprite.

The spriteImageAtCoords: method shown in Listing 6.5 implements the core mechanism for being able to retrieve a sprite.

Listing 6.5   SpriteSheet spriteImageAtCoords: Method

```
- (Image*)spriteImageAtCoords:(CGPoint)aPoint {

    if(aPoint.x > horizSpriteCount-1 || aPoint.y < 0 || aPoint.y >
        vertSpriteCount-1 ||
        aPoint.y < 0)
```

```
        return nil;

    int index = (horizSpriteCount * aPoint.y) + aPoint.x;

    return [cachedSprites objectAtIndex:index];
}
```

The first check we carry out in this class is on the coordinates that are being passed in. This method takes the coordinates for the sprite in a `CGPoint` variable. `CGPoint` has an `x` and `y` value that can be used to specify the grid coordinates in the sprite sheet.

When we know that the coordinates are within the sprite sheet, we use the coordinates of the sprite to calculate its location within the `NSMutableArray`. It's then a simple task of retrieving the image from that index and passing it back to the caller

That's it for this class. It's not that long or complex, but it does provide an important building block within our game engine.

PackedSpriteSheet Class

As mentioned earlier, the `PackedSpriteSheet` class is responsible for dealing with complex sprite sheets. These sprite sheets contain many variably sized images to which we want to get access. This often includes other sprite sheets. This class can be found in the same group within the *CH06_SLQTSOR* project, as before.

Initialization

This class uses the same caching technique as the `SpriteSheet` class. There is, however, only one initializer, which is shown in Listing 6.6.

Listing 6.6   PackedSpriteSheet initWithImageNamed:controlFile:filter Method

```
- (id)initWithImageNamed:(NSString*)aImageFileName
controlFile:(NSString*)aControlFile
      filter:(GLenum)aFilter {

   if (self = [super init]) {
      NSString *fileName = [[aImageFileName lastPathComponent]
         stringByDeletingPathExtension];

      image = [[[Image alloc] initWithImageNamed:fileName
         filter:aFilter] retain];

      sprites = [[NSMutableDictionary alloc] init];

      controlFile = [[NSDictionary alloc]
         initWithContentsOfFile:[[NSBundle mainBundle]
         pathForResource:aControlFile ofType:@"plist"]];
```

```
        [self parseControlFile:controlFile];
        [controlFile release];
    }
    return self;

}
```

Once inside the initializer, we create a new `Image` instance from the details passed in and allocate an `NSMutableDictionary` instance called `sprites` that will hold the details of the sprites in our packed sprite sheet.

The last section of the initializer grabs the contents of the control file that were passed in and loads it into an `NSDictionary` called `controlFile`. It is always assumed that the type of file is a *plist*, so the file type is hard coded. After we have the `controlFile` dictionary populated, we then parse the information inside that dictionary using the private `parseControlFile` method shown in Listing 6.7.

Listing 6.7   **PackedSpriteSheet parseControlFile: Method**

```
- (void)parseControlFile:(NSDictionary*)aControlFile {

    NSDictionary *framesDictionary = [controlFile objectForKey:@"frames"];

    for (NSString *frameDictionaryKey in framesDictionary) {

        NSDictionary *frameDictionary = [framesDictionary
            objectForKey:frameDictionaryKey];

        float x = [[frameDictionary objectForKey:@"x"] floatValue];
        float y = [[frameDictionary objectForKey:@"y"] floatValue];
        float w = [[frameDictionary objectForKey:@"width"] floatValue];
        float h = [[frameDictionary objectForKey:@"height"] floatValue];

        Image *subImage = [image subImageInRect:CGRectMake(x, y, w, h)];
        [sprites setObject:subImage forKey:frameDictionaryKey];
    }
}
```

Parsing the Control File

The `parseControlFile` method creates a dictionary from all the `frames` objects within the dictionary we passed in. There are several objects inside the *plist* file, as follows:

- Texture, which holds the dimensions of the texture.
- Frames, which hold objects keyed on the image's filename for each image in the sprite sheet.

An example of the *plist* file inside the Plist Editor can be seen in Figure 6.8.

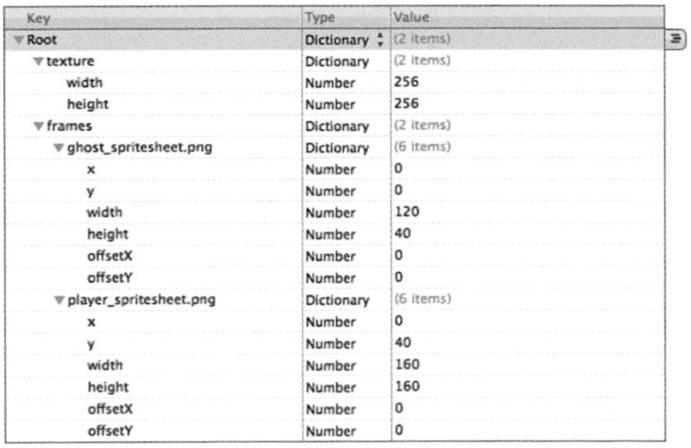

Key	Type	Value
▼ Root	Dictionary ⏷	(2 items)
▼ texture	Dictionary	(2 items)
width	Number	256
height	Number	256
▼ frames	Dictionary	(2 items)
▼ ghost_spritesheet.png	Dictionary	(6 items)
x	Number	0
y	Number	0
width	Number	120
height	Number	40
offsetX	Number	0
offsetY	Number	0
▼ player_spritesheet.png	Dictionary	(6 items)
x	Number	0
y	Number	40
width	Number	160
height	Number	160
offsetX	Number	0
offsetY	Number	0

Figure 6.8   Sprite sheet plist control file.

The details we want for the sprites are therefore held in the frame's objects.

Now that we have a dictionary called `frames`, we loop through each of them, extracting the information we need. For each frame we find, we assign another `NSDictionary` that contains the objects for the key we are dealing with. Remember that the key is a string that contains the name of the original image file that was embedded into the larger sprite sheet. This makes it easy later on to reference the image we need.

Once we have the information for the frame, we then add a new object to our `sprites` dictionary. The key is the name of the image file we have just read from the control file, and the object is an `Image` instance.

Getting a sub-image from the full sprite sheet image creates the `Image` instance. Again, we are just making use of functionality we have already built.

This process is repeated for each image in the sprite sheet control file, and we end up with a dictionary that contains an image representing each image in our packed sprite sheet.

Retrieving a Sprite

Having all our sprites in a dictionary now makes retrieving a sprite from our `PackedSpriteSheet` very simple. This is done using the `imageForKey` method. Listing 6.8 shows this method.

Listing 6.8   **PackedSpriteSheet imageForKey Method**

```
- (Image*)imageForKey:(NSString*)aKey {
    Image *spriteImage = [sprites objectForKey:aKey];
    if (spriteImage) {
        return [sprites objectForKey:aKey];
    }
```

```
    NSLog(@"ERROR - PackedSpriteSheet: Sprite could not be found for key
        '%@'", aKey);
    return nil;
}
```

We pass an `NSString` into this method containing the key to the sprite's dictionary that we created earlier. If you remember, the key is the filename of the image that was placed inside the packed sprite sheet. If an image is found for the key supplied, a reference to this image is returned. Otherwise, an error is logged, so we know that the sprite we wanted could not be found.

> **Note**
>
> Notice that, in some methods, an error is raised using `NSLog`. This is handy when debugging your game, but this is also a huge performance hog. To reduce the possibility of an `NSLog` message being called in the production code, it would be worth only generating the log messages when running in debug code.

Summary

In this chapter, we have reviewed the `SpriteSheet` and `PackedSpriteSheet` classes that continue to build out our game engine for *Sir Lamorak's Quest*. These classes enable us to retrieve sub-images from within a specified image in a number of ways:

- `SpriteSheet` **class:** As a new `Image` instance based on a sprite's grid location.
- `PackedSpriteSheet` **class:** As an `Image` reference based on a sprite's key (for example, the sub-image's original filename).

These important classes enable us to not only manage the number of textures we need, but also provide us with a mechanism for grabbing the images needed to create animation.

Classes such as `Image`, `SpriteSheet`, and `PackedSpriteSheet` are the building blocks that form the backbone of our game engine. Being comfortable with how they work and how they can be used enable you to get the most out of the game engine itself, as well as a clearer view of how to implement your own games. Although the game engine we are building for *Sir Lamorak's Quest* is not suited to all types of games, it provides you with the basis for any future games you want to develop. This enables you to take the game engine in new directions as your needs and experience grow.

The next chapter covers animation. It's not exactly Pixar Animation,[2] but animation nonetheless.

---

[2] Pixar Animation is an award-winning computer animation studio responsible for feature films such as *Toy Story*, *Monsters, Inc.*, and *Finding Nemo*, among many others.

Exercise

The example project that is provided with this chapter, *CH06_SLQTSOR*, displays three different images that have been taken from a single sprite sheet. These images are scaled, rotated, and colored using the features of the `Image` class covered in Chapter 5 to show that the `Image` instance returned is an entirely separate image in its own right.

The current project is using a couple of sprite sheets from *Sir Lamorak's Quest* that have been placed inside a complex sprite sheet.

Using this project as a guide, why not try to create your own basic sprite sheet or download one from the Internet? Once you have your sprite sheet, create a complex sprite sheet using Zwoptex and then render your sprites to the screen.

Here are the steps you need to follow:

1. Decide what fancy sprites you want to create.

2. Work out the dimensions each sprite is going to be (for example, 40×40 or 50×80) and any spacing you want to use.

3. Open up your favorite graphics package and draw your sprites, remembering to keep each sprite in a square that has the dimensions you decided.

4. Export your sprite sheet as a PNG file.

5. Open up the Zwoptex link (**www.zwoptexapp.com/flashversion/**), and add the sprite sheets that are included in the project along with your own.

6. Export the texture and coordinates from Zwoptex.

7. Add the two files you have just generated to the Xcode project. This can be done by right-clicking the Images group inside the Game Resources group and selecting **Add > Add Existing File**. Inside the panel that pops up, navigate to the file and select it. You should also select the Copy option to make sure the files are copied to the project folder.

8. Finally, follow the code example in the current project to import and start using your sprite sheet.

9. Once you are rendering your sprites, try to apply some image functions, such as scaling, rotation, and color.

7

Animation

We're starting to add all the core classes to our game engine. We can now render an image using the `Image` class and apply different functions to it, such as scale, rotation, and color. In Chapter 6, "Sprite Sheets," we looked at the `SpriteSheet` class that enables us to store multiple images that share the same dimensions in a single image and then retrieve a sub-image (sprite) using its grid location within that larger image. We also reviewed the `PackedSpriteSheet` class, which enables us to handle a sprite sheet that is made up of images that have different sizes and dimensions.

In this chapter, we build on the `Image`, `SpriteSheet`, and `PackedSpriteSheet` classes we now have and create an `Animation` class. This class enables you to string together multiple images with a delay between each, allowing us to create animation.

Animation is an important and fun side to games. There are game styles for which animation is not really needed, but to be honest, most interesting games have some kind of animation.

We all know how Apple uses animation within Mac OS X and the iOS to improve usability; this can also be done in games. Using animation to attract a player's attention when there is a lot going on can be really useful, such as flashing an icon or player sprite. It also means you have to think about the animation you are going to use. Just because you can animate it, doesn't mean you should. Too much animation can overload the player and actually harm the player's experience.

Animation Chapter Project

Open, build, and run the *CH07_SLQTSOR* project inside Xcode.

When the project runs, you see a number of images rendered to the screen, as shown in Figure 7.1.

You will recognize some of the images from those seen in the Chapter 6 project. What's new in this project are the animated sprites in the top-left and bottom-right corners of the screen. The project accompanying this chapter uses both the `PackedSpriteSheet` and `SpriteSheet` classes and creates a couple of animations from the images in those sprite sheets.

Figure 7.1   iPhone simulator running the
CH07_SLQTSOR project.

This chapter runs through the requirements for the `Animation` class and then reviews the implementation we are using for *Sir Lamorak's Quest*.

Introduction to Animation

Let's do some thinking about what it is our `Animation` class is going to need to do. There is no doubt that we could make the animation class very sophisticated indeed, but based on the game design we discussed in Chapter 1, "Game Design," we don't need to get carried away.

Next are the different features that need to exist within our `Animation` class so we can implement our game design.

Frames

First, we need to be able to create an instance of the `Animation` class and then add frames to it. A frame would be a single `Image` instance that represents one frame of the animation.

Along with the image, a *delay* would also be associated with a frame. The delay would specify how long that frame should appear on screen in seconds. We could have a single delay value that is used for all frames of the animation, but that is too restrictive. We may have animation where we want certain frames to appear on the screen longer than others. Having a delay associated with each frame will allow us to do that.

State

As with most things inside a game, our animation will need to manage its state. We don't need anything complex, but we need to be able to identify if the animation is running or is stopped.

Type

As well as defining the frames and the state of our animation, we will also want to define the type of animation. The type will define if the animation is going to run in one of three ways, as follows:

- **Repeating:** Repeating animations reach the end of the defined frames and then start again back at the beginning.
- **Ping-Pong:** Ping-pong has nothing to do with small white balls and paddles. It does, however, describe an animation characteristic. When it reaches the end, it runs backward to the beginning and then forward again.
- **Once:** As the name suggests, this type causes the animation to run once and then stop.

Direction

This enables us to identify which direction the animation is currently running. This may not be useful when using a *repeating* animation, but when using a *ping-pong* animation, it can be useful to know which direction the animation is running.

Bounce Frame

This is something introduced to help reduce the complexity of some animations. Our hero, Sir Lamorak, is going to have a number of different frames within his animation. Figure 7.2 shows the animation frames for Sir Lamorak running to the right.

Figure 7.2   Sir Lamorak's animation frames.

Notice that the first frame of the animation shows Sir Lamorak standing still. This is what we would use when he is not moving, of course. The other three frames are played in order to represent him running to the right.

When we come to develop the class that controls our hero, it would be handy to have a single animation instance that handles him running right and also standing still. To keep this simple, the concept of a bounce frame was introduced. This is a simple property that defines a frame in the animation that should cause the animation to bounce, or run in the opposite direction without that frame being drawn.

As we see later in Chapter 14, "Game Objects and Entities," we will be able to have a single animation instance for running right and also be able to render the standing still frame when the player is not moving using frames from a single `Animation` instance.

Animation Class

Because we have looked at the key features we need to cover with the `Animation` class, we now look at how this is implemented within the `Animation` class.

If you open the *CH07_SLQTSOR* project, you see a new group within the Game Engine group called Animation. This group contains the `Animation` class's *.h* and *.m* files. Open the *Animation.m* file now.

Initialization

As with the previous chapters, we start by looking at how you initialize an instance of the Animation class. For this class, we are simply overriding the `init` method; we are not taking any other parameters. Listing 7.1 shows the complete initializer method for the *Animation.m* class.

Listing 7.1   **Animation init Method**

```
- (id)init {
    if(self = [super init]) {
        maxFrames = 5;
        frameCount = 0;
        currentFrame = 0;
        state = kAnimationState_Stopped;
        type = kAnimationType_Once;
        direction = 1;
        bounceFrame = -1;

        frames = calloc(maxFrames, sizeof(AnimationFrame));

    }
    return self;
}
```

You can see that the initializer method is not that big. The key function being performed, other than setting default values for the classes' properties, is setting up the storage for the frames that are going to be loaded into the instance. You'll also notice that the method is using constants, such as `kAnimationType_Once`, that are defined in the *Animation.h* file.

By default, we are setting `maxFrames` to 5. This causes the frames array to be allocated with enough space to store five frames of animation. You may be wondering why we are setting the `maxFrames` to five when we may need more frames than that. This is just the default value for the `Aniamtion` class. We will see in the next method that deals with adding frames how we extend the storage to hold more frames as necessary. Five is not a bad number to start off with and helps reduce the amount of wasted space we have assigned but are not using.

If you know you are going to always have animations with more than five frames, you can up the `maxFrames` value in here to help reduce the number of storage extensions that need to be done.

Notice that as part of the `calloc` command, we are getting the size of a structure called `AnimationFrame`. This has been defined inside the `structures.h` file in the `Global Headers` group of the project:

```
typedef struct {
    Image *image;
    float delay;
} AnimationFrame;
```

The structure is actually very simple and just contains a pointer to an `Image` instance and a `float` that represents the delay to be used for that frame. The rest of the initializer is simply setting the default values of the class.

> **Note**
>
> We are using a C structure to store the frame information for performance reasons. Although we could have used an `NSArray` to store information about frames, animation is updated frequently during the game loop, and we want to use a method that has as little overhead as possible.

After a new `Animation` instance has been created, we can add animation frames to it.

Adding Frames

To add a frame of animation, we have the `addFrameWithImage:delay` method shown in Listing 7.2. This method is responsible, as you would expect from the name, for adding frames to the animation instance. The first check that is carried out is making sure we are not adding more frames than we have allocated storage for in the `frames` array. Trying to put more data into an array than we have allocated storage for is a bad idea and has unpredictable results.

Earlier, you saw that we set the `maxFrames` property to five. It is inside this check that we are adding more space to the `frames` array if it's necessary.

Listing 7.2   **The addFrameWithImage:delay: Method**

```
#define FRAMES_TO_EXTEND 5

- (void)addFrameWithImage:(Image*)aImage delay:(float)aDelay {

    if(frameCount+1 > maxFrames) {
        maxFrames += FRAMES_TO_EXTEND;
        frames = realloc(frames, sizeof(AnimationFrame) * maxFrames);
    }

    frames[frameCount].image = [aImage retain];
    frames[frameCount].delay = aDelay;
    frameCount++;

}
```

Once the check is complete and we know we have enough storage for a new frame, we start creating a frame, setting its properties, and incrementing the frame count.

Animation Updates

Having created a new `Animation` instance and loaded it with frames, we need a mechanism that enables us to move through those frames. In Chapter 3, "The Journey Begins," we discussed how we should break up the update and render elements of the loop. This means that for any entity in the game that needs to be updated, it will be asked to update itself from within the update element of the game loop.

We are going to model any class that can both update and render using this concept. Implementing two specific methods inside classes that can update and render themselves will do this:

- `updateWithDelta`
- `render`

The `updateWithDelta` method is called from inside the game loop's update routine. This method is passed the delta value from the game loop, and this value can then be used when performing time-based calculations. For our animation, this is going to be important because we are defining how long each frame should be shown for.

The `render` method is, as you would expect, responsible for actually rendering the entity. This method will not perform any actions on the entity's properties or state, as this is handled inside the update method. There are also convenience methods for rendering, such as `renderCenteredAtPoint`, but these are still just responsible for rendering the entity.

So, inside the *Animation.m* file, you see a method called `updateWithDelta:`, shown in Listing 7.3.

Listing 7.3   **The updateWithDelta: Method**

```
- (void)updateWithDelta:(float)aDelta {

    if(state != kAnimationState_Running)
        return;

    displayTime += aDelta;

    if(displayTime > frames[currentFrame].delay) {
        currentFrame += direction;

        displayTime -= frames[currentFrame].delay;

        if (type == kAnimationType_PingPong && (currentFrame == 0 ||
            currentFrame ==
            frameCount-1 || currentFrame == bounceFrame)) {
            direction = -direction;
        }
        else if (currentFrame > frameCount-1 || currentFrame ==
                 bounceFrame) {
            if (type != kAnimationType_Repeating) {
                currentFrame -= 1;
                state = kAnimationState_Stopped;
            } else {
                currentFrame = 0;
            }
        }
    }
}
```

The first check is on the state of the animation. If it is not running, there is no need to update its state and we can just leave the method.

> **Note**
>
> kAnimationState_Running and kAnimationState_Stopped form an enum that has been configured in the *Animation.h* file. State is a simple integer, so creating an enum enables us to use a friendlier name for the states of the animation. There is also an enum configured in the header for animation types as well.

Next, we increment the displayTime variable. This variable is tracking how much time has passed since the last update and enables us to know when to move to the next frame.

Knowing that we should move to the next frame, we increment the currentFrame based on the direction variable and reset the displayTime to the difference between displayTime and the frames delay. This means the correct frame is shown if the game slows down, causing the displayTime value to be larger, as frames may need to be skipped. The `direction` variable stores either 1 for moving forward or -1 for moving backward through the frames.

Having incremented the frame, we can update the animation based on its configured type.

If the animation type is `kAnimationType_PingPong` and the `currentFrame` is either equal to 0, the number of frames in the animation, or to the configured `bounceFrame`, the direction of animation is reversed.

If the animation is not of type `kAnimationType_PingPong` and `currentFrame`, it has either passed the last frame of the animation or is equal to the configured `bounceFrame`. If this is the case, the `currentFrame` is set to 0 being the start of the animation.

Last of all, we check to see if the type is `kAnimationType_Repeating`. If not, it must be `kAnimationType_Once` and the animation state is set to `kAnimationState_Stopped`.

That is the complete update method. It's a simple method, but it provides us with all the functionality we described at the start of this chapter for our animation class. Now we can move onto how we then render the animation.

Animation Rendering

Having dealt with updating the animation, we can now look at how we render the `currentFrame`. This is actually simple, as we make use of the render methods provided by `Image` class. All we need to do is provide some convenience methods that give us access to the different render methods in the `Image` class. Listing 7.4 shows the render methods inside the *Animation.m* file. These are convenience methods for rendering an animation to the screen.

Listing 7.4   **The Render Methods within Animation.m**

```
- (void)renderAtPoint:(CGPoint)aPoint {
    [self renderAtPoint:aPoint scale:frames[currentFrame].image.scale
        rotation:frames[currentFrame].image.rotation];
}

- (void)renderAtPoint:(CGPoint)aPoint scale:(Scale2f)aScale
    rotation:(float)aRotation {
    [frames[currentFrame].image renderAtPoint:aPoint scale:aScale
        rotation:aRotation];
}

- (void)renderCenteredAtPoint:(CGPoint)aPoint {
    [self renderCenteredAtPoint:aPoint
        scale:frames[currentFrame].image.scale
        rotation:frames[currentFrame].image.rotation];
}

- (void)renderCenteredAtPoint:(CGPoint)aPoint scale:(Scale2f)aScale
    rotation:(float)aRotation {
```

```
    [frames[currentFrame].image renderCenteredAtPoint:aPoint scale:aScale
        rotation:aRotation];
}
```

You can see that we are grabbing the current frame from the `frames` array using the `currentFrame` as the index. With that, we are then able to access the image property and from there call the necessary method on that image.

As I've said before, we are just continuing to build on the previous classes we have created, using that functionality from within the new classes. Clearly understanding what class is responsible for what function helps to simplify the process of adding more functionality later on.

Finishing Things Off

The last few methods we look at are some getters and setters and the class's `dealloc` method.

Some of the functions we may want to support need a little more effort than just setting a property. If we look at how we set either the `rotationPoint` or actual rotation for an animation, we see that it does involve more than just setting a property.

Our images do accept a point of rotation and a rotation amount, but our animation is made up of a number of images. For this reason, when setting the `rotationPoint` or `rotation` for an animation, we need to set these properties for each image that makes up the animation. This could be done manually, of course, by setting the image property for a specific frame, but it's useful to be able to set that value for all frames, and this is what our setters are doing:

```
- (void)rotationPoint:(CGPoint)aPoint {
    for(int i=0; i<frameCount; i++) {
        [frames[i].image setRotationPoint:aPoint];
    }
}

- (void)setRotation:(float)aRotation {
    for(int i=0; i<frameCount; i++) {
        [frames[i].image setRotation:aRotation];
    }
}
```

We are simply looping through all the frames in the animation and setting the necessary properties for the image associated with that frame.

A couple of other convenience getters enable us to get the image for the current frame or the image for the specified frame:

```
- (Image*)currentFrameImage {
    return frames[currentFrame].image;
}
```

```
- (Image*)imageForFrame:(NSUInteger)aIndex {
    if(aIndex > frameCount) {
        NSLog(@"WARNING - Animation: Invalid frame index");
        return nil;
    }
    return frames[aIndex].image;
}
```

Organic Growth

Not all the methods in the classes we have been through have existed from day one. I personally have found that as I develop a game, I come across handy methods that help to simplify the API to the game engine and keep the game code cleaner. I always consider if a method I am adding to the game content should be placed into the game engine code. If it is something I could reuse across classes, I usually try to identify the right class for it to live in and add it.

Adding these items to classes is not always a simple change either. There are times when you find that adding a method to a class requires other changes to that class to be made for it to still be logical. Don't be afraid to make these changes. Experience has shown me in all aspects of programming, and maybe even more so in games, that adding hacks here and there to just make things work will usually not turn out favorably for you in the end.

I have spent many hours trying to debug horrible issues that end up resulting from a hack I had introduced to get a quick fix. I normally find that I end up spending more time debugging these than I would have spent implementing the change fully from the start.

Much like everyone else, I'm always after instant gratification, and a quick hack normally hits the spot. But you must remember that in the end, you typically will live to regret it.

The last method we need to discuss is the `dealloc` method. We haven't really been looking at this method much, but it's extremely important. Managing memory on the iPhone, in general, is something to spend time on. Because we have a limited amount of resources, and as there is no garbage collection[1] to help us out, we need to think about memory all the time. How can we reduce how much we need, and how can we make sure we give back what we have taken?

Note

The Objective-C 2.0 documentation from Apple does talk about garbage collection, but this is not available in iOS.

Unlike a lot of classes where you simply release the objects you have allocated in the `dealloc` method, the `Animation` class requires us to free memory we have allocated to structures.

---

[1] Garbage collection is a form of automatic memory management. The garbage collection basically tries to reclaim memory from objects that are no longer in use.

As we added frames of animation, we were allocating memory for our `AnimationFrame` structure. To make sure we give this all back when the `Animation` instance is released, we need to loop through all the frames in our animation, freeing memory as we go:

```
- (void)dealloc {

    if (frames) {
        for(int i=0; i<frameCount; i++) {
            AnimationFrame *frame = &frames[i];
            [frame->image release];
        }
        free(frames);
    }
    [super dealloc];
}
```

After we have freed the memory for each frame, we then finish off by freeing the memory allocated to the `frames` array that held our animation frames.

Summary

The Animation class is a relatively simple class to implement. However, even though it is simple, it provides a key element to our game engine. Being able to generate animation from multiple images is a tried and tested approach to animation within 2D games.

The animation that you create could be for any use really. You don't have to limit animation to game characters or the player; you could also have animation on buttons and other GUI elements. Having a GUI element animate when the user touches it just gives them some feedback and acknowledgment of the action they have performed.

Clever use of animation can really make a game. Even a simple game can look impressive with the right mix of animation within the GUI and game itself.

The next chapter introduces another important element to our game engine. We now have all the game engine components we need to render images to the screen and handle sprite sheets and animation. The next chapter deals with rendering text to the screen.

Being able to render text to the screen is important and not something OpenGL ES provides for us, so Chapter 8, "Bitmap Fonts," runs through a well-used technique for being able to render dynamic text.

Exercise

If you have opened and run this chapter's project called *CH07_SLQTSOR*, you have seen how we built on the Chapter 6 project and added some animation elements.

If you completed the exercise in Chapter 6, you have created your own sprite sheet and rendered it to the screen. Why not use that sprite sheet to try out the new `Animation` class? Even if your sprite sheet is not animated, you could still cycle through the sprites to get the hang of how to use the `Animation` class.

You could also search the Internet and try to find some animated sprites you could use.

Once you have your own sprites in the project, try out the different animation types, as follows:

- `kAnimationType_Repeating`
- `kAnimationType_Pingpong`
- `kAnimationType_Once`

You can also try applying effects to your animation, such as scaling and rotating the images you have inside your animation. You will see that this has been done inside the Chapter 7 project. Simply applying a rotation, rotation point, color, or scale to the sprite sheet image you are going to use causes each image extracted from that sheet to have those properties.

8

Bitmap Fonts

Most games provide the player with important information during game play using text. It's important to be able to provide players with information such as their score, health, and time, as well as messages for the players.

The iPhone SDK provides great features to render very attractive text to the screen. This is used by applications that use the UIKit components available on the iPhone. If you were developing a game using just UIKit, Quartz, and Core Animation, you could use these capabilities to easily select the font, size, and color of the text you want to display.

When using OpenGL ES to render the game scene, displaying text is a little more challenging. There are no features built into the OpenGL ES API to render text. As you have already seen, OpenGL ES simply deals in triangles, points, and lines. It has no concept of fonts or the characters that make up a font.

For this reason, we need to use a concept that has been around as long as computer games themselves. This concept is called *bitmap fonts*. Bitmap fonts consist of a complex sprite sheet that contains a sub-image for each character needed to render a font. To display text, you identify the characters that are included in the text you want to render and then render the image for each character in that text to the screen.

This chapter covers the creation of bitmap fonts and also the `BitmapFont` class we are using in *Sir Lamorak's Quest*.

Bitmap Font Project

Open and run the *CH08_SLQTSOR* project that comes with this chapter. As with previous chapters, this chapter continues to build on the work we have done before. This project includes the `BitmapFont` class that can be found within the *Bitmap Font* group inside the *Game Engine* group.

Figure 8.1 shows a screenshot of this project running.

You will recognize the images from Chapter 7, "Animation," but also notice the colorful text in the middle of the screen. Being able to render all kinds of different fonts in different sizes and colors is what the `BitmapFont` class is all about. By the end of this chapter, you will have all the tools and knowledge necessary to take a font and use it within your game.

Figure 8.1   CH08_SLQTSOR project running on
the iPhone simulator.

Introduction to Bitmap Fonts

As mentioned earlier, bitmap fonts enable you to render text to the screen using OpenGL
ES. Even before OpenGL ES, developers were using the concept of bitmap fonts to render text to the screen.

Back in the 1980s, the 8-bit home computers and consoles were able to render only
very basic fonts to the screen using built-in functions. To enable games developers to use
larger, more interesting, and even colorful fonts, they came up with the concept of
bitmap fonts.

Each character in a bitmap font is represented by an image. To render text to the
screen, each character in the text message has its associated image rendered to the screen.
This sounds complicated, but it is not that difficult to implement.

For the purposes of this book, we can think of bitmap fonts as complex sprite sheets
(that is, a single image that contains smaller sub-images representing the different characters in our font). Figure 8.2 shows a bitmap font sprite sheet generated using the Hiero[1]
application.

---

[1] Hiero is a Java-based application that can create a bitmap font sprite sheet and control file from
standard as well as TrueType fonts.

Figure 8.2   Bitmap font sprite sheet.

You may be wondering if we could use the `PackedSpriteSheet` class covered in Chapter 6, "Sprite Sheets"—unfortunately, the answer is no. The `PackedSpriteSheet` class was designed specifically to parse the sprite sheet control file generated by the Zwoptex application. Because the bitmap font image is also going to be a complex sprite sheet, it too needs a control file. The problem we have is that the tool we are going to use to generate our bitmap font sprite sheets generates the corresponding control file in a different format to Zwoptex.

Although it's not impossible to implement an extra parser in the `PackedSpriteSheet` class, the way we are going to parse and then render our bitmap font lends itself to be a stand-alone class.

It's also worth mentioning that you don't have to use bitmap fonts for ALL text you want to render to the screen. It is perfectly possible to create UILabel instances and add those to your EAGLView and use them to render text to the screen. This is a simple task, and it does save a lot of time. That said, you may find the fonts and capabilities available with UIKit limiting, so understanding how to use bitmap fonts is still a good idea.

Creating the Bitmap Font Sprite Sheet

Having mentioned that we are going to be using a tool to generate our bitmap font sprite sheet, let's look at how that is done. As with the complex sprite sheets, there is nothing stopping us from generating our own sprite sheet image and control file; it's just tedious and difficult to get it right.

To make things easier, we are going to use a free Java application called Hiero (**n4te. com/hiero/hiero.jnlp**). You may remember that we touched on this tool briefly in Chapter 2, "The Three Ts: Terminology, Technology, and Tools."

> **Note**
>
> There is also a Windows-based application called BMFont (**www.angelcode.com/products/ bmfont**) that can create bitmap fonts from TrueType fonts. This application, like Hiero, generates both an image and control file. Although this application runs only under Windows, it does provide more functionality than Hiero; if you are able to run it, it's worth checking it out.

As described, Hiero enables you to take a TrueType font and generate a sprite sheet of the font's characters and the control file needed to process the sprite sheet. Figure 8.2 shows the Hiero GUI as seen when creating the bitmap font, shown previously in Figure 8.1.

The first step in creating a bitmap font is to start the Hiero app by visiting **n4te.com/ hiero/hiero.jnlp**. After Hiero has opened, you see the GUI shown in Figure 8.3. You are now able to select either a system font that's shown in the top-left corner of the interface, or select a font file that you have downloaded from the Internet.

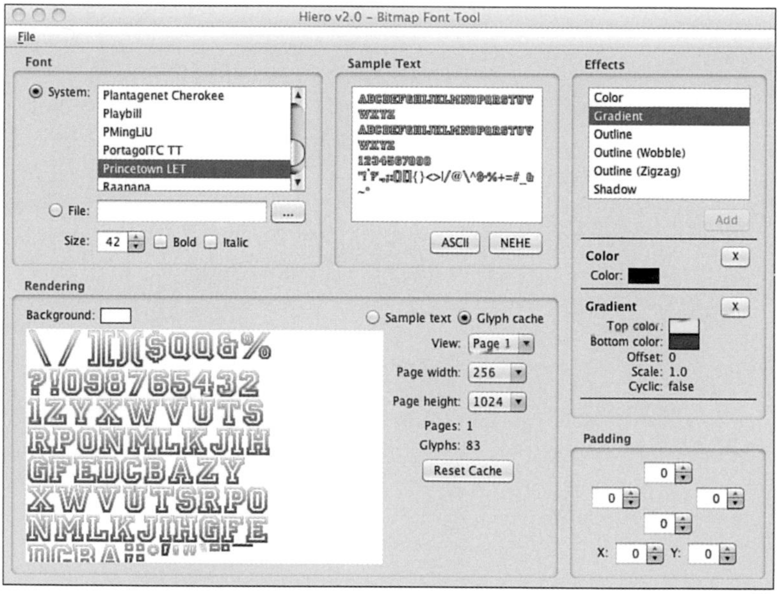

Figure 8.3   Hiero.

After you choose your font, you can then set the size of the font as well as details of how it is going to be placed within a sprite sheet.

To configure the size of the sprite sheet, select the width and the height to be used inside the rendering panel, shown in Figure 8.4.

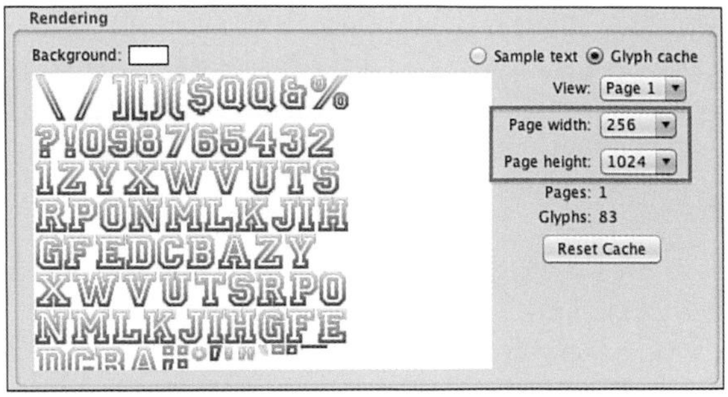

Figure 8.4   Setting texture width and height in Hiero.

Note

The maximum texture size that the iPhone 3G and all preceeding iPhone devices will handle is 1024×1024. It is important to make sure you do not exceed this size. If you do, the `Texture2D` class shrinks the texture by 50 percent to make it fit into the 1024×1024 limits. This causes the control file values that are also generated for the font to be incorrect, and you will get unknown results. From the iPhone 3GS onwards, the maximum texture size increased to 2048×2048.

You can also apply effects to the font as well, such as shadows, gradients, and outlines. Figure 8.5 shows the Effects panel in Hiero.

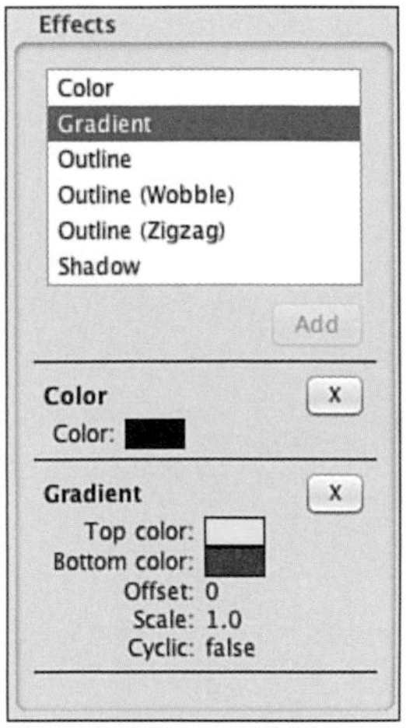

Figure 8.5   Effects panel in Hiero GUI.

Although there are only limited effects available in Hiero, it is still really useful to be able to add effects before exporting the bitmap font.

> **Tip**
>
> You could load the PNG file produced by Hiero into a graphics application and make changes to the colors or shadows directly. This can be tricky, though—you need to make sure that each character does not move or change size. If the position or size changes, the control file that's generated also needs to be updated.

After you have finished configuring how you want your font to look, it is time to export the font for use in the game. This is done using the **File > Save BMFont filts (text)**. When you select this menu option, a Save dialogue appears, allowing you to name the file and select its location.

When you hit the Save button, two files are generated. The first is a PNG file that contains the image you are going to use as the sprite sheet, and the second is the control file that holds the details of where each character of the font is located within the image file. The control file has the *.fnt* file extension.

After you have those files, you have everything you need to start using that font. Well, everything except the `BitmapFont` class used to process and render the font you just created, so let's take a look at that in the next section.

The BitmapFont Class

The `BitmapFont` class is responsible for loading the image that is to be used as the sprite sheet for the font and also the processing of the control file. Remember, the control file contains the details of where in the image each character of the font can be found. We can use this information when extracting characters.

Header File

We normally start these sections by looking at the initializer methods. This time, let's start with the header file. Header files are normally self-explanatory and don't need much coverage. For the `BitmapFont` class, however, we need to look at a structure, shown in Listing 8.1, that has been defined in the header.

Listing 8.1   **Structure of BitmapFontChar**

```
typedef struct _BitmapFontChar {
        int charID;
        int x;
        int y;
        int width;
        int height;
        int xOffset;
        int yOffset;
        int xAdvance;
        Image *image;
        float scale;
} BitmapFontChar;
```

This structure is going to be used to store information on each character in the font. Each character in the font has data that is associated with it, such as its ID, location within the font image, size, and offsets. The `BitmapFontChar` structure stores this information inside an array for each character in the font control file.

What's with the C?

Notice that we are starting to use C structures more often as we get deeper into this book. This is because when working with Objective-C objects, there is an overhead in terms of messaging to and from those objects. Asking an instance of a class for a properties value is handled using messages between those objects.

When information is to be queried or updated regularly, it is worth seeing if the information can be held in a C structure rather than creating a class with properties.

Initializer

The initializer continues to follow the same structure as those in previous classes. Listing 8.2 shows the entire initializer method.

Listing 8.2   **BitmapFonts initWithFontImageNamed:controlFile: Method**

```
- (id)initWithFontImageNamed:(NSString*)aFileName controlFile:(NSString*)aControlFile
    scale:(Scale2f)aScale filter:(GLenum)aFilter {

    self = [self init];
    if (self != nil) {

        sharedGameController = [GameController sharedGameController];

        image = [[Image alloc] initWithImageNamed:aFileName filter:aFilter];
        image.scale = aScale;

        fontColor = Color4fMake(1.0f, 1.0f, 1.0f, 1.0f);

        charsArray = calloc(kMaxCharsInFont, sizeof(BitmapFontChar));

        [self parseFont:aControlFile];
    }
    return self;
}
```

The initializer first grabs a reference to the `GameController` and then creates an `Image` instance using the image details that were passed in.

After the image has been created, the scale of the image is set along with the color. By default, all components of the color are set to `1.0`. This maximum intensity setting means that the actual colors of the font image will be used when the characters are rendered. You could change these values, but it would cause all characters to render with a colored filter applied. (A color filter could be applied later if we wanted to.)

With the scale and color set, we next allocate the space required for the `charsArray` that is configured to hold `BitmapFontChar` information. This array is sized using the maximum number of characters that can be found in a font, `kMaxCharsInFont`, and the `BitmapFontChar` structure that is going to be used to store the character information.

You may be wondering why we are not allocating this space dynamically when we have identified how many characters are in the font we are processing. The reason comes down to how we are going to be accessing the font characters later in the `BitmapFont` class which we will see shortly.

When the arrays have been set up, the initializer method then parses the control file for the font we are processing.

Parsing the Control File

As mentioned earlier, the bitmap font is made up of two components: the sprite sheet image (a PNG file) and the control file. The control file tells us where each character is within the image. Inside the *BitmapFont.m* file is a private class that is used to parse the font's control file.

If you look at the bottom of the *BitmapFont.m* file, within the private implementation you see a method called `parseFont:`, as shown in Listing 8.3.

Listing 8.3   **BitmapFont parseFont: Method**

```
- (void)parseFont:(NSString*)controlFile {

NSString *contents = [NSString stringWithContentsOfFile:
    [[NSBundle mainBundle] pathForResource:controlFile
    ofType:@"fnt"] encoding:NSASCIIStringEncoding error:nil];

    NSArray *lines = [[NSArray alloc] initWithArray:[contents
        componentsSeparatedByString:@"\n"]];

    NSEnumerator *nse = [lines objectEnumerator];

    NSString *line;

    while(line = [nse nextObject]) {
        if([line hasPrefix:@"common"]) {
            [self parseCommon:line];
```

```
        } else if([line hasPrefix:@"char id"]) {
                [self parseCharacterDefinition:line];
            }
    }
    [lines release];
}
```

The first action of the method is to load the contents of the control file into a string. It is assumed that the control file will have a *.fnt* extension, as this is the default extension used by Hiero (described earlier).

Having loaded the file into an NSString, it's now necessary to break that string into individual lines; each line within the control file represents a single character's definition. This is done by creating an NSArray and populating it with the contents string separated by \n. This is basically breaking the contents string into pieces whenever a new line marker is found. Each of these pieces is then loaded into its own element in the lines array.

Now that we have an array full of strings representing each character definition in the control file, we create an enumerator for the lines array, which we can use to move through each line in the array. We also create a variable in which to hold each line as we are processing it, called line.

The control file is a simple text file with each line representing a character definition (that is, the character's image location within the image file), its image size, and how far we need to move horizontally or vertically so we can position characters correctly next to each other. Listing 8.4 shows a sample from the bitmap font control file.

Listing 8.4   Excerpt from the Bitmap Font Control File

```
info face="TransformersNormal" size=56 bold=0 italic=0 charset=""
    unicode=0 stretchH=100 smooth=1 aa=1 padding=0,0,0,0 spacing=1,1
common lineHeight=77 base=26 scaleW=1024 scaleH=1024 pages=1 packed=0
    page id=0 file="testFont.png"
chars count=94
char id=32   x=0      y=0      width=0      height=0      xoffset=0
    yoffset=57   xadvance=31    page=0  chnl=0
```

Each line starts with a prefix that identifies the kind of information held within that line. Listing 8.3 uses an if statement to check what the prefix of the line is and then performs the necessary action.

A number of different prefixes are used within the Hiero control file, but for our implementation, we are interested in only two of them:

- common: Provides common information about the font image, such as the scaleW and scaleH of the image itself and also the lineHeight that gives us the common height in pixels of a font character.

- **char id**: Provides the character definition information for each character in the font. This includes its location within the font's image file, along with the size of the character. It also specifies how far we need to advance after rendering that character to correctly place the next character.

If we find that the prefix is `common`, we call the `parseCommon` method. If the prefix is `char id`, we call the `parseCharacterDefinition` method.

Parsing the `common` Prefix

There is a single line in the control file that has the `common` prefix. As stated earlier, this is the `common` line information on the width and height of the font's image file and the `common` height in pixels of characters in the font. Listing 8.5 shows the method used to parse this information.

Listing 8.5   **BitmapFont parseCommon: Method**

```
- (void)parseCommon:(NSString*)line {

    int scaleW;
    int scaleH;
    int pages;

    sscanf([line UTF8String], "common lineHeight=%i base=%*i scaleW=%i
        scaleH=%i pages=%i", &lineHeight, &scaleW, &scaleH, &pages);

    NSAssert(scaleW <= 1024, @"ERROR - BitmapFont: Texture atlas cannot be
        larger than 1024x1024");
    NSAssert(scaleH <= 1024, @"ERROR - BitmapFont: Texture atlas cannot be
        larger than 1024x1024");
    NSAssert(pages == 1, @"ERROR - BitmapFont: Only supports fonts with a
        single texture atlas.");
}
```

A string is passed into the `parseCommon` method that contains the line of text from the control file that has a prefix of `common`. Using the `sscanf` C function, we populate the `lineHeight`, `scaleW`, `scaleH`, and `pages` variables.

The remaining checks make sure that the image for this font is not larger than the maximum image (texture) size the older iPhone's can handle, 1024×1024, and that this font does not use multiple pages or image files, as this class can only process one. If any of these conditions are not met, an assertion error is thrown using the error text defined.

This is a good way of making sure we don't carry on regardless when we have come across a serious problem. We obviously need the font if we are creating an instance of it, but the configuration of the font would not allow it to initialize correctly, so it's best to stop and let everyone know there is a problem and where.

Parsing the `char id` Prefix

If we come across a line in the control file that has the `char id` prefix, the `parseCharacterDefinition:` method is called. This method is basically the same as the `parseCommon` method. Listing 8.6 shows that the `parseCharacterDefinition:` method is the same as the `parseCommon` method, in which we separate the line sent in using = and then create an enumerator.

Listing 8.6   BitmapFont parseCharacterDefinition: Method

```
- (void)parseCharacterDefinition:(NSString*)line {

    int charID;

    sscanf([line UTF8String], "char id=%i", &charID);

    charID -= 32;

    sscanf([line UTF8String], "char id=%*i x=%i y=%i width=%i height=%i
        xoffset=%i yoffset=%i xadvance=%i", &charsArray[charID].x,
        &charsArray[charID].y,
        &charsArray[charID].width, &charsArray[charID].height,
        &charsArray[charID].xOffset, &charsArray[charID].yOffset,
        &charsArray[charID].xAdvance);

    charsArray[charID].image =
        [[image subImageInRect:CGRectMake(charsArray[charID].x,
        charsArray[charID].y, charsArray[charID].width,
        charsArray[charID].height)] retain];

    charsArray[charID].image.scale = image.scale;
}
```

Let's look at an example `char id` line from a font control file:

```
char id=78    x=0      y=17      width=13      height=12      xoffset=1      yoffset=4
    xadvance=12     page=0   chnl=0
```

The layout for a `char id` line is the same as you saw earlier with `common`; there are just different name-value pairs.

Notice that when we calculate the `charID`, we are subtracting 32 from the value taken from the control file. Each character definition we read will be stored within the `charsArray` created in this class's initializer. To make things simple, we are going to use the ID of the character as the index into the array.

Hiero only supports characters from 32 to 255. The first 32 characters are not used within the font itself, so to save space, we are subtracting 32 from the ID of all characters we process. Doing the same calculation, when we go to look up a font character, we then need to make sure we access the correct index in the array.

We finally add the `Image` instance to the `BitmapFontChar` for the current character's ID.

Remember that the `charsArray` is made up of `BitmapFontChar` structures, and within that structure, there are variables to store the information we have just processed from the control file, along with an `Image` reference.

It's important to remember that this image needs to be retained, as the image passed back when requesting a sub-image is auto-released by the `Image` class.

The final line of code simply sets the scale of the image we have just created to match the scale provided when this font was initialized.

Rendering Text

So far, we have covered the functions needed to load a font's image file and parse its control file. It's all important stuff, but now we are going to look at something more interesting—how to actually render the text onscreen.

I'm not sure about you, but I find working on code that actually puts something on the screen much more exciting than the plumbing around it. It's just a shame that the plumbing is such an important prerequisite.

Getting text on the screen is actually going to be a lot easier than you think. The way we have built up this class means we have laid down all the necessary foundations to make the rendering of text nice and easy.

Listing 8.7 shows the `renderStringAt:text:` method used for rendering the text.

Listing 8.7   **BitmapFont renderStringAt:text: Method**

```
- (void)renderStringAt:(CGPoint)aPoint text:(NSString*)aText {

    float xScale = image.scale.x;
    float yScale = image.scale.y;

    for(int i=0; i<[aText length]; i++) {

        unichar charID = [aText characterAtIndex:i] - 32;

        int y = aPoint.y + (commonHeight * yScale) —
            (charsArray[charID].height +
            charsArray[charID].yOffset) * yScale;
        int x = aPoint.x + charsArray[charID].xOffset;
        CGPoint renderPoint = CGPointMake(x, y);

        charsArray[charID].image.color = fontColor;

        [charsArray[charID].image renderAtPoint:renderPoint];

        aPoint.x += charsArray[charID].xAdvance * xScale;
    }
}
```

The core of this method is a loop that runs through all the characters in the text provided. The first line of code in the loop creates a variable called charID. This holds the ASCII code of the character. You'll notice we are subtracting 32 from this value. This is to compensate for the fact that we are not using the first 32 ASCII character codes. You'll remember that when we were parsing the control file, we also subtracted 32 from the character's code, so we need to do the same here.

Next, we need to calculate the y position of the character. We have passed in a point, aPoint, where we want the text to be rendered, but depending on the character to be rendered, the y position needs to be adjusted.

Some letters have *descenders* that fall below the base line (such as g, j, p, q, and y), and others have *ascenders* that rise above other characters (such as d, f, h, and k). To make sure that the bottom of each character sits correctly on the base line with descenders and ascenders appearing normally, we perform a calculation that gives us the correct y offset.

Figure 8.6 highlights how characters are rendered to the screen based on the calculation. The line labeled y represents the position where you want the text to be rendered onscreen. The characters are actually rendered above that line so that letters with descenders and other characters, such as the underscore, are rendered correctly in relation to the other characters.

Figure 8.6   Character positions when rendering.

In the font control file, there is a lineHeight value. This value is a common height for all characters in the font. To calculate the correct y value for each character, the characters height plus yOffset is subtracted from the lineHeight. The result positions the character correctly when rendered next to other characters.

Now that the y position has been calculated, the renderPoint is calculated. With the renderPoint calculated, we set the color of the image for the character we are about to render and then simply render that image at renderPoint.

Next, we increase the x location of the renderPoint ready to render the next character. This is done using the xAdvance value for the character and adjusting it by any scale that may have been applied.

> **Note**
>
> Kerning information, if the font supports it, is also held within the control file produced by Hiero, making it possible to implement kerning as well. Because we aren't using a great deal of text in *Sir Lamorak's Quest*, we won't worry about kerning the text. It's good to know this information is available, though, if you need more control over the text in a game you are developing.

Rendering Justified Text

As well as being able to render text to a specified point on the screen, it would also be useful to justify the text within a defined box. This, as you can imagine, makes centering text onscreen very easy. For this, we'll use the `renderStringJustifiedInFrame:justification:text:` method, as shown in Listing 8.8.

Listing 8.8   BitmapFont renderStringJustifiedInFrame:justification:text: Method

```
- (void)renderStringJustifiedInFrame:(CGRect)aRect
justification:(int)aJustification
    text:(NSString*)aText {

  CGPoint point;

  int textWidth = [self getWidthForString:aText];
  int textHeight = [self getHeightForString:aText];

  switch (aJustification) {
    case BitmapFontJustification_TopLeft:
        point.x = aRect.origin.x;
        point.y = aRect.origin.y + (aRect.size.height - textHeight) -
          (commonHeight - textHeight);
        break;
    case BitmapFontJustification_MiddleLeft:
        point.x = aRect.origin.x;
        point.y = aRect.origin.y + ((aRect.size.height - textHeight) /
          2) - (commonHeight - textHeight);
        break;
    case BitmapFontJustification_BottomLeft:
        point.x = aRect.origin.x;
        point.y = aRect.origin.y - (commonHeight - textHeight);
        break;
    case BitmapFontJustification_TopCentered:
        point.x = aRect.origin.x + ((aRect.size.width - textWidth) /
          2);
        point.y = aRect.origin.y + (aRect.size.height - textHeight) -
          (commonHeight - textHeight);
        break;
```

```
    case BitmapFontJustification_MiddleCentered:
        point.x = aRect.origin.x + ((aRect.size.width - textWidth) /
            2);
        point.y = aRect.origin.y + ((aRect.size.height - textHeight) /
            2) - (commonHeight - textHeight);
        break;
    case BitmapFontJustification_BottomCentered:
        point.x = aRect.origin.x + ((aRect.size.width - textWidth) /
            2);
        point.y = aRect.origin.y - (commonHeight - textHeight);
        break;
    case BitmapFontJustification_TopRight:
        point.x = aRect.origin.x + (aRect.size.width - textWidth);
        point.y = aRect.origin.y + (aRect.size.height - textHeight) -
            (commonHeight - textHeight);
        break;
    case BitmapFontJustification_MiddleRight:
        point.x = aRect.origin.x + (aRect.size.width - textWidth);
        point.y = aRect.origin.y + ((aRect.size.height - textHeight) /
            2) - (commonHeight - textHeight);
        break;
    case BitmapFontJustification_BottomRight:
        point.x = aRect.origin.x + (aRect.size.width - textWidth);
        point.y = aRect.origin.y - (commonHeight - textHeight);
        break;

    default:
        break;
    }

    [self renderStringAt:point text:aText];
}
```

The CGRect defines the box inside of which the text is to be rendered. The text inside the rectangle won't be clipped; it just provides the bounds and location for the rendering to take place.

The justification value is an enum defined within the header file of the BitmapFont class. The possible justification values include the following:

- BitmapFontJustification_TopCentered

- BitmapFontJustification_MiddleCentered

- BitmapFontJustification_BottomCentered

- BitmapFontJustification_TopRight

- BitmapFontJustification_MiddleRight

- `BitmapFontJustification_BottomRight`
- `BitmapFontJustification_TopLeft`
- `BitmapFontJustification_MiddleLeft`
- `BitmapFontJustification_BottomLeft`

These values are used inside a `switch` statement to calculate the point at which to render the text onscreen. After the point has been calculated, the `renderTextAtPoint:` method is called to actually render the text.

Text Width and Height

Now that we can actually render text to the screen, there are a couple of handy functions that we need to add. When rendering text, it can be useful to know the width and height in pixels the text will be when on the screen. For example, if you wanted to center some text, you would need to know the width of the text in pixels to perform the following calculation, commonly used to center text:

`Screen width − Text width / 2`

Listing 8.9 shows the method for returning the width of a string.

Listing 8.9   **The getWidthForString: Method**

```
- (int)getWidthForString:(NSString*)string {
    int stringWidth = 0;

    for(int index=0; index<[string length]; index++) {
        unichar charID = [string characterAtIndex:index] - 32;
        stringWidth += charsArray[charID].xAdvance * image.scale.x;
    }
    return stringWidth;
}
```

This method is really simple. It loops through the characters in the string that are passed in and looks up the character's **xAdvance** value. It applies any scaling that has been defined and accumulates the value. It then returns the result. Listing 8.10 shows a similar method that returns the height of the string passed in.

Listing 8.10   **The getHeightForString: Method**

```
- (int)getHeightForString:(NSString*)string {
    int stringHeight = 0;

    for(int i=0; i<[string length]; i++) {
        unichar charID = [string characterAtIndex:i] - 32;
```

```
    if(charID == ' ')
        continue;

    stringHeight = MAX((charsArray[charID].height * image.scale.y) +
        (charsArray[charID].yOffset * image.scale.y), stringHeight);
    }
    return stringHeight;
}
```

The method in Listing 8.10 does almost the same thing as the one to calculate the width of text. The difference is that it ignores space characters, as they have no height the `stringHeight` variable only stores the maximum height found.

Deallocation

The final method to review is the `dealloc` method. Listing 8.11 shows the `dealloc` method for the `BitmapFont` class.

Listing 8.11   **The dealloc Method for the BitmapFont Class**

```
- (void)dealloc {
    if (charsArray) {
        for(int i=0; i < kMaxCharsInFont; i++) {
            if (charsArray[i].image)
                [charsArray[i].image release];
        }
        free(charsArray);
    }
    if (image)
        [image release];
    [super dealloc];
}
```

The `dealloc` method is similar to the `dealloc` method inside the `SpriteSheet` class. We have allocated space for each character in the `charsArray`, so we need to loop through that array, freeing the memory for each character. After that is done, we free the `charsArray` itself, the image we instantiated, and we call the parent's `dealloc` method.

Summary

This chapter has given us the ability to take any font we like and turn it into a bitmap font for use within our game engine. Being able to communicate with the player is important, and not having the ability to render text to the screen would leave our game engine a little lacking.

In terms of the features, our game engine needs are almost finished. The next chapter covers the `TiledMap` class, which enables us to create large complex playing areas for our game, followed by Chapter 10, "The Particle Emitter," where we will be able to start creating explosions and other organic effects.

Exercise

This chapter should have given you all the information needed to be able to use your own fonts now. To practice what we have been through during this chapter, try adding your own font to the *CH08_SLQTSOR* project and render some text to the screen.

If you don't already have any fonts that you would like to use, check out **www.dafont.com**. This great website contains thousands of different fonts to use. Some of them are free, whereas others are for limited use or requiring purchasing/licensing. Make sure you understand the license for the font you want to use if it's going to be in a game you publish and charge money for.

9

Tile Maps

Tile maps are used in computer games to both store and render a large playing area while using as little memory as possible. The technique isn't as important today as it was 15 or 20 years ago, but there are still valid reasons for using a tile map in a game, especially for things like collision detection. Knowing where an object is in relation to the player is really useful, and a tile map is a simple way of finding that information.

This chapter introduces the concept of tile maps and covers the associated classes used in *Sir Lamorak's Quest* to implement the tile maps.

Tile maps are a fundamental element of *Sir Lamorak's Quest*'s game engine, and will be used not only to render the core map Sir Lamorak is running around, but also for objects within the map, such as the baddies and other elements of the game.

Getting Started with the Tile Map Project

To get started, open the *CH09_SLQTSOR* project that accompanies this chapter and run it in the iPhone Simulator. You see a tile map slowly scrolling from right to left, as shown in Figure 9.1.

By the end of this chapter, you will understand tile maps in general and be able to create a tile map using the Tiled (**www.mapeditor.org**) tile map creation tool. You will also understand the classes required to use the maps you design using Tiled inside both *Sir Lamorak's Quest* and your own games.

Figure 9.1   iPhone Simulator running the
CH09_SLQTSOR project.

Introduction to Tile Maps

Back in the early days of game development, managing memory efficiently was not just a nice optimization; it was a necessity. With limited memory and graphical performance, those early arcade games needed to store large playing areas and graphics in a way that would allow for smooth graphics and fast game play.

It was from these requirements that the concept of the *tile map* was born. The idea is simple. A typical tile map consists of a 2D array containing references to tile objects. The actual tile object holds information about the tile, such as the following:

- The ID of the image to be rendered
- Whether the tile block is impassable
- Whether the tile causes damage to the player

By defining a map as an array, the same tile can be used over and over again rather than having every tile load up its own image. This enables you to reduce the amount of memory needed to store a large playing area. It is assumed, for example, that if you had a large open grassy area to render, you would need just a couple of different grass tiles that could be used over and over again. This is much more efficient than storing a single large image that you were rendering each frame and having to store in memory.

Figure 9.2 shows an example of a tile map that has been created from using a number of smaller images.

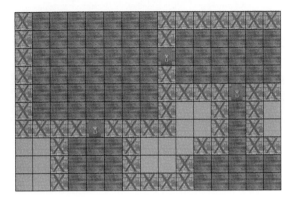

Figure 9.2   Example tile map.

Areas of the map, such as the wooden floor, are all represented by a single image. This means we only have to store that one image in memory and just render it to the screen wherever the tile map identifies it should go.

Now this is a very basic map. To make things more interesting, you could have more than a single image for the floor and walls. This enables you to introduce some variance into the tile map, making it look less like a tile map and more like a very large solid area you are walking around.

We will use many different tiles for *Sir Lamorak's Quest*. In fact, there are over 130 tiles that we'll use to draw the rooms and then object tiles on top of that. Figure 9.3 shows a small tile map created using some tiles from *Sir Lamorak's Quest*.

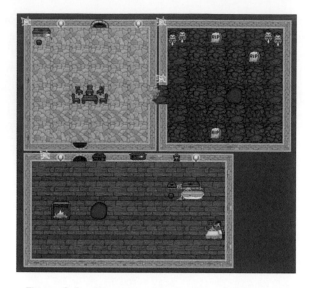

Figure 9.3   Tile map using tiles from *Sir Lamorak's Quest*.

You can see that using many different tiles, you can create nice detailed maps. What is great is that as your map grows, your memory storage requirements do not. After you have all of your tiles images loaded, no matter how many times they are used in the tile map, you don't need to store any additional image data.

As your tile map grows, only the tile map data itself gets larger.

Tile Map Editor

Chapter 2, "The Three Ts: Terminology, Technology, and Tools," covered a number of different tools we are going to use to create *Sir Lamorak's Quest*. One of these tools was called *Tiled Qt*. Tiled is an open source general tile map editor written using the Qt framework, and we'll use this tool to create the tile map for *Sir Lamorak's Quest*.

There are many different ways to create a tile map. The most basic of these is to manually populate a 2D array with values that represent the images to be drawn. The game engine then processes that array and calculates where to draw each image that is referenced. For *Sir Lamorak's Quest*, though, we need something more sophisticated.

The tile map is the backbone of our game; it's what that the player will be walking around and the primary visual the player sees. Editing a tile map by simply populating a text file with numbers to be loaded into an array is not particularly intuitive. Luckily, Tiled provides us with a WYSIWYG editor that we'll use as our level design tool.

Being able to see how the tile map looks when rendered is really important, and most complex tile map-based games also have their own level editors for doing the same job. Figure 9.4 shows a screenshot of Tiled rendering a tile map for *Sir Lamorak's Quest*.

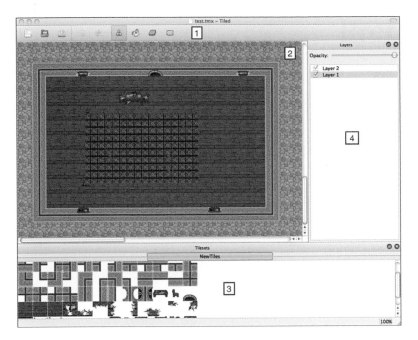

Figure 9.4   Tiled GUI with a map being edited.

Tiled has four key panels marked by red numbers in Figure 9.4. These panels are as follows:

1. Toolbar (at the top)

2. Main editor panel (in the middle)

3. Tile palette (at the bottom)

4. Layer palette (on the right)

This gives us the perfect environment to build a tile map and see how it will look before using it in our game. This really speeds up the development process. Having to run the map in the actual game every time we wanted to see how it looked would be time consuming. It also means that it's hard for someone other than the game engine developer to work on the map.

Using tools such as Tiled, you can actually get someone else to help you create the maps for your game. After all the tile images have been created, you can give the editor and the tiles to your level designer, or to someone who is willing to help you out, and get them to draw the map for you. This gives you time to carry on building the game engine.

> **Note**
>
> You will, of course, need to communicate with the person designing the level to make sure he implements things in the right way. As the game developer, you may be building functionality that causes special things to happen for certain tiles or objects on the map.

Sir Lamorak's Quest will have portals placed around the map. These portals, when walked into (or collided with), cause the player (Sir Lamorak) to be transported to another location on the map. The location of these portals is defined within the tile map using tile map objects. Also, when a door is found on the tile map, the game engine creates a door entity that manages that particular door, including when it opens and closes, and whether it is locked or not.

For this to be effective, there may be properties that need to be associated with a tile, which is where communication with the level designer becomes very important.

Tile Palette

The tile palette inside Tiled enables you to select images from tile sets and start painting with them. Creating a tile map really is as simple as picking an image and then painting the map you require using the stamp tool within Tiled.

> **Note**
>
> Tiled supports multiple tile sets within a single map. If you are creating a very large map that has more tiles that you can fit on a single 1024×1024 tile sheet, this is a handy feature. For our purposes, we will stick with a single tile sheet, supported by the `TiledMap` class.

A tile sheet is basically the same as a simple sprite sheet. It is a large image that contains smaller images, all of which have the same dimensions.

Layers

Layers are really useful when creating a tile map. Being able to draw one layer on top of another enables us to define different layers for different purposes, as well as manage how the layers are rendered; for example:

- Base map tiles (that is, floors and walls)
- Map objects (that is, chairs and tables)
- Collision information
- Portal information

Keeping these layers separate makes them easier to handle within the game engine, and it also makes maintaining the tile map within the Tiled editor easier.

With Tiled, each layer that is created takes on the dimensions of the map, allowing you to specify an image at any location on that layer.

When we run through the `Tiled` class later in this chapter, you will see that we create an object for each layer within the tile map. These layer objects are responsible for holding the data associated with each layer (that is, the layer's name and tile data). It also implements methods that enable you to query a layer's data based on a tile's coordinates.

Creating a Tile Map

After having a brief look at Tiled, let's run through how you would create a tile map.

Inside the *CH09_SLQTSOR* project, you find a tile image called *NewTiles.png*. Copy this image to your desktop, as you will need this when testing the tile map.

When you launch Tiled (the version used is Tiled Qt 0.4.0), if it is the first time you have launched the application, you are presented with an empty workspace (that is, there will be no tile sets, layers, or map image).

To create a new tile map, select **File > New**. Figure 9.5 shows the New Map dialog box, which asks for details for the map you want to create.

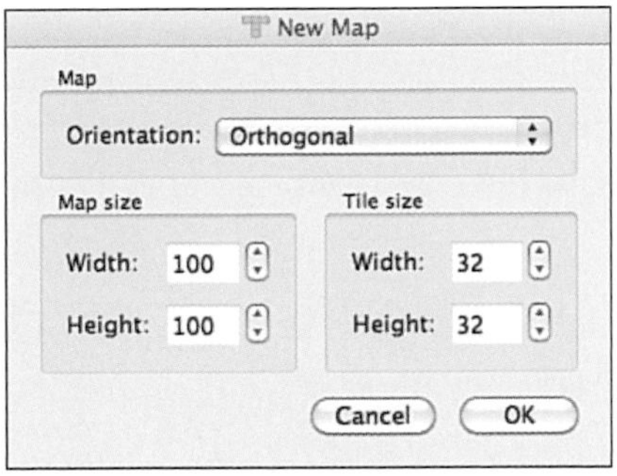

Figure 9.5   New Map dialog in the Tiled application.

Let's quickly run through the New Map dialog:

- **Map orientation:** There are two different types of map available to choose from: *Orthogonal* and *Isometric*. The only map type we will be using is Orthogonal, and this is the default value within the dialog box. The map type defines the shape of the tiles we are going to be using.
- **Map size:** The map size defines how many tiles wide and high the map is going to be. For this test, make the width and height both 50.
- **Tile size:** Tile size defines the size of the tiles in the map. You can have any size you want, and the tile height does not necessarily need to match the size of the tile images you are going to use. The normal practice, though, for Orthogonal maps is to match the tile size to the size of the tile images you are going to be using.

Our tiles are 40×40, so use that for the width and height and then click OK. The tile map panel will turn a dark gray color, signifying that you are now editing a map.

Create a New Tile Set

In the menu bar, select **Map > New Tileset**. This displays the New Tileset dialog, shown in Figure 9.6.

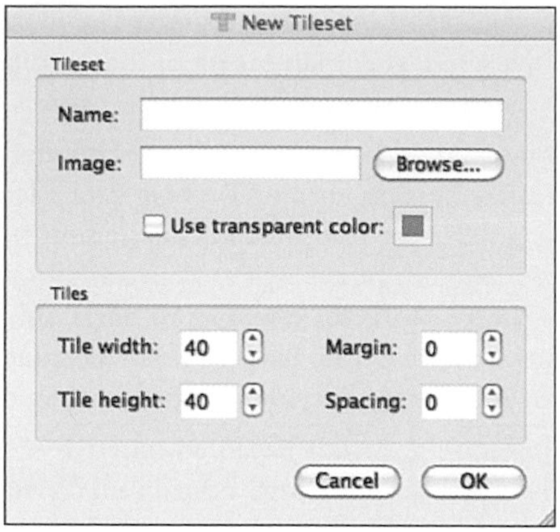

Figure 9.6   New Tileset dialog in the Tiled
application.

As the name suggests, this dialog enables you to create a new tileset. Let's quickly run through the New Tileset dialog's options, as follows:

- **Name:** This enables us to set a name for the tileset. This is most handy when you have more than one tileset, but we are only going to have a single tileset in *Sir Lamorak's Quest*. That said, it is still a good idea to give the tileset a sensible name, such as *SLQ Tiles*.

- **Image:** This section enables you to select the image you want to use for the tileset. As stated earlier, you can think of a tileset image as a simple sprite sheet. To select an image, click **Browse**, and be sure to enable the **Reference tileset image** button in the dialog that appears.

  You can also define a color within your tileset that should be treated as transparent by enabling the **Use transparent color** option. Enabling this option allows you to select a color within the image that will be transparent. We won't use this option and it will not be implemented within the Tiled class either.

- **Tile Width and Tile Height:** Notice that it is possible to change the width and height of the tile set being imported as your tiles. The tile set we are using has the same dimensions as the tile map so we will be leaving the values unchanged.

In this dialog, click **Browse** and select the *NewTiles.png* file, which you copied to your desktop earlier.

If your tileset image had spacing between the tile images, the tile spacing and margin values should be changed to match the spacing in the image.

After you finish configuring the settings, press OK. You see a palette of tile images appear at the bottom of Tiled's window, as shown in Figure 9.7.

Figure 9.7   Tileset palette containing the `NewTiles.png` tileset.

Creating Map Layers

By default, a single layer is created for us when we create a map. If you look in the Layers panel (on the right in Tiled), you see a single layer called **Layer 1**. Double-click this name to make it editable, and change the name to **TileMap**.

You can create multiple layers as described earlier, so let's see how you create a new layer within our map. In the menu bar, select **Layer > Add Tile Layer**. A new dialog appears, asking for the name of the layer. Add the **Collision** and **Objects** layers to your tile map, as shown in Figure 9.8.

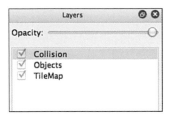

Figure 9.8   Map layers.

Creating Object Layers

Within Tiled, there are special layers called *object layers*. These layers enable you to create rectangles at any pixel location within the map and not be limited to the tile map locations. This is useful if you want to place objects within the game that are not aligned to tiles or even to define collision bounds.

You create an object layer by selecting **Map > Add Object Layer** in the menu bar, and providing the layer with a name. With this layer selected, clicking the map creates a new object within that layer. The handle on the bottom-right of the object (as shown in Figure 9.9) enables you to resize the object as necessary.

Within the Tiled configuration file, information is saved about the location of each object in an object layer, as well as the object's dimensions. Figure 9.9 shows two objects created within the tile map.

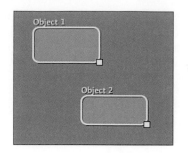

Figure 9.9   Objects within a Tiled object layer.

> **Tip**
>
> The color used to render each object layer's objects can be changed using the layer's proper-
> ties, which you can access by right-clicking a layer.

Now that we have the layers, save the map and call it *tilemap.tmx*.

Drawing the Map

Next, we can start drawing the map itself, so make sure the *TileMap* layer is selected in the
layer panel. To draw a tile, simply select the tile you want to draw from the tileset palette
and make sure that the brush tool is selected in the toolbar (along the top). Simply click
the tiles in the map view where you would like that image to be used.

Removing a tile is just as simple. Just make sure you have the eraser tool selected and
click the tile images you want to remove.

> **Tip**
>
> Make sure you have the correct layer selected before you start erasing or drawing. I have
> been caught out a number of times by drawing an entire section of map on the wrong layer
> or by going to erase something on one layer and actually removing it from another.
>
> Getting into the habit of checking the layer you have selected before you do anything will
> save lots of stress.

Placing Objects

To place an object on the map (for example, a table or chair), we need to draw the object
in the *Objects* layer. This causes the object tile to be rendered on top of any layers below it.
This is also how we will render game objects. We render the tile map one layer at a time
(that is, the *TileMap* layer followed by the *Object* layer). This causes the objects in the game
to be rendered on top of the map just as they are in the Tiled editor.

Select the *Objects* layer and then try drawing some of the object tiles onto the map. The
objects will be rendered on top of the map layer without obviously replacing the tile from
the layer underneath.

Understanding the Tiled Configuration File

When you create a map using Tiled, the output is a configuration file that describes the map you have created. This file is an XML file that contains the information necessary to recreate the map you have designed inside your game.

At this point, it is worth taking a look at this file so you understand the information it contains. Later in this chapter, you see how this file is parsed by the `Tiled` class and used to recreate the map you have designed in your game.

The standard configuration file generated by Tiled has the *.tmx* extension and is a standard XML file. This is handy because it means it is human-readable if you need to take a look inside.

The first couple of lines in the *.tmx* file are a standard XML header, as shown here:

```
<?xml version="1.0" encoding="UTF-8"?>
<!DOCTYPE map SYSTEM "http://mapeditor.org/dtd/1.0/map.dtd">
```

Map Element

The `map` element is the root element of the *.tmx* file:

```
<map version="1.0" orientation="orthogonal" width="200" height="200"
tilewidth="40" tileheight="40">
```

It provides high-level information about the map defined within the file, such as the `width` and `height` of the map in tiles and the `tileWidth` and `tileHeight`, which are the dimensions of the tiles themselves.

Within the `map` element is a properties element defining any number of properties. If there is information you would like to hold at the map level, you can create properties, which are basically name-value pairs, to hold that information. Map properties can be added using the **Map > Map Properties** menu item:

```
<properties>
    <property name="PlayerStartx" value="10"/>
    <property name="PlayerStarty" value="10"/>
</properties>
```

This example shows a couple of properties that have been added to store the players start position. This could be used rather than hard coding the location in the game code. There could be any number of `property` elements within the `properties` elements.

Tileset Element

A `map` element can contain one or more `tileset` elements. We have already discussed how Tiled supports more than one tile set per map. Each tile set used generates a `tileset` element within the *.tmx* file. Although Tiled can pass as many `tileset` elements as found in the *.tmx* file, only the first tile set is used when rendering. This is how we have implemented the `TiledMap` class and is not a restriction of the Tiled editor.

Listing 9.1 shows a `tileset` element from a *.tmx* file.

Listing 9.1   A Complete Tileset Element within a .tmx File

```
<tileset name="Tiles" firstgid="1" tilewidth="40" tileheight="40">
    <image source="NewTiles.png"/>
    <tile id="0">
        <properties>
            <property name="reducePlayersHealth" value="10"/>
        </properties>
    </tile>
</tileset>
```

The `tileset` element shown in Listing 9.1 contains the `name` and `firstgid` of the tile set, along with the `tileWidth` and `tileHeight`; these are the pixel dimensions of the tiles defined within the `tileset`. There is also an `image` element that holds the name of the `source` image of the `tileset`. This is the image that should be used as the sprite sheet for the tiles.

As well as setting `properties` at the map level, it is also possible to set `properties` on individual `tile` images within a `tileset`. These too are name-value pairs, and you are free to create as many as you need. This is handy if you want to store information that can be used during game play, such as by how much the player's health should be reduced if he hits a particular tile.

Layer Element

The `layer` element holds information about a specific layer. Just as a map can contain multiple layers, there can be multiple `layer` elements within a *.tmx* file, as shown in Listing 9.2.

Listing 9.2   Complete Layer Element within a .tmx File

```
<layer name="Map" width="200" height="200">
    <properties>
        <property name="LayerProp1" value="MyValue"/>
    </properties>
    <data encoding="base64" compression="gzip">
```
```
H4sIAAAAAAAAO3abWvbMBAAYH1KDe022Fg3RhnZW2HppyX//7/VYha9atJmt7SJ1+eBw7biCAdyOZ2dl
ADg4T6P8a0RHzrj26NcJRzHboxNI352xm+Oc5lwFEvz42NaVm96sX2GzwaPFfNjSO2cmJM3efxsmqO1jZ
HH1CHWYGn96EXJg7JfH2/SXX5Yp7EWc/Jj6IzX58e8KHlQ1w35wZq8GePLFJuwfz3G1zHeT+OX0/F5GM/
nnU3b7+G9MYbO+Nvn+HDwSL36cVO9Xv/e1+8r/UepE3Xfsam26gdr0MuPcp/qYjp+le7ff3qX2vkR+/K4
LotjQ2rfB9s+7UeFxf7Wf+zH+NWIffqzD6nzI9aS2LOXyHMcwpx5X03h1PTyo3x3x3D9V+HGv1560aMjRee
51+9zGll8nz6Uk4NU9VP1o9SO/+7m6aV/3g1HxKd7/jMX6k+/ebDtXxdXX+eWOOXBdyLl02XrsK17BL1l
esS/1c/SHPv/Mc+xnnqh+sTb3uqnNkznc5P1vVJdaG+91XHRdJ/sC45P1r3aZc8vyj1I/Yt9fYYQtuo1Ha1G
vr+p+e853udfb9O0KqPQ2cnJwf8d1FfJbh/1O8dGV91fpvofzgpfvX2sh
```
```
aCAAAAAAAAAAAAAAAAAAAAAAAAAAAAAAAAAAAAAAAAAAAAAAAAAAAAAAAAAAAAAAAAAAAAAAAAAAAAA
AAAAAAAAAAAAAAAAAAAAAAAAAAAAAAAAAAAAAAAAAAAAAAAAAAAAAAAAAAAAAAAAAAAAAAAAAAAAAAA
AAAAAAAAAAAAAAAAAAAAAAgP/JLRKhvX4AcQIA
```
```
    </data>
</layer>
```

Attributes within the `layer` element define the layer `name`, `width`, and `height`. It is normal for a `layer`'s dimension to equal the map's dimension, although nothing stops them from being different. As with the `map` and `tileset` elements, the `layer` element can have any number of `properties` defined for it. They follow the same format as with the previous elements, where each name-value pair is represented by a `property` element within the `properties` element.

The large blob of characters within the `data` element is the individual tile information for each tile inside the layer. Tiled enables you to gzip this information and store it base64 encoded within the *.tmx* file. This significantly reduces the size of the *.tmx* file, as well as the speed at which this information can be parsed.

> **Note**
>
> In a layer that is 200×200, not encoding and compressing the information results in tens of thousands of lines of XML bloating the size of the *.tmx* file from a few kilobytes to many megabytes. On a platform such as the iPhone, this is not a good idea. Parsing that amount of information would also take far too long. Keep it simple, and compress.

The `encoding` and `compression` types used are specified as attributes within the `data` element. The Tiled class detailed later in this chapter only supports gzip compression.

Object Group Element

The final element you find in a *.tmx* file is the `objectgroup`. As mentioned earlier, object layers are a special kind of layer that enable you to place objects anywhere on a map (that is, they can be located on a specific pixel rather than aligned to the tiles).

This can be useful if you have objects or images that you want to render on top of the map that are not aligned to the tiles, and you want to define their locations in the Tiled editor rather than in code. These objects could be entity spawning points, portal locations, or simple objects such as chairs and tables. Listing 9.3 shows a complete `objectgroup` element.

Listing 9.3   **Complete objectgroup Element Within a .tmx File**

```
<objectgroup name="Portals" width="0" height="0">
    <object name="Portal_1" type="PORTAL" X="179" y="496">
        <properties>
            <property name="dest_x" value="26.5"/>
            <property name="dest_y" value="289.5"/>
        </properties>
    </object>
</objectgroup>
```

The `objectgroup` element has attributes that define the `name` of the group along with the `width` and `height`. We won't be using the `width` and `height` of the `objectgroup` in *Sir Lamorak's Quest*, so there's no need to concern yourself with those elements.

A single `objectgroup` can contain any number of `object` elements. These define the `name` of the object along with their `type` and pixel location stored in the `x` and `y` attributes. Again, an object can have as many user-defined properties as you would like, and these are held as `property` elements within a single `properties` element.

You will see how `object` properties are used in Chapter 14, "Game Objects and Entities." One entity type we have in *Sir Lamorak's Quest* is a portal that can transport the player to another location on the map. The portal (a tile location) to which the player is transported is defined as `properties` within the `portal` object.

Tile Map Classes

Having covered the basics of tile maps and how to use Tiled to create a map, we can now look at the classes used in *Sir Lamorak's Quest's* Tiled map. The following three classes make up the complete tile map class set:

- **Layer:** Responsible for holding all tile and tile image data on a specific layer as well as providing functions that enable us to query that tile information.

- **TileSet:** Stores the image- and tile-related information for the tile sets we will be using. As noted earlier, even though Tiled supports multiple tile sets, we use only one in *Sir Lamorak's Quest*.

- **TiledMap:** The main class used in the game. We create an instance of this class when we want to use a tile map. **TiledMap** makes use of the **Layer** and **TileSet** classes internally, as they are not designed for direct access.

Let's examine these classes in more detail.

Layer Class

As described earlier, a single map can be made up of many layers. Each layer is responsible for storing and providing access to the actual tile data defined for that layer. To store this information and provide the functions necessary for a layer, we use the `Layer` class. This class can be found in the *CH09_SLQTSOR* project inside the *Game Engine/Tile Map* group and is called *Layer.m*.

A layer has the following properties:

- **Layer ID:** Unique ID given to each layer.
- **Layer name:** Name given to the layer inside Tiled.

- **Layer data:** Multi-dimensional array for storing the tile information within the layer.
- **Layer width:** Width of the layer in tiles.
- **Layer height:** Height of the layer in tiles.
- **Layer properties:** Properties that have been created on the layer.
- **Tile images:** Image information for each tile on the layer.

We see how these properties are used as we move through the `Layer` class's implementation.

Initialization

Initialization follows the same pattern we have seen on other classes in previous chapters. Open the *Layer.m* file that can be found in the *CH09_SLQTSOR* project. The *Layer.m* file can be found within the *Game Engine > Tile Map* group. Listing 9.4 shows the complete initialization method for the `Layer` class.

Listing 9.4   **Layer initWithName: Method**

```
- (id)initWithName:(NSString*)aName layerID:(int)aLayerID
    layerWidth:(int)aLayerWidth
    layerHeight:(int)aLayerHeight {
    if(self = [super init]) {
        layerName = aName;
        layerID = aLayerID;
        layerWidth = aLayerWidth;
        layerHeight = aLayerHeight;

tileImages = calloc(layerWidth * layerHeight,
    sizeof(TexturedColoredQuad));
    }
        return self;
}
```

Information that has been read from the Tiled map configuration file is passed into the layer's initialization method and is used to set the properties. We will be reviewing how the values are actually read from the configuration file when we review the `Tiled` class later in this chapter.

Inside the *Global.h* file, you find these two definitions at the top of the file:

```
#define kMax_Map_Width 200
#define kMax_Map_Height 200
```

These are used to define the maximum width (kMax_Map_Width) and height (kMax_Map_Height) a layer can have. These constants are used further down the header file when defining the layerData array that holds the tile data, as shown here:

```
int layerData[kMax_Map_Width][kMax_Map_Height][4];
```

The layerData array is a multi-dimensional array. The first two dimensions hold the x and y coordinates of a tile and the third-dimension is used to hold information related to the tile at that location.

Normally, the layer width and height is the same as the tile map's width and height. If you ever wanted to use a tile map larger that 200×200, you would need to change the constants in the *Layer.h* file to reflect the dimensions you wanted to use.

The initializer is also responsible for setting up an array of TexturedColoredQuad's, called tileImages, which is used to store the image information for each tile in the layer. As the TiledMap class parses the contents of a *tmx* file, it provides the layer class with image information for each tile that contains an image. This information is then used when rendering a layer.

Adding a Tile to a Layer

After the TiledMap class has initialized a layer, the layer needs to be loaded with the tile information for that layer. The TiledMap class loops through the tiles on the layer using the addTileAt:tileSetID:tileID: method, shown in Listing 9.5, to add that tile's information.

Listing 9.5   **Layer addTileAt:tileSetID:tileID: Method**

```
- (void)addTileAt:(CGPoint)aTileCoord tileSetID:(int)aTileSetID
    tileID:(int)aTileID
    globalID:(int)aGlobalID value:(int)aValue {
        layerData[(int)aTileCoord.x][(int)aTileCoord.y][0] = aTileSetID;
        layerData[(int)aTileCoord.x][(int)aTileCoord.y][1] = aTileID;
        layerData[(int)aTileCoord.x][(int)aTileCoord.y][2] = aGlobalID;
        layerData[(int)aTileCoord.x][(int)aTileCoord.y][3] = aValue;
}
```

Each tile in a Tiled map has an x and y location within a layer. It also contains four other pieces of information:

- **TileSetID**: Identifies the tile set from which the tile image was taken. You may remember that Tiled supports the use of multiple tile sets. The Layer class has been designed to handle multiple tile sets in addition to the TiledMap class itself. Let me point out that currently, though, the method of rendering a tile map layer to the screen does not support multiple tile sets. To increase performance, I wanted to keep the number of texture swaps to a minimum, and I've found that having a single tile set has not been a problem while writing *Sir Lamorak's Quest*.

The `TileSetID` starts at `0` for the first tile set and increments for each tile set used.

> **Note**
>
> Nothing is stopping you from updating the `render` method to provide the necessary perform-ance along with multiple tile set support. If you do make changes, be sure to let me know what you did.

- **`TileID`**: The ID given to each image within a tile set. This starts at `0` and increases by 1 for each tile image. This number is used to identify which image should be rendered in a given tile location on a layer.

- **`GlobalTileID`**: Related to the `TileID`. The `GlobalTileID` identifies a tile image uniquely across multiple tile sets. Each tile set has a `firstGID` value. For the first tile set in a map, this would be `0`. If the first tileset contained 45 images, indexing 0 through 44, then the `firstGID` for the second tile set would be `45`. The `GlobalTileID` is basically the `TileID` plus the tile set's `firstGID`.

- **`Value`**: Having added the `TileSetID`, `TileID`, and `GlobalTileID` to the `layerData` array, the final piece of data loaded is a simple integer. This `Value` container is some-thing I added to make it easier to store other useful information against a specific tile. You will see, in later chapters, that I make use of this value by storing an index against any tile that is identified as a door within our map. This index value is used to identify the location of that specific door object within an array of door objects. It could, however, be used to store any useful numerical information you need.

It may seem like a waste of time to explain something that is not actually being used in our game, but I wanted to implement the `TiledMap` class to handle as much of the func-tionality in a Tiled map as possible. Apart from multiple tile sets, all the functionality pro-vided within a Tiled map is supported in the `TiledMap` class and its supporting classes.

Adding a Tile Image to a Layer

In addition to adding a tile's base information to a layer, we also need to be able to add a tile image. The `Layer` class is responsible for storing the tile image information for each tile on a layer. The `TiledMap` class uses the `createLayerTileImages:` method to loop through all tiles on a layer and add the necessary image information to each layer.

The method responsible for adding these tiles to a layer is called `addTileImageAt:`, and is shown in Listing 9.6.

Listing 9.6   Layer addTileImageAt: Method

```
- (void) addTileImageAt: (CGPoint) aPoint
    imageDetails: (ImageDetails*) aImageDetails {

    int index = (int) (layerWidth * aPoint.y) + (int) aPoint.x;

    memcpy(&tileImages[index], aImageDetails->texturedColoredQuad,
        sizeof(TexturedColoredQuad));

    tileImages[index].vertex1.geometryVertex.x += (aPoint.x * kTile_Width);
    tileImages[index].vertex1.geometryVertex.y += (aPoint.y * kTile_Height);
    tileImages[index].vertex2.geometryVertex.x += (aPoint.x * kTile_Width);
    tileImages[index].vertex2.geometryVertex.y += (aPoint.y * kTile_Height);
    tileImages[index].vertex3.geometryVertex.x += (aPoint.x * kTile_Width);
    tileImages[index].vertex3.geometryVertex.y += (aPoint.y * kTile_Height);
    tileImages[index].vertex4.geometryVertex.x += (aPoint.x * kTile_Width);
    tileImages[index].vertex4.geometryVertex.y += (aPoint.y * kTile_Height);
}
```

This method is passed the `ImageDetails` structure of the image that is being used in the tile map at the position provided. The `TexturedColoredQuad` structure within `ImageDetails` is copied into the `tileImages` array that is created during the initialization of a layer. The location within the array is calculated and held in the `index` variable.

The copy is necessary because a single tile image in a tile set may be used many times in a tile map. Simply pointing to the original image in the tile set means that every change we make to the location of an image will be overwritten the next time that image is used. We therefore need to take a copy of each image's `TexturedColoredQuad` structure so that its location can be set correctly.

The `TexturedColoredQuad` information we place inside the `tileImages` array will be used when we come to render the layer.

The position of the image is defined based on its location within the tile map. This location is calculated by multiplying the tile location with the tile's width and height. This gives us the pixel location where the tile should be rendered in relation to all other tiles on the map. The tiles themselves will never move, they will always be rendered in exactly the same place as defined in the tilemap file. Whilst the player will remain in the middle of the screen, as they move their location within the tilemap is updated. Using that location, we will calculate which tiles on the tilemap are visible and render only those tiles to the screen.

Getting and Setting Tile Information

Having created an instance of the `Layer` class and shown how to add tile information, we now look at the methods used to retrieve and set tile information within a layer.

This is important, as we will want to query a layer and use the tile information returned within our game. It was mentioned earlier that we would be identifying door tiles within *Sir Lamorak's Quest*. This will be done using the tile's `TileID`. If this value is equal to a door image, we perform the necessary steps to add a door object to the game at the appropriate location.

> **Note**
>
> Using the tile map data to add objects within the game allows us to really use Tiled as our level designer. We are not simply drawing a map in Tiled, but we are also specifying where on the map dynamic objects should be placed when the game runs.
>
> Doors within *Sir Lamorak's Quest* open and close randomly. In fact, the doors have their own logic and images. The logic controls when the doors should open and close, and the images are changed accordingly.

The methods used to get and set information within the layer are simple. You will see the methods inside the `Layer.m` file, and Listing 9.7 shows the method used to get the Global Tile ID of a specific tile.

Listing 9.7   **Layer getGlobalTileIDAtX: Method**

```
- (int)globalTileIDAtTile:(CGPoint)aTileCoord {
    return layerData[(int)aTileCoord.x][(int)aTileCoord.y][2];
}
```

You can see that we simply pass in the x and y coordinates of the tile we want to query, and return the value held within the `layerData` array at that location. The last dimension is hard coded to 2, which is the index for the `GlobalTileID`.

Setting the value within the `layerData` array for a tile is also just as simple. We simply pass in the coordinates again along with a value that is assigned to the third index of the `layerData` array, as shown in Listing 9.8.

Listing 9.8   **Layer setValueAtX: Method**

```
- (void)setValueAtTile:(CGPoint)aTileCoord value:(int)aValue {
    layerData[(int)aTileCoord.x][(int)aTileCoord.y][3] = aValue;
}
```

The `tileImageAt:` method, shown in Listing 9.9, is used to retrieve a tile's image information. This is the `TexturedColoredQuad` that we saw created within the `addTileImageAt:ImageDetails:` method earlier.

Listing 9.9   **Layer tileImageAt: Method**

```
- (TexturedColoredQuad*)tileImageAt:(CGPoint)aPoint {

        int index = (int)(layerWidth * aPoint.y) + (int)aPoint.x;
        return &tileImages[index];
}
```

This method is simple but important. It forms an important part of the rendering process when we come to render a layer's tiles.

TileSet Class

Having looked at the Layer class and how it stores information relating to each layer in a Tiled map, we will now look at the `TileSet` class. This class can be found in the `CH09_SLQTSOR` project inside the `Game Engine > Tile Map` group and is called `TileSet.m`.

This class is used to store information on a single tile set that has been used within a Tiled map. One instance of the class is instantiated per tile set used in the map. Remember, though, that we are only using a single tile sheet in the map for *Sir Lamorak's Quest*.

Just like the Layer class, the `TileSet` class has a number of properties, as listed here:

- **Tile set ID:** Holds the ID of the tile set.
- **Name:** Holds the name defined for this tile set in the Tiled editor.
- **First GID:** Holds the first Global ID to be used for this tile set.
- **Last GID:** Holds the last Global ID held within this tile set.
- **Tile width:** The width of each tile image in pixels.
- **Tile height:** The height of each tile image in pixels.
- **Spacing:** The spacing used between each image in the tile set.
- **Margin:** The margin to be used within the sprite sheet.
- **Tiles:** A `SpriteSheet` instance that holds the images to be used within the tile set.

As with the Layer class, the information passed into a `TileSet` instance is read from the Tiled map file.

Initialization

The `initWithImageNamd:name:tileSetID:firstGID:tileSize:spacing:margin:` method responsible for initializing a `TileSet` instance.

Listing 9.10 shows the complete method inside the *TileSet.m* file in the *CH09_SLQTSOR* project.

Listing 9.10   **TileSet's initWithImageNamed: Method**

```
- (id)initWithImageNamed:(NSString*)aImageFileName
    name:(NSString*)aTileSetName tileSetID:(int)tsID
    firstGID:(int)aFirstGlobalID
    tileSize:(CGSize)aTileSize spacing:(int)aSpacing
    margin:(int)aMargin {
    if (self = [super init])  {
            sharedTextureManager = [TextureManager sharedTextureManager];

        tiles = [[SpriteSheet spriteSheetForImageNamed:aImageFileName
            spriteSize:aTileSize spacing:aSpacing margin:aMargin
            imageFilter:GL_LINEAR] retain];

        tileSetID = tsID;
        name = aTileSetName;
        firstGID = aFirstGlobalID;
        tileWidth = aTileSize.width;
        tileHeight = aTileSize.height;
        spacing = aSpacing;
        margin = aMargin;

        horizontalTiles = tiles.horizSpriteCount;
        verticalTiles = tiles.vertSpriteCount;

        lastGID = horizontalTiles * verticalTiles + firstGID - 1;
    }
    return self;
}
```

The first task of the initializer is to create a new SpriteSheet instance that will hold the sprites for this tile set.

With the tiles initialized as a sprite sheet, we then set the properties for this tile set using the information that has been passed in and by calculating some values such as the lastGID.

Getting Tile Set Information

There is not much information to get from a TileSet instance. The main property of the class is the sprite sheet called tiles. From this, the image information will be taken when we come to set up the rendering of a map layer inside the TiledMap class.

However, three methods provide access to tile information inside the *TileSet.m* file, as follows:

- **containsGlobalID:** Checks to see if the GlobalTileID passed exists within this tileset. This is important when there are multiple tile sets (not currently supported in the TiledMap class). When you find a tile ID, you can use this method to identify the tile set that the image comes from.

- **getTileX:** Given a `TileID`, this method returns the *x* component of where that tile is within the sprite sheet.

- **getTileY:** Same as `getTileX`, but returns the *y* component of where a tile is within the sprite sheet.

TiledMap Class

The `Layer` and `TileSet` classes are helper classes that are used within the **TiledMap** class. When you want to use a Tiled map, it is an instance of the **TiledMap** class that you create. This in turn creates instances of the `TileSet` and `Layer` classes based on the information read from the Tiled map configuration file. The **TiledMap** class can be found in the *CH09_SLQTSOR* project inside the *Game Engine > Tile Map*, and is called *TiledMap.m*.

The **TiledMap** class performs two key functions. First, it parses the *.tmx* configuration file we discussed earlier in this chapter. This stores all the information we need to recreate a map created within the Tiled editor. Second, it renders a map layer to the screen.

Although these two functions don't sound like much, they are rather involved. Parsing the *tmx* file is important because it contains all the information we need be able to reproduce a map in our game.

XML Parsing

XML parsing is an interesting subject on the iPhone. The full XML specification and its associated technologies, such as XSLT, are complex. Providing support for all the different capabilities you have with XML is memory and processor intensive. As you know, the iPhone has limited resources in terms of both memory and processor. Trying to support all the different XML capabilities is therefore difficult.

By default, Apple provides us with an event-based XML parser called NSXMLParser. This class enables us to parse any XML file and deal with the data we find in that file in an event-driven manor. This works well for small XML files, but when you start to process much larger files, performance can really suffer.

I ran into performance problems when writing *Sir Lamorak's Quest* when using NSXMLParser and needed to find a much faster way of parsing XML files. A good friend of mine (Tom Bradley) had the solution in the form of a very small and fast XML parser he had created called TBXML.

TBXML can parse any XML file that conforms to the W3C XML Specification 1.0. It can only be used to parse XML files and currently has no write capability. It also has a very simple API.

After testing TBXML, it was clear that it would give me the performance I needed and actually reduced the time to parse an uncompressed *.tmx* file considerably.

Since then, I have started to use *.tmx* files where the tile data is compressed and gzipped. Using NSXMLParser for that kind of file would not suffer from the performance problems I originally had, but because TBXML had already been implemented and was working well, I decided to stay with that.

You can find information on TBXML and download the source from **www.tbxml.co.uk**. When visiting the site, you will notice that, as well as the *TBXML.h* and *TBXML.m* files, there are several other files: *NSDataAdditions.h* and *.m*. These can also be found in the TBXML group inside the *CH09_SLQTSOR* project.

> **Note**
>
> The version of TBXML used in *Sir Lamorak's Quest,* and referenced throughout this book, is version 1.3.

The `NSDataAdditions` class extends Apple's `NSData` class, providing the ability to encode and decode `base64` data and also inflate and deflate data using gzip. Information on the original authors of this class can be found in the *NSDataAdditions.h* file.

The `NSDataAdditions` class also requires that the zlib library be added to the project. This library comes with the SDK and can simply be added to the project. View the information on a project's target in Xcode and within the general tab by pressing the plus button at the bottom of the Linked Libraries window. From the list that is displayed, select *zlib.dylib* and press OK.

Figure 9.10 shows the Target Info window that you can use to add the library.

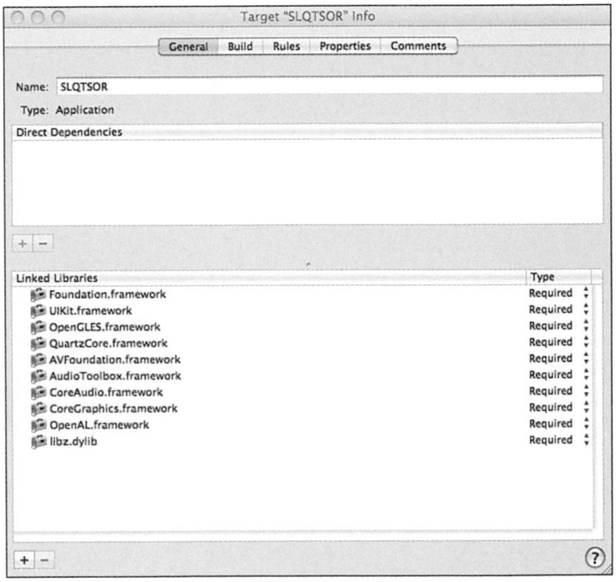

Figure 9.10   Linked libraries in the project's target info window.

These functions are really useful, and we will make use of them inside the `TiledMap` class when decoding and unzipping the tile data for a layer.

Initialization

Initialization of the `TiledMap` class continues to follow the standard pattern for initializing a class. Listing 9.11 shows the first half of the `initWithFileName:fileExtension` initialization method.

Listing 9.11   TiledMap initWithFileName:fileExtension Method (Part 1)

```
- (id)initWithFileName:(NSString*)aTiledFile
   fileExtension:(NSString*)aFileExtension {

  self = [super init];
  if (self != nil) {

    sharedGameController = [GameController sharedGameController];
    sharedImageRenderManager = [ImageRenderManager
        sharedImageRenderManager];

    tileSets = [[NSMutableArray alloc] init];
    layers = [[NSMutableArray alloc] init];
    mapProperties = [[NSMutableDictionary alloc] init];
    objectGroups = [[NSMutableDictionary alloc] init];

    NSLog(@"INFO - TiledMap: Loading tilemap XML file");
    TBXML *tmxXML = [[TBXML alloc] initWithXMLFile:aTiledFile
        fileExtension:aFileExtension];
```

At the start of the method, we grab a reference to the sharedGameController and sharedImageRenderManager and allocate the mutable arrays and dictionaries used to store the tile sets, layers, map properties, and object groups. The method then creates a new instance of TBXML using the initWithXMLFile:fileExtension method.

Listing 9.12 shows the second half of the TiledMap initialization method.

Listing 9.12   TiledMap initWithFileName:fileExtension Method (Part 2)

```
    NSLog(@"INFO - TiledMap: Started parsing tilemap XML");
    [self parseMapFileTBXML:tmxXML];
    [self parseMapObjects:tmxXML];

    NSLog(@"INFO - TiledMap: Finishing parsing tilemap XML");

    [tmxXML release];
  }

  memset(&nullTCQ, 0, sizeof(TexturedColoredQuad));

  [self createLayerTileImages];

  colorFilter = Color4fOnes;

  return self;
}
```

Having created an instance of TBXML called tmxXML, we then need to parse the *.tmx* file that has been opened. This is handled by two private methods: parseMapFile: and parseMapObjects: (covered next). The TBXML instance is released when the file has been parsed. The next line of code uses memset to initialize the nullTCQ structure we have to zeros. This will be used later when we check to see if a tile in the tile map has an associated image. With this structure initialized, the createLayerTileImages method is used to load the image data required by each tile in the tile map; these are used when the map's layers are rendered.

Finally, the colorFilter for the tile map is defaulted to all ones and the new instance is returned. We cover what colorFilter is being used for when we review the render method inside TiledMap.

Parsing a Map File

There is a lot of data within a *.tmx* file, and this makes the method used to parse this information quite long. As you saw in the initialization method, the method used to parse a *.tmx* file is called parseMapFile.

This method takes a TBXML instance that has been created using a *.tmx* file and sets up some variables that we will be using as we parse the *.tmx* file.

Parsing the Map Element

Listing 9.13 shows start of the parseMapFile method inside *TiledMap.m* that deals with parsing the map element.

Listing 9.13   **TiledMap parseMapFileTBXML: Method (Part 1)**

```
- (void)parseMapFileTBXML:(TBXML*)tbXML {

    currentLayerID = 0;
    currentTileSetID = 0;
    tile_x = 0;
    tile_y = 0;

    TBXMLElement * rootXMLElement = tbXML.rootXMLElement;

    if (rootXMLElement) {

        mapWidth = [[TBXML valueOfAttributeNamed:@"width"
            forElement:rootXMLElement] intValue];
        mapHeight = [[TBXML valueOfAttributeNamed:@"height"
            forElement:rootXMLElement] intValue];
        tileWidth = [[TBXML valueOfAttributeNamed:@"tilewidth"
            forElement:rootXMLElement] intValue];
        tileHeight = [[TBXML valueOfAttributeNamed:@"tileheight"
            forElement:rootXMLElement] intValue];
```

```
NSLog(@"INFO - TiledMap: Tilemap map dimensions are %dx%d",
    mapWidth, mapHeight);
NSLog(@"INFO - TiledMap: Tilemap tile dimensions are %dx%d",
    tileWidth, tileHeight);
```

The first step is to get the `root` object of the file being parsed. All the lookups we will do inside the document will use this `root` element as the parent.

It's then time to take the map element's attributes and put their values into `TiledMap` properties. After the attributes are processed, we output a couple of debug message to provide information on the map and move onto checking for map properties. Listing 9.14 shows the loop that checks for and processes any map properties found in the *.tmx* file.

Listing 9.14   TiledMap parseMapFileTBXML: Method (Part 2)

```
TBXMLElement * properties = [TBXML childElementNamed:@"properties"
parentElement:rootXMLElement];
if (properties) {
    TBXMLElement * property = [TBXML childElementNamed:@"property"
        parentElement:properties];

    while (property) {

        NSString *name = [TBXML valueOfAttributeNamed:@"name"
            forElement:property];
        NSString *value = [TBXML valueOfAttributeNamed:@"value"
            forElement:property];
        [mapProperties setObject:value forKey:name];
        NSLog(@"INFO - TiledMap: Tilemap property '%@' found with value
            '%@'", name, value);

        property = property->nextSibling;
    }
}
```

To find map properties, we create a new `TBXMLElement` called `properties` and populate it with the properties element if one has been found. There should only be a single properties element inside the map element, so if the properties element is not `null`, we know we have some properties to process.

If a properties element is found, we then create another `TBXMLElement` into which we place the first child `property` element. From `property`, we take the name and value attributes and load them into the `mapProperties NSMutableDictionary`. We also output some debug information to the log so we can see what has been found. These debug messages should be removed from a released version of this code.

The last command in the while loop loads the property element with the next sibling that is found. If this is `null`, we have finished finding all the properties; otherwise, we process the next property as before. This continues until there are no more properties to process.

Parsing the Tile Set Element

After we finish dealing with the `map` element, we move onto the `tileset` elements. Even though we create `TileSet` instances for all `tileset` elements found, only the first tile set will be used when rendering.

Listing 9.15 shows the code used to find the first `tileset` element and process its attributes. This is done in exactly the same way as we did for the `map` element.

Listing 9.15   **TiledMap parseMapFileTBXML: Method (Part 3)**

```
tileSetProperties = [[NSMutableDictionary alloc] init];

TBXMLElement * tileset = [TBXML childElementNamed:@"tileset"
    parentElement:rootXMLElement];
while (tileset) {
    tileSetName = [TBXML valueOfAttributeNamed:@"name" forElement:tileset];
    tileSetWidth = [[TBXML valueOfAttributeNamed:@"tilewidth"
        forElement:tileset] intValue];
    tileSetHeight = [[TBXML valueOfAttributeNamed:@"tileheight"
        forElement:tileset] intValue];
    tileSetFirstGID = [[TBXML valueOfAttributeNamed:@"firstgid"
        forElement:tileset] intValue];
    tileSetSpacing = [[TBXML valueOfAttributeNamed:@"spacing"
        forElement:tileset] intValue];
    tileSetMargin = [[TBXML valueOfAttributeNamed:@"margin"
        forElement:tileset] intValue];
```

After we assign the `tileset` attributes, we output some debug information and then retrieve information from the `image` and `source` elements. These elements are used to store the actual name of the image file to be used as the `tileset` sprite sheet.

```
NSLog(@"INFO - Tiled: -> TILESET found named: %@, width=%d,
    height=%d, firstgid=%d, spacing=%d, id=%d",
    tileSetName, tileSetWidth, tileSetHeight, tileSetFirstGID,
    tileSetSpacing, currentTileSetID);

TBXMLElement *image = [TBXML childElementNamed:@"image"
    parentElement:tileset];
NSString *source = [TBXML valueOfAttributeNamed:@"source"
    forElement:image];
NSLog(@"INFO - Tiled: --> Found source for tileset called
    '%@'.", source);
```

Once we have the image and source details for the tile set, we move onto processing any tile set properties. These properties are held at the tile image level (that is, each image inside a tile set can have any number of properties associated with it). This can be useful if you want to assign information to a tile image that maybe relates to its function in the map or maybe the amount of health that should be removed from the player should the player touch that tile.

Listing 9.16 shows the loop that is used to process any tile set properties.

Listing 9.16   **TiledMap parseMapFileTBXML: Method (Part 4)**

```
while (tile) {
    int tileID = [[TBXML valueOfAttributeNamed:@"id"
        forElement:tile] intValue] + tileSetFirstGID;

    NSMutableDictionary *tileProperties =
        [[NSMutableDictionary alloc] init];

    TBXMLElement * tstp = [TBXML childElementNamed:@"properties"
        parentElement:tile];
    TBXMLElement * tstp_property =
        [TBXML childElementNamed:@"property" parentElement:tstp];
    while (tstp_property) {

        [tileProperties setObject:
            [TBXML valueOfAttributeNamed:@"value"
            forElement:tstp_property]
            forKey:[TBXML valueOfAttributeNamed:@"name"
            forElement:tstp_property]];

        tstp_property = [TBXML nextSiblingNamed:@"property"
            searchFromElement:tstp_property];
    }
    [tileSetProperties setObject:tileProperties
        forKey:[NSString stringWithFormat:@"%d", tileID]];

    [tileProperties release];
    tileProperties = nil;

    tile = [TBXML nextSiblingNamed:@"tile"
        searchFromElement:tile];
}
```

If we look at an example of the `tile` element and its properties, you see that we need a couple of loops: one that runs through all the `tile` elements that exist within a `tileset`, and another that processes the `property` details for each `tile`. Listing 9.17 is an excerpt from a *.tmx* file that shows a `tile` element with associated `property` elements.

Listing 9.17   **Example Tile Elements with Properties**

```
<tile id="0">
    <properties>
        <property name="CollisionTile" value="true"/>
    </properties>
</tile>
<tile id="3">
    <properties>
        <property name="ReduceHealth" value="25"/>
    </properties>
</tile>
```

We loop through the `tile` and `property` elements in the same way we ran through the elements when processing the `map` element. This is a common pattern as we parse the different sections within a *.tmx* file.

Listing 9.18 shows how we finish processing the tileset.

Listing 9.18   **TiledMap parseMapFileTBXML: Method (Part 5)**

```
    currentTileSet = [[TileSet alloc] initWithImageNamed:source
                                          name:tileSetName
                                    tileSetID:currentTileSetID
                                      firstGID:tileSetFirstGID
                                      tileSize:CGSizeMake(tileWidth,
                                                          tileHeight)
                                       spacing:tileSetSpacing
                                        margin:tileSetMargin];

    [tileSets addObject:currentTileSet];

    [currentTileSet release];

    currentTileSetID++;

    tileset = [TBXML nextSiblingNamed:@"tileset" searchFromElement:tileset];
}
```

Having parsed the information from the `tileset` element, we then create a new `TileSet` instance, `currentTileSet`, using the information we have retrieved. We then add that `currentTileSet` to the `tileSets` array so that we can access it later.

Having added the tile set to our array, we then release `currentTileSet` because its retain count would have been increased when adding it to the `tileSets` array.

We finish off by incrementing the `currentTileSetID` counter and then looking for
any other `tileset` elements.

Parsing the Layer Element

The layer element is processed in the same way as the map and `tileset` elements, as
shown in Listing 9.19.

Listing 9.19   **TiledMap parseMapFileTBXML: Method (Part 6)**

```
TBXMLElement * layer = [TBXML childElementNamed:@"layer"
    parentElement:rootXMLElement];
while (layer) {
    layerName = [TBXML valueOfAttributeNamed:@"name" forElement:layer];
    layerWidth = [[TBXML valueOfAttributeNamed:@"width" forElement:layer]
        intValue];
    layerHeight = [[TBXML valueOfAttributeNamed:@"height" forElement:layer]
        intValue];

    currentLayer = [[Layer alloc] initWithName:layerName
        layerID:currentLayerID layerWidth:layerWidth
        layerHeight:layerHeight];

    NSLog(@"INFO - Tiled: -> LAYER found called: %@, width=%d, height=%d",
        layerName, layerWidth, layerHeight);

    TBXMLElement * layerProperties = [TBXML childElementNamed:@"properties"
        parentElement:layer];
    if (layerProperties) {
        TBXMLElement * layerProperty = [TBXML childElementNamed:@"property"
            parentElement:layerProperties];
        NSMutableDictionary *layerProps = [[NSMutableDictionary alloc] init];

        while (layerProperty) {
            NSString *name = [TBXML valueOfAttributeNamed:@"name"
                forElement:layerProperty];
            NSString *value = [TBXML valueOfAttributeNamed:@"value"
                forElement:layerProperty];
            [layerProps setObject:value forKey:name];
            layerProperty = layerProperty->nextSibling;
        }
        [currentLayer setLayerProperties:layerProps];

        [layerProps release];
}
```

As each layer is processed, we create a new Layer instance. This is loaded with the information we parse from the *.tmx* file. We also parse any properties that have been defined for the layer and pass them to the Layer instance.

Having parsed the layer element and created the Layer instance, next you'll need to parse the tile information for that layer. This is a little more complex than the previous loops because the information about each tile could be base64 encoded and gzipped or simply plain XML.

Inside each layer element is a single data element. This contains the information for each tile inside an array. Listing 9.20 shows how we are searching for the data element and then checking to see if the information is encoded and gzipped.

Listing 9.20   TiledMap parseMapFileTBXML: Method (Part 7)

```
TBXMLElement * dataElement = [TBXML childElementNamed:@"data"
    parentElement:layer];
if (dataElement) {
    if ([[TBXML valueOfAttributeNamed:@"encoding" forElement:dataElement]
        isEqualToString:@"base64"]) {

        NSData * deflatedData = [NSData dataWithBase64EncodedString:[TBXML
            textForElement:dataElement]];
        if ([[TBXML valueOfAttributeNamed:@"compression"
            forElement:dataElement] isEqualToString:@"gzip"])
            deflatedData = [deflatedData gzipInflate];
```

If we find a data element, we then check the encoding and compression attributes to see how the information has been stored. If the information has been encoded in base64, we decode it into an NSData instance called deflatedData. We then check to see if the compression is gzip, which is the only supported compression currently in our implementation. If it is gzip, we inflate the data held in deflatedData. The ability to inflate information held inside NSData is provided by the NSDataAdditions method that we discussed earlier in the sidebar, "*XML Parsing*."

With the data now inflated, we allocate memory that holds the tile information for our layer. The information we are interested in is the GlobalID for each tile. By simply loading the inflated data into bytes, we have created an integer array that contains the GlobalID for each tile in the layer:

```
long size = sizeof(int) * (layerWidth * layerHeight);
int *bytes = malloc(size);
[deflatedData getBytes:bytes length:size];
```

With this new array, we can now loop through the data and add each tile to the layer using the addTileAtX:y:tileSetID:tileID:globalID:Value method provided by the Layer class.

Listing 9.21 shows the loop we use to add the tiles to the layer we are currently processing.

Listing 9.21   TiledMap parseMapFileTBXML: Method (Part 8)

```
    long y;
for (tile_y=0, y=0;y<layerHeight*layerWidth;y+=layerWidth,tile_y++) {
    for (tile_x=0;tile_x<layerWidth;tile_x++) {
        int globalID = bytes[y+tile_x];
        if(globalID == 0) {
            [currentLayer addTileAt:CGPointMake(tile_x, (layerHeight - 1) -
                tile_y)
                tileSetID:-1 tileID:-1 globalID:-1 value:-1];
        } else {
            TileSet *tileSet = [self tileSetWithGlobalID:globalID];
            [currentLayer addTileAt:CGPointMake(tile_x, (layerHeight - 1) -
                tile_y)
                            tileSetID:[tileSet tileSetID]
                              tileID:globalID - [tileSet firstGID]
                            globalID:globalID
                               value:-1];
        }
    }
}
```

Notice that we are checking to see if the globalID is equal to zero or not. If globalID equals zero, it means that no tile image has been defined for that tile. If that is the case, we add a tile to the layer that has a tileSetID and tileID of -1. When rendering the tiles, a value of -1 indicates a blank tile and the rendering method will deal with it as necessary. We see how this is done when we cover *layer rendering* later in this chapter.

If the globalID is not zero, a tile image has been defined. We use the tileSetWithGlobalID: method defined in the **TiledMap** class to find out which tile set contains the tile image being used. Remember, we are supporting only a single tileset when rendering, even though the code necessary to load more tile sets has been implemented.

Having found the tile set that contains the tile image, we add the tile to the layer using the globalID and the information from the tile set.

Note

When we add a tile to the layer, you will notice that we are subtracting the tileY value from the full height of the layer. The reason for this is that a Tiled map has its origin in the top-left corner (that is, tile 0, 0). Everything else that we do in OpenGL ES has an origin in the bottom-left corner. To simplify things later on, this small calculation reverses the y value so the map still has the same orientation as normal, but tile 0, 0 becomes the bottom-left corner rather that the top-right. This enables you to render and perform calculations based on the origin being in the bottom-left corner.

If the data information was not `base64` encoded, it means we need to process the tile data as plain XML.

> **Note**
>
> For large maps, this can create a significant performance problem, so `base64` encoding should be used at all times. The preferences for saving a tile map can be changed from within `Preferences`.

Listing 9.22 shows the code necessary to process plain XML tile information.

Listing 9.22   TiledMap parseMapFileTBXML: Method (Part 9)

```
    } else {

        tile_x = 0;
        tile_y = 0;

        TBXMLElement * tileElements = [TBXML childElementNamed:@"tile"
            parentElement:dataElement];

        while (tileElements) {
            int globalID = [[TBXML valueOfAttributeNamed:@"gid"
                forElement:tileElements] intValue];

            if(globalID == 0) {
                [currentLayer addTileAt:CGPointMake(tile_x, (layerHeight - 1) -
                    tile_y) tileSetID:-1 tileID:-1 globalID:-1 value:-1];
            } else {
                TileSet *tileSet = [self tileSetWithGlobalID:globalID];
                [currentLayer addTileAt:CGPointMake(tile_x, (layerHeight - 1) -
                    tile_y)
                            tileSetID:[tileSet tileSetID]
                               tileID:globalID - [tileSet firstGID]
                            globalID:globalID
                                value:-1];
            }
            tile_x++;
            if(tile_x > layerWidth - 1) {
                tile_x = 0;
                tile_y++;
            }

            tileElements = tileElements->nextSibling;
        }
    }
}
```

Processing the plain XML tile information is almost identical to processing the other *.tmx* file elements. We loop through all the tile elements and use the attribute information to add tiles to the layer, just as we did when processing the compressed tile information.

You will see that for both the compressed and plain loops, we are responsible for calculating `tileID` for each tile. This is a simple calculation that uses the `globalID` and subtracts the `firstGID` from the tileset the image is within.

After we finish dealing with all the tile data, we finally add the layer we have created to the layers array and release it. We then increment the layer counter, `currentLayerID`, and see if there are any more layers to process:

```
[layers addObject:currentLayer];
[currentLayer release];
 currentLayerID++;

layer = [TBXML nextSiblingNamed:@"layer" searchFromElement:layer];
    }
  }
}
```

Parsing Object Group Elements

The final elements we need to parse are the object groups. As described earlier in the chapter when we reviewed the Tiled configuration file, object groups enable us to create objects within a special object group layer. Objects within these object groups can be positioned pixel-perfect rather than aligned to the map tiles. They can also have any number of properties defined that can be used to hold useful information.

If you review the code at the end of the `parseMapFileTBXML` method, you see that we deal with object groups in the same way we dealt with map, `tileset`, and `layer` elements.

We create three mutable dictionaries called `objectGroupDetails`, `objectGroupAttribs`, and `objectGroupObjects`, which we load with the information we find within object groups in the *.tmx* file.

The code to loop through the object groups is long, so I won't reproduce the code in the book. You can review the code in the *TiledMap.m* file.

Creating the Layer Images

Having parsed the *.tmx* file, we now have all the information we need to configure the rendering of each layer within our map. The `createLayerTileImages:` method shown in Listing 9.23 is used to load the tile image information into the tile maps layers.

Listing 9.23   **TiledMap createLayerTileImages: Method**

```
- (void) createLayerTileImages {

    int x = 0;
    int y = 0;

    TileSet *tileSet = [tileSets objectAtIndex:0];

    for(int layerIndex=0; layerIndex < [layers count]; layerIndex++) {

        Layer *layer = [layers objectAtIndex:layerIndex];
        for(int mapTileY=0; mapTileY < mapWidth; mapTileY++) {
            for(int mapTileX=0; mapTileX < mapHeight; mapTileX++) {
                int tileID = [layer tileIDAtTile:CGPointMake(mapTileX,
                    mapTileY)];
                if (tileID > -1) {
                    SpriteSheet *tileSprites = [tileSet tiles];
                    Image *tileImage = [tileSprites
                        spriteImageAtCoords:CGPointMake([tileSet
                        getTileX:tileID],
                        [tileSet getTileY:tileID])];
                    [layer addTileImageAt:CGPointMake(mapTileX, mapTileY)
                        imageDetails:tileImage.imageDetails];
                }
                x += tileWidth;
            }
            y += tileHeight;
            x = 0;
        }
        y = 0;
    }
}
```

This loop is responsible for running through all tiles in a layer and identifying the image within the tile map's tile set that is being used at each tile location. If a tile image has been set, its image is found in the tile map's tile set. The ImageDetails structure for that image is then sent to the layer's addTileImageAt: method that we saw earlier.

Note

To help performance, only layers that have a property called visible with a value of 1 are processed. A layer that does not have the property—or has it, but is not set to 1—will be ignored by this method. This enables us to skip layers that are never going to be rendered (for instance, the Collision layer in *Sir Lamorak's Quest*).

Rendering a Layer

We've certainly covered a lot so far in this chapter. You'll be glad to know that we are approaching the end now as we look at how we render a layer.

Having done all this hard work, we really want to start to see the results. For this, we need to be able to render our map layers to the screen. This is done by using the `renderLayer:mapx:mapy:width:height:useBlending:` method, shown in Listing 9.24.

Listing 9.24   **TiledMap renderLayer:mapx:mapy:width:height:useBlending Method**

```
(void) renderLayer: (int) aLayerIndex mapx: (int) aMapx mapy: (int) aMapy
width: (int) aWidth
    height: (int) aHeight useBlending: (BOOL) aUseBlending {

    if (aMapx < 0)
        aMapx = 0;
    if (aMapx > mapWidth)
        aMapx = mapWidth;
    if (aMapy < 0)
        aMapy = 0;
    if (aMapy > mapHeight)
        aMapy = mapHeight;

    int maxWidth = aMapx + aWidth;
    int maxHeight = aMapy + aHeight;

    Layer *layer = [layers objectAtIndex:aLayerIndex];

    TileSet *tileSet = [tileSets objectAtIndex:0];
    uint textureName = [tileSet tiles].image.textureName;

    for (int y=aMapy; y < maxHeight; y++) {
        for (int x=aMapx; x < maxWidth; x++) {
            TexturedColoredQuad *tcq = [layer tileImageAt:CGPointMake(x, y)];

            if (memcmp(tcq, &nullTCQ, sizeof(TexturedColoredQuad)) != 0)
                [sharedImageRenderManager
                    addTexturedColoredQuadToRenderQueue:tcq
                textureName:textureName];
        }
    }
}
if (!aUseBlending)
    glDisable(GL_BLEND);
```

```
[sharedImageRenderManager renderImages];

if (!aUseBlending)
    glEnable(GL_BLEND);
}
```

When we render a tile map layer, we are actually rendering a small part of the map. It makes no sense to render the whole layer, which could be hundreds of tiles wide and high, when you are only going to actually see an 8x13 section of the map on the screen.

I have experimented in different ways to render the tile map, including trying to get OpenGL ES to render the whole map, letting it work out which tiles should and should not be visible. The best performance I got was by limiting the tiles being rendered to just those visible on the screen.

This method first of all checks to make sure that the start and end locations within the tile map are within tile map bounds. If this is the case, the layer object specified is re-trieved, along with the tile set and its texture name.

The method then loops through all the rows and columns defined by the tile map x and y location provided and the width and height. These are parameters passed in, so you can very easily change the tiles that should be visible.

For each tile in this grid, a check is performed to see if the tile's image has been de-fined. The odd-looking memcmp command is being used for this. The tileImages array is just a chunk of memory that can store TextureColoredQuad structures. If a tile does not have an associated image, the TexturedColoredQuad structure at that location within the array will not be initialized. By comparing each entry in the tileImages array against a blank TexturedColoredQuad created during the initialization of the layer, we can see if an image exists for each tile in the layer.

If a tile image does exist, its TexturedColoredQuad information is added to the ImageRenderManager's render queue. As you saw in Chapter 5, "Image Rendering," the ImageRenderManager has a specific method called addTexturedColoredQuadToRenderQueue:texture:. This method is used to take infor-mation and place it in the render queue.

With all the visible tile images added to the render queue, a quick check is performed to see if blending should be disabled for this layer because it is enabled in the game engine by default.

Tip

If you have a layer of the tile map that does not contain any transparent tiles, such as the floor and walls in *Sir Lamorak's Quest*, there is no need to have blending enabled. Blending is an expensive process on the iPhone, so turning off blending when it is not needed really helps performance.

With the blending set and the images loaded, the renderImages method is called on the ImageRenderManager, and the tiles for the layer are rendered to the screen.

The last check ensures that blending is re-enabled.

Getting Tile Informaiton

The final methods to discuss are those that let us query map information; for this, we'll use the following methods:

- **tileSetWithGlobalID:**: Returns the tile set that contains the global tile ID provided.
- **layerIndexWithName:**: Returns the index of a layer that has a name that matches the name provided.
- **mapPropertyForKey:**: Returns the value of a map property identified by the supplied key.
- **layerPropertyForKey:**: Returns the value of a layer property identified by the supplied key.
- **tilePropertyForGlobalTileID:**: Returns the value of a tile property identified by the global tile ID supplied.

These methods provide us with access to any properties that have been defined in the map. They are very basic in that they use the key provided to search the dictionaries that were created when the Tiled map was parsed using the key provided.

Summary

Although the techniques for parsing *.tmx* map files is not complex, the amount of information held within the map file and making sure that the tile map class can be used for more than just a single game has caused the class to become complex.

Tile maps are still an important element in 2D games today. Having a robust tile map-editing tool, such as Tiled, and the ability to reproduce the maps designed in that tool in your game is a great asset. By making use of properties and object groups, it is possible to create a game that is data-driven for which the map provides a lot of this data.

Being able to change how your game functions by simply changing the tile map enables you to make game changes very quickly. When it comes to play testing and tuning the game, being able to make changes in the tile map and not having to dig through your game engine code will speed things up.

In the next chapter, we review the ParticleEmitter class. This class enables us to generate organic effects, such as smoke and fire, dynamically and is a great deal of fun to play with. We will be using particles in *Sir Lamorak's Quest* to produce the effect of a baddie appearing and dying, as well as for the teleportation effects when Sir Lamorak gets bounced from one room to the next.

Exercise

The *CH09_SLQTSOR* project that accompanies this chapter moves over the top of a tile map, rendering two layers. The first layer is the map itself (that is, the floors and walls), and the second layer contains the objects, such as pictures, chairs, and so on.

Remember that the actual layers in a tile map are always rendered at 0,0, so movement inside the project is achieved by translating the OpenGL ES viewport before rendering. This gives the effect of moving over the tile map.

Try changing the values that are being used to translate the OpenGL ES world coordinates using the glTranslate command. It is important that you understand how using glTranslate affects what is rendered to the screen, as this technique is used within *Sir Lamorak's Quest* to move the player around the map.

> **Note**
>
> The tile map in the project has the rooms drawn in the top-left corner of the tile map. For anything to be seen on the screen, we therefore need to translate the world coordinates so that when rendered, that area of the map is visible on the screen. Remember that the top of the tile map in pixels will be as follows:
>
> ```
> Tile height * map height in tiles
> ```

10

The Particle Emitter

This chapter focuses on what has to be my favorite part of the game engine: the particle system. As mentioned in Chapter 2, "The Three Ts: Terminology, Technology, and Tools," a particle system in the world of games does not involve expensive particle accelerators or the collision of exotic particles at the speed of light. Particle systems are actually used in games to generate very dynamic, and almost organic, visual effects for things such as the following:

- Fire
- Smoke
- Rain
- Snow
- Sparks
- Explosions

Each of these visual effects is made up from a number of individual particles (images) moving independently of each other but following the same set of basic rules. This is the basis for any particle system.

The particle system we review in this chapter for *Sir Lamorak's Quest* is actually a relatively basic system compared to some of the highly sophisticated systems used in many modern games, such as *Halo* or *World of Warcraft*. That said, even this basic system can be used to generate some pretty impressive visual effects.

I spent a great deal of time researching particle systems for *Sir Lamorak's Quest*. Having reviewed many articles and code examples, I eventually created the class we will run through in this chapter based on the particle system in the Cocos2D (**www.cocos2d. org**) game engine. Cocos2D is an open source iPhone game engine, written in Objective-C. Although it isn't a complex engine, Cocos2D provided everything I needed and was simple to understand.

> **Note**
>
> To learn more about Cocos2D, look for *Learning Cocos2D: A Hands-on Guide to Building iPhone & iPad Games with Cocos2D, Box2d, and Chipmunk* by Rod Strougo. This book is currently in development and will be available in early 2011 from Addison-Wesley. Keep an eye on **www.informit.com/learnmac** for more news about upcoming Mac/iPhone developer titles from Addison-Wesley.

Particle Emitter Project

Open and run the project that accompanies this chapter called *CH10_SLQTSOR* in the iPhone Simulator. When the project starts, you see a colorful particle fountain erupting onscreen, as shown in Figure 10.1.

Figure 10.1   iPhone simulator running the
CH10_SLQTSOR project.

What you are looking at is a particle system generating 750 particles that have been configured to move up the screen at a specified speed and also to be affected by gravity over time. These particles have also been configured to change color and size during their four-second life span.

This chapter explores the **ParticleEmitter** class inside *Sir Lamorak's Quest*. By the end of this chapter, you will be familiar with what a particle system is, have reviewed in detail the **ParticleEmitter** class we are using, and also learned how to configure the particle emitter using XML configuration files.

Introduction to Particle Systems

Particle systems have become more and more popular over the years. As both CPUs and GPUs have increased in speed, it has been possible for game designers and programmers to come up with more and more clever uses of particle systems.

It is unlikely that you will play any game today that does not use a simple particle system somewhere. In space shooters, these particle systems can be used to generate explosions, engine trails, star fields, and galaxies, to name a few.

In *Sir Lamorak's Quest*, we also have a number of areas where we can use a particle system. Rather than create a fixed animation to show when a baddie is appearing or dying, we could use a particle system to dynamically produce the effect we are after, as shown in Figure 10.2.

Figure 10.2   Particle emitter configured to show
a strange flame as baddies appear in *Sir Lamorak's
Quest*.

> **Note**
>
> Particle systems are all about their organic look and movement. Unfortunately, a static picture does not do a particle system justice. If you want to see this particle configuration in action, you can edit the *CH10_SLQTSOR* project.

Open the *CH10_SLQTSOR* project and then open the *GameScene.m* file. Within the init method, you see the following lines of code:

```
// Particle fountain configuration
pe = [[ParticleEmitter alloc]
    initParticleEmitterWithFile:@"emitterConfig.pex"];
emitterType = @"Particle Fountain";
pe.sourcePosition = Vector2fMake(160, 25);


// Appearing emitter configuration
//pe = [[ParticleEmitter alloc]
//    initParticleEmitterWithFile:@"appearingEmitter.pex"];
//emitterType = @"Appearing Emitter";
//pe.sourcePosition = Vector2fMake(160, 25);
```

Comment out the three lines of code under the particle fountain configuration comment and then uncomment the three lines of code under the Appearing emitter configuration comment. When you then run the project again, you will see the particle emitter shown in Figure 10.2 in action.

Although the particle fountain and appearing emitter look very different, they are all using exactly the same particle system. It is only the configuration details for each that are different. Being able to produce different effects by simply changing configuration files is a very handy tool when making a game.

> **Warning**
>
> Particle systems can be addictive. It is easy to spend hours just changing the settings and watching the pretty particles move around the screen. I personally enjoy configuring particle systems, although I've wasted many hours in the process. Be warned.

Particle System Parameters

I've talked about the fact that particle systems are normally very configurable, so we should look at the parameters we will implement inside our **ParticleEmitter** class:

- **Texture:** Texture to be used to render each particle.
- **Source Position:** Position from which particles will be emitted.
- **Source Position Variance:** Variance that should be applied to each particle's source position on creation.
- **Particle Life Span:** Time in seconds the particle should live for.
- **Particle Life Span Variance:** Variance applied to a particle's life span on creation.
- **Speed:** Speed at which the particle should move.
- **Speed Variance:** Variance applied to a particle's speed on creation.
- **Angle:** Angle at which the particle should be emitted from the source position.
- **Angle Variance:** Variance applied to a particle's angle at creation.
- **Gravity:** Amount of gravity in the x and y planes that should be applied to a particle.
- **Start Color:** Particle's color at the start of its life span.
- **Start Color Variance:** Variance to be applied to a particle's start color at creation.
- **Finish Color:** Particle's color at the end of its life span.
- **Start Particle Size:** Particle's size at the start of its life span.
- **Start Particle Size Variance:** Variance applied to a particle's start size at creation.
- **Finish Particle Size:** Particle's size at the end of its life span.
- **Finish Particle Size Variance:** Variance applied to a particle's end size at creation.
- **Max Particles:** Maximum number of particles the particle emitter will control.
- **Max Radius:** Maximum radius from the source position for a particle.

- **Max Radius Variance:** Variance applied to a particle's radius at creation.
- **Min Radius:** Minimum radius a particle can be from the source position.
- **Radius Speed:** Speed at which a particle moves from Max Radius to Min Radius.
- **Rotate Per Second:** Number of degrees per second a particle will rotate around the source position.
- **Rotate Per Second Variance:** Variance applied to a particle's Rotate Per Second at creation.
- **Duration:** Amount of time in seconds that the particle emitter should emit particles.

There are a lot of parameters we can change that affect how particles are rendered from a particle emitter. Remember that this is only a simple particle system. More complex systems not only handle many more rendering parameters, but also physical interaction of the particles and their surroundings. This allows you to generate particles for sparks. As each spark (particle) hits a floor or wall, it can bounce to really give the impression of hot sparks bouncing around a room.

For *Sir Lamorak's Quest*, we don't need the particles to be that advanced. We are sticking with the previous list of parameters, which will make it easier to understand what the particle system is doing and how it works.

Life Cycle of a Particle

At this point, we should look at the life cycle of a particle and at how the parameters we have just reviewed are actually used.

At a basic level, a particle is born, lives for a specified period of time, and then dies.

A Particle Is Born

When a particle is born, its properties are given their initial values based on the parameters that have been set. These values have been defined in the parameters for the particle emitter that are adjusted by the specified variance.

As an example of a parameter with a variance, we'll look at a particle's life span. We will look at a particle that has a lifeSpan of 4 seconds and a lifeSpanVariance of 2. When a particle is born or added to a particle emitter, a calculation is performed using the lifeSpan and lifeSpanVariance; for example:

```
timeToLive = lifespan + lifeSpanVariance * RANDOM_MINUS_1_TO_1
```

This calculation first multiplies the lifeSpanVariance by RANDOM_MINUS_1_TO_1. RANDOM_MINUS_1_TO_1 is a macro we see later that randomly returns a number between 1 and -1, oddly enough.

After we have our variance calculated, we than add it to the lifeSpan. With a lifeSpan of 4, a lifeSpanVariance of 2 and -1 returned from our macro, timeToLive would be equal to

2. The next time that calculation is performed, we may get 6 as the answer if the macro returned 1.

This technique is applied whenever there is a variance in our particle emitter, so that we can create randomness to the particle's properties within bounds we have control over.

That handles the situation where we want to randomly create a single value at the start of a particle's life, but what about when we know both the start value of a particle's property and its end value? This is the case when we look at the color properties of a particle. We can specify both the start and end color, which means we need to make sure the particle will transition smoothly from the start color to the end color during its lifetime.

For this, we need to calculate a delta. This delta will tell us how much we need to change the red, green, blue, and alpha values over the lifetime of the particle. As with the life span example, the initial red, green, blue, and alpha values can be specified for both the start and end colors, along with a variance. The same calculation would be used on each of these color elements as was used for the life span.

The difference is that once we have the start and end color, we need to calculate a delta value that can be applied to the particle over its lifetime. The easiest approach for this is to calculate a delta value that will be added to the start color each time a particle is updated. We look at the update method in a moment.

For calculating the delta, we can perform the following calculation:

```
deltaRed = ((end.red — start.red) / timeToLive) * delta
```

`delta` is the number of milliseconds since the last update of this particle and would normally be provided by the game loop.

> **Note**
>
> Calculating the delta to be used each time a particle is updated will only work if your game loop is using a fixed delta value. If you remember from Chapter 4, "The Game Loop," our game loop is using a fixed delta value rather than a variable delta value. If you were using a variable delta value, you would need to perform the calculation to work out the color of a particle during its lifetime inside the update method of a particle.

This approach to setting up a particle's initial properties can equally be applied to the location parameters, which we see when we review the **ParticleEmitter** class later in this chapter.

A Particle Lives

We have looked at what happens when we create a particle; we now need to consider what will happen when we update particles. Just like any other entity within our game, we need to update particle emitters during the game loop. The **ParticleEmitter** class itself will be responsible for updating all the particles it owns; we just need to tell each emitter we have that it should perform an update and pass in the delta value to be used.

The update function will carry out a couple of functions. The first one creates new particles to be emitted based on an emission rate. The emission rate in the particle system is calculated when a particle emitter is created as follows:

```
emissionRate = maxParticles / particleLifeSpan;
```

This value is then used to work out how many particles are going to be added to this emitter during this update. We will see the code that performs this when we review the **ParticleEmitter** code later in this chapter.

The update method ensures that the particle emitter itself should still be running. One of the parameters we mentioned earlier was duration. The duration tells the particle emitter how long it should emit particles for. For the particle fountain example in this chapter's project, the duration is set to –1, which causes it to run continuously. Providing a positive number causes the emitter to emit particles for that number of seconds. When that time is up, the emitter will stop emitting.

Having performed these initial checks, the update method will then need to loop through all particles that still have a life span and update their properties. Each particle's properties will be updated based on the rules defined when the particle emitter was created.

We review the rules and calculations performed in our **ParticleEmitter** class later in this chapter, but to give you an idea of what's involved, the update method will calculate a new direction for the particle using the particle's current position and applying a direction vector along with a gravity vector. It also includes the calculations necessary to change the particle's color based on the particle's current time left to live.

A Particle Dies

As with all things, a particle will eventually die. In this context, that means that it has been alive for longer than its defined life span and now needs to be removed from the active list of particles being processed. Each particle has a state that is simply set to identify that it should no longer be included in the particle update routine or rendered to the screen.

This doesn't mean, however, that we will not see that particle again.

A Particle Is Reborn

An important aspect of a particle system is speed. As you can imagine, you could end up with many particle emitters, each controlling many tens or even hundreds of particles. One performance hog is the initial creation of an object. This could be the creation of a new class instance or just the initialization of memory to be used for a structure. We want to reduce the number of new allocations performed during game play as much as possible, and this includes the creation of particles in our particle emitter as well.

To help with this in our particle emitter, we actually create all the particles our emitter will ever need up front, when the emitter is first created. These particles are placed into an array that is looped through during each update, and the state of the particle is used to see if it should be updated or not. We also make sure that the array is packed so that all active particles (that is, those with a positive lifespan) are held together at the start of the array. We'll see how this is done later in this chapter.

Because of this, a particle never really dies; it is simply set to inactive. When we then need to emit a new particle, we simply grab an inactive particle from our array and set it up to be emitted again, kind of like being reincarnated. It's still a particle, but it will have a completely new set of properties the next time it is used.

Particle Emitter Configuration

We have seen that a number of properties are needed to configure a particle emitter. These could all be defined in code, of course, but for Sir Lamorak's Quest, I decided to use an external XML file to hold the configuration. For me, having configuration of the emitters outside of the code made the code easier to read, as well as making configuration changes to the emitters very simple.

Listing 10.1 shows a complete particle configuration file containing all the configurable parameters for an emitter.

Listing 10.1   Particle Emitter XML Configuration File

```
<particleEmitterConfig>
    <texture name="defaultTexture.png"></texture>
    <sourcePosition x="164.00" y="0.00"></sourcePosition>
    <sourcePosition x="164.00" y="0.00"></sourcePosition>
    <sourcePositionVariance x="7.00" y="7.00"></sourcePositionVariance>
    <speed value="625.00"></speed>
    <speedVariance value="10.00"></speedVariance>
    <particleLifeSpan value="4.0000"></particleLifeSpan>
    <particleLifespanVariance value="2.0000"></particleLifespanVariance>
    <angle value="90.00"></angle>
    <angleVariance value="8.00"></angleVariance>
    <gravity x="0.00" y="-500.00"></gravity>
    <startColor red="0.00" green="0.00" blue="0.00"
        alpha="0.00"></startColor>
    <startColorVariance red="1.00" green="1.00" blue="1.00"
        alpha="0.00"></startColorVariance>
    <finishColor red="0.00" green="0.00" blue="0.00"
        alpha="1.00"></finishColor>
    <finishColorVariance red="1.00" green="1.00" blue="1.00"
        alpha="0.00"></finishColorVariance>
    <maxParticles value="500"></maxParticles>
    <startParticleSize value="30.00"></startParticleSize>
    <startParticleSizeVariance value="5.00"></startParticleSizeVariance>
    <finishParticleSize value="7.16"></finishParticleSize>
    <FinishParticleSizeVariance value="0.00"></FinishParticleSizeVariance>
    <duration value="-1.00"></duration>
    <blendAdditive value="1"></blendAdditive>
```

```
    <maxRadius value="0.00"></maxRadius>
    <maxRadiusVariance value="0.00"></maxRadiusVariance>
    <minRadius value="0.00"></minRadius>
    <rotatePerSecond value="0.00"></rotatePerSecond>
    <rotatePerSecondVariance value="0.00"></rotatePerSecondVariance>
</particleEmitterConfig>
```

The root element for the file is called `particleEmitterConfig` and this contains elements representing all the parameters that need to be set up for a particle emitter. These parameters relate directly to the list of parameters we saw earlier in this chapter.

The element name represents the parameter being defined and the attributes for each element hold the values that should be used for that parameter in the particle emitter.

This is a simple XML file that makes editing a particle emitter's configuration very easy.

There are no real rules about how to configure a particle emitter. Just play with the values in the configuration file until you get the result you want. The configuration files included with the Chapter 10 sample project should help you get started.

The key message here is to have fun. When you have your particle emitter up and running, simply play with the values. I've been surprised at what you can produce with simple value changes. It must be said, though, that many hours can be wasted playing with these settings, so be warned.

Particle Emitter Classes

Let's now review the **ParticleEmitter** classes we are going to use for *Sir Lamorak's Quest*. The two classes we'll use are as follows:

- ParticleEmitter
- TBXMLParticleAdditions

ParticleEmitter contains all the code necessary to create and control our particle emitter. **TBXMLParticleAdditions** is a class that adds a category to the TBXML class we saw back in Chapter 9, "Tile Maps."

TBXMLParticleAdditions Class

TBXML is a lightweight XML parsing class that we used in Chapter 9 to process tile map XML files. To make the particle emitters easier to configure, the **ParticleEmitter** class also uses an XML file to hold the configuration for a particle emitter. Although we could simply use TBXML as we did inside the tile map class, it is sometimes cleaner to extend a class by adding your own methods. We are going to add our own methods to TBXML using Objective-C categories.

Listing 10.2 shows the header file for the *TBXMLParticleAdditions.h* file. You see that we are importing the *TBXML.h* file and also creating an interface that has the same name as TBXML class along with a category name in parenthesis.

Listing 10.2   **TBXMLParticleAdditions Header File**

```
#import "TBXML.h"
#import "Global.h"

@interface TBXML (TBXMLParticleAdditions)

// Returns a float value from the processes element
- (float) floatValueFromChildElementNamed:(NSString*)aName
  parentElement:(TBXMLElement*)aParentXMLElement;

// Returns a bool value from the processes element
- (BOOL) boolValueFromChildElementNamed:(NSString*)aName
  parentElement:(TBXMLElement*)aParentXMLElement;

// Returns a vector2f structure from the processes element
- (Vector2f) vector2fFromChildElementNamed:(NSString*)aName
  parentElement:(TBXMLElement*)aParentXMLElement;

// Returns a color4f structure from the processes element
- (Color4f) color4fFromChildElementNamed:(NSString*)aName
  parentElement:(TBXMLElement*)aParentXMLElement;

@end
```

The category name in parenthesis is really the only change to what is a normal interface declaration. The rest of the header file deals with defining the methods this class is going to contain. By using a category, these methods will become available to anything using the TBXML class, even though you have not physically altered that class at all.

> **Note**
> A category name must be unique throughout your application, just like class names.

The methods that have been defined are basically specialist methods for dealing with the kind of data that will be found in a particle emitter configuration file. Each method is responsible for reading an element from the XML file and returning the data read in a specific format. This enables us to reduce the amount of code duplication within our `ParticleEmitter` class that we will be reviewing in the next section of this chapter.

Listing 10.3 shows the code for the `color4fFromChildElementNamed:parentElement` method.

Listing 10.3   **TXMLParticleAdditions color4fFromChildElementNamed:parentElement Method**

```
- (Color4f)color4fFromChildElementNamed:(NSString*)aName
      parentElement:(TBXMLElement*)aParentXMLElement {
      TBXMLElement * xmlElement = [TBXML childElementNamed:aName
```

```
            parentElement:aParentXMLElement];

    if (xmlElement) {
        float red = [[TBXML valueOfAttributeNamed:@"red"
         forElement:xmlElement] floatValue];
        float green = [[TBXML valueOfAttributeNamed:@"green"
         forElement:xmlElement] floatValue];
        float blue = [[TBXML valueOfAttributeNamed:@"blue"
         forElement:xmlElement] floatValue];
        float alpha = [[TBXML valueOfAttributeNamed:@"alpha"
         forElement:xmlElement] floatValue];
        return Color4fMake(red, green, blue, alpha);
    }

    return Color4fMake(0, 0, 0, 0);
}
```

This method can be used to retrieve an XML element that contains color information. It retrieves four attributes from the element—called red, green, blue, and alpha—and then returns those values inside a color4f structure. This could be done when reading the data from the XML file, but it would need to be repeated many times, which can be messy and easily allow for the introduction of awkward bugs.

The other methods inside the **TBXMLParticleAdditions** class all work in the same way by returning a specific element's attribute in a defined structure (for example, BOOL, float, vector2f, and color4f).

ParticleEmitter Class

Having seen the XML configuration file and reviewed the **TBXMLParticleAdditions** class that we will be using to parse this file, it's time to review the **ParticleEmitter** class itself. As mentioned earlier, the **ParticleEmitter** class is responsible for the creation, update, and rendering of particles that belong to this emitter.

Structures

Before we look at the contents of the **ParticleEmitter** implementation, we need to review the key structures we will be using to manage our particles. We are using structures for performance reasons. It would be simple enough to create a class that holds all the information we are placing into these structures, but there is a performance penalty for doing that.

As mentioned in Chapter 8, "Bitmap Fonts," messaging between Objective-C objects carries an overhead. When handling many hundreds of particles per second, using Objective-C classes and messaging can introduce a significant overhead.

To reduce the overhead, we use structures in memory that we can simply reference or look up. It may not have the flexibility of classes and objects, but it's quick.

The first structure is shown in Listing 10.4 and is called `PointSprite`.

Listing 10.4   **PointSprite Structure**

```
typedef struct {
    GLfloat x;
    GLfloat y;
    GLfloat size;
    Color4f color;
} PointSprite;
```

You may wonder why we have called the structure `PointSprite`. We are going to be using something called point sprites to render the particles for each particle emitter. We cover these in more detail when we cover rendering of particles later in this chapter.

A single `PointSprite` structure will be created for each particle in an emitter. It stores the particle's *x* and *y* location along with the size of the particle. This information is used when the particles are rendered with OpenGL ES.

The second structure can be seen in Listing 10.5 and is called `Particle`.

Listing 10.5   **Particle Structure**

```
typedef struct {
    Vector2f position;
    Vector2f direction;
    Color4f color;
    Color4f deltaColor;
    GLfloat radius;
    GLfloat radiusDelta;
    GLfloat angle;
    GLfloat degreesPerSecond;
    GLfloat particleSize;
    GLfloat particleSizeDelta;
    GLfloat timeToLive;
} Particle;
```

The `Particle` structure stores all information related to a particle during its lifetime. Whereas the `PointSprite` structure is simply the location and size of a particle that will be sent to OpenGL ES, the `Particle` structure stores the other details required to manage a particle during its lifetime. It stores elements such as the particle's current position, direction of travel, color, and time left to live. Each particle will have its own `Particle` structure that stores that particle's detail.

Initialization

The first stage of using our particle emitter is to initialize it. The `initParticleEmitterWithFile:` method shown in Listing 10.6 is the designated initializer for the `ParticleEmitter` class.

Listing 10.6   **ParticleEmitter initParticleEmitterWithFile: Method**

```
- (id)initParticleEmitterWithFile:(NSString*)aFileName {
    self = [super init];
    if (self != nil) {

        TBXML *particleXML = [[TBXML alloc] initWithXMLFile:aFileName];

        [self parseParticleConfig:particleXML];

        [self setupArrays];

        [particleXML release];
    }
    return self;
}
```

Inside our initializer, we first create a new instance of TBXML using the name of the passed-in configuration file. These details relate to an XML particle configuration file.

Having created a new instance of TBXML, we then parse the particle configuration file. This populates all the properties needed by the particle emitter based on what is in the configuration file. It also performs some initial calculations that we see shortly.

After the configuration file has successfully been passed, the arrays that are needed to hold the particle details are configured, as well as the information needed by OpenGL ES. Having completed these steps, the method then releases the TBXML instance we were using, `particleXML`, and returns `self`.

Parsing Particle Configuration

The `parseParticleConfig` method is responsible for parsing the XML configuration file. It starts out by making sure that there is a root element inside the configuration file of the type we expect. Listing 10.7 shows the start of the `parseParticleConfig` method and the check performed on the root element.

Listing 10.7   **ParticleEmitter parseParticleConfig: Partial Method (Part 1)**

```
- (void)parseParticleConfig:(TBXML*)aConfig {

    TBXMLElement *rootXMLElement = aConfig.rootXMLElement;

    // Make sure we have a root element or we can't process this file
    if (!rootXMLElement) {
        NSLog(@"ERROR - ParticleEmitter: Could not find root element in
            particle config file.");
    }
```

Having made sure that we at least have a configuration file with a valid root element, we then start to process the other elements we need. Listing 10.8 shows the texture element being processed, along with a number of other configuration elements.

Listing 10.8   ParticleEmitter parseParticleConfig Method (Part 2)

```objc
- (void)parseParticleConfig:(TBXML*)aConfig {

    TBXMLElement *rootXMLElement = aConfig.rootXMLElement;

    // Make sure we have a root element or we cant process this file
    if (!rootXMLElement) {
        NSLog(@"ERROR - ParticleEmitter: Could not find root element in
            particle config file.");
    }
    // First thing to grab is the texture that is to be used for the point sprite
    TBXMLElement *element = [TBXML childElementNamed:@"texture"
        parentElement:rootXMLElement];
    if (element) {
        NSString *fileName = [TBXML valueOfAttributeNamed:@"name"
         forElement:element];

        if (fileName) {
        // Create a new texture which is going to be used as the texture for the
        point sprites
            texture = [[Image alloc] initWithImageNamed:fileName
                filter:GL_LINEAR];
        }
    }

    sourcePosition = [aConfig
      vector2fFromChildElementNamed:@"sourcePosition"
                    parentElement:rootXMLElement];
    sourcePositionVariance = [aConfig
        vector2fFromChildElementNamed:@"sourcePositionVariance"
                    parentElement:rootXMLElement];
    speed = [aConfig floatValueFromChildElementNamed:@"speed"
                                    parentElement:rootXMLElement];
    speedVariance = [aConfig
      floatValueFromChildElementNamed:@"speedVariance"
                    parentElement:rootXMLElement];
    particleLifespan = [aConfig
      floatValueFromChildElementNamed:@"particleLifeSpan"
                    parentElement:rootXMLElement];

    // Calculate the emission rate
    emissionRate = maxParticles / particleLifespan;}
```

This method simply populates each property by using the appropriate method inside our **TBXMLParticleAdditions** class. Using methods such as `vector2fFromChildElement` saves us from repeating the code we have actually placed inside the `TBXMLParticleAdditions` category.

The last line of this method is something we should also understand, as follows:

```
emissionRate = maxParticles / particleLifespan;
```

This line is responsible for calculating the emission rate that our particle emitter is going to use. The emission rate allows us to make sure we are emitting the correct number of particles per update. It is a simple calculation but an important one.

Setting Up Particle and Render Arrays

Having now loaded all the properties we need from the configuration file, we need to set up the arrays needed to hold our particle's information for both updating the particles as well as rendering them. Listing 10.9 shows the `setupArrays` method that is used to perform this setup.

Listing 10.9   **ParticleEmitter setupArrays Method**

```
- (void)setupArrays {
    particles = malloc( sizeof(Particle) * maxParticles);
    vertices = malloc( sizeof(PointSprite) * maxParticles);

    NSAssert(particles && vertices, @"ERROR - ParticleEmitter: Could not
        allocate arrays.");

    glGenBuffers(1, &verticesID);

    active = YES;

    particleCount = 0;

    elapsedTime = 0;
}
```

The first couple of lines in this method allocate the memory needed for two arrays: `particles` and `vertices`. The particles array holds a `Particle` structure for every particle required by the particle emitter. The vertices array holds a `PointSprite` structure for the same number of particles, and it's this information that will be used to tell OpenGL ES where each point sprite needs to be rendered and at what size.

Point Sprites

I've already mentioned point sprites a couple of times in this chapter, so it would be helpful to run through what they are. Up until now, when we want to render something to the screen, we create a quad using four vertices and then map a texture into that quad. This works well, and we could easily use the same approach for our particle system.

We could define a quad for each particle and then update that quad's properties during the update method, as well as create a vertex array of those quads when we render to the screen. This method does have some benefits in that you can control the vertices yourself, enabling you to scale and rotate each particles quad as you wish, just as we do in the **Image** class. If you need to rotate your particles, this is the method you would need to use.

Another approach is to use point sprites. A point sprite enables you to render an axis-aligned (not rotated) textured quad to the screen using just a single vertex. This single vertex is used as the center point of the texture to be rendered. Therefore, point sprites enable you to render a quad using only 25 percent of the information you would need to provide if you were rendering quads manually. This is important because in most cases, the biggest bottleneck for performance is actually copying this information to the GPU's memory.

Point sprites are regularly used in high-performance particle systems because of this saving and the ease with which they can be rendered.

There are some rules around using point sprites in OpenGL ES 1.1. The first is that the texture you specify to be used with a point sprite must have dimensions that are power of 2. The second rule is that point sprites must have a maximum size of 64 pixels. If you need your particles to render larger than 64×64, you would need to use normal quads rather than point sprites.

Apart from a point sprites texture needing to have dimensions that are power of 2, and having a maximum size of 64 pixels if using OpenGL ES 1.1, the texture can be anything you want. The texture being used inside this chapter's example project is a white radial gradient that moves from fully opaque in the center to fully transparent at the edges.

Having allocated the memory, we then need to check to make sure that the allocation was successful. If either of the arrays was not allocated, the method throws an assertion. If we can't allocate the memory needed for the arrays, our particle emitter will not work. This is not a good thing, so we throw the assertion.

After the arrays have been allocated, we then create a Vertex Buffer Object (VBO) that holds the vertex and point size data when we render the particles. There is no real reason why we could not have used a vertex array rather than a VBO. Using VBOs on devices other than the iPhone 3GS, iPhone 4 and iPad doesn't really give us much of a benefit from a performance perspective. That said, there is no harm in using them for the particle system, with the added benefit that if a player is using an iPhone 3GS, iPhone 4 or iPad, he should benefit from improved performance.

The last few lines of the method simply make the particle system active by default, and set up the particle count and the elapsed time. The active property of the **ParticleEmitter** specifies whether the emitter should update when its update method is called.

Updating Particles

With our particle configuration having been parsed and the storage setup, we can now deal with how to update the particles. Listing 10.10 shows the start of the `ParticleEmitter` `updateWithDelta` method.

Listing 10.10   **ParticleEmitter updateWithDelta Method (Part 1)**

```
- (void)updateWithDelta:(GLfloat)aDelta {

    if(active && emissionRate) {
        float rate = 1.0f/emissionRate;
        emitCounter += aDelta;
        while(particleCount < maxParticles && emitCounter > rate) {
            [self addParticle];
            emitCounter -= rate;
        }

        elapsedTime += aDelta;
        if(duration != -1 && duration < elapsedTime)
            [self stopParticleEmitter];
    }
```

This method is called whenever we need to update all the particles within a `ParticleEmitter` instance. The first check to perform is to see whether the particle emitter is active. We also ensure that we have a positive `emissionRate`. The `emissionRate` controls how many particles are emitted each time we update the particle emitter. Remember that the `emissionRate` was calculated at the end of the `ParticleEmitter` `parseParticleConfig` method.

If both of these checks are positive, we calculate a rate and update the `emitCounter` by the delta value passed into the method. The while loop then checks to make sure we have not exceeded the maximum number of particles we have said this emitter should handle and also check that the `emitCounter` is greater than the rate we calculated. Although these are true, we add a new particle to the emitter and reduce the `emitCounter` by the rate. This loop is how we add new particles to the particle emitter, and it enables us to have a nice constant flow of particles being emitted.

Having added as many particles as necessary for this update, we then increase the `elapsedTime` by aDelta. This is used in the next check to see if the emitter has run out of time. You may remember that within the XML configuration file, there was a duration property. This specifies how long the particle emitter will emit particles. If the value is –1, the emitter continues to emit particles until told to stop. Any other value represents the number of seconds the emitter should run for.

If the emitter has been running for longer than the defined duration, we call the `stopParticleEmitter` method.

The code so far has made sure the particle emitter is active and within its defined duration and also that particles have been emitted based on the emitter's configuration. The next task is to run through all active particles and update their location, size, and color.

Listing 10.11 shows the start of the while loop that updates all active particles.

Listing 10.11   ParticleEmitter updateWithDelta Method (Part 2)

```
while(particleIndex < particleCount) {

    // Get the particle for the current particle index
    Particle *currentParticle = &particles[particleIndex];

    // If the current particle is alive then update it
    if(currentParticle->timeToLive > 0) {

        // If maxRadius is greater than 0 then the particles are going to
        // spin otherwise they are effected by speed and gravity
        if (maxRadius > 0) {
            Vector2f tmp;
            tmp.x = sourcePosition.x - cosf(currentParticle->angle) *
                currentParticle->radius;
            tmp.y = sourcePosition.y - sinf(currentParticle->angle) *
                currentParticle->radius;
            currentParticle->position = tmp;

            // Update the angle of the particle from the sourcePosition and
            // the radius. This is only done of the particles are rotating
            currentParticle->angle += currentParticle->degreesPerSecond *
                aDelta;
            currentParticle->radius -= currentParticle->radiusDelta;
            if (currentParticle->radius < minRadius)
                currentParticle->timeToLive = 0;
        } else {
            // Calculate the new position of the particle based on the
            // particles current direction and gravity
            Vector2f tmp = Vector2fMultiply(gravity, aDelta);
            currentParticle->direction =
                Vector2fAdd(currentParticle->direction, tmp);
            tmp = Vector2fMultiply(currentParticle->direction, aDelta);
            currentParticle->position =
                Vector2fAdd(currentParticle->position, tmp);
        }
```

The while loop continues while the `particleIndex` ivar is less than the `particleCount`. `particleCount` is updated whenever a new particle is added to the particle emitter. Inside the while loop, the particle at `particleIndex` within the particle's array is referenced, and we check to see if that particle's `timeToLive` value is greater than 0. If this is the case, we move onto updating that particle's position and color. If it is not greater than 0, we move that particle to the end of the `particle` array. We see how this is done later at the end of the `updateWithDelta` method.

The particle emitter has two ways of updating a particle's position. If within the particle configuration file we specified a radius, this tells the emitter that we are going to rotate the particles around the source position. With this update, the configuration of the emitter specifies how the particles orbit around the source position and if they should decay over time. This functionality was added specifically to support the portals we are going to be using in *Sir Lamorak's Quest*. Figure 10.3 shows the effect used in the game.

Figure 10.3   Portal emitter.

Note

As before, it's hard to imagine how this looks with a static image. Go back to the *CH10_SLQTSOR* and uncomment the lines beneath the Portal emitter configuration comment. This can be found in the init method inside the *GameScene.m* file, as shown here:

```
// Particle fountain configuration
//pe = [[ParticleEmitter alloc]
      initParticleEmitterWithFile:@"emitterConfig.pex"];
//emitterType = @"Particle Fountain";
//pe.sourcePosition = Vector2fMake(160, 25);


// Appearing emitter configuration
//pe = [[ParticleEmitter alloc]
      initParticleEmitterWithFile:@"appearingEmitter.pex"];
//emitterType = @"Appearing Emitter";
//pe.sourcePosition = Vector2fMake(160, 25);

// Portal emitter configuration
pe = [[ParticleEmitter alloc]
      initParticleEmitterWithFile:@"portalEmitter.pex"];
emitterType = @"Portal";
pe.sourcePosition = Vector2fMake(160, 240);
```

Run the project, and you will see a green swirling mist, which is what the portals in *Sir Lamorak's Quest* are going to look like.

The code to support this effect is specific to the needs of the portal, but it is still possible to generate effects that could be used in other situations by changing the configuration file of the emitter.

If the emitter was not configured with a radius value, the emitter will be updated using the particle's current position and direction along with the configured gravity and speed.

You will notice that we are using some new functions when updating the particles (for example, Vector2fAdd and Vector2fMultiply). These functions have been defined inside the *Global.h* file. They are defined as static inline functions to help with performance.

A number of other functions have been defined in *Global.h* that we are not using at the moment (for example, Vector2fDot, Vector2fNormalize, and Vector2fSub). These are useful functions to have when you start moving into more advance functions when dealing with your geometry. These functions are not restricted to the **ParticleEmitter** class and can be used anywhere that has imported the *Global.h* file.

Having updated the position of the particle, we can now finish off performing the updates. Listing 10.12 shows the final part of the updateWithDelta method.

Listing 10.12   ParticleEmitter updateWithDelta Method (Part 3)

```
// Update the particle's color
currentParticle->color.red += currentParticle->deltaColor.red;
currentParticle->color.green += currentParticle->deltaColor.green;
currentParticle->color.blue += currentParticle->deltaColor.blue;
currentParticle->color.alpha += currentParticle->deltaColor.alpha;

// Reduce the life span of the particle
currentParticle->timeToLive -= aDelta;

// Place the position of the current particle into the
 // vertices array
vertices[particleIndex].x = currentParticle->position.x;
vertices[particleIndex].y = currentParticle->position.y;

// Place the size of the current particle in the size array
currentParticle->particleSize += currentParticle->particleSizeDelta;
vertices[particleIndex].size = MAX(0, currentParticle->particleSize);

// Place the color of the current particle into the color
 // array
vertices[particleIndex].color = currentParticle->color;

// Update the particle counter
```

```
                particleIndex++;
        } else {

                // As the particle is not alive anymore replace it with the
                // last active particle in the array and reduce the count of
                // particles by one. This causes all active particles to be
                // packed together at the start of the array so that a
                // particle which has run out of life will only drop into
                // this clause once
            if(particleIndex != particleCount - 1)
                particles[particleIndex] = particles[particleCount - 1];
            particleCount--;
        }
    }
}
```

The first update is done to the color of the particle. Each component of the particle's color is updated by the delta value we calculated for that particle when it was created. If you were using a particle engine that was not using a fixed delta, this calculation would need to be done based on the delta value being passed in to get the best results. Not doing this could cause timing issues with the particles being rendered.

Having updated the color, the particle's timeToLive is reduced and is followed by updates to the particle's position and size. Notice that the particle's position and size information is placed inside the vertices array at the particle's index. The reason is that the information inside the vertices array is going to be passed to OpenGL ES as part of the rendering method and therefore needs to contain all the information necessary to render the particle (that is, the particle's x, y, size, and color).

You will also notice that we are making sure that the particle's size is between 0 and the particle's current size. During the development process, I found that if the particle size became negative for some reason, odd effects (random flashes of light, for example) would appear onscreen when using the iPhone 3GS. Other devices were not affected.

With all updates done, we increment the particle index and move onto the next particle.

The end of this method deals with particles that are no longer alive. It basically replaces the dead particle in the array with the last active particle. This keeps all active particles grouped together at the start of the particles array to help performance.

Adding Particles

Particles are added during the updateWithDelta method inside the **ParticleEmitter** class. Adding a particle basically means we are configuring a particle within the particle's array ready to be used. This involves setting up the particle's position, direction, color, and size. These properties are configured based on the information in the configuration file.

Listing 10.13 shows the code inside the addParticle method that is used to set up a particle's position and start color.

Listing 10.13   **ParticleEmitter addParticle Method Exert**

```
particle->position.x = sourcePosition.x + sourcePositionVariance.x *
    RANDOM_MINUS_1_TO_1();
particle->position.y = sourcePosition.y + sourcePositionVariance.y *
    RANDOM_MINUS_1_TO_1();

float newAngle = (GLfloat)DEGREES_TO_RADIANS(angle + angleVariance *
    RANDOM_MINUS_1_TO_1());

Vector2f vector = Vector2fMake(cosf(newAngle), sinf(newAngle));

float vectorSpeed = speed + speedVariance * RANDOM_MINUS_1_TO_1();

particle->direction = Vector2fMultiply(vector, vectorSpeed);

Color4f start = {0, 0, 0, 0};
start.red = startColor.red + startColorVariance.red *
    RANDOM_MINUS_1_TO_1();
start.green = startColor.green + startColorVariance.green *
    RANDOM_MINUS_1_TO_1();
start.blue = startColor.blue + startColorVariance.blue *
    RANDOM_MINUS_1_TO_1();
start.alpha = startColor.alpha + startColorVariance.alpha *

    RANDOM_MINUS_1_TO_1();
```

You see that we are performing some basic calculations using the information from the configuration file to set up the particle. Remember that this is not actually creating a new particle in the particles array; it is simply setting up the next available particle to be ready for use. Physically creating an object or allocating memory in the middle of an intensive operation (that is, it's not a good idea to update the particles in the particle emitter because doing so would have a negative impact on performance).

Rendering Particles

With all the updates done to the emitter particles, we have come to the point where they need to be rendered. Nothing in this method should be new to you if you have read Chapter 5, "Image Rendering."

Listing 10.14 shows the first part of the renderParticles method.

Listing 10.14   **ParticleEmitter renderParticles Method (Part 1)**

```
- (void)renderParticles {

    glDisableClientState(GL_TEXTURE_COORD_ARRAY);
```

```
glBindBuffer(GL_ARRAY_BUFFER, verticesID);
glBufferData(GL_ARRAY_BUFFER, sizeof(PointSprite) * maxParticles,
    vertices, GL_DYNAMIC_DRAW);

glVertexPointer(2, GL_FLOAT, sizeof(PointSprite), 0);
glColorPointer(4,GL_FLOAT,sizeof(PointSprite),
    (GLvoid*) (sizeof(GLfloat)*3));

GLint currentlyBoundTexture;
GLint textureName = (GLuint)[[texture texture] name];
glGetIntegerv(GL_TEXTURE_BINDING_2D, &currentlyBoundTexture);
if (currentlyBoundTexture != textureName) {
    glBindTexture(GL_TEXTURE_2D, textureName);
}

glEnableClientState(GL_POINT_SIZE_ARRAY_OES);

glPointSizePointerOES(GL_FLOAT,sizeof(PointSprite),
    (GLvoid*) (sizeof(GL_FLOAT)*2));

if(blendAdditive) {
    glBlendFunc(GL_ONE_MINUS_SRC_ALPHA, GL_ONE);
}

glEnable(GL_POINT_SPRITE_OES);
glTexEnvi( GL_POINT_SPRITE_OES, GL_COORD_REPLACE_OES, GL_TRUE );
```

The one area you will not have seen before is how we set up and use point sprites. Having bound to the right VBO and set up the vertex and color pointers, we then enable a client state called `GL_POINT_SIZE_ARRAY_OES`. This tells OpenGL ES that we are going to be providing the point sizes for each particle in an array configured using `glPointSizePointerOES`. This works in the same was as `glVertexPointer` or `glColorPointer`.

Note

The OES means this is an optional part of the OpenGL ES 1.1 specification and that it's not guaranteed to be implemented on all devices that support OpenGL ES 1.1. That said, I personally don't know of any devices that support OpenGL ES without the OES extensions.

You will also see that we are enabling `GL_POINT_SPRITE_OES` and setting up `glTexEnvi` for `GL_POINT_SPRITE_OES` so that OpenGL ES knows how to render the particles themselves. Having set up the rendering, we then simply ask OpenGL ES to perform the render and then tidy up, as shown in Listing 10.15.

Listing 10.15   **ParticleEmitter renderParticles Method (Part 2)**

```
- (void)renderParticles {
    glDrawArrays(GL_POINTS, 0, particleIndex);
```

```
    glBindBuffer(GL_ARRAY_BUFFER, 0);

    glDisableClientState(GL_POINT_SIZE_ARRAY_OES);
    glDisable(GL_POINT_SPRITE_OES);

    if(blendAdditive) {
        glBlendFunc(GL_SRC_ALPHA, GL_ONE_MINUS_SRC_ALPHA);
    }

    glEnableClientState(GL_TEXTURE_COORD_ARRAY);
}
```

You'll see that we are using `glDrawArrays` to render the particles. Having loaded all the data into a VBO and not needing to jump around in the VBO to render, `glDrawArrays` is an efficient way to render the array's contents. Once the rendering has been set off, we then unbind the VBO, disable the states we no longer need, and then re-enable the `GL_TEXTURE_COORD_ARRAY` state. The blend function is also set back to our default mode if the blend additive blend mode was used for the particles.

> **Note**
>
> The rendering of this particle system is done separately from the rendering that is used for images. There is no real reason why they cannot be merged into a single render engine, and this is in fact what some people do. The main reason for keeping this separate was to allow this class to be implemented on its own and to be re-usable and also to keep things simple. Because we are using point sprites and need to set up the state of OpenGL ES before we use them, keeping their rendering separate from the rendering of images has simplified our rendering engine. This approach also means that the particles need to be rendered last and, therefore, on top.

Stopping the Particle Emitter

The smallest method in the **ParticleEmitter** class is `stopParticleEmitter`. This method is called if we wanted to stop a particle emitter that was set up with duration of –1. Listing 10.16 shows the `stopParticleEmitter` method.

Listing 10.16   **ParticleEmitter stopParticleEmitter Method**

```
- (void)stopParticleEmitter {
    active = NO;
    elapsedTime = 0;
    emitCounter = 0;
}
```

This is certainly the most straightforward method in the **ParticleEmitter** class. It simply sets active to NO and resets the `elapsedTime` and `emitCounter` ivars. With this done, the particle emitter stops emitting or rendering particles and is ready to be started again if needed in the future.

Have a Play

In this book, the last section of a chapter is normally called "*Exercise.*" However, there aren't any exercises for this chapter. Instead, you get to play with the particle emitter. (Lucky you!)

See what different effects you can generate (for example, smoke or fire). Figure 10.4 shows you a flame emitter created by changing the configuration file to give you something to aim for.

Figure 10.4   Flame particle system.

While creating particle effects was great fun, I soon realized that it was also time consuming and fiddly. Trying to get the effect you are after by changing numbers in an XML file is actually hard and it can take come time to get the effect you are after. Because of this, I decided that it would be great to build a visual designer that would allow me to tweak the parameters for a particle emitter and see the effect on the emitter in real time.

The result is a product called Particle Designer, available from http://particledesigner. 71squared.com. This is a Mac OS X application that I developed with Tom Bradley that lets you load and save particle configurations and edit them visually. This really does speed up the process of creating particle effects and makes the whole process even more fun than it already was.

Particle Designer actually uses a slightly more advanced version of the ParticleEmitter class I used in SLQ. This class is provided with Particle Designer and can simply be swapped with the ParticleEmitter class already in the SLQ engine. This will then allow you to use the extra features of this particle engine inside SLQ or your own games.

Figure 10.5 shows a screen shot of a particle emitter being edited using Particle Designer.

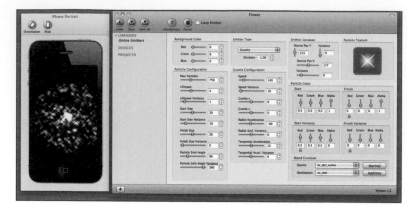

Figure 10.5   Particle Designer GUI.

Summary

As I said at the start of this chapter, particle systems are great fun to play with. The amazing effects you can get by simply changing a few parameters are both a blessing and a curse. On the one hand, you can easily change settings to get the effect you are after without needing to change the code, unless you are doing something very different. On the other hand, the simple fact that they are so simple to change means you can spend hours tweaking the settings until you get something you want, or simply have fun seeing what you can create—if you're anything like me, that is.

This is by no means a complex particle engine. Plenty of other features could be added, such as using images rather than point sprites so that particles can be rotated. Also, collision detection between particles could be added. This would need to be done carefully, of course, as collision detection for a high number of objects can be very processor intensive.

Using images rather than point sprites would also allow other features to be added, such as the ability to change the shape of the particle in flight. An example of this would be when creating sparks. Sparks normally appear as long trails of light, so with stretching the quad between its last position and next position, and using the right kind of texture, you could get a pretty good spark effect.

As you can imagine, particle systems could be used for many different effects and are only limited by your imagination. Well, that is not completely true, as we have the limitations of the device to consider, but you get the idea.

In the next chapter, we will finish off the last of the classes that make up our core engine: the **SoundManager** class. This class enables you to play background music and sound effects within your game. The **SoundManager** class implements both the AVAudioPlayer for playing background music as well as OpenAL for shorter sound effects and positional sound.

11

Sound

This is the final chapter that deals with the underlying technology we need to make *Sir Lamorak's Quest* and most 2D games. Sound is one of the most important elements in a game. Although it's possible to create a game that has no sound at all, sound really can take your game to a new level.

Many of the games in the early 1980s didn't have sound, or the sound was as simple as clicks and buzzes. Even though the sound was not that advanced, just having something really made a difference to the player's experience.

During this chapter, we review the **SoundManager** class and look at how we can play both music and sound effects. This involves using both the **AVAudioPlayer** class and OpenAL.[1]

Sound Project

The project for this chapter introduces the **SoundManager** class and demonstrates how to load music, create a playlist, and also a sound effect.

Open the *CH11_SLQTSOR* project and run it. When the app loads, you see a message on the screen telling you that the music is playing. The music gently fades up over a period of five seconds. If you then tap the screen, you hear a sound effect of a door slamming.

Even if you tap the screen repeatedly, you hear the sound effect playing correctly, overlapping with the previous sound effect if necessary.

As we see in this chapter, the music is playing using the **AVAudioPlayer** class, and the sound effects are played using OpenAL. Using OpenAL allows us to play sound effects very quickly and in parallel, up to a maximum of 32, as well as being able to play those effects in 3D.

---

[1] OpenAL is a cross-platform 3D audio API for use with gaming applications and many other types of audio applications. More information can be found at http://connect.creativelabs.com/openal/default.aspx.

Introduction to Sound on the iPhone

Sound on the iPhone can be a daunting subject. When I first looked at how to get sound on the iPhone, I found it to be confusing because a number of different approaches could be taken.

The sound requirements for the iPhone are complicated. The device needs to handle different output routes—that is, internal speaker, wired headset, or Bluetooth headset. It also needs to handle sound that is playing from the iPod library, alarms, phone calls, and whatever app is running at the time.

All this needs to be handled without the user needing to do anything apart from setting his required volume and maybe selecting if he wants sound to play or not using the toggle switch on the side of the iPhone.

Luckily for us, the iPhone SDK provides us with a couple of APIs that enable us to easily interact with the iPhone's sound features, helping to keep all the complexity out of our game.

Audio Sessions

The iPhone handles the audio behavior for us at the application, inter-application, and device levels. Access to these behaviors and settings is done through *audio sessions*. The audio session API allows us to define the behavior of sound in our game. The behavior of our sound and, therefore, the settings that need to be used can be defined by answering a few simple questions:

- Should the ring/silent switch silence the audio?
- Should iPod audio continue when our game audio starts?
- What should be done if audio is interrupted?
- Do we want to make use of the hardware decoding capabilities of the iPhone?

After we answer these questions, we are able to decide which audio session category needs to be set and also define the actions that should take place during an interruption (for example, a phone call or alarm).

We define the game's audio intentions by setting the audio session's category. When the application starts, its audio session is given a default category called `AVAudioSessionCategorySoloAmbient`. Table 11.1 shows the details of each available category. This information has been taken from Apple's *Audio Session Programming Guide*, which is part of the SDK documentation. The highlighted row in Table 11.1 is the default category used when a new audio session is created.

Table 11.1   **Audio Session Category Behavior**

Category Identifiers[2]	Silenced by the ring/silent switch and by screen locking	Allows audio from other applications	Allows audio input (recording) and output (playback)
AVAudioSessionCategoryAmbient kAudioSessionCategory_Ambient Sound	Yes	Yes	Output only
AVAudioSessionCategorySolo Ambient kAudioSessionCategory_Solo AmbientSound	Yes	No	Output only
AVAudioSessionCategoryPlayback kAudioSessionCategory_Media Playback	No	No by default; Yes by using override switch	Output only
AVAudioSessionCategoryRecord kAudioSessionCategory_Record Audio	No (recording continues with the screen locked)	No	Input only
AVAudioSessionCategoryPlayAnd Record kAudioSessionCategory_PlayAnd Record	No	No by default; Yes by using override switch	Input and output
AVAudioSessionCategoryAudio Processing kAudioSessionCategory_Audio Processing	-	No	No input and no output

Note

`AVAudioSessionCategorySoloAmbient` makes use of the iPhone's hardware decoding capabilities. This is important if you are going to be playing a compressed sound or music file during your game, such as an MP3. Playing a compressed music file without using this category can cause very noticeable lag within your game.

Understanding how to use audio sessions gives you the ability to tightly control how the game will behave with other audio generated on the iPhone, such as alarms or phone calls.

---

[2] In each row, the first identifier is for the Objective-C-based `AVAudioSession` API and the second is for the C-based Audio Session Services API.

Playing Music

When playing the game, it would be great to play some music. This is not mandatory and depends on the style of the game you are writing. For *Sir Lamorak's Quest,* music can really add atmosphere to the game, so it is something we will want our sound manager handle.

Luckily, there is a simple Objective-C API for playing back audio data from a file or memory. The class is called **AVAudioPlayer**. This API was introduced in iPhone OS 2.2.

This is a great multi-purpose API that Apple recommends you use for all audio, unless you need to provide 3D sound or very precise synchronization between your sound and other aspects of your game. It's possible to use multiple instances of this class to play multiple sounds at the same time, but it should be noted that playing multiple compressed sounds at the same time does have an impact on performance.

Some of the characteristics of **AVAudioPlayer** are as follows:

- Play sounds of any duration
- Play sounds from files or memory buffers
- Loop sounds
- Play multiple sounds simultaneously, one sound per audio player
- Control relative playback level for each sound being played
- Seek a particular point within a sound file
- Obtain data that you can use for playback-level metering

These capabilities make the **AVAudioPlayer** a great general-purpose API for generating sound. Although multiple audio players can be playing at the same time, the latency they each have does not always make it the best option for generating sound within a game. I have found that **AVAudioPlayer** is best used for playing background music. If this is a compressed file, such as MP3, using an audio session category of SoloAmbient means that the audio player will make use of the hardware to decode the file, and you will not get any lag. Lag in this case is an interruption to the smooth rendering of your game.

Generating short in-game sound effects is best left to a different API. This is the OpenAL API available in the iOS OpenAL framework.

Playing Sound Effects

In addition to playing a cool background track, it would also be great to play sound effects such as when a baddie dies, a door opens or closes, or when the player dies. In-game sound effects normally end up playing simultaneously because multiple sound-generating events could happen at the same time. This is the kind of work the OpenAL API was designed for.

OpenAL is a cross-platform 3D audio API that can be used within games and many other types of audio applications. It has the advantage of being very quick and is, for example, implemented using the iPhone I/O unit for playback. This results in the lowest latency, which is important when writing games.

OpenAL is made up of three core objects that are used to generate a sound:

- Listener
- Source
- Buffer

There is only one listener object (per context[3]), and all sound is rendered (generated) based on the location of this listener in relation to a source. The source defines the location at which a sound is generated, and the buffer is the actual sound data to be used to generate that sound.

There can be many buffers created, storing all the different sound effects we may need. When we want to play a sound, the appropriate sound buffer is bound to a source, and the sound source's location is set. The source is then asked to play, and it will play the contents of the sound buffer to which it has been bound. Just as there can be multiple buffers, it is possible to generate multiple sound sources. The iPhone supports 32 sources playing simultaneously. You can generate more than 32 sources, but only 32 can be played simultaneously.

What the player hears depends on the location of the listener object (see Figure 11.1)—usually the player's location (for example, the further away the source from the listener, the quieter the sound will be). There are a number of different algorithms defined within OpenAL that can be used to handle all these calculations without us needing to worry about how it works.

OpenAL even handles sound that moves. If the listener or sources are moving, the sound played is updated as necessary. A great example of this is the sound of a police siren as it moves toward you. The siren appears to get both louder and higher in pitch; then, as it passes and moves away, the pitch gets lower, as does the volume. This Doppler effect is handled for us by OpenAL.

I mentioned at the start of this section that OpenAL is a 3D audio API. The coordinate system of the listener and sound sources is the same as OpenGL; in fact, the API for OpenAL is similar to that of OpenGL. The listener and sources can be given a location made up of the x, y, and z coordinates. This means that it's easy to assign a sound source to a game object, set the location of that object, and then let OpenAL worry about whether the player (listener) can hear the sound and at what volume and pitch.

This also means that sound played behind the player in the game world will sound as though it is behind the player in the real world. We get all this functionality for free by using OpenAL, and it's something we will be taking advantage of in the sound manager we review in this chapter.

---

[3] The OpenAL context can be thought of as a session that all sounds are going to be played in. You could also think of it as the world the sound sources and listener are in.

Figure 11.1   Different sound source in relation to a single listener.

Creating Sound Effects

Knowing that we have APIs that can play music and sound effects for us is great, but we need to have music and sound effects that we can actually play. Putting sound into your game does not need to be expensive. There are many sources of sound and music on the Internet that can be used. Some are free and give you permission to use the sounds as you want, even in commercial applications, whereas others ask you to pay a fee for unlimited use of the sound or music.

> **Note**
>
> A quick Google search brings back many different sites that you can search through for the music or sound effects. One site that I used for sound effects in *Sir Lamorak's Quest* was **www.sound-effect.com**.

You don't always have to grab a pre-built sound effect. With tools such as GarageBand on the Mac, it's possible to create your own music and sound effects. Although I'm not going to run through how to use something like GarageBand, it is important to understand how you get something you have downloaded or created ready for use in your game.

The **AVAudioPlayer** API will play any format of music that is supported by iOS. Details of the audio codecs supported up to iOS 4 are shown in Table 11.2.

Table 11.2   **Audio Playback Formats and Codecs**

Audio Decoder/Playback Format	Hardware-Assisted Decoding	Software-Based Decoding
AAC (MPEG-4 Advanced Audio Coding)	Yes	Yes, starting in iPhone OS 3.0
ALAC (Apple Lossless)	Yes	Yes, starting in iPhone OS 3.0
AMR (Adaptive Multi-Rate, a format for speech)	-	Yes
HE-AAC (MPEG-4 High Efficiency AAC)	Yes	-
iLBC (Internet Low Bitrate Codec, another format for speech)	-	Yes
IMA4 (IMA/ADPCM)	-	Yes
Linear PCM (uncompressed, linear pulse-code modulation)	-	Yes
MP3 (MPEG-1 audio layer 3)	Yes	Yes, starting in iPhone OS 3.0
µ-law and a-law	-	Yes

It's important to understand how these formats are being handled (that is, are they being decoded using software or hardware? This will have a big impact on performance). Most people tend to use an MP3 format for their background music because the compression helps keep the size of these long tracks down. Decoding an MP3 sound file takes a fair amount of work, so decoding in software will have a noticeable effect on the performance of your game.

In *Sir Lamorak's Quest*, not using the hardware to decode MP3 files caused a noticeable pause in the game every one second for about half a second. It may not sound like much, but it is very noticeable. Using software to decode compressed files is normally visible as small pauses in game play every one second or so.

As you saw in the previous section on audio sessions, we can define how we want the audio to behave by setting the audio session category. Doing this lets us specify for instance that we want to use hardware to decode compressed files with a category of SoloAmbient.

> **Note**
>
> It is only possible to decode a single instance of one of the supported audio formats using hardware at any one time. If you play more than one MP3 sound, for example, the first sound will be decoded using hardware, but the second, third, and so forth will use software. For this reason, it is a good idea to use the hardware to decode your longer music tracks and use uncompressed sound for other sounds that will be played alongside the music.

You may wonder what you can do if you have a music track or sound effect that is not in the format you need. Although a number of applications on the Internet let you convert from one format to another, Apple provides a great command-line tool in Mac OS X, *afconvert* (located in */usr/bin*), which you can use to convert audio files. *afconvert* is perfect for converting any sound into a format that is preferred in iOS.

> **Tip**
>
> iOS does have a preferred full-quality format, which is 16-bit, little-endian, linear PCM packaged as a CAF. Making sure that your sounds are all converted to this format and with the same sample rate reduces the amount of mixing that needs to be done and, therefore, improves performance.

To convert an audio file to the CAF format using a sample rate of 22050, you would run the following command in the Terminal:

```
$ afconvert -f caff -d LEI16@22050 {inputfile} {outputfile}
```

> **Note**
>
> To learn more about afconvert and its options, run `man afconvert` (or `afconvert -h`) in the Terminal.

Stereo Versus Mono

Most audio tools output sound in stereo by default. For background music, this is perfect, as you want to give players the enjoyment of listening to your background music in their headphones in glorious stereo. What you need to make sure is that when you are creating sound effects you are going to play using OpenAL, they are saved as mono.

The reason for this is that OpenAL needs to decide through which channel to play the sound based on its location relative to the listener. If the sound already has the stereo split built in, it acts against the work OpenAL is trying to do, and you either get nothing or not the effect you were hoping for.

It is normally simple to specify that you want a sound to be saved in mono and not stereo, but it is something to watch out for.

Sound Manager Classes

Having had a look at sound on the iPhone, let's review the two classes we'll use to manage sound in *Sir Lamorak's Quest,* as follows:

- `MyOpenALSupport`
- `SoundManager`

MyOpenALSupport is an example class provided by Apple. It takes audio data from an audio file and places it into a format that can be used with an OpenAL sound buffer.

The **MyOpenALSupport** class takes care of identifying a number of important properties the sound file may have, including the following:

- Sample Rate
- Channels Per Frame
- Format (for example, PCM)
- Frames Per Packet
- Bytes Per Frame
- Bits Per Channel

This is useful information if you want to get deep and technical with audio data, formats, and so on. For our needs, though, we just want to provide a sound file and have the audio data from that file made available for our OpenAL sound buffer. This is exactly what the **MyOpenALSupport** class does, and it's not something we review in any detail.

The core of what we are going to review in this chapter is inside the **SoundManager** class. This class is a wrapper around the **AVAudioPlayer** class and OpenAL. It provides a simple API that can be used to play both music and sound effects, as well as manage music playlists, manage music and sound effects volumes, and manage music and sound effects libraries.

To make use of **AVAudioPlayer** and OpenAL, a number of frameworks need to be added to the project. These are the following:

- CoreAudio
- OpenAL
- AVFoundation
- AudioToolbox

These can be added by right-clicking the project target and selecting **Add > Existing Frameworks**. From the selection panel that appears, highlight the frameworks you want to use and press add.

SoundManager Class

This class is a singleton, and as such, there will only be a single instance of this class while the game is running. Using the singleton pattern means that we can have a single place across our entire game that manages sounds. Just as using the singleton pattern made it easier to share textures or render images, the singleton sound manager makes it easier to manage sound with *Sir Lamorak's Quest*.

Initialization

The initialization of this class follows the singleton pattern that we covered in Chapter 4, "The Game Loop." Although the creation of the singleton is the same, specific initialization is being carried out within the `init` method.

Listing 11.1 shows the first section of the init method.

Listing 11.1   **SoundManager init Method (Part 1)**

```
- (id)init {
    self = [super init];
        if(self != nil) {

            soundSources = [[NSMutableArray alloc] init];
            soundLibrary = [[NSMutableDictionary alloc] init];
            musicLibrary = [[NSMutableDictionary alloc] init];
            musicPlaylists = [[NSMutableDictionary alloc] init];
```

The first task in the `init` method is to set up the arrays and dictionaries that are going to be used to store the sounds, music, sound sources, and playlists in the sound manager.

The `soundSources` array will store a reference to the OpenAL sound sources that we generate later in this method. Generating sound sources up front and storing their details in an array is a good way to reduce the overhead of creating resources during game play. This is especially useful when you have sound that may need to be played very rapidly.

The `soundLibrary` dictionary stores the name of the OpenAL buffers we create when we load a sound to play using OpenAL. The buffer ID will be stored, along with a key to make it easy to reference.

The `musicLibrary` array stores the file name and path of any music we want to play. Music will be played using the `AVAudioPlayer` class that takes in a URL to the music we want to play. We are storing that URL in this dictionary along with a simple key for reference.

Finally, the `musicPlaylists` dictionary will store other dictionaries that contain the list of keys in the `musicLibrary` that are to be played in order. This allows for multiple playlists to be defined.

Listing 11.2 shows the next section of the `init` method, in which the audio session and category is set up.

Listing 11.2   **SoundManager init Method (Part 2)**

```
        audioSession = [AVAudioSession sharedInstance];
        isExternalAudioPlaying = [self isExternalAudioPlaying];

        if (!isExternalAudioPlaying) {
            soundCategory = AVAudioSessionCategorySoloAmbient;
            audioSessionError = nil;
            [audioSession setCategory:soundCategory
```

```
            error:&audioSessionError];
        if (audioSessionError)
            NSLog(@"WARNING - SoundManager: Error setting the
                sound category to SoloAmbientSound");
    }
```

Just as the **SoundManager** class is a singleton, the **AVAudioSession** class is also a singleton, so we grab a reference to its shared instance. After we have the reference to the audio session, we do a check to see if any music is already playing. This would be the case if the iPod was playing music when the game started. Listing 11.3 shows the simple method that checks this for us.

Listing 11.3   **SoundManager isExternalAudioPlaying Method**

```
- (BOOL)isExternalAudioPlaying {
    UInt32 audioPlaying = 0;
    UInt32 audioPlayingSize = sizeof(audioPlaying);
    AudioSessionGetProperty(kAudioSessionProperty_OtherAudioIsPlaying,
        &audioPlayingSize, &audioPlaying);
    return (BOOL)audioPlaying;
}
```

There are two APIs available when dealing with the audio session: Objective-C-based and C-based. It is perfectly normal and appropriate to use both APIs interchangeably and together.

If the check for external audio playing is negative, the init method sets the audio session category to SoloAmbient, thereby giving us access to the hardware decoder for any compressed music we may have. If music were playing, the default audio session category would have been left in place, which is Ambient. Listing 11.4 shows the final section of the init method.

Listing 11.4   **SoundManager init Method (Part 3)**

```
        BOOL success = [self initOpenAL];
        if(!success) {
            NSLog(@"ERROR - SoundManager: Error initializing OpenAL");
            return nil;
        }

        currentMusicVolume = 0.5f;
        musicVolume = 0.5f;
        fxVolume = 0.5f;
        playlistIndex = 0;

        isFading = NO;
        isMusicPlaying = NO;
```

```
                  stopMusicAfterFade = YES;
                  usePlaylist = NO;
                  loopLastPlaylistTrack = NO;
        }
        return self;
}
```

In this final section, you can see that we initialize OpenAL and check for the success of that initialization before moving on. We see what the `initOpenAL` method does next.

Once OpenAL has been initialized, the sound manager's ivars are given default values. Listing 11.5 shows Part 1 of the `initOpenAL` method.

Listing 11.5 **SoundManager initOpenAL Method (Part 1)**

```
- (BOOL)initOpenAL {
    NSLog(@"INFO - Sound Manager: Initializing sound manager");

    uint maxOpenALSources = 16;

    device = alcOpenDevice(NULL);

    if(device) {
        context = alcCreateContext(device, NULL);
        alcMakeContextCurrent(context);
        alDistanceModel(AL_LINEAR_DISTANCE_CLAMPED);
```

The first thing you notice is that `maxOpenALSources` is defined as 16. OpenAL sources are generated in much the same way as OpenGL textures. The same is also true for OpenAL buffers. Because we don't want to hit performance issues in the middle of the game by generating OpenAL sources, we define here how many sources we want to create upfront. The iPhone is capable of playing 32 sources simultaneously, but for the purposes of *Sir Lamorak's Quest*, we only need around 16. If this number ever appeared to be too small, it could easily be increased.

The maximum number of sources is not limited to 32. That is only the maximum number of sources that can be played simultaneously.

Next, we grab a device to use for our OpenAL sound rendering. The `alcOpenDevice` command looks for a device driver/device to use when rendering OpenAL sound. Passing in `NULL` causes the command to pass back the details of the first available device it finds. It's expected that only a single device would ever be present on the iPhone.

If `alcOpenDevice` returns `NULL`, something has gone wrong, and no device was found.

If a device has been found, we then create a context and make it the current context. You could think of the context as the environment in which the sounds will be generated. It is possible to have multiple contexts but the sound from one context will not be rendered in any of the other contexts that may have been created. For our needs, we just have one context.

The last command in Listing 11.5 sets up the distance model that we want to use. There are a number of different distance models available within OpenAL. They define how sound should be affected by the distance of the listener from the source.

Details of all the different models are outside the scope of this book, but more information can be found in the OpenAL documentation on the OpenAL website.[4] Listing 11.6 shows Part 2 of the `initOpenAL` method, where the OpenAL sources are generated.

Listing 11.6   **SoundManager initOpenAL Method (Part 2)**

```
NSUInteger sourceID;
for(int index = 0; index < maxOpenALSources; index++) {
    alGenSources(1, &sourceID);

    alSourcef(sourceID, AL_REFERENCE_DISTANCE, 25.0f);
    alSourcef(sourceID, AL_MAX_DISTANCE, 150.0f);
    alSourcef(sourceID, AL_ROLLOFF_FACTOR, 6.0f);

        [soundSources addObject:[NSNumber
numberWithUnsignedInt:sourceID]];
    }
```

To generate the sources, we have a simple loop that on each pass generates a single OpenAL source and sets some of its parameters. The `alGenSources` command should feel familiar to you, as it is almost identical to the OpenGL ES command `glGenBuffers`. As with `glGenBuffers`, you specify how many sources you want to create using the first parameter and then provide somewhere for the resulting source ID to be stored.

We could have created all the buffers we wanted in a single command by using the `maxOpenALSources` value in the `alGenSources` command. The only reason we are using a loop is that we are setting the parameters for each source as it is created.

The parameters being configured are `AL_REFERENCE_DISTANCE`, `AL_MAX_DISTANCE`, and `AL_ROLLOFF_FACTOR`. These are all related to the distance algorithm that has been set. After you have selected the algorithm you want to use, it is possible to refine it to meet your exact requirements. These settings can be tricky to get right, and normally trial and error is the best way to get the values that work for you.

After a source has been generated and configured, its ID is added to the `soundSources` array ready for us to associate with a buffer when we want to play a sound.

Listing 11.7 shows the final part of the `initOpenAL` method that configures the listener location.

---

[4] OpenAL documentation can be found at http://connect.creativelabs.com/openal/Documentation/Forms/AllItems.aspx.

Listing 11.7   SoundManager initOpenAL Method (Part 3)

```
        float listener_pos[] = {0, 0, 0};
        float listener_ori[] = {0.0, 1.0, 0.0, 0.0, 0.0, 1.0};
        float listener_vel[] = {0, 0, 0};
        alListenerfv(AL_POSITION, listener_pos);
        alListenerfv(AL_ORIENTATION, listener_ori);
        alListenerfv(AL_VELOCITY, listener_vel);

        NSLog(@"INFO - Sound Manager: Finished initializing the sound
            manager");
      return YES;
   }


    NSLog(@"ERROR - SoundManager: Unable to allocate a device for
        sound.");
    return NO;
}
```

The final task in initializing OpenAL is to set the listener to a default location. This also includes setting the orientation and velocity. As you will remember, OpenAL supports positioning of the listener and sound sources in 3D space. This means that the listener does not only have a location but also an orientation (that is, which way is the listener facing). This allows OpenAL to work out which speaker it should play sound from based on the position and orientation of the listener in relation to the sound.

Music Management

There are many different ways music management could be implemented, but I've gone for a simple approach. I wanted to keep the API and code as simple as possible, so music is managed using **NSDictionaries** and the core **AVAudioPlayer** features. Depending on your needs, you may require more than the basic features in this sound manager, but you could easily add your own features at a later date.

The music functions the sound manager needs to support are the ability to load, play, stop, pause, and resume music as well as manage playlists. A number of methods in the **SoundManager** class deal with these functions:

- loadMusicWithKey:musicFile:
- removeMusicWithKey:
- playMusicWithKey:timesToRepeat:
- stopMusic
- pauseMusic
- setMusicVolume:
- setFxVolume:

- resumeMusic
- fadeMusicVolumeFrom:toVolume:duration:stop:
- addToPlaylistNamed:track:
- startPlaylistNamed:
- removedFromPlaylistNamed:track:
- removePlaylistNamed:
- clearPlaylistNamed:
- playNextTrack:
- shutDownSoundManager:

Loading Music

We start by looking at the loadMusicWithKey:musicFile: method shown in Listing 11.8.

Listing 11.8   **SoundManager loadMusicWithKey:musicFile Method**

```
- (void)loadMusicWithKey:(NSString*)aMusicKey
    musicFile:(NSString*)aMusicFile {

    NSString *fileName = [[aMusicFile lastPathComponent]
        stringByDeletingPathExtension];
    NSString *fileType = [aMusicFile pathExtension];

    NSString *path = [musicLibrary objectForKey:aMusicKey];

    if(path != nil) {
        NSLog(@"WARNING - SoundManager: Music with the key '%@' already
            exists.", aMusicKey);
        return;
    }

    path = [[NSBundle mainBundle] pathForResource:fileName
        ofType:fileType];
    if (!path) {
        NSLog(@"WARNING - SoundManager: Cannot find file '%@.%@'",
        fileName, fileType);
         return;
    }

    [musicLibrary setObject:path forKey:aMusicKey];
    NSLog(@"INFO - SoundManager: Loaded background music with key '%@'",
        aMusicKey);
}
```

This method takes the key passed in and checks to see if an entry already exists within the `musicLibrary` dictionary for the key.

If a match was found, a message is logged, explaining that the music has already been loaded. If no match is found, the path of the file is calculated within the main bundle of the application and an entry is added to the `musicLibrary` dictionary. This does mean that any music you are going to use needs to be included within the Xcode project.

Removing Music

If you can load music, you also need to be able to remove music. This is done using `removeMusicWithKey:`, as shown in Listing 11.9.

Listing 11.9   SoundManager removeMusicWithKey: Method

```
- (void)removeMusicWithKey:(NSString*)aMusicKey {
    NSString *path = [musicLibrary objectForKey:aMusicKey];
    if(path == NULL) {
        NSLog(@"WARNING - SoundManager: No music found with key '%@' was
            found so cannot be removed", aMusicKey);
        return;
    }
    [musicLibrary removeObjectForKey:aMusicKey];
    NSLog(@"INFO - SoundManager: Removed music with key '%@'", aMusicKey);
}
```

This method simply removes the entry from the `musicLibrary` dictionary with the matching key. If no match is found for the key, a message is logged to give you some clue as to what is happening. It's simple to create a typo in filenames or keys. If no music plays when you expect it to, simple messages like this in the log can help speed up the debugging process. These messages should, of course, be removed when testing is complete and the game goes to production.

Playing Music

We can now load and remove music, so the next step is to play music. The main method used to play music is `playMusicWithKey:timesToRepeat:`, as shown in Listing 11.10.

Listing 11.10   SoundManager playMusicWithKey:timesToRepeat: Method

```
- (void)playMusicWithKey:(NSString*)aMusicKey timesToRepeat:(NSUInteger)aRepeatCount {

    NSError *error;
    NSString *path = [musicLibrary objectForKey:aMusicKey];
    if(!path) {
        NSLog(@"ERROR - SoundManager: The music key '%@' could not be
            found", aMusicKey);
```

```
            return;
    }

    if(musicPlayer)
        [musicPlayer release];

    musicPlayer = [[AVAudioPlayer alloc] initWithContentsOfURL:[NSURL
        fileURLWithPath:path] error:&error];

    if(!musicPlayer) {
        NSLog(@"ERROR - SoundManager: Could not play music for key
            '%d'", error);
        return;
    }

    musicPlayer.delegate = self;
    [musicPlayer setNumberOfLoops:aRepeatCount];
    [musicPlayer setVolume:currentMusicVolume];
    [musicPlayer play];
    isMusicPlaying = YES;
}
```

This method takes a key string that it uses to search the `musicLibrary` dictionary. If a match is found, a check is carried out to see if an instance of `musicPlayer` (**AVAudioPlayer**) exists. If so, it is released, and a new instance is created using the path returned from the `musicLibrary` dictionary. To finish, the number of repeats is set, along with the volume and delegate.

Setting the delegate is important because it means we can respond to **AVAudioPlayer** interruptions, audio decoding errors, and to the completion of the music's playback. This has been used to implement the playlist functionality reviewed later in this chapter.

> **Note**
>
> To use the delegate methods of **AVAudioPlayer**, you need to make sure that the class implements the `AVAudioPlayerDelegate` protocol. This can be seen in the *SoundManager.h*.

Controlling Music

The other common functions needed for controlling music include stopping, pausing, and resuming, along with setting the volume of music being played. Listing 11.11 shows the methods responsible for these functions.

Listing 11.11   **SoundManager stopMusic, pauseMusic, resumeMusic, and setMusicVolume: Methods**

```
- (void)stopMusic {
    [musicPlayer stop];
```

```
        isMusicPlaying = NO;
        usePlaylist = NO;
}

- (void)pauseMusic {
    [musicPlayer pause];
    isMusicPlaying = NO;
}

- (void)resumeMusic {
    [musicPlayer play];
    isMusicPlaying = YES;
}
}
- (void)setMusicVolume:(float)aVolume {

    if (aVolume > 1)
        aVolume = 1.0f;

    currentMusicVolume = aVolume;
    musicVolume = aVolume;

    [musicPlayer setVolume:currentMusicVolume];
}
```

The **AVAudioPlayer** class provides methods that let us stop, play, and pause the currently
playing track. The SoundManager methods simply wrap these, enabling us to set ivars that
we can use to manage the state of the sound manager in relation to playing music.

When setting the volume, the method ensures that the volume does not exceed 1.0f,
and it sets both the currentMusicVolume and musicVolume ivars. The reason there are
two values for the music volume is to handle fading. The musicVolume ivar stores the volume as set by the player or by default. The player would set the currentMusicVolume ivar
through the settings screen that we see in Chapter 13, "The Game Interface."

Fading Music

When we fade music out and then in, we want to be able to identify what the set volume
was so that we can match that volume when the music fades in. There is nothing worse
than to set the volume and then have a game override that whenever it feels like it. For
this reason, we use musicVolume to store the set volume and currentMusicVolume to
hold the actual volume we are using. currentMusicVolume can then be reduced and increased over time, but we don't lose the set volume.

Listing 11.12 shows the fadeMusicVolumeFrom:toVolume:duration:stop: method
that is used to fade the volume of music up or down over a defined period.

Listing 11.12   **SoundManager fadeMusicVolumeFrom: toVolume: duration: stop: Method**

```
- (void)fadeMusicVolumeFrom:(float)aFromVolume toVolume:(float)aToVolume
    duration:(float)aSeconds stop:(BOOL)aStop {

    if (timer) {
        [timer invalidate];
         timer = NULL;
    }

    fadeAmount = (aToVolume - aFromVolume) / (aSeconds / kFadeInterval);
    currentMusicVolume = aFromVolume;

    fadeDuration = 0;
    targetFadeDuration = aSeconds;
    isFading = YES;
    stopMusicAfterFade = aStop;

    timer = [NSTimer scheduledTimerWithTimeInterval:kFadeInterval
        target:self selector:@selector(fadeVolume:)
        userInfo:nil repeats:TRUE];
}
```

The first check is to see if the timer, which is a global parameter, already exists. If so, then it's invalidated. This destroys it, and it becomes ready for a new timer to be created. This current implementation, therefore, can only handle one fade at a time.

The key to this method is the calculation of the `fadeAmount`. This calculates the amount that `currentMusicVolume` should be adjusted by each time the timer calls the `fadeVolume` method. The last line of the method sets up this new timer and tells it to call the `fadeVolume` method each time it fires. The interval it fires on is a constant defined in the *SoundManager.h* file.

```
#define kFadeInterval (1.0f/60.0)
```

Setting up `kFadeInterval` in this way causes the fade timer to fire 60 times per second. I've found that 60 times per second seems to work well in most situations, but you can change this to meet your own needs. Listing 11.13 shows the `fadeVolume` method itself.

Listing 11.13   **SoundManager fadeVolume Method**

```
- (void)fadeVolume:(NSTimer*)aTimer {
        fadeDuration += kFadeInterval;
        if (fadeDuration >= targetFadeDuration) {
                if (timer) {
                        [timer invalidate];
                        timer = NULL;
                }
```

```
                isFading = NO;
                if (stopMusicAfterFade) {
                        [musicPlayer stop];
                        isMusicPlaying = NO;
                }
        } else  {
                currentMusicVolume += fadeAmount;
        }

        if(isMusicPlaying) {
                [musicPlayer setVolume:currentMusicVolume];
        }
}
```

You can see that this method simply increments the `fadeDuration` ivar and checks to see if `fadeDuration` has reached or exceeded the target duration. If so, the timer is destroyed and the music is stopped if required. If the duration has not been reached, the `currentMusicVolume` ivar is adjusted by the `fadeAmount` calculated earlier.

Finally, if music is playing, the volume of the music is set to `currentMusicVolume`.

Music Playlists

In terms of the basic controls, the methods we have just covered are sufficient enough to handle music. The following methods deal with playlists, which is functionality added to the sound manager for a specific reason.

The music that is being used for the main menu, win screen, and lose screen for *Sir Lamorak's Quest* is made up of two tracks. The first track is an introduction, which is then followed by a track that can be looped for as long as necessary. To simplify the playing of one track after another, and to specify that the second track should loop, the playlist feature was added.

Creation of a new playlist is done using the `addToPlaylistNamed:track:` method shown in Listing 11.14.

Listing 11.14   SoundManager addToPlayListName:track: Method

```
- (void)addToPlaylistNamed:(NSString*)aPlaylistName
track:(NSString*)aTrackName {

    NSString *path = [musicLibrary objectForKey:aTrackName];
    if (!path) {
        NSLog(@"WARNING - SoundManager: Track '%@' does not exist in the
            music library and cannot be added to the play list.");
        return;
    }
```

```
    NSMutableArray *playlistTracks = [musicPlaylists
objectForKey:aPlaylistName];

    BOOL newPlayList = NO;

    if (!playlistTracks) {
        newPlayList = YES;
        playlistTracks = [[NSMutableArray alloc] init];
    }

    [playlistTracks addObject:aTrackName];

    [musicPlaylists setObject:playlistTracks forKey:aPlaylistName];

    if (newPlayList)
        [playlistTracks release];
}
```

A playlist is basically an NSMutableArray that contains the name of all the tracks within the musicLibrary that should be played in order. Each playlist dictionary is held within the musicPlaylists dictionary under a key that is the name given to that playlist.

The addToPlaylistNamed:track: method first checks to see if a playlist already exists with the same name. If so, the track specified is added to that playlist and the musicPlaylists dictionary is updated. If no playlist with the specified name is found, a new NSMutableArray is created that will hold that playlists tracks.

Having created a playlist, we need to be able to play its contents. This is done using the startPlaylistNamed: method, shown in Listing 11.15.

Listing 11.15   **SoundManager startPlaylistNamed: Method**

```
- (void)startPlaylistNamed:(NSString*)aPlaylistName {

    NSMutableArray *playlistTracks = [musicPlaylists
        objectForKey:aPlaylistName];

    if (!playlistTracks) {
        NSLog(@"WARNING - SoundManager: No play list exists with the
            name '%@'", aPlaylistName);
        return;
    }

    currentPlaylistName = aPlaylistName;
    currentPlaylistTracks = playlistTracks;
    usePlaylist = YES;
    playlistIndex = 0;
```

```
[self playMusicWithKey:[playlistTracks objectAtIndex:playlistIndex]
    timesToRepeat:0];
}
```

Starting a playlist is very similar to creating one. The method in Listing 11.15 first searches for a playlist with the name provided. If nothing is found in the musicPlaylists dictionary, a message is logged.

If an entry was found, the playlist ivars are set up. The key item here is the currentPlaylistTracks dictionary. This is set to the dictionary pulled back from musicPlaylists for the playlist name provided.

The usePlaylist ivar is used within the SoundManager class to identify if a playlist is being played, and the playlistIndex ivar is used to keep track of the currently playing track's index in the playlist.

The final line of the method actually uses the playMusicWithKey:timesToRepeat: method we saw earlier to actually play the first track in the playlist.

Having started to play tracks from a playlist, we need to move to the next track when the first track is finished. This is handled using an **AVAudioPlayer** delegate method. The method is called audioPlayerDidFinishPlaying:successfully: and is shown in Listing 11.16.

Listing 11.16   **SoundManager audioPlayerDidFinishPlaying:successfully: Method**

```
- (void)audioPlayerDidFinishPlaying:(AVAudioPlayer *)player
successfully:(BOOL)flag {

    if (!flag) {
        NSLog(@"ERROR - SoundManager: Music finished playing due to an
            error.");
        return;
    }

    isMusicPlaying = NO;

    if (usePlaylist) {
        [self playNextTrack];
    }
}
```

Whenever the **AVAudioPlayer** finishes playing a track, this method is called. If the flag ivar is set to NO, the playing stopped due to an error, which is logged. If flag is set to YES, we set the isMusicPlaying ivar to NO; if the usePlaylist flag is set, we call the playNextTrack method, as shown in Listing 11.17.

Listing 11.17   **SoundManager playNextTrack Method**

```
- (void)playNextTrack {
    if (playlistIndex + 1 == [currentPlaylistTracks count]-1 &&
loopLastPlaylistTrack) {
        playlistIndex += 1;
        [self playMusicWithKey:[currentPlaylistTracks
objectAtIndex:playlistIndex]
            timesToRepeat:-1];
    } else if (playlistIndex + 1 < [currentPlaylistTracks count]) {
        playlistIndex += 1;
        [self playMusicWithKey:[currentPlaylistTracks
objectAtIndex:playlistIndex]
            timesToRepeat:0];
    } else if (loopPlaylist) {
        playlistIndex = 0;
        [self playMusicWithKey:[currentPlaylistTracks
objectAtIndex:playlistIndex]
            timesToRepeat:0];
    }
}
```

The `playNextTrack:` method checks to see if more tracks are available in the playlist. If the next track is not the last in the playlist, it simply plays it. If the next track is the last track and the sound manager ivar `loopLastPlaylistTrack` has been set, the last track is played and set to repeat continuously; otherwise, the last track is just played.

If all the tracks have been played but the `loopPlaylist` ivar is set, the `playlistIndex` is set to 0 and the playlist is started again.

Managing the Playlist

Having created and played a playlist, we now need to look at the methods that manage a playlist. Listing 11.18 shows the `removeFromPlaylistNamed:track:` that is used, as you may have guessed already, to remove a track from a playlist.

Listing 11.18   **SoundManager removeFromPlaylistNamed:track:**

```
- (void)removeFromPlaylistNamed:(NSString*)aPlaylistName
track:(NSString*)aTrackName {

    NSMutableArray *playlistTracks = [musicPlaylists
        objectForKey:aPlaylistName];

    if (playlistTracks) {
        int indexToRemove;

        for (int index=0; index < [playlistTracks count]; index++) {
            if ([[playlistTracks objectAtIndex:index]
```

```
            isEqualToString:aTrackName]) {
                indexToRemove = index;
                break;
            }
        }

        [playlistTracks removeObjectAtIndex:indexToRemove];
    }
}
```

Removing a track from a playlist is pretty straightforward. The only trick to watch out for is that you cannot change the contents of an NSDictionary while you are looping through its contents. This is why the removeFromPlaylistName:track: method loops through the playlistTracks dictionary and sets the indexToRemove variable to the index of the track found with a matching name. This track is then removed outside the loop.

The methods needed to remove entire playlists or clear them are shown in Listing 11.19.

Listing 11.19   SoundManager removePlaylistNamed: and clearPlaylistNamed: Methods

```
- (void)removePlaylistNamed:(NSString*)aPlaylistName {
    [musicPlaylists removeObjectForKey:aPlaylistName];
}

- (void)clearPlaylistNamed:(NSString*)aPlaylistName {
    NSMutableArray *playlistTracks = [musicPlaylists
        objectForKey:aPlaylistName];

    if (playlistTracks) {
        [playlistTracks removeAllObjects];
    }
}
```

The removePlaylistNamed: method removes the named playlist from the musicPlaylists dictionary. Removing the playlist in this way causes the NSDictionary instance for that playlist to be released completely. This is why we made sure there were no extra retains on that dictionary in the addToPlaylistNamed:track: method.

Clearing a playlist simply removes all the entries inside that playlist's dictionary.

Music Management Summary

We have covered a number of methods in this last section, all related to the management of music in the sound manager. Although using AVAudioPlayer is not complex, wrapping the methods around its functionality as we have both simplifies how we can use music in the game, as well as provides some useful functionality with limited work.

The next section covers how to manage the sound effects used within the game. For this, we make use of OpenAL, as mentioned earlier in this chapter.

Sound Effect Management

So far, we have covered the features and technology needed to support music within the sound manager. We now look at the sound effect features.

For high-performance, 3D sound, OpenAL is a perfect fit. If, however, you have just a few sound effects and no need for the positional nature of OpenAL, there is no reason you cannot use instances of **AVAudioPlayer** to play those sounds.

Even if you don't want to use the positional features of OpenAL, it's still a good fit for sound effects. Having the listener and sound sources all sharing the same location causes sounds to play as normal with no adjustments made on volume and direction. It's also possible to play up to 32 sounds simultaneously using limited resources, which is another bonus when using OpenAL.

> **Audio Services**
>
> This section would not be complete without mentioning `AudioServices` for playing sounds. If you are going to be playing only a few simple sounds, the `AudioServicesCreateSystemSoundID`, `AudioServicesPlaySystemSound`, and `AudioServicesDisposeSystemSoundID` functions are worth reviewing.
>
> `AudioServices` is a C interface for playing short sounds and invoking vibration, if supported by the device. These services can be used when you have sounds that are less than 30 seconds. The interface doesn't provide any level, positioning, or timing control, but it is very simple to use if you have some kind of simple or user interface sound to play.
>
> This API uses the technique of lazy loading—that is, it doesn't bother doing any setup such as creating sound buffers until you call the function for the first time. This means when you first load a sound, it causes a pause while all the setup is done.
>
> If you want to have multiple sounds playing and more flexibility and control, you should use OpenAL.

As with the music features of the sound manager, a number of functions need to be supported to manage and use sound effects. These include playing, removing, and stopping a sound effect, and the methods are as follows:

- `loadSoundWithKey:soundFile:`
- `playSoundWithKey:`
- `playSoundWithKey:location:`
- `playSoundWithKey:gain:pitch:location:shouldLoop:`
- `stopSoundWithKey:`
- `removeSoundWithKey:`
- `setListenerPosition:`
- `setOrientation:`

Loading Sound Effects

We follow the same order as the music features and look at how to load a sound. Listing 11.20 shows the first part of the loadSoundWithKey:soundFile: method.

Listing 11.20   SoundManager loadSoundWithKey:soundFile: Method (Part 1)

```
- (void)loadSoundWithKey:(NSString*)aSoundKey soundFile:(NSString*)aMusicFile {

    NSNumber *numVal = [soundLibrary objectForKey:aSoundKey];

    if(numVal != nil) {
        NSLog(@"WARNING - SoundManager: Sound key '%@' already exists.",
            aSoundKey);
        return;
    }

    alError = AL_NO_ERROR;
    alGenBuffers(1, &bufferID);

    if((alError = alGetError()) != AL_NO_ERROR) {
        NSLog(@"ERROR - SoundManager: Error generating OpenAL buffer with
            error %x for
            filename %@\n", alError, aMusicFile);
    }

    ALenum format;
    ALsizei size;
    ALsizei frequency;
    ALvoid *data;

    NSBundle *bundle = [NSBundle mainBundle];

    NSString *fileName = [[aMusicFile lastPathComponent]
        stringByDeletingPathExtension];
    NSString *fileType = [aMusicFile pathExtension];
    CFURLRef fileURL = (CFURLRef)[[NSURL fileURLWithPath:[bundle
      pathForResource:fileName
        ofType:fileType]] retain];
```

The real work when loading a sound effect starts when we generate a new buffer using the alGenBuffers command. This is similar to the glGenBuffers command in OpenGL ES. The parameters it takes are very similar, with the first parameter specifying how many buffers you want to generate and the second parameter being the location where the buffer names are written. We load only a single buffer, so we need to generate only a single buffer name.

Having generated a buffer, we then check for any errors that may have occurred. The `alError` variable was set to `AL_NO_ERROR` at the start of the method to make sure that any previous OpenAL errors were reset.

> **Note**
>
> When you query OpenAL for any errors, it returns only the very last error. There may have been a number of errors generated over the previous OpenAL commands, but only the latest one is returned. For this reason, it is important to regularly check for errors so you can identify where—and when—a problem is occurring.
>
> Checking for errors does produce some overhead, so make sure your error-checking is removed from the production code before you ship the app to the App Store for approval.

Next, we set the variables used to store information about the sound file we are loading. These include the `format`, `size`, and `frequency`.

The next four lines of code create a `CFURLRef` that we use to locate the file that contains the sound data. Listing 11.21 shows the remaining code of the `loadSoundWithKey:soundFile:` method.

Listing 11.21   SoundManager loadSoundWithKey:soundFile: Method

```
if (fileURL) {
data = MyGetOpenALAudioData(fileURL, &size, &format, &frequency);
CFRelease(fileURL);

alBufferData(bufferID, format, data, size, frequency);

if((alError = alGetError()) != AL_NO_ERROR) {
    NSLog(@"ERROR - SoundManager: Error attaching audio to
        buffer: %x\n", alError);
}

    free(data);
} else {
    NSLog(@"ERROR - SoundManager: Could not find file '%@.%@'",
        fileName, fileType);
    if (data);
        free(data);
     data = NULL;
}

[soundLibrary setObject:[NSNumber numberWithUnsignedInt:bufferID]
    forKey:aSoundKey];
    NSLog(@"INFO - SoundManager: Loaded sound with key '%@' into
```

```
            buffer '%d'",
        aSoundKey, bufferID);
}
```

We check to make sure that a `fileURL` was returned and then deal with loading the sound data from the file. The `MyGetOpenALAudioData` function is used for this, which is part of the *MyOpenALSupport.c* file. This sample Apple function handles the identification of the data held within the supplied file, such as the size, format, and frequency.

The `data` variable is loaded with the actual sound data from the supplied file, and the `size`, `format`, and `frequency` parameters are loaded with the discovered information from the same file. We're now in a position to actually associate the sound data with the buffer that has been created, using the `alBufferData` command.

alBufferData Versus alBufferDataStaticProc

The `alBufferData` command is used to load the audio data into the buffer. The command specifies the buffer ID along with the format, data, size, and frequency. OpenAL needs this information because the actual sound data itself is just raw data and does not include this information once it is loaded into a buffer.

When you use `alBufferData`, OpenAL becomes responsible for the management of that data for the sound buffer. The contents of our data variable are copied to a location managed by OpenAL. So, once we have performed `alBufferData`, we can release the memory we were using for the data. This makes things super easy for us, as we don't have to worry about managing that data and all the hassle that can be involved.

If you want to manage the buffer data yourself, you can use the `alBufferDataStaticProc` command. This doesn't take a copy of the data, and it is up to you to manage the memory as necessary.

Unless you really need to control the memory of these buffers yourself, I recommend that you stick with `alBufferData`.

After the buffer data has been loaded, a check is performed to see if any errors were raised. You can query the last error reported by OpenAL using the `alGetError` command. If there are no errors, it's time to release the memory that was used when loading the sound data. At this point, OpenAL has its own copy of the sound data that it will manage.

The last task of the method is to add the generated buffer ID to the `soundLibrary` dictionary using the key provided. This enables us to grab the buffer that contains that sound when we want to play it.

Playing Sound Effects

With the sound loaded, we need a way to play it. This is handled by the `playSoundWithKey:gain:pitch:location:shouldLoop:` method, the first part of which is shown in Listing 11.22.

Listing 11.22   **SoundManager playSoundWithKey:gain:pitch:location:shouldLoop: Method (Part 1)**

```
- (NSUInteger)playSoundWithKey:(NSString*)aSoundKey gain:(float)aGain
    pitch:(float)aPitch
    location:(CGPoint)aLocation shouldLoop:(BOOL)aLoop {

    alError = alGetError(); // Clear the error code

    NSNumber *numVal = [soundLibrary objectForKey:aSoundKey];
    if(numVal == nil) return 0;
    NSUInteger bufferID = [numVal unsignedIntValue];
    // Find the next available source
    NSUInteger sourceID;
    sourceID = [self nextAvailableSource];
    // If 0 is returned then no sound sources were available
    if (sourceID == 0) {
        NSLog(@"WARNING - SoundManager: No sound sources available to
            play %@", aSoundKey);
        return 0;
    }
```

Notice that this method takes in a number of parameters. When you play a sound through a sound source, it is possible to individually set the source's gain (volume), pitch, and location, along with parameters such as AL_LOOPING. This method can take those parameters in one hit and configure the sound source as necessary.

For convenience, there are also a couple of methods that take just the sound key, or the key and location. The other values are defaulted in. These can be seen in the *SoundManager.m* file in the *CH11_SLQTSOR* project for this chapter. The method names are as follows:

- playSoundWithKey:
- playSoundWithKey:location:

When the method starts, any OpenAL errors are read using alGetError. A lookup is then done in the soundLibrary dictionary for the key that has been supplied. If nothing is found, the method simply returns.

Next, the sourceID is set to the next available source ID by calling the nextAvailableSource method. This method is shown in Listing 11.23.

Listing 11.23   **SoundManager nextAvailableSource Method**

```
- (NSUInteger)nextAvailableSource {

    NSInteger sourceState;
```

```
    for(NSNumber *sourceNumber in soundSources) {
        alGetSourcei([sourceNumber unsignedIntValue], AL_SOURCE_STATE,
        &sourceState);
        if(sourceState != AL_PLAYING)
            return [sourceNumber unsignedIntValue];
    }
}
```

The `nextAvailableSource` method loops through all the sources that have been added to the `soundSources` dictionary, looking for a source that is not currently playing. As soon as a source is found, its ID is returned to the caller. If no sources are found, 0 is returned.

Depending on your needs, if no available source is found in the first loop, you may want to loop through the sources again, looking for one that is looping. If that fails, you may just want to take the last source from the list. The specifics depend on your needs but could be easily implemented within this method.

Listing 11.24 shows the second part of the `playSoundWithKey:gain:pitch:location:shouldLoop:` method.

Listing 11.24   SoundManager playSoundWithKey:gain:pitch:location:shouldLoop Method (Part 2)

```
    alSourcei(sourceID, AL_BUFFER, 0);

    alSourcei(sourceID, AL_BUFFER, bufferID);

    alSourcef(sourceID, AL_PITCH, aPitch);
    alSourcef(sourceID, AL_GAIN, aGain * fxVolume);

    if(aLoop) {
        alSourcei(sourceID, AL_LOOPING, AL_TRUE);
    } else {
        alSourcei(sourceID, AL_LOOPING, AL_FALSE);
    }

    alSource3f(sourceID, AL_POSITION, aLocation.x, aLocation.y, 0.0f);

    alSourcePlay(sourceID);

    alError = alGetError();
    if(alError != 0) {
        NSLog(@"ERROR - SoundManager: %d", alError);
            return 0;
    }

    return sourceID;
}
```

With the source ID found, the rest of the method deals with configuring that source to play the sound. First, the source is bound to buffer 0, which ensures it is not bound to another sound source (this is similar to binding an OpenGL ES texture to texture ID 0). The source is then bound to the buffer, and the pitch and gain are set. The gain is multiplied by fxVolume, which is a global volume value used to control the overall volume of all sound effects. This enables you to set the volume of individual sound effects and change them all using this global value (for example, using a sound effect's volume slider in a Settings screen).

Notice that most of the source parameters are set using alSourcef. This command takes the source ID as parameter one, the attribute to set as parameter two, and the value to be used as parameter three. The f at the end of the command specifies that the value in parameter three will be a *float*. If it were an i, the value would be an *integer*. As such, 3f specifies that three float values will be used.

With the source now configured, we ask the source to play using alSourcePlay. At this point, OpenAL uses the sound data stored in the buffer we have associated with the source to play the sound. The configuration of the source is used, as well as other environmental effects, such as the distance algorithm.

Having asked the source to play, a check is performed to see if any errors have been reported and the source ID used to play the sound returned to the caller.

> **Note**
>
> During development, it is wise to check for an OpenAL error after every OpenAL command. This helps with tracking down when errors occur. After the code is stable, you can remove all those error checks (or comment them out) since they will affect the performance of your game.

Stopping Sound Effects

To stop playing a sound effect, the stopSoundWithKey: method is used, shown in Listing 11.25.

Listing 11.25   **SoundManager stopSoundWithKey: Method**

```
- (void)stopSoundWithKey:(NSString*)aSoundKey {

    alError = alGetError();
    alError = AL_NO_ERROR;

    NSNumber *numVal = [soundLibrary objectForKey:aSoundKey];

    if(numVal == nil) {
        NSLog(@"WARNING - SoundManager: No sound with key '%@' was found
            so cannot be
            stopped", aSoundKey);
```

```
            return;
    }

    NSUInteger bufferID = [numVal unsignedIntValue];
    NSInteger bufferForSource;
    NSInteger sourceState;
    for(NSNumber *sourceID in soundSources) {
        NSUInteger currentSourceID = [sourceID unsignedIntValue];

        alGetSourcei(currentSourceID, AL_BUFFER, &bufferForSource);

        if(bufferForSource == bufferID) {
            alSourceStop(currentSourceID);
            alSourcei(currentSourceID, AL_BUFFER, 0);
        }
    }

    if((alError = alGetError()) != AL_NO_ERROR)
        NSLog(@"ERROR - SoundManager: Could not stop sound with key '%@'
            got error %x", aSoundKey, alError);
}
```

There are two ways to stop a sound that is playing. The simple way is to use the
`alSourceStop` command and pass in the source ID you want to stop. The more complex
way is to loop through all the sources and stop those that are playing in the buffer you
want to stop.

The first method could be implemented using the source ID passed back from the
`playSoundWithKey:` method. However, if you have the same sound playing on multiple
sound sources, you need to work out which sound sources are playing that particular
sound and stop each one. There are many different ways to accomplish this (for example,
keeping track of the source IDs used to play a sound buffer), but this means you need to
update that list when the sound starts and when it ends. There is no simple method for
knowing when a sound has finished playing in OpenAL, so that's not the approach I took.

The simplest solution was to loop through all the sound sources and query the currently bound buffer. If it matched the one I wanted to stop, I would simply stop the
source and unbind the buffer.

Setting Sound Effect and Listener Position

The final two methods needed to manage sound effects are as follows:

- `setListenerLocation:`
- `setOrientation:`

Listing 11.26 shows these two methods in use.

Listing 11.26   **SoundManager setListenerLocation and setOrientation Methods**

```
- (void)setListenerPosition:(CGPoint)aPosition {
    listenerPosition = aPosition;
    alListener3f(AL_POSITION, aPosition.x, aPosition.y, 0.0f);
}

- (void)setOrientation:(CGPoint)aPosition {
    float orientation[] = {aPosition.x, aPosition.y, 0.0f, 0.0f, 0.0f, 1.0f};
    alListenerfv(AL_ORIENTATION, orientation);
}
```

These methods take a `CGPoint` and use it to set the position and orientation of the listener. These may be simple methods, but they are important. The `setListenerPosition:` method is how we update the location of the listener based on the location of the player, for example.

By moving the listener with the player and having objects in the game, such as doors, play sound at their given location, OpenAL will manage the playback of these sounds to give us a full 3D experience. Sounds that are behind the player will be heard behind the player, as well as sounds getting quieter as you move away from their source.

By making use of these concepts in OpenAL, the sound in *Sir Lamorak's Quest* will create a much better atmosphere for the player.

Handling Sound Interruptions

One area of sound management on the iPhone that can catch people off guard is how to handle sound interruptions—such as when a phone call is received or an alarm goes off.

If a call comes in during game play, we want all music and sounds to be paused while the phone rings. The same is true if an alarm goes off. At the start of this chapter, you learned how to define sound behavior in these circumstances by setting the audio category. This is only half of the answer, though.

Because we are using OpenAL in *Sir Lamorak's Quest*, there is work that needs to be done when a sound is interrupted to ensure that if the phone call or alarm is cancelled, the sound playing in the game resumes.

It's actually not that hard, but if you don't manage the sound interruption, you will end up with no sound at all once the sound interruption has finished, leaving the player confused and in a cone of silence.

As you saw earlier, the **SoundManager** class adopts the AVAudioSessionDelegate protocol. This contains a number of optional methods that enable you to respond to the following changes in state:

- Changes to the audio session category
- Changes to the audio hardware route (such as headset plugged in or unplugged)
- Changes to the audio input
- Changes to the number of audio hardware input or output channels

The methods associated with these are as follows:

- beginInterruption:
- endInterruption:
- categoryChanged:
- inputIsAvailableChanged:
- currentHardwareSampleRateChanged:
- currentHardwareInputNumbrOfChannelsIsChanged:

To deal with interruptions such as phone calls, we need to implement the beginInterruption and endInterruption methods. The implementation used in *Sir Lamorak's Quest* is shown in Listing 11.27.

Listing 11.27   **SoundManager AVAudioSessionDelegate Methods**

```
- (void)beginInterruption {
      [self setActivated:NO];
}

- (void)endInterruption {
      [self setActivated:YES];
}
```

As you can see, these are not complicated and call the setActivated: method when an interruption begins or ends. It's this method shown in Listing 11.28 that deals with making sure the sound is shut down and restarted correctly.

Listing 11.28   **SoundManager setActivated: Method**

```
- (void)setActivated:(BOOL)aState {

   OSStatus result;
```

```
   if(aState) {
       NSLog(@"INFO - SoundManager: OpenAL Active");

           [audioSession setCategory:soundCategory
               error:&audioSessionError];
       if(audioSessionError) {
           NSLog(@"ERROR - SoundManager: Unable to set the audio session
               category");
           return;
       }

           [audioSession setActive:YES error:&audioSessionError];
           if (audioSessionError) {
           NSLog(@"ERROR - SoundManager: Unable to set the audio session
               state to YES with error %d.", result);
           return;
       }

           if (musicPlayer) {
                   [musicPlayer play];
           }

       alcMakeContextCurrent(context);
   } else {
       NSLog(@"INFO - SoundManager: OpenAL Inactive");

        alcMakeContextCurrent(NULL);
   }
}
```

The main responsibility of this method is to make sure that the audio session category is correctly set when reactivating sound, and that the OpenAL context is correctly shutdown and restarted.

If NO is passed to this method, the OpenAL context is set to NULL, causing it to be shut down. When YES is sent to the method, the audio session category is set using the category that was defined during initialization of the SoundManager class. The OpenAL context created during initialization of the class is also made current.

Without these basic steps, you will end up with no sound after an interruption.

Summary

This has been another long chapter with a lot of information covered. Sound can appear to be a daunting subject on the iPhone when you first start to read through the documentation. By reviewing the sound manager for *Sir Lamorak's Quest* and having looked at some of the APIs available under iOS, you should now be more confident to tackle sound and have seen how a reasonably simple wrapper around those APIs can provide a powerful sound manager.

In the next chapter, we examine how elements of *Sir Lamorak's Quest* are implemented rather than looking at the underlying game engine. Chapter 12, "User Input," deals with the handling of touches by the player. It covers how a touch is registered using `UITouch`, and how this information is made available inside *Sir Lamorak's Quest*.

12

User Input

This chapter covers capturing user input for use in *Sir Lamorak's Quest*. For any game to work, there needs to be some kind of input from the player. This could be simply moving a game piece on a board game, selecting options, or moving a player around a 3D environment.

Until the arrival of the iPhone, most handheld consoles had one or more joypad controls built into the device, along with a number of buttons. Input from these would be processed by the game to identify what the player wants to do. There were some devices that also had basic touch capability using a stylus of some type, but this was not normally the primary input device for the player.

The iPhone introduced two unique methods for interacting with the device: multi-touch (without the need for a stylus) and the accelerometer. With touch, the player's finger becomes the main input mechanism by tapping, sliding, or gesturing one or more fingers onscreen. The accelerometer allows the player to tilt and move the iPhone to provide input. This has been used in many different ways, such as using the iPhone as a steering wheel, or shaking the device to shake a dice. Measuring how the iPhone is being moved has also been enhanced with iPhone 4 with the inclusion of a gyroscope, making it possible to calculate the iPhone 4's position relative to the person holding it much more accurately.

This chapter reviews both touch and accelerometer input, but the focus will be on touch input, as this is the core input mechanism used in *Sir Lamorak's Quest*.

User Input Project

The project accompanying this chapter, called *CH12_SLQTSOR*, demonstrates how to use touch to implement a joypad. It has become common to see joypads implemented in iPhone games. Although there are other unique forms of input, such as gestures or the accelerometer, the joypad is one of the most recognizable control mechanisms.

One big advantage of the iPhone is that the joypad is a virtual control; it doesn't need a fixed shape, size, or location. One example of where this is useful is in dealing with left- or right-handed players. Being able to move the joypad based on user preference allows the player to select his dominant hand. Figure 12.1 shows the location of the joypad onscreen.

Figure 12.1   iPhone Simulator running the
CH12_SLQTSOR project.

This project is very basic, but it shows the building blocks necessary to introduce touch into your game. The joypad is a good mechanism to control a game such as *Sir Lamorak's Quest*, but you should not feel limited to this. It's always a good idea to think hard about how your game will be controlled, and I encourage you to experiment with new and unique ways to employ both touch and accelerometer controls into your game.

> **Note**
>
> As mentioned earlier, the accelerometer is not used in *Sir Lamorak's Quest*. However, this sample project does demonstrate how to read accelerometer data and use this to move the player.
>
> Also note that this project mixes OpenGL ES and UIKit controls in the same view. Mixing UIKit and OpenGL ES can speed up development. Being able to make use of all the UIButton features for example and just skin the button to match the game is a great way of providing the player with a familiar control and its behavior, although it may have been skinned to match your games look and feel.
>
> Always make sure that you don't mix too much UIKit content on top of your OpenGL ES view. This can introduce performance issues on older hardware.

Introduction to User Input

Handling user touches is fundamental to the iPhone. Without the ability to recognize one or more touches on the screen, you would not be able to interact with the iPhone, essentially making it an attractive paperweight.

Because of this, Apple has provided a framework that enables you to capture and process touch events. We see throughout this chapter how this framework and the events generated can be used to control a game.

We will also briefly see how accelerometer data can be read and processed, providing a second mechanism to interact with a game.

Touch Events

To get an understanding of the overall touch framework on the iPhone, it is worth reading Apple's *iPhone Application Programming Guide*.[1] This is included in the SDK documentation and has a section on event handling.

The iPhone currently supports two types of events, as follows:

- Touch events
- Motion events

These events are all instances of the `UIEvent` class. As a user event takes place (for example, fingers touching and moving across the screen), the system continually sends event objects to the current application registered to handle these events. These event objects contain important information, such as a touch's state and information on specific touches that have been identified (for example, their location). Four key methods are used to process touch events:

- `touchesBegan:withEvent:`
- `touchesMoved:withEvent:`
- `touchesEnded:withEvent:`
- `touchesCancelled:withEvent:`

To handle touch events, your class needs to be part of the `UIResponder` chain and implement one or more of these methods. These events contain the logic necessary to process the touch, such as tracking movement over a joypad.

Each of these methods represents a different phase of a touch event, which can be seen in their name (that is, `touchesBegan`, `touchesMoved`, `touchesEnded`, and `touchesCancelled`). Figure 12.2 shows the phases that a single touch can have.

---

[1] Apple's *iPhone Application Programming Guide* can be found online at **developer.apple.com/iphone/ library/documentation/iPhone/Conceptual/iPhoneOSProgrammingGuide/ iPhoneAppProgrammingGuide.pdf**.

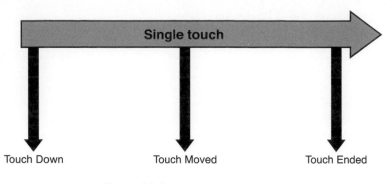

Figure 12.2   Single-touch phases.

Events can also contain multiple touches. Figure 12.3 shows how touch phases can be tracked on multiple touches at the same time.

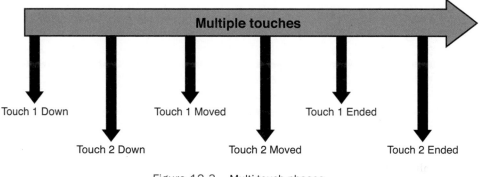

Figure 12.3   Multi-touch phases.

For each of the methods already mentioned, data is passed in that allows you to identify all the touches that have occurred:

```
- (void)touchesBegan:(NSSet*)touches withEvent:(UIEvent*)event
```

The first data item sent is an NSSet. This set contains all the UITouch objects that have been identified by the iOS for the starting phase of the event. The starting phase means that these touches did not previously exist (that is, a new touch has been detected on-screen).

If a touch was already identified but the location of the touch changed, the touchesMoved method is called and details of the touch that has moved are provided. As you would expect, the touchesEnded method is called when a touch ends and the user's finger is lifted from the screen.

By now, you're probably wondering when the `touchesCancelled` method is called, as there is no obvious way to cancel a touch. This method is called if the system itself has to cancel a touch (for example, an event, such as an incoming phone call, occurs that causes the application to no longer be active or the view is removed). A view being removed could occur if a low memory warning is received or a text message is received, causing another view to pop up.

Processing Touch Events

Having received a touch event, the next step is to take that touch and use it to make something happen in the game. This could be moving the player or simulating a button press. One of the most important pieces of information, therefore, is the touch's location. For example, you'll need to identify if the touch happened on the joypad or on a button.

Getting the location of the touch is really simple. `UITouch` has a method called `locationInView:`, which enables you to obtain the coordinates of the touch. The method accepts a `UIView` reference that specifies the coordinate system in which you want the touch located.

> **Note**
>
> If a custom view is handling the touch, you should specify `self`.

Inside the game engine for *Sir Lamorak's Quest*, we have a concept of **AbstractScene** that we reviewed in Chapter 4, "The Game Loop." This supports different scenes for different aspects of the game, such as the main menu or the main game.

To process touch events, we need to implement the touch methods inside a class that is part of the **UIResponder** chain. This normally means the methods are implemented in a class that inherits from **UIView**. The **UIView** class is a subclass of **UIResponder**, and therefore receives touch events. **UIViewController**, along with other controllers, are not and thus would not receive touch events.

The **AbstractScene** class is not an eventual subclass of **UIResponder** and will therefore also not receive touch events. Because we need to process touch events differently in each of the game's scenes, we need to get the touch events pushed into the class responsible for each scene, such as the **GameScene** class.

The only **UIView** we have implemented in *Sir Lamorak's Quest* is **EAGLView**. This is the main view of the game and inherits from **UIView**.

Listing 12.1 shows the touch methods implemented within **EAGLView** inside Chapter 12's project, *CH12_SLQTSOR*.

Listing 12.1   **EAGLView Touch Methods**

```
- (void)touchesBegan:(NSSet*)touches withEvent:(UIEvent*)event {

  [[sharedGameController currentScene] touchesBegan:touches withEvent:event
      view:self];
}

- (void)touchesMoved:(NSSet*)touches withEvent:(UIEvent*)event {
  [[sharedGameController currentScene] touchesMoved:touches withEvent:event
      view:self];
}

- (void)touchesEnded:(NSSet*)touches withEvent:(UIEvent*)event {
  [[sharedGameController currentScene] touchesEnded:touches withEvent:event
      view:self];
}

- (void)touchesCancelled:(NSSet*)touches withEvent:(UIEvent*)event {
  [[sharedGameController currentScene] touchesCancelled:touches
      withEvent:event view:self];
}
```

When the game loop was implemented in Chapter 4, we created a `GameController` class. This class was responsible for knowing which scenes were available and for keeping track of the current scene. Using this, we can now easily pass touch events registered inside `EAGLView` to the current scene.

Listing 12.1 shows the four touch methods and how they call the touch methods inside the class identified as the `currentScene`. The methods implemented inside each scene are very similar to the touch methods inside `EAGLView`, except that they accept a third parameter. This parameter is a reference to `EAGLView` itself and can be used in the `locationInView:` method we saw earlier.

The methods inside `EAGLView` are not responsible for any processing at all. They simply pass details of the touch events to the current scene. This allows the current scene to then process these touch events as necessary.

The `touchesBegan` Phase

After receiving the touch events, the scene's next job is to process the touches. Listing 12.2 shows the `touchesBegan:withEvent:view:` method inside the `GameScene` class of the *CH12_SLQTSOR* project.

Listing 12.2   **GameScene touchesBegan:withEvent:view: Method**

```
- (void)touchesBegan:(NSSet*)touches withEvent:(UIEvent*)event
   view:(UIView*)aView {

   for (UITouch *touch in touches) {
       CGPoint originalTouchLocation = [touch locationInView:aView];

       CGPoint touchLocation = [sharedGameController
           adjustTouchOrientationForTouch:originalTouchLocation];

       if (CGRectContainsPoint(joypadBounds, touchLocation) &&
           !isJoypadTouchMoving) {
           isJoypadTouchMoving = YES;
           joypadTouchHash = [touch hash];
           break;
       }
   }
}
```

Once inside the method, a loop runs through all touches in the `touches` set. The location of each touch is retrieved using the `locationInView:` method. The location is based upon the `UIView` coordinates, which are not the same as the OpenGL ES coordinates. In OpenGL ES, the `y` coordinate goes from `0` at the bottom of the screen (in portrait mode) to `480` at the top of the screen. Within a `UIView`, the `y` coordinate is reversed.

To handle this, a call is made to the `adjustTouchOrientationForTouch:` method inside the **GameContoller** class. This custom method currently adjusts the `y` coordinate and returns a corrected `CGPoint`. In Chapter 13, "The Game Interface," you see how this method is extended to adjust the location of touches if the orientation of the phone has been changed (for example, from landscape left to landscape right).

The location of the `touch` is then checked against the bounds of a `CGRect`. Using a `CGRect` makes it really simple to check for points inside a rectangle using the `CGRectContainsPoint` function. The rectangle needs to be big enough to easily pick up a touch at the center of the joypad, but small enough not to be accidentally touched or confused with another rectangle.

If the point is within the rectangle and no other touch has been detected in the joypad, the `isJoypadTouchMoving` flag is set to `YES` and the `joypadTouchHash` value is set.

Tracking Touches Between Phases

When implementing an onscreen joypad, it is necessary to track touches between phases (for example, once a touch has been registered on the joypad, we need to track where that touch moves to calculate the direction the player wants to move). The initial touch is handled by the `touchesBegan` method, and movement is handled by the `touchesMoved` method.

The `NSSet` of touches in the `touchesMoved` method contains all current touches, but not necessarily in the same order as they were in the `touchesBegan` method. As such, you'll need another way to identify a touch between phases because you can't simply use the touch's location within the set.

To handle this, we grab the `hash` of the touch that has been identified as touching the joypad. The `hash` is a unique number that stays with a touch through its entire lifecycle. This enables you to identify a touch using its `hash` rather than its location in the `NSSet`.

With the touches `hash` value recorded, we break from the loop because we are not interested in processing any more touches in this example. If you were tracking multiple touches, you would not break from the loop, so you could continue to process each touch.

Note

To track more than one touch at a time, you need to make sure that the view has been set to handle multiple touches. Inside the *CH12_SLQTSOR* project, this is done inside the *SLQTSORAppDelegate.m* file. In that file, you see the following line in the `applicationDidFinishLaunching:` method:

```
[glView setMultipleTouchEnabled:YES];
```

glView is an instance of `EAGLView`. If `setMultipleTouchEnabled:` is set to `NO`, the view will be sent only the first touch event.

The `touchesMoved` Phase

After the player has touched the joypad, he will start to move his finger in the direction he wants the player to move. This generates events that are sent to the `touchesMoved:withEvent:` method. Listing 12.3 shows the `touchesMoved:withEvent:view` method inside `GameScene`, which handles these events.

Listing 12.3   GameScene touchesMoved:withEvent:view Method

```
- (void)touchesMoved:(NSSet*)touches withEvent:(UIEvent*)event view:(UIView*)aView {

    for (UITouch *touch in touches) {

        if ([touch hash] == joypadTouchHash && isJoypadTouchMoving) {

            CGPoint originalTouchLocation = [touch
                locationInView:aView];
```

```
        CGPoint touchLocation = [sharedGameController
        adjustTouchOrientationForTouch:originalTouchLocation];

        float dx = (float)joypadCenter.x - (float)touchLocation.x;
        float dy = (float)joypadCenter.y - (float)touchLocation.y;

        // Manhattan Distance
        joypadDistance = abs(touchLocation.x - joypadCenter.x) +
            abs(touchLocation.y - joypadCenter.y);

        directionOfTravel = atan2(dy, dx);
    }
  }
}
```

This method works in a similar way to the `touchesBegan` method. It loops through the set of touches that were passed in, and a check is made is to see if the hash of the current touch matches the hash of the touch registered inside the joypad rectangle. It also checks to make sure that the `isJoypadTouchMoving` flag is set. This flag is used to make sure we don't start tracking two touches in the joypad; we only want to handle one. If these conditions are true for the current touch, we can start to process it.

So, what does processing really mean for our joypad? Well, first of all, we want to get the touch's location and then adjust it to make sure it's using the same coordinates as OpenGL ES.

We then want to work out the direction in which the touch has moved from the center of the joypad. Determining the angle from the joypad's center to the touch gives us an angle and therefore a direction.

The `dx` and `dy` values are calculated first using the joypad's center and touch locations. Using these new values, the `atan2` function calculates the angle of the touch from the center of the joypad.

The distance of the touch from the center is also calculated. The current distance calculation uses the *Manhattan distance* algorithm,[2] which is good enough for our needs with the joypad.

The reason for getting the distance is that we can use this to calculate the speed at which the player wants to move. The smaller the distance from the center of the joypad, the slower the player moves; the greater the distance, the faster the player moves. This gives the joypad a much more realistic feel than just a binary moving or not moving.

---

[2] Manhattan Distance, as defined on Wikipedia: **en.wikipedia.org/wiki/Manhattan_distance**.

The `directionOfTravel` and `joypadDistance` values are used within the scenes `updateSceneWithDelta:` method. This is basically linking the joypad movement to the movement of the player.

The `touchesEnded` Phase

At some point, the player will either lift his finger from the screen, or slide it off. When this happens, the `touchesEnded:withEvent` method is triggered. Listing 12.4 shows the `touchesEnded:withEvent:view` method.

Listing 12.4   GameScene touchesEnded:withEvent:view Method

```
- (void)touchesEnded:(NSSet*)touches withEvent:(UIEvent*)event
    view:(UIView*)aView {

    for (UITouch *touch in touches) {
        if ([touch hash] == joypadTouchHash) {
            isJoypadTouchMoving = NO;
            joypadTouchHash = 0;
            directionOfTravel = 0;
            joypadDistance = 0;
            return;
        }
    }
}
```

As with the previous methods, we loop through the touches, looking for one that has a hash that matches the joypad touch's hash. If a match is found, it means the player has lifted his finger from the joypad. That being the case, we set the `isJoypadTouchMoving` flag to `NO` and clear the `joypadTouchHash`, `directionOfTravel`, and `joypadDistance` variables.

Processing Taps

So far, we have covered how to deal with touches and movement, but what if you wanted to capture an event when a player taps on the screen? This is actually really easy, because each touch event has a `tapCount` property. This property captures how many times the player has tapped the screen in the same place.

Listing 12.5 shows the `touchesBegan:withEvent:view` method from the `GameScene` class, but this time, a check has been added to the end of the `for` loop.

Listing 12.5   GameScene touchesBegan:withEvent:view Method Handling Taps

```
- (void)touchesBegan:(NSSet*)touches withEvent:(UIEvent*)event view:(UIView*)aView {
```

```
for (UITouch *touch in touches) {
    CGPoint originalTouchLocation = [touch locationInView:aView];

    CGPoint touchLocation = [sharedGameController
        adjustTouchOrientationForTouch:originalTouchLocation];

    if (CGRectContainsPoint(joypadBounds, touchLocation) &&
        !isJoypadTouchMoving) {
        isJoypadTouchMoving = YES;
        joypadTouchHash = [touch hash];
        continue;
    }

        if (touch.tapCount == 2) {
            NSLog(@"Double Tap at X:%f Y:%f", touchLocation.x,
                touchLocation.y);
        }
}
}
```

The code we have added checks the `tapCount` of each touch and prints a message to the log if a double tap is found.

Single taps would mean you just check for a `tapCount` of 1. If a single tap is found, you could then perform checks to see if the tap happened inside a specified `CGRect` and perform actions as necessary (for example, a button press).

When creating your own GUI controls, you need to consider how the UIKit controls work. Introducing controls that work differently to the normal controls on the iPhone can be confusing to the user. An example of this is the button tap. When you tap a UIKit button, the tap is not registered until you lift your finger off the button. If the user touches a button by mistake, he can slide his finger off the button and then lift it from another area of the screen to stop the button touch from registering.

When implementing the touch functionality within *Sir Lamorak's Quest*, this same behavior was copied into the OpenGL ES buttons created. Placing the check for a touch in the `touchesEnded` method enables us to check where the touch was when it ended. If the user's finger is not within the bounds of a button, no button press is carried out.

Chapter 13 also demonstrates how touches can be used to handle button presses as a way to interact with the game's main menu, as well as other game items, such as the inventory.

With this in mind, it does make sense to review the use of UIKit controls on top of your OpenGL ES view to handle the GUI elements e.g. a *UIButton* that is skinned to look the same as your game. Skinning the button could be a simple as using an Image for the button which looks like other elements in your game, or actually sub-classing *UIButton* and creating your own drawRect: method that can render whatever you want to the screen.

Accelerometer Events

The accelerometer is a great feature on the iPhone, and many games use this as a mechanism for player control. This section briefly covers how you can get information from the accelerometer. Although not used in *Sir Lamorak's Quest*, this book would not be complete without covering how to access the accelerometer.

The first thing you'll need to do is enable the accelerometer, which is done in Chapter 12's sample project using the `GameController` class. If you look inside the *GameController.m* file and the `initGameController` method, you see the following two lines that set up the accelerometer:

```
[[UIAccelerometer sharedAccelerometer] setUpdateInterval:1.0 / 100.0];
[[UIAccelerometer sharedAccelerometer] setDelegate:currentScene];
```

The first command sets the interval. This specifies how many times per second the delegate method for the accelerometer is called. In this example, the interval is set to 100 times per second.

The second command sets the class used as the delegate. This class must implement the `UIAccelerometerDelegate` protocol. We want to have the current scene process the accelerometer events so the **AbstractScene** class has been updated to implement this protocol.

This is a formal protocol, so the delegate method must be implemented. This has been done inside the **GameScene** class, as shown in Listing 12.6.

Listing 12.6   **GameScene accelerometer:didAccelerate: Method**

```
- (void)accelerometer:(UIAccelerometer *)accelerometer
didAccelerate:(UIAcceleration
    *)acceleration {

  accelerationValues[0] = acceleration.x * 0.1f + accelerationValues[0] *
      (1.0 - 0.1f);
  accelerationValues[1] = acceleration.y * 0.1f + accelerationValues[1] *
      (1.0 - 0.1f);
  accelerationValues[2] = acceleration.z * 0.1f + accelerationValues[2] *
      (1.0 - 0.1f);
}
```

This method receives two parameters. The first is the application-wide accelerometer object and the second provides the most recent acceleration data. This data can be used to identify how the iPhone has been moved and then used to adjust the movement of the player.

The sample project's implementation employs a very basic low-pass filter on the data to remove sharp accelerations due to say the jostling of the device. Much more sophisticated filters are available, and some of these can be seen in the `AccelerometerGraph` project included within the iPhone SDK.

Having captured the accelerometer data, we now have to use it. Listing 12.7 shows the scenes `updateSceneWithDelta:` method.

Listing 12.7   **GameScene updateSceneWithDelta: Method**

```
- (void)updateSceneWithDelta:(float)aDelta {

    if (!sharedGameController.eaglView.uiSwitch.on) {
        knightLocation.x -= (aDelta * (20 * joypadDistance)) *
            cosf(directionOfTravel);
        knightLocation.y -= (aDelta * (20 * joypadDistance)) *
            sinf(directionOfTravel);
    }

    if (sharedGameController.eaglView.uiSwitch.on) {
        knightLocation.x += aDelta * (accelerationValues[0] * 1000);
        knightLocation.y += aDelta * (accelerationValues[1] * 1000);
    }

    if (knightLocation.x < 0)
        knightLocation.x = 0;
    if (knightLocation.x > 320)
        knightLocation.x = 320;
    if (knightLocation.y < 0)
        knightLocation.y = 0;
    if (knightLocation.y > 480)
        knightLocation.y = 480;
}
```

This method checks to see which form of input is being used. The .xib file, called *MainWindow.xib*, was edited using Interface Builder to add a `UISwitch` and `UILabel` to the view. `UISwitch` was then wired up to the `uiSwitch` ivar inside the **EAGLView** class. Figure 12.4 shows the change being made in Interface Builder.

Figure 12.4   Interface Builder linking the UISwitch control to EAGLView.

Having linked the switch and exposed it as a property in **EAGLView**, we can then use that property to check if the switch is on or off. This can be seen in the code in Listing 12.7, where we check the `sharedGameController.eaglView.uiSwitch.on` value.

If the accelerometer is off, the joypad information is used to move the player; otherwise, the accelerometer information is used.

Summary

This has been a small, but important, chapter. A game that has no way for players to interact with it is pretty useless. The framework and examples we have been through in this chapter provide the basis for how player control is implemented in *Sir Lamorak's Quest* and for how it could be implemented in other projects.

The accelerometer is an interesting control method. When prototyping *Sir Lamorak's Quest*, the accelerometer was originally used to control Sir Lamorak. However, feedback from the beta testers proved that it was awkward to control the game by tilting the device. Reflections on the screen and not being able to clearly see what was going on, along with the control being either too sensitive or sluggish, lead me to move to an onscreen joypad for control.

Chapter 13 looks at how the interface for *Sir Lamorak's Quest* is created. It reviews GUIs made using OpenGL ES for the main menu and main game, as well as the `UIViews` used for things like credits, instructions, high scores, and settings. Chapter 13 also covers how *Sir Lamorak's Quest* handles changes in the iPhone's orientation and how the interface is rotated to deal with a new orientation.

13

The Game Interface

This chapter covers the interface elements of *Sir Lamorak's Quest*, including how the different interfaces were built and implemented. There are two types of interface in *Sir Lamorak's Quest*. The first type is those built using OpenGL ES, such as the main menu and main game interfaces. The second type is those built using UIKit controls, such as `UISlider` and `UIButton` inside their own `UIView`. These interfaces, for example, are used for displaying and handling the settings within the game, such as volume and joypad position.

This chapter also covers how these interfaces handle rotation of the device. This is not always as easy as it sounds, so we review the approach taken to handle this within *Sir Lamorak's Quest*.

Game Interface Project

The project we review throughout this chapter has taken a big leap from the previous chapter. The project for Chapter 13 is called *SLQTSOR* and is the complete game project for *Sir Lamorak's Quest*.

At this point, we have covered all the key building blocks and are now reviewing the specific implementations for the game. Trying to pick apart the game and show these elements in isolation would be complex and not in context. By reviewing the complete game, however, we can see how the interface items have been implemented in the context of the completed game.

Figure 13.1 shows the iPhone Simulator running the *SLQTSOR* project. The interface being displayed is the Settings view, where the player can set the music and FX volume along with the location of the joypad.

When you run this project, you arrive at the Games main menu. Selecting the *High Score*, *Instructions*, and *Information* buttons brings up `UIViews` that are used to display that information. Pressing the gear icon in the bottom-left corner of the screen shows the *Settings* view, as seen in Figure 13.1.

Figure 13.1   iPhone Simulator running the SLQTSOR project.

With one of these views visible, rotating the iPhone causes the views to rotate and maintain the correct orientation to the player. You'll also notice that the main menu in the background flips to maintain its orientation. This is also true when you are playing the game.

As you look through the *SLQTSOR* project, you see a great deal of new code—code that we have not reviewed yet. This chapter and the rest of this book look at this new code and how it's used to implement the features we need for *Sir Lamorak's Quest*.

Going through every line of code would take too long, but we cover all the important areas you need to understand. The remaining code is commented, and it should be reasonably easy to see what is being done and why.

OpenGL ES Interface

We start by looking at how the OpenGL ES interfaces have been created. There is no magic to this, and it simply uses techniques that we have already reviewed. The big difference between an OpenGL ES interface and something using the UIKit is that you have to build everything in OpenGL ES from scratch.

With UIKit, you get sliders and buttons that you can simply add to a view and start using. They handle the look and feel, as well as the actions that the controls provide. With OpenGL ES, you need to create the interface and controls manually using your own graphics and code for handling events.

You can make this as simple or as complex as you want. A simple button would consist of an image that is rendered to the screen and a CGRect that defines the bounds of the button. When a touch ends, the touch location is then checked against each button's defined bounds. If the touch occurred inside a button's bounds, you carry out the actions of that button.

If you wanted to make a more comprehensive control, you could create a new button class, for example, that would contain all the processing logic needed for your buttons.

This class would be able to take care of rendering and identifying if a touch landed within the buttons bounds using some kind of visual highlight on the button.

What you implement is really down to the requirements for your game. It is amazing, though, what can be created using simple techniques.

The following sections cover the three elements that are needed to handle interface controls:

- Rendering
- Defining bounds
- Handling touches

Rendering the Interface

Rendering the interface in OpenGL ES is no different from actually rendering the game itself and any other OpenGL ES image. You design the graphics that you want to represent your buttons or other interface elements and then render these to the screen as normal.

Figure 13.2 shows the sprite sheet used for the main menu of *Sir Lamorak's Quest*.

Figure 13.2   Sprite sheet used in *Sir Lamorak's Quest* main menu.

These images are used to generate the floating clouds, background, and the menu post. For the menu, I decided to have a fixed image for the majority of the options. These options never move and are always displayed, so having a single image was a simple solution. The *Resume Game* button appears only when there is a game to resume, so this needed to be a separate element in the sprite sheet. You can see that the *Resume Game* button has several chains on top. This makes the menu option look like it is hanging from the other panels on the signpost.

You will also notice that there is a logo and gear image in the sprite sheet. These images are both used as buttons. When the logo graphic is tapped, the credits for the game appear, and the gear displays the settings.

Inside the sample project is a group called Game Scenes. Inside this group are two further groups: Menu and Game. Inside the Menu group is the class that implements the main menu called *MenuScene.m*.

This class inherits from **AbstractScene** and contains all the logic and rendering code for the menu. The rendering code can be found in the renderScene method, shown in Listing 13.1.

Listing 13.1   **MenuScene renderScene Method**

```
- (void)renderScene {

    [background renderAtPoint:CGPointMake(0, 0)];

    for (int index=0; index < 7; index++) {
        Image *cloud = [clouds objectAtIndex:index];
        [cloud renderAtPoint:(CGPoint)cloudPositions[index]];
    }

    [castle renderAtPoint:CGPointMake(249, 0)];
    [logo renderAtPoint:CGPointMake(25, 0)];
    [settings renderAtPoint:CGPointMake(450, 0)];
    [menu renderAtPoint:CGPointMake(0, 0)];

    if ([sharedGameController resumedGameAvailable]) {
        [menuButton renderAtPoint:CGPointMake(71, 60)];
    }

    if (state == kSceneState_TransitionIn ||
        state == kSceneState_TransitionOut ||
        state == kSceneState_Idle) {
        [fadeImage renderAtPoint:CGPointMake(0, 0)];
    }

    [sharedImageRenderManager renderImages];

    if (SCB) {
        drawBox(startButtonBounds);
        drawBox(scoreButtonBounds);
        drawBox(instructionButtonBounds);
        drawBox(resumeButtonBounds);
        drawBox(logoButtonBounds);
        drawBox(settingsButtonBounds);
    }
}
```

This is basic code, and you should recognize it from what has already been covered in the previous chapters. The core elements in this method deal with rendering the clouds that move in different directions. This is handled by the `for` loop at the start of the method.

This method also checks the current state of the scene to decide on what needs to be rendered. The **AbstractScene** class has a property called `state` that can have a number of different values associated with it. These values are defined as an `enum` in the *Global.h* file inside the `Global Headers` group and are shown in Listing 13.2.

Listing 13.2   Scene States as Defined in the Global.h File

```
enum {
    kSceneState_Idle,
    kSceneState_Credits,
    kSceneState_Loading,
    kSceneState_TransitionIn,
    kSceneState_TransitionOut,
    kSceneState_TransportingIn,
    kSceneState_TransportingOut,
    kSceneState_Running,
    kSceneState_Paused,
    kSceneState_GameOver,
    kSceneState_SaveScore,
    kSceneState_GameCompleted
};
```

Within the `renderScene` method, we check to see if the state of the scene is `kSceneState_TransitionIn` or `kSceneState_TransitionOut`. If either of these states is set, the `fadeImage` is rendered. The `fadeImage` is a single black pixel that is scaled up to the size of the screen. This means that we can render an entire black image over the screen without the need for an image the size of the actual screen, which would use more memory.

The `fadeImage` is rendered above everything else when we need to fade in or out of this scene. As fading takes place, the alpha value of this image is changed, causing the underlying images that are being rendered to show through. This provides a very simple way of fading the entire screen.

As discussed in Chapter 4, "The Game Loop," the rendering and logic are handled in separate methods. The state of the scene is used in both the render and update methods to make sure that the correct actions are taking place based on the state.

If you look at the `updateWithDelta:` method inside *MenuScene.m*, you see that a switch statement has been used to check the state of the scene. The scene state determines which actions are carried out. This method is employed throughout *Sir Lamorak's Quest* to manage state within a scene.

Defining Button Bounds

Inside the *MenuScene.h* file, a number of CGRect variables have been created. These are shown in Listing 13.3.

Listing 13.3   **CGRect Variables Defined in MenuScene.h**

```
CGRect startButtonBounds;
CGRect resumeButtonBounds;
CGRect scoreButtonBounds;
CGRect instructionButtonBounds;
CGRect logoButtonBounds;
CGRect settingsButtonBounds;
```

These variables hold the bounds defined for each of our buttons, and each is initialized within the `init` method inside *MenuScene.m*, as shown in Listing 13.4.

Listing 13.4   **Initialization of Button Bounds**

```
startButtonBounds = CGRectMake(74, 235, 140, 50);
   scoreButtonBounds = CGRectMake(71, 178, 135, 50);
   instructionButtonBounds = CGRectMake(74, 120, 144, 50);
   resumeButtonBounds = CGRectMake(74, 61, 142, 50);
   logoButtonBounds = CGRectMake(15, 0, 50, 50);
   settingsButtonBounds = CGRectMake(430, 0, 50, 50);
```

With the scene elements being rendered on the screen, it was a matter of working out where each button on the signpost was located and then defining the bounds for that button using those coordinates. The coordinates were worked out inside of a graphics package. Each screen was laid out using the images from the game inside an image the same size as the iPhone screen. Once items were where I wanted them, I was able to take the coordinates of each object and use them in the game code.

Handling Touches

With the interface buttons being rendered and their bounds defined, we can move onto processing touches.

The methods used to process touches were covered in Chapter 12, "User Input." Each time a touch ends, we need to check if the touch occurred in any of the buttons bounds and then carry out actions associated with that button.

The `touchesEnded:` method is similar to the examples from the last chapter. The key difference is that we are only interested in single touches. This means that we don't need to loop through all touches that are sent to the method; we just take any object from the `UIEvent` using the following command.

```
UITouch *touch = [[event touchesForView:aView] anyObject];
```

This takes any touch from the set of touches that may exist and is therefore not an approach to be used if you want to deal with multiple touches together. In this situation, you would need to loop through each touch, processing it as you go.

From the touch, we then grab its location and adjust the coordinates based on the orientation of the iPhone. (We review the orientation code a little later.)

Having obtained the location of the touch, we then check the state of the scene. We want touches to be processed only while the scene is running, not transitioning in or out. If the scene's state is running, checks are made against the touch location and each button's bounds. Listing 13.5 shows the check performed on the start button's bounds.

Listing 13.5   **Checking The Bounds Of The Start Button**

```
if (CGRectContainsPoint(startButtonBounds, touchLocation)) {
    [sharedSoundManager playSoundWithKey:@"interfaceTouch"];
    state = kSceneState_TransitionOut;
    sharedGameController.shouldResumeGame = NO;
    alpha = 0;
    return;
}
```

We are using the `CGRectContainsPoint` function to check if the touch was inside the button's bounds. If so, a sound effect is played and a number of variables are modified.

The scene's state is changed to `kSceneState_TransitionOut`, which causes the menu to fade out, and the game scene to fade in. The code that handles the transition from the main menu to game can be found inside the `updateWithDelta:` method.

As part of transitioning to the main game, the iPhone's idle timer is disabled using the following command:

```
[[UIApplication sharedApplication] setIdleTimerDisabled:YES];
```

This timer causes the screen to dim during inactivity, which can be annoying during game play.

> **Tip**
>
> Apple recommends that you enable the idle timer when displaying items such as the main menu, settings, or high score screens in your game. Having the screen fade to save battery while these items are displayed is good practice. However, having them fade during game play is not so helpful.
>
> With touches being made on the screen, the timer does not normally dim the screen during game play. However, if you are using the accelerometer to control a game with no touches, the timer will assume inactivity and dim the screen, eventually putting the iPhone to sleep.

Handling touches is exactly the same for the other buttons on the main menu. The only difference is the code that is executed when a button is pressed.

Visualizing Boundaries

Setting up the boundaries for buttons and other elements does sound easy, but I found that identifying where boundaries were during testing was not so easy. I eventually came up with a simple method that let me visualize the boundaries for interface items, allowing me to easily see where they were onscreen. This was also extended to in game entities as well so that I could see where collision bounds were for objects within the game. Figure 13.3 shows the main game interface with boundary information switched on.

Figure 13.3   In-game screenshot showing the debug boundary information for touch areas.

The green boxes shown in Figure 13.3 represent the boundaries of the elements on the screen. This helped in fine-tuning those boundaries.

One important lesson was to make sure that the touch areas for interface items are large enough to be easily touched. An example of this can be seen with the Settings button in the bottom-right corner of the screen. The boundary for this item is large compared to the size of the image. This helps to ensure that when the user taps in the lower-right corner, the Settings appear.

Adding code to visualize these boundaries was very straightforward. I created a new class called `Primitives` and implemented a C function called `drawBox`. You can find the code for this inside the sample project inside the *Game Engine > Primitives* group. Listing 13.6 also shows the code for this function.

Listing 13.6   **Primitives drawBox Function**

```
void drawBox(CGRect aRect) {
```

```
    GLfloat vertices[8];
    vertices[0] = aRect.origin.x;
    vertices[1] = aRect.origin.y;
    vertices[2] = aRect.origin.x + aRect.size.width;
    vertices[3] = aRect.origin.y;
    vertices[4] = aRect.origin.x + aRect.size.width;
    vertices[5] = aRect.origin.y + aRect.size.height;
    vertices[6] = aRect.origin.x;
    vertices[7] = aRect.origin.y + aRect.size.height;

    glDisableClientState(GL_COLOR_ARRAY);
    glDisable(GL_TEXTURE_2D);
    glVertexPointer(2, GL_FLOAT, 0, vertices);
    glDrawArrays(GL_LINE_LOOP, 0, 4);
    glEnableClientState(GL_COLOR_ARRAY);
    glEnable(GL_TEXTURE_2D);
}
```

The method simply takes the `CGRect` passed in and creates the vertices necessary to render it to the screen. These vertices are held inside the `vertices` array and passed to the `glDrawArrays` command. The key item here is the use of the `GL_LINE_LOOP` mode. This tells OpenGL ES to draw a line between each vertex, giving us a rectangle. None of these calls are batched, so this method of drawing lines is not suitable for large numbers of lines as part of the game itself, but is fine for debugging purposes.

With this function in place, I then placed code inside the `MainMenu` and `GameScene` classes that drew the boundaries for the interface elements. Listing 13.7 shows the code used inside the *MainMenu.m* file.

Listing 13.7   **Code to Render Interface Element Boundaries Inside MainMenu.m**

```
#ifdef SCB
    drawBox(startButtonBounds);
    drawBox(scoreButtonBounds);
    drawBox(instructionButtonBounds);
    drawBox(resumeButtonBounds);
    drawBox(logoButtonBounds);
    drawBox(settingsButtonBounds);
#endif
```

The commands to render the boundaries were wrapped inside an `ifdef` compiler directive. If Show Collision Bounds (`SCB`) is not defined, this code won't be compiled and the boxes aren't drawn. `SCB` is defined within the *Global.h* file.

Having added this to the interface items, it was then a simple task to add the same feature to the game items, such as entities and objects. This allowed me to visualize collision boundaries for these items, which again was great for testing.

The code to render the boundaries was added to the **AbstractEntity** class inside the render method. Each entity in the game has two different boundaries: Movement bounds are checked against the map and stop the entity moving into a blocked tile, and collision bounds are checked against other entities and are used to see if one entity has collided with another. Movement bounds are rendered blue and collision bounds are rendered green. More detail about how and why this was done can be found in Chapter 14, "Game Objects and Entities."

Handling Transitions

Transitions between scenes in *Sir Lamorak's Quest* are handled using methods inside the **GameController** class and scene classes.

Inside the **GameController** class, the transitionToSceneWithKey: method is used to change the current scene. This method retrieves the scene with the matching key from the gameScenes dictionary and then calls the transitionIn method on the new scene.

The transitionIn method inside each scene is responsible for setting up the scenes state, as well as any other initialization that needs to be done. This provides a simple mechanism for switching between scenes and adding effects such as fading.

Transitions to UIViews, such as the high score, instructions, credits, and settings, are handled differently. A transition to these non-OpenGL ES views is done using the iOS notification center.

NSNotificationCenter provides a mechanism for broadcasting notifications. Classes can register with the notification center to listen for (observe) specific messages. This allows more than one class to be notified when a single message is broadcast.

When requesting the settings view, for example, there are a couple of actions we want to carry out. The first is to pause the game, and the second is to show the settings view.

Both the **SettingsViewController** and **EAGLView** classes register as observers for the showSettings message and get notified when the message is sent. On receiving this message, **EAGLView** pauses the game and **SettingsViewController** makes itself visible. If the hideSettings message was received, **EAGLView** would start the game and **SettingsViewController** would hide itself.

Notifications are a robust and quick way to pass notifications between classes and are used in *Sir Lamorak's Quest* primarily for requesting a UIView to display or hide itself.

More detail on how these messages are processed will be provided in the next section.

OpenGL ES Orientation

When running the sample project and rotating the iPhone, you will have noticed how the OpenGL ES interface also flipped to maintain the correct orientation for the player. This is something that can cause people a lot of problems either around how to actually achieve it or with performance issues.

First of all, we need to look at how we can find out what the orientation of the iPhone is and then how to adjust the view to match it.

Manually Setting Orientation

By default, *Sir Lamorak's Quest* starts up in landscape mode. This has been defined in the sample project's *SLQTSOR-Info.plist* file, located in the *Resources* group, as shown in Figure 13.4.

Key	Value
▼ Information Property List	(14 items)
Localization native development re	English
Bundle display name	${PRODUCT_NAME}
Executable file	${EXECUTABLE_NAME}
Icon file	icon.png
Bundle identifier	com.daley-uk.slqtsor
InfoDictionary version	6.0
Bundle name	${PRODUCT_NAME}
Bundle OS Type code	APPL
Bundle creator OS Type code	????
Bundle version	0.6b
Application requires iPhone enviror	☐
Main nib file base name	MainWindow
Initial interface orientation	Landscape (right home button)
Status bar is initially hidden	☑

Figure 13.4   Plist file for the SLQTSOR project.

In the property list, you see a line called *Initial interface orientation* that has a value of *Landscape (right home button)*. This sets the iPhone's screen orientation when the application launches. This *plist* file can also contain other useful settings. The last setting you will see in Figure 13.4 is *Status bar is initially hidden*. If you have this option enabled (that is, checked) in the *plist* file, the status bar will not be visible when you run your game.

This orientation does not, however, affect the orientation of the OpenGL ES view implemented within **EAGLView**. Only when using a UIViewController does the associated view automatically rotate to the orientation of the phone and only if the UIViewController is configured to support it.

It is possible to manually rotate the view associated with **EAGLView** using a CGAffineTransform on the view. This is not recommended, however. The performance overhead created when applying a CGAffineTransform onto a view displaying OpenGL ES content is high and can seriously degrade the performance of the application.

The recommended way to rotate the contents of an OpenGL ES view is to use OpenGL ES itself by applying a rotation matrix. A rotation matrix is far more efficient at rotating the view itself and is the recommended approach by Apple.

To apply the rotation, we first need to know the orientation of the iPhone. Luckily, we can ask the iPhone to start generating orientation notifications that are sent to the NSNotificationCenter. This is done inside the applicationDidFinishLaunching: method of the **SLQTSORAppDelegate** class, found in the *Classes* group of the sample project:

```
[[UIDevice currentDevice] beginGeneratingDeviceOrientationNotifications];
```

This asks the iPhone to switch on the accelerometer and to start sending notifications when the orientation changes. The name of the notification that gets sent is the following:

```
UIDeviceOrientationDidChangeNotification
```

To capture those notifications, the **ES1Renderer** class, found in the *Classes > Views* group of the sample project, registers an observer during initialization for that message. During registration, the method that should be called on receipt of that notification is also defined:

```
[[NSNotificationCenter defaultCenter] addObserver:self
selector:@selector(orientationChanged:)
name:@"UIDeviceOrientationDidChangeNotification" object:nil];
```

The orientationChanged method, which is inside the **ES1Renderer** class (and is shown in Listing 13.8), is called when the device orientation changes. This enables you to make changes to the OpenGL ES configuration. Of course, you could have as many classes as you want responding to this notification; they just need to register an observer.

Listing 13.8   ES1Renderer orientatonChanged Method

```
- (void) orientationChanged:(NSNotification *)notification {

    UIDeviceOrientation orientation = [[UIDevice currentDevice] orientation];
    if (orientation == UIDeviceOrientationLandscapeRight) {
        sharedGameController.interfaceOrientation =
            UIInterfaceOrientationLandscapeLeft;
        glLoadIdentity();
        glTranslatef( 160, 240, 0);
        glRotatef(90, 0, 0, 1);
        glTranslatef(-240,-160,0);
    }

    if (orientation == UIDeviceOrientationLandscapeLeft) {
        sharedGameController.interfaceOrientation =
            UIInterfaceOrientationLandscapeRight;
        glLoadIdentity();
        glTranslatef( 160, 240, 0);
        glRotatef(-90, 0, 0, 1);
        glTranslatef(-240,-160,0);
    }
}
```

This method grabs the device's orientation and then checks to see if it is equal to one of the two supported landscape modes (for example, `UIDeviceOrientationLandscapeLeft` or `UIDeviceOrientationLandscapeRight`).

When a match is found, the `interfaceOrientation` property of the **GameController** class is set, which will be used when orienting the UIKit views when they first appear. Finally, the OpenGL ES `ModelView` matrix is rotated.

With the rotation matrix applied, the OpenGL ES content will now be rendered in landscape mode with no other changes needed.

Tip

Even though the OpenGL ES content has been rotated, the view itself has not. For this reason, touch events and frame dimensions will still be reported as if in portrait mode. This means that the location of a touch event needs to be adjusted. In addition, the width of the view becomes the height, and the height becomes the width.

You'll remember that when dealing with touch events, we called the GameController `adjustTouchOrientationForTouch:` method, which adjusted the touch location. Listing 13.9 shows this method and how it adjusts the touch locations to handle the game running in landscape mode.

Listing 13.9   **GameController adjustTouchOrientationForTouch: Method**

```
- (CGPoint)adjustTouchOrientationForTouch:(CGPoint)aTouch {

    CGPoint touchLocation;

    if (interfaceOrientation == UIInterfaceOrientationLandscapeRight) {
        touchLocation.x = aTouch.y;
        touchLocation.y = aTouch.x;
    }

    if (interfaceOrientation == UIInterfaceOrientationLandscapeLeft) {
        touchLocation.x = 480 - aTouch.y;
        touchLocation.y = 320 - aTouch.x;
    }

    return touchLocation;
}
```

The method simply checks on the interface's current orientation and then adjusts the touch location accordingly.

UIKit Interfaces

Building and using the OpenGL ES-based interface builds on what we have reviewed so far in the book by making use of images as interface elements and tracking touches against defined bounds. Building interfaces with UIKit is different in that a lot of the work you need to do in OpenGL ES is done for you by the UIKit framework and its controls.

This section reviews how to build a UIKit interface and integrate it into an OpenGL ES game. Integrating UIKit with OpenGL ES can be tricky—not so much technically in mixing the two, but when trying to maintain performance. Apple's documentation states that mixing UIKit and OpenGL ES content can cause performance issues (and it indeed does), so we'll tread carefully. These performance problems have been reduced with the increased power of new devices such as the iPhone 4 and iPad, but care should be taken not to mix too many UIKit controls over OpenGL ES, especially transparent ones as the blending required has a larger hit on performance.

Creating the Interface

UIKit interfaces can be hand-coded, but it is much easier to use Interface Builder. This allows you to graphically build your interface and then wire it up to a view controller. Most of the time, you will have two parts to your view: the view itself (as defined in a *.xib* file), and the view controller code file.

The view controller is a class that inherits from **UIViewController**. Inside this class, the code is placed that joins the view and its controls to the data to be used in your game. This is a standard approach used in creating iPhone applications and follows the Model-View-Controller (MVC) design pattern.

> ### Know Your Design Patterns
>
> If you want to learn more about design patterns and how they apply to the apps you develop for the iPhone, iPad, or Mac, I highly recommend picking up a copy of *Cocoa Design Patterns* by Erik M. Buck and Donald A. Yacktman (Addison-Wesley, 2009).

Because each view will normally have an associated view controller, they can be created at the same time within Xcode. Figure 13.5 shows the **New File** panel that is displayed when you create a new file in an Xcode project.

By selecting *Cocoa Touch Class* from the iPhone OS panel, and then the *UIViewController subclass*, you have the option to also create a *.xib* file for the user interface. By default, the *.xib* file will have the same name as the view controller class. If you are creating a view for the iPad, make sure you tick the Targeted for iPad option in the Options panel.

Inside the *Resources* group of the sample project, you find the Interface Builder files for the views used in *Sir Lamorak's Quest*. Their associated view controller classes can be found in the sample project's **Classes > Views** group. Figure 13.6 shows Interface Builder with the *SettingsView.xib* file opened.

Figure 13.5   New File panel in Xcode.

Figure 13.6   SettingsView.xib inside Interface
Builder.

> **Note**
>
> If you open these *.xib* files from outside of Xcode, the images they use will not be found because they are stored within the Xcode bundle.

You see that this view was created from a number of different elements. A `UIImageView` was used for the background image of the wooden panel. On top of that, the labels and sliders were added along with the `UISegmentedControl` for the joypad position and then two buttons.

The buttons were configured with a background image. This allows us to theme the buttons to match the rest of the game. The `UISlider` controls stand out as not being themed in this screenshot.

To theme the `UISlider` controls, the thumb images need to be changed along with the slider track the thumb image moves along. The thumb image is changed using the following lines of code inside the `viewDidLoad` method of the **SettingsViewController** class:

```
[musicVolume setThumbImage:[UIImage imageNamed:@"ui_scrollbutton.png"]
    forState:UIControlStateNormal];
[fxVolume setThumbImage:[UIImage imageNamed:@"ui_scrollbutton.png"]
    forState:UIControlStateNormal];
```

Skinning the UISlider Track

As well as setting the thumb image using code, it is also possible to set the slider track images using code. The `UISlider` `setMaximumTrackImage:forState:` and `setMinimumTrackImage:forState:` methods can be used to set the end caps of the `UISlider` control along with the slider itself.

The image to be used with these methods needs to be carefully designed to get the effect you are after. The image needs to contain both the minimum and maximum end caps, along with a single pixel band after the left end cap that is stretched for the length of the slider to make the track.

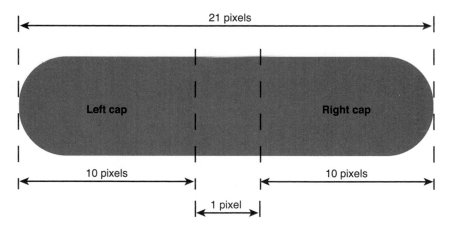

When creating the image to be passed to these methods you use a `UIImage` method that specifies the size of the left end cap. The right end cap is automatically calculated as the width of the image minus the width of the left end cap and the one pixel-wide stretchable region. The `UIImage` is created as follows:

```
UIImage *capImage = [[UIImage imageNamed:@"RedTrack.png"]
    stretchableImageWithLeftCapWidth:10 topCapWidth:0];
```

Using a different image when defining the minimum track image enables you to have the slider to the left of the slider thumb rendered in red and the track to the right rendered in white, or whatever colors your choose.

This is the method I used to skin the UISlider in Sir Lamorak's Quest to make the UISlider control fit with the rest of the game.

Tip

When using images inside Interface Builder, they need to be part of the project or they will not be available to select in the Interface Builder GUI.

Setting up your view really is just a case of dragging around controls and laying them out as you need. One item worth noting is that the background color of the view itself has been changed. When this view appears, it will be over the top of the main menu of the game, and I want the game to show through so the background's color has been made 55 percent transparent. This allows some of the background to be visible when this view is displayed.

Wiring Up the Interface

With the view built in Interface Builder, it is now time to write the code that joins the interface to the game. Within the *Settings View.xib* file, there are several `UISlider` controls, a `UISegmentedControl`, and two `UIButton` controls. If you look inside the *SettingsViewController.h* file, you find that variables have been declared using `IBOutlet`, as shown in Listing 13.10.

Listing 13.10   **SettingsViewController.h IBOutlets**

```
IBOutlet UISlider *musicVolume;
IBOutlet UISlider *fxVolume;
IBOutlet UISegmentedControl *joypadPosition;
IBOutlet UIButton *menuButton;
```

`IBOutlet` is a hint that tells Interface Builder that these variables will be linking to objects in the view. After these have been created and the class has been saved, it is possible to link the objects in Interface Builder with the variables defined in the controller.

Figure 13.7 shows the music volume slider being linked to the `musicVolume` variable in *Settings ViewController.h*.

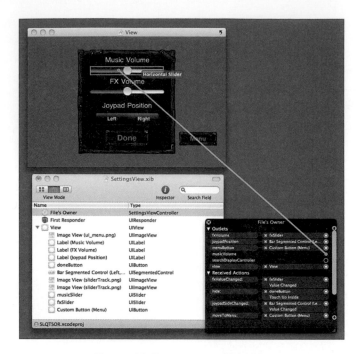

Figure 13.7   Linking an IBOutlet.

Right-clicking the File's Owner in the *Settings View.xib* panel causes the File's Owner panel to pop up. This is the black panel on the bottom right of Figure 13.7. Under the Outlets section, you see all the variables defined in the *Settings ViewController.h* file as `IBOutlets`. If you don't see the outlets there, make sure that `IBOutlet` has been specified in the header file of your view controller class and that the class has been saved. Also, make sure that File's Owner has been configured to point to the `SettingsViewController` class.

To link the `musicVolume` variable with the music volume `UISlider` in the view, the empty circle to the right of the `musicVolume` item in the File's Owner panel was clicked. While keeping the mouse button down, the circle was dragged to the music volume `UISlider` control. The mouse button was then released and the connection is made.

The same process is performed for all the controls on the view.

This process simply links the control on the view to a variable in the view controller, which enables us to access information about the control using that variable. Controls can also perform actions (for example, a button can be pressed and slider value changed). To capture these, we need to link these actions to methods inside the view controller.

The process is exactly the same. Inside the view controller header, the methods that are going to be linked to control actions are defined, as shown in Listing 13.11.

Listing 13.11   **Action Methods Defined in SettingeViewController.h**

```
- (IBAction)hide:(id)aSender;

- (IBAction)moveToMenu:(id)sender;

- (IBAction)musicValueChanged:(UISlider*)sender;

- (IBAction)fxValueChanged:(UISlider*)sender;
- (IBAction)joypadSideChanged:(UISegmentedControl*)sender;
```

You can see that the IBAction keyword has been used when defining these methods. Again, this is a hint to Interface Builder that these methods will be linked to actions. The process of linking the method to an action is almost identical to the one used to link a variable to an IBOutlet. The only difference is that on releasing the mouse button over a control, a new pop-up window is displayed, in which you can select the action that will trigger the linked method. Figure 13.8 shows this being done.

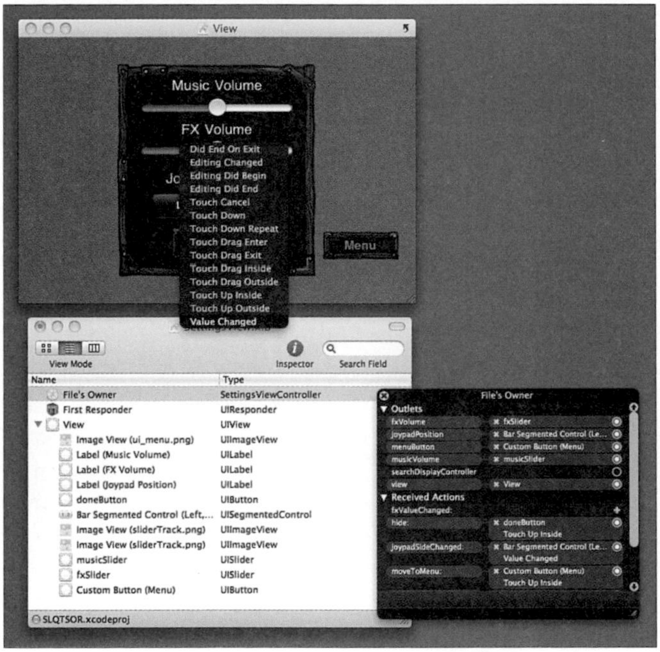

Figure 13.8   Linking an IBAction.

As you can see, there are a number of different actions supported by the control. We are interested when the value of the slider changes, so *Value Changed* is the action selected. The action for the buttons was *Touch Up Inside* (which is triggered when the button is pressed), and the action for the segmented control was (again) *Value Changed*. Listing 13.12 shows the IBAction methods in the **SettingsViewController** class.

Listing 13.12   SettingsViewController IBAction Methods

```
- (IBAction)musicValueChanged:(UISlider*)sender {
    sharedSoundManager.musicVolume = [sender value];
}

- (IBAction)fxValueChanged:(UISlider*)sender {
    sharedSoundManager.fxVolume = [sender value];

}

- (IBAction)joypadSideChanged:(UISegmentedControl*)sender {
    sharedGameController.joypadPosition = sender.selectedSegmentIndex;
}
```

These methods simply set the value of properties in the GameController class that are then referenced to get the different volume settings or the joypad location.

All the UIKit views used in *Sir Lamorak's Quest* are set up this way. The only difference is what they display. The credits and information views contain UIScrollView controls that allow the player to scroll up and down an image. The most complex view is the high scores view. This has a UITableView within it, which means it must implement the UITableViewDelegate and UITableViewDataSource protocols. This allows it to feed the UITableView with the data it needs.

This data is provided by the high scores table maintained in the **GameController** class. Even the cells that are used within the UITableView are defined using Interface Builder. The *.xib* file for the high scores table is called *HighScoreCell.xib*.

UIKit Orientation

As mentioned earlier, the process for managing orientation with a UIKit interface was different from that of an OpenGL ES interface. The reason for this is that the UIViewController class that sits behind each of our UIKit interfaces handles the rotation for us.

When the iPhone is rotated, the topmost view controller also rotates based on its configuration. On rotation, the shouldAutorotateToInterfaceOrientation: method is called in the view controller. This method returns a Boolean that identifies if the view should rotate to match the orientation of the iPhone. This enables you to limit rotation to an orientation supported by your application. Listing 13.13 shows this method inside the SettingsViewController class.

Listing 13.13   SettingsViewController shouldAutorotateToInterfaceOrientation: Method

```
- (BOOL)shouldAutorotateToInterfaceOrientation:
    (UIInterfaceOrientation)interfaceOrientation {
```

```
        return UIInterfaceOrientationIsLandscape(interfaceOrientation);
}
```

There really isn't too much to this method. It simply returns YES if the orientation of the iPhone is landscape. The UIInterfaceOrientationIsLandscape macro is defined within the *UIKit.h* file and is a simple way to identify if the orientation passed in is landscape, regardless of it being landscape left or right.

Having set up the view controller to rotate when we want it to, we have to deal with the orientation of the view when it appears. We want the views to appear in the correct orientation and not have to rotate when they first appear. To make sure the views are oriented correctly when they first appear, we can rotate them to the correct orientation within the viewWillAppear: method, shown in Listing 13.14.

Listing 13.14   SettingsViewController viewWillAppear: Method

```
- (void)viewWillAppear:(BOOL)animated {
    self.view.alpha = 0;

    [self updateControlValues];

    if (sharedGameController.interfaceOrientation ==
        UIInterfaceOrientationLandscapeRight){
        [[UIApplication sharedApplication]
            setStatusBarOrientation:UIInterfaceOrientationLandscapeRight];
        self.view.transform = CGAffineTransformIdentity;
        self.view.transform = CGAffineTransformMakeRotation(M_PI_2);
        self.view.center = CGPointMake(160, 240);
    }
    if (sharedGameController.interfaceOrientation ==
        UIInterfaceOrientationLandscapeLeft){
        [[UIApplication sharedApplication]
            setStatusBarOrientation:UIInterfaceOrientationLandscapeLeft];
        self.view.transform = CGAffineTransformIdentity;
        self.view.transform = CGAffineTransformMakeRotation(-M_PI_2);
        self.view.center = CGPointMake(160, 240);
    }
}
```

Tip

Notice that M_PI_2 is used in the rotation transformation. This is a constant that holds PI divided by 2 and saves you from performing a calculation to find PI/2. This is defined in *math.h*.

This method first sets the alpha value of the view to 0. These views are going to fade into view using Core Animation, so when they initially appear, we need to make sure that they are transparent. With the alpha value set each of the controls on the view are updated with the values held in the `GameController`. This makes sure that the controls display the correct values when the view appears.

Next are the checks on the orientation of the iPhone. We check the value of `interfaceOrientation` in the `GameController`, which is updated when the iPhone is rotated inside `ES1Renderer`. Depending on the current orientation, the status bar orientation is set and then the view is rotated. Without doing both of these, the views will not appear in the correct orientation.

The view has a `transform` property that is first reset using `CGAffineTransformIdentity`. This is the same as the OpenGL ES command `glLoadIdentity`. The transform property is then given a rotation matrix that rotates it either 180 degrees to the left or right, and we make sure that the center of the view is set to the center of the screen. This now means that when the view does appear, it is positioned correctly in the middle of the screen with the correct orientation.

If the iPhone's orientation changes while a `UIKit` view is visible, the view controller deals with rotating the view for us. We don't need to worry about how that is handled.

Showing and Hiding a UIKit Interface

Having set up the orientation of a view that is about to appear, we need to actually make it appear. You'll remember that a notification (such as `showSettings`) was sent when a button was pressed on the game's main menu. Each view controller registers an observer in its `initWithNibNamed:` method. For example, `SettingsViewController` registers for the `showSettings` notification using the following:

```
[[NSNotificationCenter defaultCenter] addObserver:self
selector:@selector(show) name:@"showSettings" object:nil];
```

When the `showSettings` notification is received, the `show` method is called that is used to display the view, as illustrated in Listing 13.15.

Listing 13.15   **SettingsViewController show Method**

```
- (void)show {

    [sharedGameController.eaglView addSubview:self.view];

    if (![sharedGameController.currentScene.name
        isEqualToString:@"game"]) {
        menuButton.hidden = YES;
    } else {
        menuButton.hidden = NO;
    }

    [UIView beginAnimations:nil context:NULL];
    self.view.alpha = 1.0f;
    [UIView commitAnimations];
}
```

The first task this method carries out is to add this view as a subview to **EAGLView**. Remember that **EAGLView** is the primary view onscreen, so we want to add this view as a subview. A check is performed to see which scene is currently active. If the settings view is displayed from the game scene, we want the menu button to be visible; otherwise, it should be hidden. The menu button on this view gives the player the opportunity to quit the game and return to the main menu; thus, it doesn't need to be visible from the main menu.

The last task of this method is to actually fade in the view. This is done using Core Animation, which is perfect for this task. You simply make a call to the `beingAnimations:context:` class method and then make changes to the view.

In this example, we are setting the alpha to `1.0f`, but you could also be rotating, scaling, or even changing color. When you then call the `commitAnimations` class method, the view is transformed from the original state to the end state, as defined between the `begin` and `commit` commands. This is not instant, though; this is done smoothly over time, creating a really slick animation.

More on Core Animation

Core animation is a complete topic in itself. If you're looking for deeper coverage, I highly recommend reading *Core Animation: Simplified Animation Techniques for Mac and iPhone Development* by Marcus Zarra and Matt Long (Addison-Wesley, 2009).

Having the view on the screen, we need to be able to hide it. This is done using the `hide:` method. This method is wired to the *Touch Up Inside* action of the Done button on the view and is shown in Listing 13.16.

Listing 13.16   **SettingsViewController-hide Method**

```
- (IBAction)hide:(id)sender {

    [[NSNotificationCenter defaultCenter]
        postNotificationName:@"startGame" object:self];
    [[NSNotificationCenter defaultCenter]
        postNotificationName:@"hidingSettings" object:self];

    [UIView beginAnimations:nil context:NULL];
    [UIView setAnimationDelegate:self];
    [UIView setAnimationDidStopSelector:@selector(hideFinished)];
    self.view.alpha = 0.0f;
    [UIView commitAnimations];
}
```

At this point, the game has been paused by **EAGLView**, so we post a `startGame` notification that causes **EAGLView** to start the game again. This is followed by the hidingSettings notification that is observed by **GameScene**. Inside **GameScene**, this notification causes the checkJoypadSettings method to be called, which is shown in Listing 13.17.

Listing 13.17   GameScene checkJoypadSettings Method

```
- (void)checkJoypadSettings {

    if (sharedGameController.joypadPosition == 0) {
        joypadCenter.x = 50;
        settingsButtonCenter.x = 465;
        settingsBounds = CGRectMake(430, 0, 50, 50);
    } else if (sharedGameController.joypadPosition == 1) {
        joypadCenter.x = 430;
        settingsButtonCenter.x = 15;
        settingsBounds = CGRectMake(0, 0, 50, 50);
    }

    joypadBounds = CGRectMake(joypadCenter.x - joypadRectangleSize.width,
        joypadCenter.y - joypadRectangleSize.height,
        joypadRectangleSize.width * 2,
        joypadRectangleSize.height * 2);
}
```

This method is used to make sure that the joypad and settings buttons are positioned correctly on the screen. Based on the joypadPosition property of the **GameController** class, it alters the position of the joypad and settings button and also their bounds.

With the notifications sent, the final task of the hide method is to fade out the view. This is almost identical to the fade that was used in the show: method. The key difference is that we want to know when the fade has completed.

Part of the clean up of this method is to remove this view from **EAGLView**. This is because only the topmost view controller within **EAGLView** will respond to the iPhone rotating. If we simply left all the view controllers attached to **EAGLView** as subviews, only the topmost view would rotate when the iPhone is rotated. To overcome this, we remove each view controller from **EAGLView** when it is hidden.

The trick here is that we don't want to remove the view before it has finished fading out, so we need to be notified when the view has finished fading out. Luckily, Core Animation has a great way of handling this. You simply provide an animation delegate—which, in this example, is self—and then set the animationDidStopSelector to the method you want to run when the animation finishes.

In Listing 13.16, you see that we defined this method to be hideFinished:, which then runs the following command to remove the view from **EAGLView**:

```
[self.view removeFromSuperview];
```

Summary

This chapter covered how interface elements are created using both OpenGL ES in combination with UIKit. We have seen the differences between the two and looked at how you build interface elements, such as buttons from scratch using OpenGL ES, and how tracking the player's touches can activate them.

For the UIKit interface elements, you saw how they were created in Interface Builder and then wired up to the view controller class responsible for managing the view's actions and data.

We also saw how to handle the rotation of the iPhone while maintaining the screen's orientation to the player, and how this needed to be implemented differently for OpenGL ES than it does for the UIKit interfaces. We also covered the use of Core Animation to fade the UIKit interfaces into and out of view.

Even with the detail we have covered in this chapter, we have only scratched the surface of what is possible. With this base knowledge, you are now in a position to experiment and take your interface design and implementation even further.

Chapter 14 reviews how entities were built in *Sir Lamorak's Quest*. This includes the player, baddies, and game objects.

Game Objects and Entities

We are now at the point where we need to start thinking about how to populate our game world with game objects and entities. *Game objects* are items in the game, such as energy pickups, parchment pieces, and animated tile map game objects (such as lamps). *Game entities* include the player (Sir Lamorak), the baddies roaming around the castle, the axe Sir Lamorak throws, and the castle's doors that open and close on their own.

These entities and game objects form the backbone of the game play. How they interact with each other and the role they play in the game is important in bringing the game to life.

We know from the game design we covered in Chapter 1, "Game Design," that we want the player to perform some basic actions such as throwing an axe, collecting items such as keys, and eating energy game objects. We also wanted to have baddies that roam around the castle, getting in the player's way, as well as doors that are either locked and require the correct key to open, or those that simply open and close on their own, or maybe are helped by the resident ghosts.

This chapter covers how these objects and entities are created and implemented within *Sir Lamorak's Quest.*

Game Objects and Entities Project

The project for this chapter is the same as for Chapter 13, "The Game Interface," (*SLQTSOR*). Running this project and starting a new game, and you will immediately see the doors that open and close at will. Walking around the castle, you find energy items that can be collected and see baddies that start to appear in a cloud of purple smoke. You will also come across colored keys that Sir Lamorak needs to collect in order to escape from the castle.

Figure 14.1 shows the iPhone Simulator running *Sir Lamorak's Quest* with a ghost entity moving around and another entity appearing.

Figure 14.1   iPhone Simulator running SLQTSOR.

Game Objects

Before we start looking at how game objects have been implemented, we take a look at the different game objects that are used within *Sir Lamorak's Quest*, including the following:

- **Map:** Implements the flickering lamps that can be seen on the walls and also the gravestone that appears when the player dies.
- **Key:** Implements the colored keys that are located around the map. These keys are needed to unlock colored doors.
- **Energy:** Implements the food items that can be collected by the player. These items replenish the player's health and are used as soon as the player walks into them.
- **Parchment:** Implements the parchment pieces that the player must collect to escape from the castle.

These game objects perform specific tasks within the game so each one has its own class. These classes contain the logic and graphics specific to the game objects and allow us to easily change their behavior as required.

Game objects that share behaviors have been implemented in the same class, and each game object inherits from the **AbstractObject** class that we see later in this chapter. This abstract class contains *type*, *subtype*, *state* and *energy* properties. By setting the *type type* and *subtype*, the class knows which game object it should be representing. This changes the graphics used to render the game object, as well as the logic that controls it.

Game objects are held in an array in the **GameScene** class, called `gameObjects`.

AbstractObject Class

All game objects inherit from the **AbstractObject** class. This class contains all the properties that are common between game objects and the methods that these game objects can override. It also implements the NSCoding protocol. This is useful when information about a game object needs to be saved and restored at a later stage. More information about this can be found in the *Saving a Game Object or Entity* later in this chapter.

The **AbstractObject** class can be found in the sample project in the Abstract Classes group. Listing 14.1 shows the properties that the **AbstractObject** class defines.

Listing 14.1   **AbstractObject Properties**

```
//////////////////// Instance variables
CGPoint tileLocation;   // Tile position of the game object in the map
CGPoint pixelLocation;  // Pixel position of the game object in the map
int state;              // Game object state
int type;               // Game object type
int subType;            // Game object subtype
int energy;             // Energy passed to the player if this game
                        // object is an
                        // energy object


//////////////////// Flags
BOOL isCollectable;     // Can this object be collected by the player
```

Each game object has a tileLocation that specifies the game objects location in terms of tiles on the tile map. It also has a pixelLocation that is calculated from the tileLocation. The pixel location is used when rendering the object to the screen. There is a common function used to convert the tileLocation to the pixelLocation called tileMapPositionToPixelPosition that is defined in the *Global.h* file. This function is called within the initWithTileLocation: method of the game object classes themselves (for example, **EnergyObject**).

You may have noticed that there is no member to store an image. The reason for this is that an object could have multiple images or use animation.

The valid types, subtypes, and states are defined as enums inside the *Global.h* file within the Global Headers group. These are shown in Listing 14.2.

Listing 14.2   **Game Object Type and Subtype enums in Global.h**

```
// Game object types
enum  {
    kObjectType_Key,
    kObjectType_Energy,
    kObjectType_General
};
```

```
// Game object subtypes
enum  {
    kObjectSubType_RedKey = 0,
    kObjectSubType_GreenKey = 1,
    kObjectSubType_BlueKey = 2,
    kObjectSubType_YellowKey = 3,
    kObjectSubType_Candy = 4,
    kObjectSubType_Cake = 5,
    kObjectSubType_Chicken = 6,
    kObjectSubType_Drink = 7,
    kObjectSubType_LolliPop = 8,
    kObjectSubType_Ham = 9,
    kObjectSubType_Grave = 10,
    kObjectSubType_BottomLamp = 11,
    kObjectSubType_RightLamp = 12,
    kObjectSubType_TopLamp = 13,
    kObjectSubType_LeftLamp = 14,
    kObjectSubType_ParchmentTop = 15,
    kObjectSubType_ParchmentMiddle = 16,
    kObjectSubType_ParchmentBottom = 17,
    kObjectSubType_Exit = 18
};

// Game object states
enum {
    kObjectState_Active,
    kObjectState_Inactive,
    kObjectState_Inventory
};
```

The values assigned to each of these type and subtype enums are used within the game code and also within the tile map editor. Game objects and their location are defined within the tile map, and it's necessary to set their properties to specify their type and sub-type. This is processed when the tile map is parsed as the game starts and the necessary game objects are created.

As the value of these enums is used outside the game code, specifying the number manually in a large list of enums, such as the subtype, makes it easier to read what the values are when creating game objects in the tile map.

The **AbstractObject** class also defines a number of common methods, shown in Listing 14.3.

Listing 14.3   **AbstractObject Methods**

```
- (id)initWithTileLocation:(CGPoint)aTileLocation type:(int)aType
    subType:(int)aSubType;
- (void)updateWithDelta:(float)aDelta scene:(AbstractScene*)aScene;
- (void)render;
- (void)checkForCollisionWithEntity:(AbstractEntity*)aEntity;
- (CGRect)collisionBounds;
- (id)initWithCoder:(NSCoder *)aDecoder;
- (void)encodeWithCoder:(NSCoder *)aCoder;
```

Each game object is responsible for its own `updateWithDelta:` and `render` methods that override the methods in the abstract class. Most of these methods are empty, and you would override them in the subclasses that inherit from **AbstractObject**.

Two methods that do contain code are the `initWithTileLocation:` and `render` methods.

The `initWithTileLocation:` method simply initializes the class and creates a reference to the shared sound manager. It is assumed that all game objects will want to play a sound at some point, so the shared sound manager reference is created within the abstract class.

The `render` method contains the code necessary to render a box around the game object that matches the game objects collision bounds. We discussed the visualization of boundaries in Chapter 13. If the `SCB` constant is defined in *Global.h*, the `drawBox` function is called and renders the supplied `CGRect`.

EnergyObject Class

Although there are four different game object classes within *Sir Lamorak's Quest* that inherit from the **AbstractObject** class, for starters, we review the **EnergyObject** class as an example of how the game object classes have been implemented.

> **Note**
>
> The game object implementations can be found inside the **Game Objects** group of the sample project.

Initializing

When a game object is created, its `initWithTileLocation:` method checks to see what type and subtype the game object should be. This allows the game object class to then configure the necessary graphics to be used when rendering the game object to the screen. Listing 14.4 shows this method from the **EnergyObject** class.

Listing 14.4   **EnergyObject initWithTileLocation: Method**

```objc
- (id) initWithTileLocation:(CGPoint)aTileLocation type:(int)aType
    subType:(int)aSubType {
  self = [super init];
  if (self != nil) {
      type = aType;
      subType = aSubType;

      tileLocation.x = aTileLocation.x + 0.5f;
      tileLocation.y = aTileLocation.y + 0.5f;
      pixelLocation = tileMapPositionToPixelPosition(tileLocation);

      PackedSpriteSheet *pss = [PackedSpriteSheet
          packedSpriteSheetForImageNamed:@"atlas.png"
              controlFile:@"coordinates" imageFilter:GL_LINEAR];

      switch (subType) {
          case kGame objectSubType_Cake:
              image = [[[pss imageForKey:@"item_cake.png"]
                  imageDuplicate] retain];
              energy = 20;
                break;

          case kGame objectSubType_Drink:
              image = [[[pss imageForKey:@"item_drink.png"]
                  imageDuplicate] retain];
              energy = 10;
                break;

          case kGame objectSubType_Candy:
              image = [[[pss imageForKey:@"item_chocolate.png"]
                  imageDuplicate]
                  retain];
              energy = 15;
                break;
```

```
    case kGame objectSubType_Chicken:
       image = [[[pss imageForKey:@"item_chicken.png"]
          imageDuplicate] retain];
       energy = 25;
         break;

    case kGame objectSubType_Ham:
       image = [[[pss imageForKey:@"item_ham.png"]
          imageDuplicate] retain];
       energy = 20;
         break;

    case kGame objectSubType_LolliPop:

       image = [[[pss imageForKey:@"item_lollipop.png"]
          imageDuplicate] retain];
       energy = 10;
         break;

    default:
         break;
    }
  }
  return self;
}
```

You can see that a simple switch statement is performed on the subtype. Based on this, the image for the game object is set, along with the energy amount the player will receive when the game object is collected.

You'll also notice that we are taking a copy (duplicate) of the image from the sprite sheet. If we didn't, we would end up referencing the same image for all energy objects that share the same sprite sheet. Changing the image in one of those instances would end up changing the image for *all* instances.

> **Note**
>
> This was a bug that took me a while to track down. Once I realized they were all sharing the same image, I implemented the imageDuplicate method inside the Image class.

Because a copy is being taken, the energy object becomes responsible for retaining and releasing that image as necessary.

> **Note**
>
> There are more sophisticated ways to create this configuration that remove the hard-coding from the values of the class (for example, the information is configured in some form of file that is parsed by the game object class). Given that there were not going to be that many game objects in *Sir Lamorak's Quest*, I decided that hard-coding the values was not a bad option.

The `MapObject`, `KeyObject`, and `ParchmentObject` classes also use this same process when they are initialized to identify what type of game object they are.

Updating

During the game scenes update method, all game objects that are within the visible screen have their update method called. The check to make sure that an object is visible or not is done within the updateSceneWithDelta: method inside the GameScene method. The `updateWithDelta:` method is responsible for implementing the logic for a game object, as shown in Listing 14.5.

Listing 14.5   **EnergyObject updateWithDelta: Method**

```
- (void)updateWithDelta:(float)aDelta scene:(AbstractScene *)aScene {

    if (state == kGameObjectState_Active) {
        Scale2f scale = image.scale;
        if (scaleUp) {
            scale.x += 0.75 * aDelta;
            scale.y += 0.75 * aDelta;
        } else {
            scale.x -= 0.75 * aDelta;
            scale.y -= 0.75 * aDelta;
        }

        image.scale = scale;
        if (scale.x > 1.35) {
            scaleUp = NO;
        }

        if (scale.x < 1) {
            scaleUp = YES;
        }
    }
}
```

This update method is used to scale the game object's image up and down if they are active. An `EnergyObject` has a state of `kObjectState_Active` while it is on the tile map and available to be picked up. When a game object collides with the player, the game object's state is set to `kObjectState_Inactive` and a sound effect is played. This is done in the `checkForCollisionWithEntity:`, which we will see later.

As you can see, it's simple to place any logic required for a specific game object into these methods. The approach here is that all energy game objects are implemented in the same class, but there is nothing to stop you from creating separate classes for each of your game objects, with each implementing their own logic.

My key reason for keeping the game objects in a single class was ease of maintenance. Having a single class I could update to change behavior during play testing was quicker and easier than having many different classes. Architecting the game in this way, and using abstraction and inheritance, is also just a good design pattern to use.

Rendering

Rendering of the energy game object could not be easier; the `render` method is shown in Listing 14.6.

Listing 14.6   **EnergyObject render Method**

```
- (void)render {
    if (state == kGameObjectState_Active) {
        [image renderCenteredAtPoint:pixelLocation];
    }
    [super render];
}
```

The image associated with the game object is rendered centered on the `pixelLocation`. The only check performed is that the game object is active. Only active energy game objects are rendered. The `render` method is then called in the abstract class, which takes care of rendering the bounding box if SCB has been defined. This is done by the [super render] command.

Dealing with Collisions

During the game scene update loop, the player game object is asked to check for collisions against each game object that is visible on the screen. Each visible game object is also asked to check for a collision with the `Player` entity using the `checkForCollisionWithEntity:`, shown in Listing 14.7.

The `Player` entity is responsible for identifying and responding to collisions with game objects, as are the game objects. This means that the response to a collision can be implemented differently in each case.

Listing 14.7   **EnergyGame Object checkForCollisionWithEntity: Method**

```
- (void)checkForCollisionWithEntity:(AbstractEntity*)aEntity {

    if ([aEntity isKindOfClass:[Player class]]) {

        if (CGRectIntersectsRect([self collisionBounds],
            [aEntity collisionBounds])) {
            state = kGame objectState_Inactive;
```

```
        [sharedSoundManager playSoundWithKey:@"eatfood"
            location:CGPointMake(aEntity.pixelLocation.x,
                aEntity.pixelLocation.y)];
    }
  }
}
```

The `collision` method checks to see if the entity that has possibly collided with it is an instance of the `Player` class. In *Sir Lamorak's Quest*, the only entity that will ever be passed to this method is the `Player`. This means that the first check is redundant, but I left that in there just in case I ever wanted to have other entities interact with game objects.

If the entity is the player, a further check is made to see if the bounds of the game object have intersected the bounds of the player. That being the case, the state of the game object is changed and a sound effect is played.

The bounds for each game object are defined within the `collisionBounds` method shown in Listing 14.8. In *Sir Lamorak's Quest*, the bounds are the same for all game objects, but it is possible to have different bonds for different-sized game objects.

Listing 14.8   **EnergyObject collisionBounds Method**

```
- (CGRect)collisionBounds {
    return CGRectMake(pixelLocation.x - 10, pixelLocation.y - 10, 20, 20);
}
```

This method is as simple as it gets and simply returns a `CGRect`. The size of this is hard-coded, but bounds could be dynamic. For example, you may want to implement a game object that has an animated image with some frames being larger than others. An example of this can be seen within the `collisionBounds` method of the **Pumpkin** class found in the sample project under the *Game Entities > Moving* group.

Game Objects and the Tile Map

The game objects we have discussed in this chapter are all located within the tile map and then collected by the player. We, therefore, need a way to specify where these objects are in the map. Having some kind of hard-coded list that specifies the type, subtype, and location for each game object could do this. This is OK, but can quickly become complex to manage.

In Chapter 9, "Tile Maps," we looked at how the Tiled tile map editor can create tile maps for *Sir Lamorak's Quest*. Being able to graphically position game objects on the map is a more efficient process, and one that makes changing an object's position and details much easier.

The Tiled map editor supports the concept of layers, as well as a special kind of layer called an *object layer*. An object layer allows objects to be placed on the tile map at any pixel location. They are not limited to being positioned using tile locations.

By making use of an object layer, we can create and position game objects anywhere within the tile map. These objects are then parsed from within the tile map *.tmx* file during game initialization and loaded into the `gameObjects` array. We cover how the game objects are initialized in Chapter 16, "Pulling It All Together."

Figure 14.2 shows the Tiled editor with the map for *Sir Lamorak's Quest*. The tile map file can be found in the sample project and is called *slqtsor.tmx*.

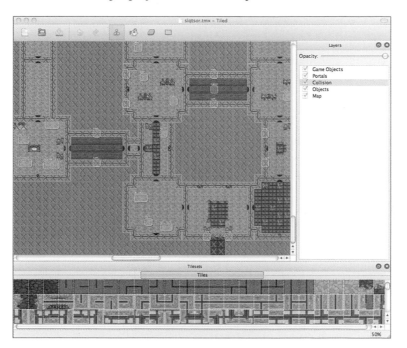

Figure 14.2   Tiled editing the slqtsor.tmx file.

In Figure 14.2, you can see the different layers listed in the layers panel on the right. The layer called *Game Objects* is the layer that contains the game objects for the game. In the large center panel, where the map itself can be seen, the yellow boxes represent the different game objects that have been added to the map.

To add an object layer to the map, the *Add Object Layer* option should be selected from the *Layer* menu. A dialog appears, asking for the layer's name. Enter a name for the layer, and when you click OK, the object layer is created.

With the object layer highlighted, clicking anywhere on the map creates a new object. A colored box represents each object. These boxes have a handle on the bottom-right corner, enabling you to change the box size. Figure 14.3 shows two objects within the map.

Figure 14.3   Objects within the Tiled map editor.

The location and dimensions for these object boxes are written to the tile map's *.tmx* file. This allows object layers to be used for different purposes (for example, collision detection).

The location of objects in the *.tmx* file are stored as pixel locations, not tile locations. When the objects are created, the pixel location of the bottom-left corner is converted to a tile location. When an object is initialized, `0.5` is added to that tile location so that the object is rendered in the center of that tile. The dimensions of the object (that is, the width and height) are not used in *Sir Lamorak's Quest*. The different sizes you can see in the editor simply allow the name to be seen clearly.

Having created an object, it is then possible to add properties. Figure 14.4 shows the context menu that appears when you right-click an object.

Figure 14.4   Object context menu.

Through the context menu, it is possible to duplicate and remove the object and set the object's properties. When you have an object with a number of properties, it is useful to be able to duplicate it and just change the property values on the new object.

Selecting the properties option brings up the *Object Properties* dialog, shown in Figure 14.5.

The name of the object is important, as it will help identify what the object is when you are working within the map editor.

> **Note**
>
> Object names *must* be unique because they are used as keys within the `TileMap` class. These keys are used to gain access to the properties that have been defined for each object. This is a restriction within the `TileMap` class and not of the Tiled editor itself.

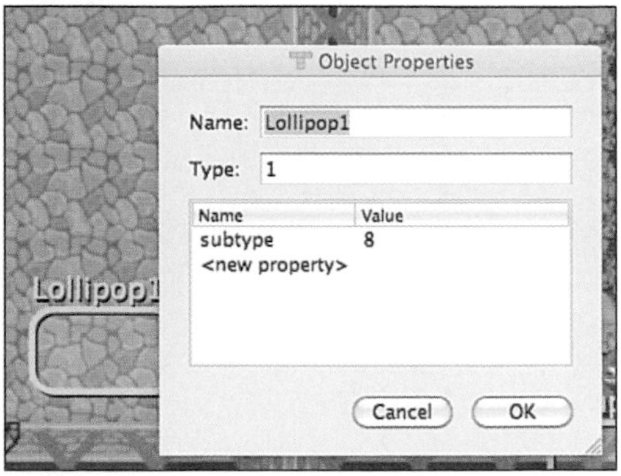

Figure 14.5   Object Properties dialog box.

The `type` field is used to store the object type value. Remember that an object can be one of three different types:

- `kObjectType_Key = 0`
- `kObjectType_Energy = 1`
- `kObjectType_General = 2`

The item selected in Figure 14.5 is a lollipop, so the type should be 1 (that is, `kObjectType_Energy`). To store the `subtype`, a property has been added to the list of properties called `subtype`. This defines what type of energy object this will be. If you review Listing 14.2, you see that an object `subtype` value of 8 is a lollipop.

> **Note**
>
> Any number of properties can be added to an object, and it's a great way of extracting configuration information from the game's code to the map editor. This kind of approach really can help make the tile map editor your level editor.

By adding objects to the tile map and configuring their type and subtype, you can easily populate the game with all the objects needed. It's also really easy to change their location when play testing shows they need to be moved, removed, or added.

Game Object Summary

We've not covered the implementation of all the game objects in *Sir Lamorak's Quest* in this chapter, but having reviewed the **AbstractObject** and **EnergyObject** class, you should now have everything you need to investigate the other objects and see how their specific implementations differ.

Game Entities

Game entities in *Sir Lamorak's Quest* are very similar to game objects—so similar, in fact, that there is no reason why they could not have shared the same abstract class with just a few changes. Although that may be true, I decided to keep them separate to denote the fact that objects are static and don't proactively perform any actions. Entities, on the other hand, can both move and perform actions.

For this reason, the **AbstractEntity** class was created. A number of different entities in *Sir Lamorak's Quest* inherit from this class:

- `Player`
- `Axe`
- `Ghost`
- `Pumpkin`
- `Bat`
- `Zombie`
- `Witch`
- `Frank`
- `Vampire`
- `Portal`
- `Door`

These entities and their classes are used to represent active elements in the game. The baddie entities should be easy enough to recognize in the list. These entities roam around the castle, getting in the player's way. If the player runs into any of these guys, they vanish, and the player's energy levels are reduced—a little like getting slimed.

Defining Doors

Each door in the castle is represented by an instance of the `Door` class. This class is responsible for handling the different doors in the castle (that is, locked doors that you need a key to move through, and those that simply open and close randomly).

Door locations and types are defined within the tile map. The doors are added to the tile map on the *Collision layer*. Within the maps tile set, the door tiles are given a property called `type`. Right-clicking on a tile brings up a context menu that enables you to view the properties that have been created for that tile.

The value of type relates to another set of `enum` values defined within the *Global.h* file. The value tells the `Door` class what type of door it should be representing and also the behavior of that door.

Only door tiles that show a closed door are used to specify the location of doors on the map. During initialization of the **GameScene**, door instances are created and added to the `doors` array while processing the collision layer of the map.

The `Axe` class is self-explanatory. This class represents the player's axe that can be thrown. It handles the fact that an axe can bounce off walls and only exists for a defined period of time.

The last two classes in the list are `Door` and `Portal`. These entities don't move, but they perform an action.

The Portal class controls the rendering of a particle effect that looks like some kind of spooky portal, and that when the player walks into one, he gets transported to another location on the map. How this transportation works, given Heisenberg's Uncertainty Principle, no one knows—it just works.[1]

AbstractEntity Class

As stated earlier, this class is similar to the **`AbstractObject`** class. It defines a number of properties that are common among entities, as shown in Listing 14.9.

Listing 14.9   **AbstractEntity Properties in AbstractEntity.h**

```
//////////////////// Singleton Managers

SoundManager *sharedSoundManager;
GameController *sharedGameController;

////////////////// Images
Image *image;
SpriteSheet *spriteSheet;
Animation *animation;

////////////////// Entity location
CGPoint tileLocation;
CGPoint pixelLocation;

////////////////// Entity state/ivars
GameScene *scene;
uint state;
float energyDrain;
float speed;
float angle;
```

---

[1] Heisenberg's Uncertainty Principle: **en.wikipedia.org/wiki/Uncertainty_principle**.

```
ParticleEmitter *dyingEmitter;
ParticleEmitter *appearingEmitter;
float offScreenTimer;
float appearingTimer;
float distanceFromPlayer;
```

These common properties are used by a large number of the entities in *Sir Lamorak's Quest*. Apart from the `Player`, `Axe`, `Portal` and `Door` classes, no other entity uses its own properties, just those defined in the abstract class.

As with the game objects, entities have a state that is used to identify if they are *alive* or *dead*, among other things. Listing 14.10 shows the entity states as defined in *Global.h*.

Listing 14.10   **Entity State enums Defined in Global.h**

```
// Entity states
enum entityState {
    kEntityState_Idle,
    kEntityState_Dead,
    kEntityState_Dying,
    kEntityState_Alive,
    kEntityState_Appearing
};
```

The **AbstractEntity** class also defines a number of methods, as did the **AbstractObject** class. Listing 14.11 shows the methods that are implemented within **AbstractEntity**.

Listing 14.11   **AbstractEntity Methods**

```
- (id)initWithTileLocation:(CGPoint)aLocation;
- (void)updateWithDelta:(float)aDelta scene:(AbstractScene*)aScene;
- (void)render;
- (BOOL)isEntityInTileAtCoords:(CGPoint)aCoords;
- (CGRect)movementBounds;
- (CGRect)collisionBounds;
- (BoundingBoxTileQuad)getTileCoordsForBoundingRect(CGRect aRect, CGSize
      aTileSize);
- (void)checkForCollisionWithEntity:(AbstractEntity*)aEntity;
- (void)checkForCollisionWithObject:(AbstractObject*)aObject;
```

You'll notice that the `getTileCoordsForBoundingRect` method is defined as a C function, not Objective-C. This function gets called a lot, so making it a C function reduces the messaging overhead that Objective-C introduces when calling methods on a class.

The `getTileCoordsForBoundingRect` method, along with the `isEntityInTileAtCoords`, `initWithEncoder`, and `encodeWithEncoder` are actually implemented inside the abstract class. These methods are the same across all entities, so they only need to be written once.

There is a new method called `movementBounds`. This defines a different bounding rectangle to that of `collisionBounds`. The `movementBounds` rectangle is used when checking to see if an entity has collided with a blocked tile on the map. This enables us to check for map collisions using one bounding box, and collisions with entities and objects using another.

> **Note**
>
> This is important, as I wanted the bounding box to be larger when checking to see if an entity had hit a blocked tile than when I was checking for collisions with entities and objects. The larger box for movement bounds allowed me to stop the graphics from the entities clipping from under doors when they passed through. With too small a bounding box, the edges of entities could be seen peeking from under the door graphics when they were in a doorway.

There are also two collision methods: one is used to check for a collision with another entity, and the other checks for a collision with an object. These could be merged, but having them split apart was part of the original design, and I've just stuck with it. The only class that actually uses the `checkForCollisionWithObject:` method is **Player**.

Artificial Intelligence

The use of artificial intelligence in games is a huge subject that has continually evolved since its inception. Since the 1950s, when the first programs using some form of Artificial Intelligence (AI) were written, such as checkers, game playing has been an area of research.

There are many books this topic, and it is too large to cover in any detail in this book, but it's worth understanding where AI can be implemented.

As you have seen, each entity is responsible for its own updates and rendering, and it's within the update method of the entities that the AI can be implemented. *Sir Lamorak's Quest* doesn't contain anything complex in terms of AI. The update routines for the game entities just deal with allowing the entity to move around the map, dealing with collisions.

It is a stretch to say that these entities have any form of intelligence. They really don't have any understanding of what is around them. There is, however, one of the baddies that does implement more than just simple movement code.

The witch entity chases the player if they get too close. Listing 14.12 shows the code responsible for chasing the player in the `Witch` classes `updateWithDelta:scene:` method.

Listing 14.12   **Witch Chase Code in the updateWithDelta:scene: Method**

```
if (distanceFromPlayer <= 3) {
    entityAIState = kEntityAIState_Chasing;
} else {
    entityAIState = kEntityAIState_Roaming;
}
 if (entityAIState == kEntityAIState_Chasing) {
     speed = 1 * MOVEMENT_SPEED;
     float dx = tileLocation.x - scene.player.tileLocation.x;
     float dy = tileLocation.y - scene.player.tileLocation.y;
     angle = atan2(dy, dx) - DEGREES_TO_RADIANS(180);
     tileLocation.x += (speed * aDelta) * cos(angle);
     tileLocation.y += (speed * aDelta) * sin(angle);
}


  if (entityAIState == kEntityAIState_Roaming) {
     changeDirSpeed = (int)(99 * RANDOM_0_TO_1());
       if(changeDirSpeed == 1) {
          angle = (int)(360 * RANDOM_0_TO_1()) % 360;
          speed = (float)(RANDOM_0_TO_1() * MOVEMENT_SPEED);
      }
     tileLocation.x += (speed * aDelta) * cos(DEGREES_TO_RADIANS(angle));
     tileLocation.y += (speed * aDelta) * sin(DEGREES_TO_RADIANS(angle));
}
```

The distance the player is from the witch is calculated anyway, so we know if the entity is too far from the player and it needs to be re-spawned. If this distance is less than three tiles, the entity's `entityAIState` variable is set to the `kEntityAIState_Chasing` enum. If it's greater than three, the `entityAIState` variable is set to the `kEntityAIState_Roaming` enum.

When the entity is chasing, its speed is adjusted and the direction is calculated based on the location of the player. This causes the witch to chase the player should he get too close.

If the player manages to get more than three tiles between him and the witch, the witch gives up chasing and returns to just roaming around, until the player gets too close again.

This is a simple form of AI, but it can be used effectively to give the player a shock when the entity suddenly locks onto him. One consideration missing from this AI is blocked tiles. The logic does not check to see if there is a wall between the witch and the player; this means that the witch can cheat and see through walls.

Most games available have a form of AI cheating in them. This could be that the AI always knows where the player is, even if they can't see the player, or that the AI entity gets a speed boost over the player when chasing him. These can seem unfair at times, but it is one way of making the AI more challenging. Without these little tricks, it is relatively easy for humans to overcome the AI within games. That said, AI is getting better and better all the time, so it may not be long before you come downstairs to find that your Mac has become self-aware overnight and has turned your kitchen appliances into an army of terminators.

Most AI makes use of a state machine. By using a number of input parameters, a specific state is set that causes the entity to exhibit specific behavior. In the `Witch` class, the entity's AI state is held in the `entityAIState` variable, and an `enum` is used to define the current AI state. This can, of course, get much more complex when many more AI states and input parameters exist.

An addition that could be made for the entity's AI is path finding. This is the process of finding a path through the map from the entity's current location to some kind of target location. This could be a specific location in the map or the player's current position. At the moment, the witch simply heads to the player and can get stuck behind walls. Using a path-finding algorithm would allow the witch to identify a route to the player without getting stuck.

A popular algorithm for finding a route through a map is called A★ (pronounced *A-star*). This algorithm is well-suited to using a tile map to identify passable and blocked tiles. Using this information, the entity is then able to calculate a route from its current location to another location in the tile map.

The A★ algorithm allows for different types of routes to be calculated by defining a cost for each move (for example, either a quickest route or a route that avoids specific types of tiles). Although we are not going cover the A★ path-finding algorithm in this book, more information can be easily found on the Internet.[2]

Player Entity Class

The `Player` class is central to everything that goes on in *Sir Lamorak's Quest*. It is responsible for the logic, rendering, movement, and inventory for Sir Lamorak. Although it does inherit from `AbstractEntity`, it does define a number of its own properties, as shown in Listing 14.13.

Listing 14.13   **Player Class Properties**

```
//////////////////// Animation
Animation *leftAnimation;
Animation *rightAnimation;
Animation *downAnimation;
Animation *upAnimation;
Animation *currentAnimation;

//////////////// Instance variables
float playerSpeed;
float energy;
float angleOfMovement;
float speedOfMovement;
float energyTimer;
float deathTimer;
```

[2] Once such resource is **www.policyalmanac.org/games/aStarTutorial.htm**.

```
float blinkTimer;
int lives;
float stayDeadTime;
CGPoint beamLocation;

///////////////// Inventory
AbstractObject *inventory1, *inventory2, *inventory3;

///////////////// Flags
BOOL renderSprite;
BOOL hasParchmentTop, hasParchmentMiddle, hasParchmentBottom;
```

The animation properties store the different animations used when Sir Lamorak is moving up, down, left, and right. currentAnimation simply points to one of the four animations set up, depending on the direction the player is moving.

The inventory properties are used as pointers to objects inside the gameObjects array in **GameScene**. When an object is picked up, a reference to that object is held in the appropriate inventory slot. This means that no copy is needed of the object, as it is updated directly.

Initializing

Initializing the **Player** class is pretty standard now based on what we you have already seen. The animation is set up for the different directions. I didn't want to have lots of if statements later in the code to decide which animation should be rendered or updated, so I decided to have a currentAnimation ivar that would point to one of the animations that has been set up. When the player changes direction, currentAnimation is updated to point to the new animation that needs to be used.

This means that the movement and render methods just deal with currentAnimation and don't need to worry that different animations have been set up.

Updating

The updateWithDelta: method has a simple switch statement based on the state of the player. If the player is alive, his location and energy are updated. Listing 14.14 shows Part 1 of this method.

Listing 14.14   **Player updateWithDelta: Method (Part 1)**

```
switch (state) {
    case kEntityState_Appearing:
    case kEntityState_Alive:

        if (state == kEntityState_Appearing) {
            appearingTimer += aDelta;

            if (appearingTimer >= 4) {
                state = kEntityState_Alive;
                appearingTimer = 0;
            }
```

```
        blinkTimer += aDelta;
        if (blinkTimer >= 0.10) {
            renderSprite = (renderSprite == YES) ? NO : YES;
            blinkTimer = 0;
        }
    }
    [self updateLocationWithDelta:aDelta];

    energyTimer += aDelta;
    if (energyTimer > 3) {
        energy -= 1;
        energyTimer = 0;
    }

    if (energy <= 0) {
        state = kEntityState_Dead;
        energy = 0;
        MapObject *grave = [[MapObject alloc] initWithTileLocation:tileLocation
            type:kObjectType_General subType:kObjectSubType_Grave];
        [aScene.gameObjects addObject:grave];
        [grave release];

        lives -= 1;
        if (lives < 1) {
        aScene.state = kSceneState_GameOver;
    }

    [sharedSoundManager playSoundWithKey:@"scream" location:pixelLocation];
    }
```

When the player's energy has fallen to 0 or lower, his state is set to kEntityState_Dead. The energy value is set to 0 to make sure there is no residual value left that could cause the health bar to display some health, even though the player is dead.

Because the player has died, a gravestone needs to be added to the gameObjects array in GameScene. This object will then be rendered as a constant reminder of where the player bit the dust. You can see that when creating the MapObject instance, the type and subtype being used define the object as the gravestone.

With the gravestone added. the player's lives are reduced and a check is made to make sure that he has some lives left. If not, the GameScene state is set to kSceneState_GameOver, and the sound of a harrowing scream is played to let the player know that he has failed miserably.

If the player did have lives left, the next time the player is updated, the switch statement will see that the state of the player is kEntityState_Dead and run the code shown in Listing 14.15.

Listing 14.15   **Player updateWithDelta: Method (Part 2)**

```
    case kEntityState_Dead:
       deathTimer += aDelta;
        if (deathTimer >= stayDeadTime) {
           deathTimer = 0;
           state = kEntityState_Alive;
           energy = 100;
        }
         break;
    default:
       break;
  }
}
```

When the player dies, we don't want him to immediately reappear. It would be good to give him some time to compose himself and carry on. For this reason, we have a simple timer that waits for a period of time and then sets the player's status back to `kEntityState_Alive` and resets his health. The timer is implemented by simply incrementing an ivar each update using the delta value. When the player finally does appear, it's also not a good idea to make him immediately vulnerable to attack. It's common to give the player a few seconds where they can move around without getting hit by the baddies. This can be seen in Listing 14.14 when the player's state is kEntityState_Appearing.

An ivar is updated that specifies if the player's sprite should be rendered or not. This is changed every 0.1 seconds for a period of 4 seconds. This causes the players sprite to flash for 4 seconds telling the player that they are not going to get hit by baddies while flashing. Once the flashing stops, the player's state is set to kEntityState_Alive and its then game on.

Updating the Player's Location

Inside the `updateWithDelta:` method was a call to the `updateLocationWithDelta:` method. This is a private method and is used to update the player's location based on the joypad input. It also handles the player colliding with blocked tiles. Listing 14.16 shows Part 1 of this method.

Listing 14.16   **Player updateLocationWithDelta: Method (Part 1)**

```
- (void)updateLocationWithDelta:(float)aDelta {

    BoundingBoxTileQuad bbtq;

    CGPoint oldPosition = tileLocation;
    if (speedOfMovement != 0) {

        tileLocation.x -= (aDelta * (playerSpeed * speedOfMovement)) *
            cosf(angleOfMovement);

        CGRect bRect = [self movementBounds];
        bbtq = getTileCoordsForBoundingRect(bRect, CGSizeMake(kTile_Width,
            kTile_Height));
        if ([scene isBlocked:bbtq.x1 y:bbtq.y1] ||
            [scene isBlocked:bbtq.x2 y:bbtq.y2] ||
            [scene isBlocked:bbtq.x3 y:bbtq.y3] ||
            [scene isBlocked:bbtq.x4 y:bbtq.y4]) {
                tileLocation.x = oldPosition.x;
        }

        tileLocation.y -= (aDelta * (playerSpeed * speedOfMovement)) *
            sinf(angleOfMovement);
        bRect = [self movementBounds];
        bbtq = getTileCoordsForBoundingRect(bRect, CGSizeMake(kTile_Width,
            kTile_Height));
        if ([scene isBlocked:bbtq.x1 y:bbtq.y1] ||
            [scene isBlocked:bbtq.x2 y:bbtq.y2] ||
            [scene isBlocked:bbtq.x3 y:bbtq.y3] ||
            [scene isBlocked:bbtq.x4 y:bbtq.y4]) {
                tileLocation.y = oldPosition.y;
```

First of all, the player's current position is stored in the `oldPosition` ivar. When trying to move the player, we may find that he has entered a blocked tile and need to move him back to where he was. This ivar is used to restore the player's position if necessary.

Next, the `speedOfMovement` ivar is checked. If this isn't `0`, the player is moving, so we need to update his location. There is no point in running through all movement checks if the player isn't moving.

If he is moving, we start to calculate the player's new position. We do this one axis at a time (that is, `x` first followed by `y`). Checking one axis at a time enables the player to slide along walls.

The calculation of the new `x` location uses the player's speed, the speed received from the joypad, and the angle delta value:

```
tileLocation.x -= (aDelta * (playerSpeed * speedOfMovement)) *
    cosf(angleOfMovement);
```

A little math is used to work out the new position based on the `angleOfMovement`. With a new x location calculated, the player's current movement bounds are retrieved and the `getTileCoordsForBoundingRect` is called. This method converts the four corners of the rectangle into tile coordinates. This enables you to verify whether the tile in which that corner is located is blocked or not.

Figure 14.6 shows a diagram of what the collision check is doing.

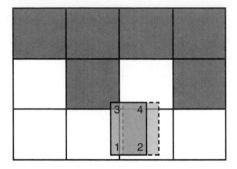

Figure 14.6   Movement bounds checked against
a blocked tile.

Figure 14.6 shows a tile map with blocked tiles colored red. The blue rectangle shows the movement bounds after applying the x movement, and the gray rectangle shows the original location.

You can see that Corner 3 on the blue rectangle is within a blocked tile. The check performed after the movement bounds have been converted to tile coordinates will spot this and set the player's x position back to the original position. This is a very quick and simple way to react to a collision with a wall. Depending on how far the player moves in a single update, there could be a gap left between the player's bounding box and the wall.

Within *Sir Lamorak's Quest*, the speeds used mean the gap cannot be seen, but in games with faster-moving objects, it would be necessary to position the player so that his bounding box was up against the wall when a collision is detected, not back at its original position.

If the y movement were then applied, and it was in a positive direction (that is, going up the tiles), no corners would have entered a blocked tile, and the movement would be allowed. This demonstrates how checking each axis individually enables you to slide along walls and other objects. Stopping dead on all axes as soon as you can't move in one of them is not a good feeling.

Listing 14.17 shows Part 2 of the `updateLocationWithDelta:` method that deals with switching the animation being used and setting the location of the OpenAL listener.

Listing 14.17   **Player updateLocationWithDelta: (Part 2)**

```
    if (angleOfMovement > 0.785 && angleOfMovement < 2.355) {
        currentAnimation = downAnimation;
    } else if (angleOfMovement < -0.785 && angleOfMovement > -2.355) {
        currentAnimation = upAnimation;
    } else if (angleOfMovement < -2.355 || angleOfMovement > 2.355) {
        currentAnimation = rightAnimation;
    } else {
        currentAnimation = leftAnimation;
    }
    [currentAnimation setState:kAnimationState_Running];
    [currentAnimation updateWithDelta:aDelta];

    [sharedSoundManager setListenerPosition:CGPointMake(pixelLocation.x,
        pixelLocation.y)];
} else {
    [currentAnimation setState:kAnimationState_Stopped];
    [currentAnimation setCurrentFrame:4];
}
```

> **Note**
>
> The odd-looking numbers used in Listing 14.17 are radians. These angles are used to define the quadrants shown in Figure 14.7.

When the joypad is touched, the player will run in the direction of the touch. To enhance the look of the game, we want to have the player animation that is used match the direction of travel. In *Sir Lamorak's Quest*, we only have four different animations, covering up, down, left, and right. To make things look as good as possible, we set the animation that should be used based on the angle at which the player is moving.

Figure 14.7 shows the angles that are being used to define the animation that should be used.

The `angleOfMovement` is checked against the radian value of the angles shown in Figure 14.7. The quadrant in which the joypad angle lays defines the animation that is going to be used. The quadrants are actually defined using 45-degree angles. I tried a few different values, but 45-degree seemed to work best. The values used in the `if` statement are in radians because the angle passed from the joypad is also in radians.

With the animation sorted out, the appropriate animation is updated and the position of the OpenAL listener is moved to the new player location. This is important because the listener is used to work out what OpenAL sounds can be heard, as you remember from Chapter 11, "Sound."

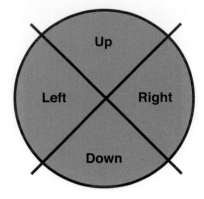

Figure 14.7   Joypad quadrants used to define
animation based on the character's direction.

If the player was not moving, the current animation's state is set to stopped and the animation frame is set to 4, which is the standing pose.

Inventory

The `Player` class is also responsible for handling the player's inventory. The following two classes are used to manage inventory:

- `placeInInventoryObject:`
- `dropInventoryInSlot:`

When the player adds an inventory item, the `placeInInventory:` method is called, as shown in Listing 14.18.

Listing 14.18   **Player placeInInventory: Method**

```
- (void)placeInInventoryObject:(AbstractObject*)aObject {

    if (aObject.state == kObjectState_Active) {
        if (!self.inventory1) {
            self.inventory1 = aObject;
            aObject.state = kObjectState_Inventory;
            aObject.isCollectable = NO;
            aObject.pixelLocation = CGPointMake(180, 303);
            [self checkForParchment:aObject pickup:YES];
        } else if (!self.inventory2) {
            aObject.state = kObjectState_Inventory;
            aObject.isCollectable = NO;
            aObject.pixelLocation = CGPointMake(240, 303);
            self.inventory2 = aObject;
            [self checkForParchment:aObject pickup:YES];
```

```
        } else if (!self.inventory3) {
            aObject.state = kObjectState_Inventory;
            aObject.isCollectable = NO;
            aObject.pixelLocation = CGPointMake(300, 303);
             self.inventory3 = aObject;
            [self checkForParchment:aObject pickup:YES];
        }
    }
}
```

First of all, the object being added has its state checked. If it is not marked as active, it's not added. If it is active, each of the three slots is checked to see if any are available. If an available slot is found, the state of the object is set to `kObjectState_Inventory`, marking it as being in the inventory. It is also marked as not collectible as you already have it, and its `pixelLocation` is set to the screen location used for that inventory slot.

A check is also performed to see if the object is a piece of parchment. Because the parchment pieces are important to finish the game, they are tracked. The `checkForParchment:pickup:` method is used to see if the object being picked up or dropped is a piece of parchment. If the player has all three pieces of parchment, a sound effect is played, letting the player know. Three flags are used to track which pieces of parchment the player is carrying. Only with all three flags set to `YES` can the player escape through the main entrance of the castle.

When dropping an inventory object, the `dropInventoryFromSlot:` method is called, as shown in Listing 14.19.

Listing 14.19   Player dropInventoryFromSlot: Method

```
- (void)dropInventoryFromSlot:(int)aInventorySlot {

    AbstractObject *invObject = nil;

    if (aInventorySlot == 0) {
        invObject = self.inventory1;
    } else if (aInventorySlot == 1) {
        invObject = self.inventory2;
    } else if (aInventorySlot == 2) {
        invObject = self.inventory3;
    }
    if (invObject) {
        invObject.pixelLocation = pixelLocation;
        invObject.tileLocation = tileLocation;
        invObject.state = kObjectState_Active;
    }
```

```
    if (aInventorySlot == 0) {
          self.inventory1 = nil;
    } else if (aInventorySlot == 1) {
          self.inventory2 = nil;
    } else if (aInventorySlot == 2) {
          self.inventory3 = nil;
    }

    [self checkForParchment:invObject pickup:NO];
}
```

The slot number is passed into the method from **GameScene**. The object associated with the inventory slot passed in is selected, and it has its `pixelLocation` set to the player's current `pixelLocation`. Its tile location is also updated, along with its state.

Entity Summary

Again, we have not been through all the entities implemented within *Sir Lamorak's Quest*, but we have reviewed the **AbstractEntity** and **Player** classes. This should provide you with the information you need to investigate the other entities to see how they work.

The entity classes we have not reviewed are very basic. The key activity takes place in their update routines that controls how they move and react to collisions with the tile map. The collision detection they perform on the map is the same as that used by the `Player` class.

Saving a Game Object or Entity

Being able to save the current state of a game object or entity is an important feature. This enables us to save the state of these objects and entities mid-game and then resume from where we left off later. This is actually easier than you may think.

You saw earlier that the **AbstractObject** and **AbstractEntity** classes implement the `NSCoding` protocol. This is a formal protocol, meaning that the class must implement the `NSCoding` methods. These are as follows:

- initWithCoder:
- encodeWithCoder:

Implementing this protocol means that the game object or entity can be archived using the `NSKeyedArchiver` to disk. When you have an array of objects or even single objects that you want to save, this is by far the easiest way to do it.

After an `NSKeyedArchiver` has been created, just a single command is needed to archive an entire array of objects or entities to a file. Listing 14.20 shows a snippet of code from the **GameController** saveGameState method.

Listing 14.20   **GameScene saveGameState Method NSKeyedArchiver Creation Snippet**

```
NSArray *paths = NSSearchPathForDirectoriesInDomains(NSDocumentDirectory,
    NSUserDomainMask, YES);
NSString *documentsDirectory = [paths objectAtIndex:0];
NSString *gameStatePath = [documentsDirectory
    stringByAppendingPathComponent:@"gameState.dat"];

NSKeyedArchiver *encoder;
gameData = [NSMutableData data];
encoder = [[NSKeyedArchiver alloc] initForWritingWithMutable Data:gameData];
[encoder encodeObject:gameScene.entities forKey:@"gameEntities"];
[encoder finishEncoding];
[gameData writeToFile:gameStatePath atomically:YES];
[encoder release];
```

This code snippet is creating a new instance of NSKeyedArchiver that is going to place its data into an NSMutableData store called gameData. It then encodes an array of entity objects and gives it the key gameEntities.

That's it—nothing else needs to be done, apart from asking the encoder to finish and then writing the data in the gameData structure to disk.

Each object inside the gameEntities array is asked to encode itself, which results in the encodeWithCoder: method being called for each object. This method is responsible for encoding each of the instance variables that need to be saved so that the object can be recreated at a later date.

iPhone Application Directories

For security reasons, when an application is loaded onto the iPhone, it only has a few locations to which it can write data. When an application is installed, it creates a home directory and a number of subdirectories that you may need to access. Table 14.1 shows the directories created and their intended purpose.

It's worth noting how the directories available to you should be used, so that your data gets backed up when necessary and is not removed when you least expect it.

Table 14.1   iPhone Application Directories

Directory	Description
<Application_Home>/ `AppName.app`	This bundle directory contains the application itself. The contents of this directory should not be changed because this could cause the application to stop launching later.
<Application_Home>/ `Documents/`	This directory should be used to store any application-specific data files. This directory is backed up by iTunes and should, therefore, store any information that you want to have backed up with your application.
<Application_Home>/ `Library/Preferences`	This directory stores the application-specific preferences files. You should not write directly to this directory but instead use the `NSUserDefaults` class to get and set preferences. You will see how this is done in *Sir Lamorak's Quest* in Chapter 16.
<Application_Home>/ `Library/Caches/`	This directory should be used to store any application-specific support files that you want to persist between launches. You are generally responsible for adding and removing these files, although iTunes will remove files from here during a full restore.
<Application_Home>/ `tmp/`	This directory can be used to store temporary data that does not need to be persisted between launches of the application. Your application should remove files from this directory when they are no longer needed. The system may also purge this directory when your application is not running.

Both the **AbstractObject** and **AbstractEntity** classes implement these methods. The encodeWithCoder: method from the **AbstractEntity** class is shown in Listing 14.21.

Listing 14.21   AbstractEntity encodeWithCoder: Method

```
- (void)encodeWithCoder:(NSCoder *)aCoder {
    [aCoder encodeCGPoint:tileLocation forKey:@"position"];
    [aCoder encodeFloat:speed forKey:@"speed"];
    [aCoder encodeFloat:angle forKey:@"angle"];
    [aCoder encodeInt:state forKey:@"entityState"];
    [aCoder encodeFloat:offScreenTimer forKey:@"offScreenTimer"];
    [aCoder encodeFloat:appearingTimer forKey:@"appearingTimer"];
}
```

This class simply encodes each instance variable in the object using the NSCoder passed into the method. Each instance variable is given a key, and it is this key that is used to access that information when you come to decode.

When an object is asked to decode itself, the `initWithCoder:` method is called instead. Listing 14.22 shows this method from the `AbstractEntity` class.

Listing 14.22   **AbstractEntity encodeWithCoder: Method**

```
- (id)initWithCoder:(NSCoder *)aDecoder {
    [self initWithTileLocation:[aDecoder decodeCGPointForKey:@"position"]];
    speed = [aDecoder decodeFloatForKey:@"speed"];
    angle = [aDecoder decodeFloatForKey:@"angle"];
    state = [aDecoder decodeIntForKey:@"entityState"];
    if (state == kEntityState_Dying)
        state = kEntityState_Dead;
    offScreenTimer = [aDecoder decodeFloatForKey:@"offScreenTimer"];
        pearingTimer = [aDecoder decodeFloatForKey:@"appearingTimer"];
    return self;
}
```

This class is provided with a decoder that is used to retrieve the instance variables for the class being created. This method needs to create a new instance of itself by calling its initializer, using the stored data if possible, and then sets the values of the remaining instance variables by using the key that was used when encoding the data.

By implementing `NSCoder` in the game object and entity classes, we have basically given them everything they need to encode and decode as necessary. The `Player`, `Door`, and `Axe` classes implement their own encode and decode classes because the data they save is different from that saved by the abstract class they inherit from.

We review how this is used to save the entire game state for *Sir Lamorak's Quest* in Chapter 16.

Summary

As said at the beginning of this chapter, game objects and entities provide the core playability of the game. Their behaviors and interaction with the player really define how the game works. By splitting them up into separate classes, we have the ability to uniquely tune their behaviors so that they each take on their own AI or function within the game.

We saw that some classes are used to implement similar objects if their behaviors are the same, but we also saw how the entities were implemented separately so that their behaviors or AI can be tuned, almost providing each of the baddies with its own personality. The fact that the witch character starts to chase Sir Lamorak when he gets within a certain range is an example of some unique behavior that has been implemented.

Although we have not been able to review all the game objects and entities in *Sir Lamorak's Quest*, having reviewed the abstract classes they use and a couple of examples, you should now be able to navigate the remaining classes to see how they work.

You should also not be afraid to make changes. Take something like the `Ghost` class and see if you can alter its behavior—maybe always chasing Sir Lamorak or altering how it roams around the castle. (Hint: Try making changes within the `update` method.)

In Chapter 15, "Collision Detection," we will review the collision detection strategy being used within *Sir Lamorak's Quest* and look at some other strategies that can be applied to the problem.

15

Collision Detection

This chapter reviews how collision detection has been implemented within *Sir Lamorak's Quest*, as well as the common problems that need to be solved. Without collision detection, the player and game characters would be able to wander through walls, and we'd have no way of knowing when the player or entities hit each other.

Although this chapter is titled "Collision Detection," it is important to remember that *collision response* should also be included. Detecting a collision and then responding are two different stages that need to be managed separately. This doesn't mean that they cannot physically be managed together in code, but that they should be considered separately when designing and implementing collision detection into your game.

Because *Sir Lamorak's Quest* is a 2D game, the collision detection covered in this chapter is also designed around 2D. Although some of the concepts of 2D collision detection can be applied to 3D, the problems associated with 3D collision detection are beyond the scope of this book.

Introduction to Collision Detection

Collision detection in 2D is not that complex when you break down the problem. You basically need to identify when two objects intersect each other. Back in the 1980s, a lot of collision detection was done at the pixel level. If a pixel in one sprite overlapped a pixel in another sprite, a collision had taken place. On some platforms, there was even hardware that helped to do these checks quickly.

Today, much of what is rendered to the screen is built from triangles, so it's not really a case anymore of just seeing if pixels have overlapped. That doesn't mean that this cannot be done, as it can, but scanning pixels inside a texture and checking for overlaps is a time-consuming process.

A key point about most games is that they are a simulation. Therefore, if something can be done that looks good enough, then it is good enough. The fact that a collision is detected that's not pixel perfect is not really a problem in games, especially in fast moving games where a mater of a few pixels is most likely not even going to be noticed by the player.

Some games model the real world much more accurately using physics engines, but again, some physics engines still cheat when checking for collisions and responses and just do enough to give the illusion of a real-world interaction between objects.

Luckily for us, *Sir Lamorak's Quest* isn't trying to be clever and uses just basic collision detection techniques.

Collision Pruning

As you can imagine, in a game with a lot of entities running around the screen (and maybe even off the screen), checking for collisions with each of them can become a big job. For this reason, it's recommended that you prune the number of actual collisions that you check for.

There are many different ways of doing this, from using a basic tile map and identifying in which tile an entity may be through to *spatial partitioning*[1] used to divide space into smaller areas.

With the tile-based approach, you can find out what tile an entity is in and compare that to the tile the player is in. If the tiles are the same or within a set distance of each other, you know that a collision is likely, so you perform the actual collision test. If the entity is in a tile, that means they could not possibly collide with the player and no collision check is necessary.

Reducing the number of collision checks done is a great way to improve performance. Although it may take more code to prune the checks that are carried out, it almost always improves overall performance, unless the pruning checks are carrying out even more complex calculations than the collision check.

This pruning done within *Sir Lamorak's Quest* is based on an object's tile location. The coordinates of the visible tile map are calculated within the GameScene's updateWithDelta: method. Only objects that are located within those coordinates are updated and checked for collision with the player. Listing 15.1 shows the code within that method that calculates the boundaries and loops through the objects.

Listing 15.1   **GameScene updateSceneWithDelta: Method—Object Update**

```
int minScreenTile_x = CLAMP(player.tileLocation.x - 8, 0,
    kMax_Map_Width-1);
int maxScreenTile_x = CLAMP(player.tileLocation.x + 8, 0,
    kMax_Map_Width-1);
int minScreenTile_y = CLAMP(player.tileLocation.y - 6, 0,
    kMax_Map_Height-1);
int maxScreenTile_y = CLAMP(player.tileLocation.y + 6, 0,
    kMax_Map_Height-1);
```

---

[1] Information on spatial portioning can be found at **en.wikipedia.org/wiki/Spatial_partitioning**.

```
isPlayerOverObject = NO;
for(AbstractObject *gameObject in gameObjects) {

    if (gameObject.tileLocation.x >= minScreenTile_x &&
        gameObject.tileLocation.x <= maxScreenTile_x &&
        gameObject.tileLocation.y >= minScreenTile_y &&
        gameObject.tileLocation.y <= maxScreenTile_y) {

        // Update the object
        [gameObject updateWithDelta:aDelta scene:self];

        if (gameObject.state == kObjectState_Active) {
            [player checkForCollisionWithObject:gameObject];
            [gameObject checkForCollisionWithEntity:player];
             if (gameObject.isCollectable) {
                isPlayerOverObject = YES;
            }
        }
    }
}
```

First, the `min` and `max` tile coordinates are calculated based on the player's position. The `CLAMP` macro means that if the player reaches the edge of the map, the tile coordinates won't fall below 0 or above the map's bounds.

With the coordinates calculated, we then loop through all the objects in the `gameObjects` array. If we have an object that is located within those bounds, it is updated. This stops us from wasting time updating objects that are not visible. This implementation is specific to *Sir Lamorak's Quest*. Other games may require entities that are not visible on-screen to still be updated. In this situation, you could update the entity but still not render it because it's not visible anyway.

After the object is updated, we then check it to see if it has collided with the player. We could prune further by only performing the collision check on objects that are even closer to the player, but given there are never that many objects on screen at once, the performance boost would be minimal.

This same test is also used later in this method when updating doors. There are many doors within the map, so updating only those that are near the player helps improve performance.

Frame-Based Versus Time-Based

In Chapter 4, "The Game Loop," you saw the problems caused by updating the game per-frame, as opposed to updating based on time. With a fast-moving object, it may have completely passed through a wall in between frames and the collision checks may miss that altogether.

Breaking the link between frame rate and update rate really helps us with collision detection. The game loop being used in *Sir Lamorak's Quest* actually uses a fixed delta rather than calculating the amount of time between frames and using that value as the delta.

Instead, the game loop updates the game more than once per frame using this fixed delta. The render method is called only after the update has run enough times to meet the frame rate set. This means that the entities in the game move at a constant rate during each update.

As more updates are performed per frame, fast-moving entities are updated and checked more frequently, reducing the chances of missing a collision with another entity or map object.

A nice side effect of this is easier testing. Because the delta passed in is constant, you are able to step through the game one frame at a time and see how the entities move and the game reacts. Using a variable delta value doesn't let you do this. It could be some seconds between updating frames when skipping through the code, so using a delta of this size would create some crazy situations with entities never spotting collisions.

Axis-Aligned Bounding Boxes

Axis-Aligned Bounding Boxes (AABB) are a popular way of managing simple collision detection in 2D games. It can even be used in a 3D game by extending the bounding box to be three-dimensional surrounding the 3D object. Figure 15.1 shows *Sir Lamorak's Quest* with the entities' bounding boxes being rendered.

Figure 15.1   Bounding boxes in *Sir Lamorak's Quest*.

Two different bounding boxes are being rendered in Figure 15.1. The blue boxes around the player and ghosts show the movement bounds, and the green boxes indicate collision bounds. Each of these is an AABB (basically, a rectangle that has not been rotated).

As you saw in Chapter 14, "Game Objects and Entities," each object and entity is responsible for providing its movement and collision bounds. These are simple CGRect structures that provide details of the rectangle to be used.

> **Tip**
>
> Although *Sir Lamorak's Quest* uses boxes, it is possible to use other shapes as well. Bounding circles are another common approach to detecting if a collision has taken place. Some games also use multiple bounding boxes or circles for a single entity. This is useful if an entity is a complex shape. Having a single bounding box around a complex shape can cause large areas to be included in the bounding box that contain no part of the entity. This could cause collisions to occur that make no sense.

Using multiple shapes reduces the amount of dead space included in the bounding box. This is a technique 2D fighting games have used for years. The arms, legs, body, and head of each fighter have their own bounding box to make for more accurate "collisions" during a fight sequence.

Detecting Collisions

When using AABBs, it's really easy to check if they intersect, and this intersection indicates they have collided. You could roll your own algorithm that checks for an intersection or, as I have done in *Sir Lamorak's Quest*, use the `CGRectIntersectsRect` function provided by the SDK.

This function takes two rectangles and returns 1 if they intersect. Now this only handles AABBs if the bounding boxes being used have not been rotated.

If you wanted to check for *Oriented Bounding Boxes* (OBB; that is, rotated rectangles), you would need to roll your own algorithm. There are many different ways this can be done using things such as the *separating axis theorem*.[2] This is beyond the scope of this book, but there is plenty of material and tutorials on the Internet.

If you wanted to be able to rotate a sprite, you could move to using circles to define the bounds of the entity. This doesn't work on all shapes—only shapes that would fill the majority of the bounding circle—but using circles means that you can rotate the entity without worrying about rotating the bounds. The only problem left to solve is circles intersecting rectangles. Listing 15.2 shows a function that could be used for this test.

Listing 15.2   Circle-to-Rectangle Collision Detection Function

```
static inline BOOL RectIntersectsCircle(CGRect aRect, Circle aCircle) {

    float testX = aCircle.x;
    float testY = aCircle.y;

    if (testX < aRect.origin.x)
        testX = aRect.origin.x;
    if (testX > (aRect.origin.x + aRect.size.width))
        testX = (aRect.origin.x + aRect.size.width);
```

[2] The separating axis theorem: **en.wikipedia.org/wiki/Separating_axis_theorem**.

```
    if (testY < aRect.origin.y)
        testY = aRect.origin.y;
    if (testY > (aRect.origin.y + aRect.size.height))
        testY = (aRect.origin.y + aRect.size.height);

    return ((aCircle.x - testX) * (aCircle.x - testX) +
        (aCircle.y - testY) * (aCircle.y - testY)) < aCircle.radius *
        aCircle.radius;
}
```

If you were using circles for all entities, you would need to also handle collisions between circles. Listing 15.3 shows a function that checks for intersections between circles.

Listing 15.3   **Circle-to-Circle Collision Detection Function**

```
static inline BOOL CircleIntersectsCircle(Circle aCircle1, Circle aCircle2) {
    float dx = aCircle2.x - aCircle1.x;
    float dy = aCircle2.y - aCircle1.y;
    float radii = aCircle1.radius + aCircle2.radius;

    return ((dx * dx) + (dy * dy)) < radii * radii;
}
```

It is important that these functions are quick. They are likely to be called many times per second, so they need to be as speedy as possible. You'll notice that we have stayed away from using the `sqrtf` function when calculating distances, as calculating the square root is an expensive task in terms of performance. Both of these functions have been included within the code for *Sir Lamorak's Quest* in the *Global.h* file. They are not used within the game but are included for completeness. These functions have also been defined as static C functions to cut down on the messaging used to call them, again helping with performance.

The `Circle` structure used to hold details of a circle is included in the `Structures.h` file found in the `Global Header` group.

Collision Map

Detecting if an entity has collided with a blocked tile on the map is a core use case in *Sir Lamorak's Quest*. We need to stop entities and the player walking through walls, tables, doors, and other items around the castle.

Tiles that are blocked are defined within the tile map. Inside the map for *Sir Lamorak's Quest*, there is a layer called `Collision`. This layer is used to both define what tiles are blocked and where doors should be placed. Figure 15.2 shows this layer in the Tiled editor.

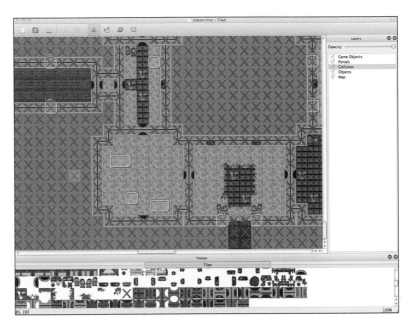

Figure 15.2   Tiled showing the collision layer in sqltsor.tmx.

Any tile that contains a red cross is blocked. This is a nice visual aid when editing the map. You'll notice that in the tile sheet at the bottom of the screen, there is a tile that contains a simple red cross. This is what I paint in the Collision layer to mark a blocked tile.

During game initialization, a collision map is built using a simple 2D array. This array simply holds 1 for a blocked tile and 0 for a clear tile. Listing 15.4 shows the initCollisionMapAndDoors: method inside GameScene.

Listing 15.4   GameScene initCollisionMapAndDoors: Method

```
- (void)initCollisionMapAndDoors {

    SLQLOG(@"INFO - GameScene: Creating tilemap collision array and doors.");

    int collisionLayerIndex = [castleTileMaplayerIndexWithName:@"Collision"];

    Door *door = nil;


    Layer *collisionLayer = [[castleTileMap layers]
        objectAtIndex:collisionLayerIndex];
    for(int yy=0; yy < castleTileMap.mapHeight; yy++) {
        for(int xx=0; xx < castleTileMap.mapWidth; xx++) {
            int globalTileID = [collisionLayer
                globalTileIDAtTile:CGPointMake(xx, yy)];
```

```
        if(globalTileID == kBlockedTileGloablID) {
            blocked[xx][yy] = YES;
        } else  {
            if (!sharedGameController.shouldResumeGame) {
                if (globalTileID >= kFirstDoorTileGlobalID &&
                    globalTileID <= kLastDoorTileGlobalID) {
                    int doorType = [[castleTileMap
                        tilePropertyForGlobalTileID:globalTileID
                                            key:@"type"
                                defaultValue:@"-1"] intValue];
                    if (doorType != -1) {
                      door = [[Door alloc]
                          initWithTileLocation:CGPointMake(xx, yy)
                          type:doorType arrayIndex:[doors count]];
                      [doors addObject:door];
                      [door release];
                    }
                }
            }
        }
    }
}
    SLQLOG (@"INFO - GameScene: Finished constructing collision array
        and doors.");
}
```

This method basically loops through the layer called `Collision` in the tile map. Any tile that has a `globalTileID` of `160` is marked as blocked. This is a little trick to speed things up. I could have easily added a property to the blocking tile image in Tiled. This would make changing the tile used much easier. The problem is that this is very slow. Querying the properties of each tile for an entire map is not quick, and I wanted to reduce the load times of the game as much as possible. To speed things up, I simply use the `globalTileID` instead. This requires no queries and speeds up processing time by over 300 percent!

Note

Another approach is to only parse the map file once. After the map file has been parsed, the first time the game is played, the contents of the map's objects created could be saved. The next time the game is played, this pre-processed data could then be loaded, removing the need to parse the tile map again. This could even be a pre-process that you perform so only this parsed data is placed into the game, not the tmx file.

The same approach is used when parsing the doors. To identify that a tile is actually a door, I check the tiles `globalTileID` to see if it is within a set range. It does tie the tileset tightly to the code, but it really does improve performance.

Inside the **GameScene** class is a method called `isBlocked:y:`, which is used to identify whether a tile is blocked or not, as shown in Listing 15.5.

Listing 15.5   **GameScene isBlocked:y: Method**

```
- (BOOL)isBlocked:(float)x y:(float)y {
    if (x < 0 || y < 0 || x > kMax_Map_Width || y > kMax_Map_Height) {
        return YES;
    }

    return blocked[(int)x][(int)y];
}
```

By passing in the tile coordinates, this method first checks that the coordinates are within the tile maps dimensions and then returns the contents of that location in the `blocked` array. You may remember from the last chapter that this method is used when moving the player to identify blocked tiles.

Entity-to-Map Collision Detection

Having the collision map, we can now test an entity's collision bounds to see if they have entered a blocked tile. As you'll remember, each entity has a defined collision bound, and these bounds can be the same size or smaller than a tile on the tile map. You can't have collision bounds that are larger than a map tile because the collision testing being done checks the corners of the bounding rectangle. If a tile could lie between these corners, a collision would not be detected, as seen in Figure 15.3.

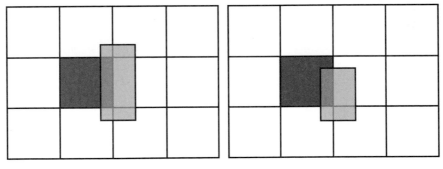

Example A   Example B

Figure 15.3   Bounding boxes on a tile map.

In Example A, checking if each corner of the blue bounding box has collided with a blocked red tile would fail because no corners are inside the blocked tile. We can clearly see, though, that the bounding box has collided with the tile.

In Example B, the bounding box has the same dimensions as a tile, and now no matter if the bounding box is slightly below or above the blocked tile, a collision will be registered.

There is nothing stopping us from altering the collision checks that are being done to not just focus on the corners, but also to look for intersection anywhere between the blocked tile and the collision bounds. This is, however, more complex and not implemented in *Sir Lamorak's Quest*.

Listing 15.6 shows how to check if a collision bounds rectangle has collided with a blocked tile.

Note

To remove the constraint of a moving entity's collision bounds not being larger than a map tile, the AABB collision check could be used when checking collisions with the tile map rather than the collision check shown in Listing 15.6.

Listing 15.6   **Entity-to-Map Collision Check**

```
CGRect bRect = [self movementBounds];


BoundingBoxTileQuad bbtq = getTileCoordsForBoundingRect(bRect,
CGSizeMake(kTile_Width, kTile_Height));

if([scene isBlocked:bbtq.x1 y:bbtq.y1] ||
   [scene isBlocked:bbtq.x2 y:bbtq.y2] ||
   [scene isBlocked:bbtq.x3 y:bbtq.y3] ||
   [scene isBlocked:bbtq.x4 y:bbtq.y4]) {
       // Collision detected
}
```

First of all, an entity's movement bounds are retrieved and the corners converted into tile map locations. Then each corner's location is checked using the `isBlocked:y:` method to see if it is inside a blocked tile.

If a collision occurs, the entity needs to respond. In the case of the entities in *Sir Lamorak's Quest*, this simply involves moving in a different direction. Each entity has an angle that specifies the direction in which they are moving. If they collide with a blocked tile, their angle is updated to move them in the opposite direction.

Entity-to-Entity Collision Detection

This is the most straightforward collision detection you'll find in *Sir Lamorak's Quest*. Given the collision bounds for the entity and also details of the entity we could be colliding with, the entities `checkForCollisionWithEntity:` method is called. Listing 15.7 shows this method inside the **Ghost** class.

Listing 15.7   Ghost checkForCollisionWithEntity: Method

```
- (void)checkForCollisionWithEntity:(AbstractEntity *)aEntity {

        if(([aEntity isKindOfClass:[Player class]] ||
            [aEntity isKindOfClass:[Axe class]]) &&
            aEntity.state == kEntityState_Alive) {
            if (CGRectIntersectsRect([self collisionBounds], [aEntity
                collisionBounds])) {

            [sharedSoundManager playSoundWithKey:@"pop"
                location:CGPointMake(tileLocation.x*kTile_Width,
                tileLocation.y*kTile_Height)];
            state = kEntityState_Dying;
            dyingEmitter.sourcePosition = Vector2fMake(pixelLocation.x,
                pixelLocation.y);
            [dyingEmitter setDuration: kDyingEmitterDuration];
            [dyingEmitter setActive:YES];
            scene.score += 150;

        }
    }
}
```

If the entity passed in is the player or the axe, a check is performed to see if the entity's bounding boxes intersect. If they do, a sound effect is played at the entity's position and their state is set to `kEntityState_Dying`. The `dyingEmitter` also has its position changed to match the entities position and is started. Finally, the player's score is increased by 150. (This value could be different for each entity, allowing the player to score more points for killing specific entities.)

As noted earlier, collision detection and collision response need to be treated differently. Having detected a collision between two entities, the next step of the process is to determine what happens immediately following that collision. Listing 15.7 showed the action the `Ghost` entity will take, and Listing 15.8 shows the action the **Player** entity will take.

Listing 15.8   Player checkForCollisionWithEntity: Method

```
- (void)checkForCollisionWithEntity:(AbstractEntity*)aEntity {

    if (CGRectIntersectsRect([self collisionBounds],
        [aEntity collisionBounds])) {
```

```
       if((([aEntity isKindOfClass:[Ghost class]] ||
          [aEntity isKindOfClass:[Frank class]] ||
          [aEntity isKindOfClass:[Witch class]] ||
          [aEntity isKindOfClass:[Pumpkin class]] ||
          [aEntity isKindOfClass:[Bat class]] ||
          [aEntity isKindOfClass:[Vampire class]] ||
          [aEntity isKindOfClass:[Zombie class]]) &&
          state == kEntityState_Alive) {
          energy -= aEntity.energyDrain;
       }
    }
}
```

As you can see, how the `Player` deals with a collision is very different from how the `Ghost` deals with a collision. If the `Ghost` is hit, the ghost dies and Sir Lamorak gets 150 points. If the `Player` is hit, the player's health is reduced using `energyDrain`, which defines for the entity that has been passed in.

Summary

In this chapter, we have reviewed the basics necessary for collision detection. We have seen how even the game loop has a role to play in terms of enabling us to perform updates that are either frame or time based. We have also seen how pruning the number of collision checks that need to be performed is important and can significantly improve performance when dealing with a large number of entities.

This chapter has also covered the common shapes that 2D games use for bounding sprites and the detection functions needed, such as rectangle-to-rectangle, rectangle-to-circle, and circle-to-circle.

More specifically for *Sir Lamorak's Quest*, we also reviewed how a collision map is created using the tile map, and how to detect entity collisions with the map and entities colliding with other entities.

Chapter 16, "Pulling It All Together," covers all the last details we need to review in *Sir Lamorak's Quest*. These include the scoring system, saving game state, beta testing, and performance tuning.

16

Pulling It All Together

This chapter covers the areas needed to finish off *Sir Lamorak's Quest*. The features discussed include saving the game's state, saving the player's scores, performance tuning, and getting the game beta tested.

We have come a long way since the start of this book, and a lot of detail has been covered. From my own experience, and the experience of many other programmers I've spoken to on forums, the last 10 percent of a game is the hardest. Finishing off those little touches, tweaking the game play, checking for memory leaks, and so on all need to be done—and they can make or break a game.

The "Camera"

No, I'm not going to describe how to become a professional photographer, but I am going to run through one of the most important elements of *Sir Lamorak's Quest*—the camera. By *camera*, I mean the process by which Sir Lamorak is rendered in the middle of the screen, and how the map scrolls around in relation to Sir Lamorak's position.

How a camera is implemented really depends on the game. For *Sir Lamorak's Quest*, I chose to keep the knight in the middle of the screen at all times. Another approach could have been to let the knight move to the edge of the screen when he reached the edge of the tile map, causing the tile map to never scroll beyond its bounds.

The implementation of the camera for *Sir Lamorak's Quest* is actually very basic and is handled within the `renderScene` method in the **GameScene** class. Listing 16.1 shows the code in this method that is used to position Sir Lamorak in the middle of the screen.

Listing 16.1 **GameScene's renderScene Method Positions the Player in the Middle of the Screen**

```
glClear(GL_COLOR_BUFFER_BIT);
glPushMatrix();
glTranslatef(240 - player.pixelLocation.x, 160 -
    player.pixelLocation.y, 0);
```

After clearing the screen, the current model view matrix is pushed onto the stack, saving its contents. This is followed by a glTranslate command that takes half the width and height of the iPhone screen and subtracts the player's pixel location.

Remember that our tile map is 200×200 tiles. With each tile being 40×40 pixels, that gives us an area that is 8000×8000 pixels.

By translating in this way, when we render the knight at its current pixel location, it will be in the middle of the screen, even though it is being rendered based on our world coordinates. Each time a scene is rendered, we are positioning the camera (that is, the iPhone's screen) directly above Sir Lamorak's location, with the knight in the middle of the screen. This gives the impression that the knight is stationary and the map is moving around the knight.

With our translation now set up, we can render the map layers. For this, we need to calculate which tiles are going to be visible based on the knight's location. Listing 16.2 shows the tile map rendering code used to render the map and object layers.

Listing 16.2   **GameScene's renderScene Method (Tile Map Rendering)**

```
[castleTileMap renderLayer:0
            mapx:playerTileX - leftOffsetInTiles - 1
            mapy:playerTileY - bottomOffsetInTiles - 1
            width:screenTilesWide + 2
            height:screenTilesHeight + 2
            useBlending:NO];
[castleTileMap renderLayer:1
            mapx:playerTileX - leftOffsetInTiles - 1
            mapy:playerTileY - bottomOffsetInTiles - 1
            width:screenTilesWide + 2
            height:screenTilesHeight + 2
            useBlending:YES];
```

As you saw when we covered the **TiledMap** class in Chapter 9, "Tile Maps," the location of each tile is calculated when the tile map is initialized. Having used glTranslate to move the world's coordinates, as long as we render tiles around the player, they will be visible onscreen. This means that we need to work out which tiles will be visible based on the player's location.

Knowing the player's tile location, the leftOffsetInTiles and bottomOffsetInTiles are calculated when GameScene is initialized using the following:

```
bottomOffsetInTiles = screenTilesHeight / 2;
leftOffsetInTiles = screenTilesWide / 2;
```

This enables us to calculate the x and y tile within the tile map from where we need to start rendering. We also use the screenTilesWide and screenTilesHigh variables, which were calculated during initialization using the following:

```
screenTilesWide = screenBounds.size.width / kTile_Width;
screenTilesHeight = screenBounds.size.height / kTile_Height;
```

Notice that we are actually subtracting 1 from the x and y tile location, and adding 2 to the `width` and `height`. As the player moves around, the tile map changes by a minimum of one pixel at a time if the player is moving slowly. This causes the map to move smoothly around the player. By adjusting the x and y tile map location along with the `width` and `height`, we can render a section of tile map that is a little larger than the screen. This means that as the player moves around, you won't see tiles suddenly disappear as they leave the screen or suddenly appear as they enter the screen.

Having rendered the tile map, the `renderScene` method then renders each of the entities and objects whose positions are relative to the tile map. Remember that we still have our translation in place so these entities and objects will be rendered in relation to the player and the map correctly.

After we render all the game objects and entities, we then pop the model view matrix from the stack using `glPopMatrix`. This puts the model view matrix back to the state it was in before we started to render the scene. We can start to render the game's interface items that need to float above the game and that we don't need to render in relation to the game objects and entities.

> **Note**
>
> It can take a while to get your head around how the camera works, but this implementation is actually very simple. Other games implement much more complex cameras, where it may be possible to move the camera independently from the player.
>
> *Sir Lamorak's Quest* implements a fixed camera with the camera's position being calculated within the render method. To achieve more complex camera behavior, you would need to implement a separate camera method that is responsible for calculating the position of the camera base on as many parameters and options as were necessary.

Saving the Game State and Settings

One of the key design points noted back in Chapter 1, "Game Design," was that the game had to be casual. This meant that the game had to be simple enough that the player could pick it up and put it down without needing to read pages of instructions. It also meant that the player should be able to stop playing at any time and have his progress saved.

Hitting the Home button on the iPhone when your train arrives and losing your progress is annoying, and chances are the user will soon delete your game (and hopefully not give it a one-star rating). Hitting the Home button and then being able to either start from scratch or continue from where you left off is much more friendly.

Saving Game State

To make this happen, we need to be able to save the game's state as soon as the player hits the Home button, or returns to the main menu from the settings screen. As discussed in Chapter 14, "Game Objects and Entities," each object in the game can be written to handle its own archiving by implementing the `NSCoding` protocol.

What we now need is the ability to save and restore those objects. Saving the games state is implemented in the **GameScene** class. All the information we want to save is in the GameScene, so it makes sense to place the method in that class. We also need to save the game settings, but this is done within the **GameController** class and covered later in this chapter.

The method responsible for saving our games state is called, well, saveGameState: and can be seen in Listing 16.3.

Listing 16.3   **GameScene saveGameState: Method**

```
- (void)saveGameState {
    SLQLOG(@"INFO - GameScene: Saving game state.");

    NSArray *paths = NSSearchPathForDirectoriesInDomains(NSDocumentDirectory,
        NSUserDomainMask, YES);
    NSString *documentsDirectory = [paths objectAtIndex:0];
    NSString *gameStatePath =
    [documentsDirectory stringByAppendingPathComponent:@"gameState.dat"];

    NSMutableData *gameData;
    NSKeyedArchiver *encoder;
    gameData = [NSMutableData data];
    encoder = [[NSKeyedArchiver alloc] initForWritingWithMutableData:gameData];

    // Archive the entities
    [encoder encodeObject:gameEntities forKey:@"gameEntities"];

    // Archive the player
    [encoder encodeObject:player forKey:@"player"];

    // Archive the players weapon
    [encoder encodeObject:axe forKey:@"weapon"];

    // Archive the games doors
    [encoder encodeObject:doors forKey:@"doors"];

    // Archive the game objects
    [encoder encodeObject:gameObjects forKey:@"gameObjects"];

    // Archive the games timer settings
    NSNumber *savedGameStartTime = [NSNumber numberWithFloat:gameStartTime];
    NSNumber *savedTimeSinceGameStarted =
    [NSNumber numberWithFloat:timeSinceGameStarted];
    NSNumber *savedScore = [NSNumber numberWithFloat:score];
    [encoder encodeObject:savedGameStartTime forKey:@"gameStartTime"];
    [encoder encodeObject:savedTimeSinceGameStarted
        forKey:@"timeSinceGameStarted"];
```

```
[encoder encodeObject:savedScore forKey:@"score"];
[encoder encodeInt:locationName forKey:@"locationName"];

// Finish encoding and write the contents of gameData to file
[encoder finishEncoding];
[gameData writeToFile:gameStatePath atomically:YES];
[encoder release];

// Tell the game controller that a resumed game is available
sharedGameController.resumedGameAvailable = YES;
}
```

The first task for this method is to create a path to the file that is going to store the games data. This is going to be called *gameState.dat*, and will be saved to the game's sandbox *documents* directory. Remember that every application on the iPhone has its own sandbox directory structure that is created with the application and also deleted when the application is deleted. The commonly used directory in this sandbox for saving data is the *documents* directory.

With the path set up, an `NSKeyedArchiver` is created along with a storage area where the archived data is going to be held. This is an `NSMutableData` variable called `gameData`.

With those in place, we simply ask each of the arrays that store game data to encode themselves and provide a key for getting to that data when we come to decode the information. When encoding an object that is an array, each object in the array that supports `NSCoding` is asked to encode itself using the code we saw in Chapter 14. This enables us to encode an entire array with just this one line of code.

After all the important arrays are encoded, we also encode the single objects and values that we want to save. These include the player, axe, score, and times. With this information all encoded, we then finish encoding and write the contents of `gameData` to the `gameStatePath` calculated at the start of the method. That's it—all the data required to run our game is now ready to be loaded when we want to resume a game.

Loading Game State

With our game state saved, we now need a mechanism to load it back again. This really is just the reverse of what we have just seen. This is handled by the `loadGameState:` method inside `GameScene`, shown in Listing 16.4.

Listing 16.4   **GameScene loadGameState: Method**

```
- (void)loadGameState {

    [self initGameContent];

    // Set up the file manager and documents path
    NSArray *paths =
        NSSearchPathForDirectoriesInDomains(NSDocumentDirectory,
        NSUserDomainMask, YES);
    NSString *documentsDirectory = [paths objectAtIndex:0];

    NSMutableData *gameData;
    NSKeyedUnarchiver *decoder;

// Check to see if the ghosts.dat file exists and if so load the contents into the
    // entities array
    NSString *documentPath = [documentsDirectory
        stringByAppendingPathComponent:@"gameState.dat"];
    gameData = [NSData dataWithContentsOfFile:documentPath];

    decoder = [[NSKeyedUnarchiver alloc] initForReadingWithData:gameData];

    SLQLOG(@"INFO - GameScene: Loading saved player data.");
    player = [[decoder decodeObjectForKey:@"player"] retain];
    [self calculatePlayersTileMapLocation];

    SLQLOG(@"INFO - GameScene: Loading saved weapon data.");
    axe = [[decoder decodeObjectForKey:@"weapon"] retain];

    SLQLOG(@"INFO - GameScene: Loading saved entity data.");
    if (gameEntities)
    [gameEntities release];
    gameEntities = [[decoder decodeObjectForKey:@"gameEntities"] retain];

    SLQLOG(@"INFO - GameScene: Loading saved game object data.");
    if (gameObjects)
     [gameObjects release];
    gameObjects = [[decoder decodeObjectForKey:@"gameObjects"] retain];

    SLQLOG(@"INFO - GameScene: Loading saved door data.");
    if (doors)
        [doors release];
    doors = [[decoder decodeObjectForKey:@"doors"] retain];

    SLQLOG(@"INFO - GameScene: Loading saved game duration.");
    timeSinceGameStarted =
        [[decoder decodeObjectForKey:@"timeSinceGameStarted"]
        floatValue];
```

```
    SLQLOG(@"INGO - GameScene: Loading saved game score.");
    score = [[decoder decodeObjectForKey:@"score"] floatValue];

    SLQLOG(@"INFO - GameScene: Loading game time data.");
    locationName = [decoder decodeIntForKey:@"locationName"];

    SLQLOG(@"INFO - GameScene: Loading game time data.");
    [decoder release];

    // Init the localDoors array
    [self initLocalDoors];
}
```

The start of this method calls the `initGameContent` method that sets up the tile map, collision map, and portals. With these configured, we then generate a path to the *gameState.dat* file that was created when we saved the game state. A `decoder` is then set up and the data that was saved is reloaded using the keys we defined when saving the information. Decoding the object with the key `gameEntities` causes the appropriate entity class to be called with `initWithCoder:coder:`, which creates a new instance of the class. That instance is then loaded into the `gameEntities` array. Once this is finished, the array and its entities are in exactly the same state it was when it was saved.

Finally, the `initLocalDoors` method is called. This is responsible for populating the `localDoors` array. This array is populated with doors that are within the visible tile map. Only these doors are updated and rendered, which helps with performance. The local door's array is updated each time the player moves.

Saving Game Settings

As well as saving game data that allows us to restore a game, we also need to save the game's settings. These are the music volume, sound effect's volume, the location of the joypad, and the fire direction. Rather than use the same method we used when saving the game state (which is perfectly valid), I decided to use `NSUserDefaults`.

`NSUserDefaults` provides a way to programmatically interact with the defaults system. Information stored in `NSUserDefaults` is written to the `<Application_Home>/Library/Preferences` directory.

Using `NSUserDefaults` makes it extremely easy to store the settings values for our game. The settings values are managed inside the **GameController** class, so that is where the `saveSettings` method has been implemented, as shown in Listing 16.5.

Listing 16.5   **GameController saveSettings Method**

```
- (void)saveSettings {
    [settings setFloat:sharedSoundManager.musicVolume forKey:@"musicVolume"];
    [settings setFloat:sharedSoundManager.fxVolume forKey:@"fxVolume"];
    [settings setInteger:self.joypadPosition forKey:@"joypadPosition"];
    [settings setInteger:self.fireDirection forKey:@"fireDirection"];
}
```

The settings variable is configured in the `initGameController` method of the
GameController class using the following:

```
settings = [[NSUserDefaults standardUserDefaults] retain];
```

With settings initialized, we can use the methods available within `NSUserDefaults` to
store the setting's values. You'll notice that we defined a key for each entry stored. This information will be used when reading the settings when the game is loaded.

Loading Game Settings

Having saved the game settings, we need to be able to load them. This is done when the
game first loads. Inside the `SLQTSORAppDelegate` class, the
`applicationDidFinishLaunching:` method calls the `GameController loadSettings`
method, shown in Listing 16.6.

Listing 16.6   GameController loadSettings Method

```
- (void)loadSettings {

    SLQLOG(@"INFO - EAGLView: Loading settings.");

    if (![settings boolForKey:@"userDefaultsSet"]) {
        [settings setBool:1 forKey:@"userDefaultsSet"];
        [settings setFloat:0.5f forKey:@"musicVolume"];
        [sharedSoundManager setMusicVolume:0.5f];
        [settings setFloat:0.75f forKey:@"fxVolume"];
        [sharedSoundManager setFxVolume:0.75f];
        [settings setInteger:0 forKey:@"joypadPosition"];
        self.joypadPosition = 0;
        [settings setInteger:0 forKey:@"fireDirection"];
        self.fireDirection = 0;
    } else {
        [sharedSoundManager setMusicVolume:[settings
            floatForKey:@"musicVolume"]];
        [sharedSoundManager setFxVolume:[settings
            floatForKey:@"fxVolume"]];
        self.joypadPosition = [settings integerForKey:@"joypadPosition"];
        self.fireDirection = [settings integerForKey:@"fireDirection"];
    }

    [[NSNotificationCenter defaultCenter]
        postNotificationName:@"updateSettingsSliders"
        object:self];
}
```

The method first checks to see if the NSUserDefaults entry with the key userDefaultsSet has a value of 1. If not, the games settings have never been saved, so default values are used and the userDefaultsSet entry is updated to 1.

If the userDefaultsSet preference does have a value of 1, the values for the games settings are read.

Last of all, a notification is posted called updateSettingsSliders. At this point, the **SettingsViewController** class will have been initialized, so we need the controls on that view to be updated with the values read from the settings file. That class observes the notification, and the controls are updated using the values now managed by the GameController.

Saving High Scores

So far, we have looked at how to save the game's state and settings. There is more information that needs to be saved: the player's high score.

The player and his friends will play the game and fail, at least when they first start playing. They will also eventually win and want to improve their score or time. For them to do this, they need to be able to look back at what they have achieved in the past.

This is done by providing them with a high scores table. You will have seen this when trying out the *SLQTSOR* project. The score is held as in integer within the **GameScene** class and is incremented by each entity when it is killed.

Within the **GameScene** class, an instance variable called score holds the players score. This score is updated by each entity as they are killed. When the game ends, either because the player won or lost, they are presented with a screen that provides them with information on their game (that is, how long they played for and what their score was). The Game Over screen can be seen in Figure 16.1.

When the player then taps the screen, he is asked to enter his name, which is shown in Figure 16.2.

Figure 16.1   Game Over screen in *Sir Lamorak's Quest.*

Figure 16.2   Name entry screen.

If the user presses the Dismiss button, the score is thrown away and not recorded. If he enters a name, the current date and time, score, game time, and whether he won or lost is recorded.

Listing 16.7 shows the `alertView:clickedButtonAtIndex:` method used to capture input from the player.

Listing 16.7   **GameScene alertView:clickedButtonAtIndex: Method**

```
- (void)alertView:(UIAlertView*)alertView clickedButtonAtIndex:(NSInteger)buttonIndex {

    UITextField *nameField = (UITextField *)[alertView viewWithTag:99];

// If the OK button is pressed then set the playersname
    if (buttonIndex == 1) {
       playersName = nameField.text;
         if ([playersName length] == 0)
           playersName = @"No Name Given";

        if (playersName) {
           BOOL won = NO;
            if (state == kSceneState_GameCompleted)
              won = YES;
           [sharedGameController addToHighScores:score
               gameTime:gameTimeToDisplay
               playersName:playersName didWin:won];
        }
    }

    [nameField resignFirstResponder];

    state = kSceneState_TransitionOut;
}
```

> **Note**
>
> I chose to use an arbitrary number for the tag value given to the `UITextField`. Feel free to use another number, if you'd like.

This method is the delegate method for the `UIAlertView`. When the game is over or completed and the user touches the screen, a new `UIAlertView` is created in the `touchesBegan:withEvent:` method in `GameScene`. This creates an alert view with the necessary controls, including a text box, and positions it onscreen so the keyboard will not cover it.

It also sets its delegate to `self`, and it's the `alertView:clickedButtonAtIndex:` method that is called when any buttons are pressed.

The first activity the method performs is to grab a reference to the `UITextField` that was placed on the alert view. A check is then performed on the `buttonIndex` to see which one was pressed. Button index 1 means the OK button was pressed. If that is the case, the text is taken from the text field and its length is checked. If the length is 0, then a default name is set.

The next step is to save the high score information. This is done by calling the `addToHighScores:gameTime:playersName:didWin:` method in `GameController`. The information provided in this method call is taken from the values in `GameScene`.

The text field responder is then resigned, any saved game state is deleted, and the scene is set to transition out, back to the main menu.

Adding a Score

Listing 16.8 shows the method inside `GameController` that adds a score to the high score list.

Listing 16.8   GameController addToHighScores:gameTime:playersName:didWin: Method

```
- (void)addToHighScores:(int)aScore gameTime:(NSString*)aGameTime
      playersName:(NSString*)aPlayerName didWin:(BOOL)aDidWin {
   Score *score = [[Score alloc] initWithScore:aScore gameTime:aGameTime
      playersName:aPlayerName didWin:aDidWin];
   [unsortedHighScores addObject:score];
   [score release];
   [self saveHighScores];
   [self sortHighScores];
}
```

This method creates a new instance of the `Score` class, which can be found in the *Game Scene > Menu* group of the project. The **Score** class is used to store the information we want to record about the players score, including the following:

- The player's name
- Date and time the score occurred

- Duration of the game
- Score

It also implements the NSCoding protocol so that it can encode and decode itself. This is how we are going to save the information to disk.

The GameController class has an instance variable called unsortedHighScores. This NSMutableArray stores the instances of **Score** that have been loaded when the game started and those created during game play.

After the new **Score** instance has been added, the contents of the array are saved and then sorted. Sorting the array is done using the sortHighScores array, as shown in Listing 16.9.

Listing 16.9   GameController sortHighScores Method

```
- (void)sortHighScores {

    NSSortDescriptor *scoreSortDescriptor = [[[NSSortDescriptor alloc]
        initWithKey:@"score" ascending:NO] autorelease];
    NSSortDescriptor *dateSortDescriptor = [[[NSSortDescriptor alloc]
        initWithKey:@"dateTime" ascending:NO] autorelease];
    NSArray *sortDescriptors = [NSArray
        arrayWithObjects:scoreSortDescriptor,
        dateSortDescriptor, nil];

    [highScores release];
    highScores = [[unsortedHighScores
        sortedArrayUsingDescriptors:sortDescriptors]
        retain];
}
```

This method makes use of the NSSortDescriptor class to create a sort descriptor on the properties of the Score object. This is a simple way to sort arrays. Two sort descriptors are recreated: one on the score, and the other on the date and time. These are added to an NSArray. The order of the sort descriptors in the array defines the order in which they are applied to the objects.

The highScores array is then released, and is ready to be populated with a new sorted list of high scores. Sorting the unsortedHighScores array is done using the sortedArrayUsingDescriptors: method.

That's it; we now have a sorted array of scores. It is the highScores array that is accessed from within the **HighScoreViewController** class and used to feed the UITableView.

Saving High Scores

The method to save the scores is exactly the same as saving the game state. The **Score** class implements the NSCoding protocol and the saveHighScores method in GameController is used to archive the contents of unsortedHighScores to disk, as shown in Listing 16.10.

Listing 16.10   **GameController saveHighScores Method**

```
- (void)saveHighScores {
    NSArray *paths =
NSSearchPathForDirectoriesInDomains(NSDocumentDirectory,
        NSUserDomainMask, YES);
    NSString *documentsDirectory = [paths objectAtIndex:0];
    NSString *scoresPath = [documentsDirectory
        stringByAppendingPathComponent:@"highScores.dat"];

    NSMutableData *scores;
    NSKeyedArchiver *encoder;
    scores = [NSMutableData data];
    encoder = [[NSKeyedArchiver alloc]
        initForWritingWithMutableData:scores];

    [encoder encodeObject:unsortedHighScores forKey:@"highScores"];

    [encoder finishEncoding];
    [scores writeToFile:scoresPath atomically:YES];
    [encoder release];
}
```

Loading High Scores

Loading the high scores when the game starts is just as simple as saving them. Listing 16.11 shows the loadHighScores method inside the GameController.

Listing 16.11   **GameController loadHighScores Method**

```
- (void)loadHighScores {
    NSArray *paths =
        NSSearchPathForDirectoriesInDomains(NSDocumentDirectory,
        NSUserDomainMask, YES);
    NSString *documentsDirectory = [paths objectAtIndex:0];

    NSMutableData *highScoresData;
    NSKeyedUnarchiver *decoder;

    NSString *documentPath = [documentsDirectory
        stringByAppendingPathComponent:@"highScores.dat"];
    highScoresData = [NSData dataWithContentsOfFile:documentPath];

    if (highScoresData) {
        decoder = [[NSKeyedUnarchiver alloc]
            initForReadingWithData:highScoresData];
        unsortedHighScores = [[decoder
            decodeObjectForKey:@"highScores"]
            retain];
```

```
        [decoder release];
    } else {
        unsortedHighScores = [[NSMutableArray alloc] init];
    }

    [self sortHighScores];
}
```

When the **GameController** is first initialized, any high scores are loaded. From that point, the unsortedHighScores array is managed by **GameController** and then saved back to disk when new scores are added.

Performance and Tuning

When writing software for a mobile device, such as the iPhone or iPad, it's important to make the best use possible of the resources you have available. This is where Instruments (located in */Developer/Applications*) can be used. Instruments provides a number of really helpful tools that can be used to monitor different aspects of your application, including the following:

- Object allocations
- Memory leaks
- OpenGL ES
- CPU

These Instruments are great for tracking down performance issues or memory leaks within your application.

I first started using Instruments when I was testing the ImageRenderManager class. I wanted to see how much I was using the GPU. The **OpenGL ES** instrument is perfect for checking to see how the GPU is being used, and it enables you to spot where you may need to make changes.

Another instrument I regularly use is **Leaks**. This instrument enables you to see leaks within your code and track down where they are. Leaks are caused when your application loses track of memory that it has asked the OS to allocate. If you remove or overwrite a pointer to a block of memory, there is no way to then be able to free the memory and return it to the OS. Therefore, you have leaked this memory. It's basically telling you that spending hours optimizing code, before you even know that it needs to be optimized, can delay projects; this can also result in complicated and difficult-to-understand code.

Tip

Something I keep in mind while developing is a saying that my old computer science teacher told my class many years ago: *"Premature optimization is the root of all evil."* He was not the one to coin that phrase, but it has stuck with me over the years.

Optimizing your application, especially a game, is important, but it should be done on the basis of evidence (that is, profiling) and an obvious need, not just because a piece of code looks like it may be slow.

There are areas in *Sir Lamorak's Quest* that I believe can be optimized—making more use of C functions rather than Objective-C methods, for example, could further optimize the particle system. Having said that, the game runs fine on all the different iPhone platforms currently available, so I felt no need to complicate the code further by introducing more optimizations in that area.

When it comes to finding the bottlenecks in your code, Instruments can help.

This section is not intended as a complete guide to using Instruments; rather, it's intended as a primer to let you see the kind of checks that can be made using Instruments and how to get information about the most common areas of interest (for example, OpenGL ES, CPU, and memory).

Using Instruments

Using Instruments could not be easier. With your project open in Xcode, select *Run > Run With Performance Tool* in Xcode's menu bar. This brings up a list of template instrument configurations, as shown in Figure 16.3.

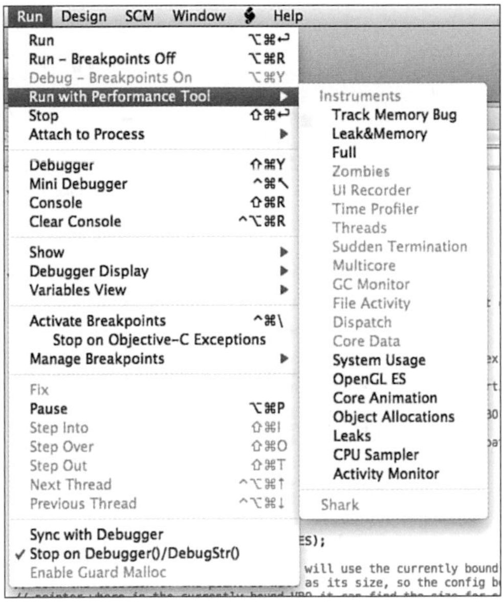

Figure 16.3   Selecting a template instrument in Xcode.

There are a number of different templates, including a few that I created myself (that is, Track Memory Bug, Leak&Memory, and Full). You can add as many instrument templates in Instruments as you need. After you have added and configured your instruments, you can save it as a template so it shows up in the list in Xcode.

> **Note**
>
> The existing templates contain a number of different instruments already in place that you can immediately put to use .

Leaks Instrument

Selecting the Leaks instrument starts the Instruments application using that template. It also runs the current project in the iPhone Simulator or on the iPhone, depending on which you have selected. Figure 16.4 shows Instruments when the Leaks template is selected.

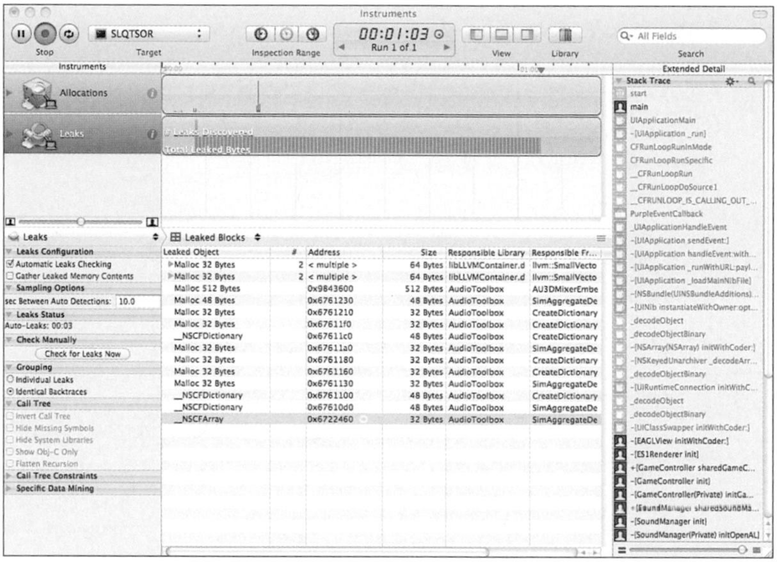

Figure 16.4   Instruments running the Leaks template on SLQTSOR.

The top of the interface shows the graphical view of object allocations that are being made. The spike that can be seen is when *Sir Lamorak's Quest* starts creating new objects and allocating space for images and sprite sheets.

The second graphical view is the leaks that have been found. The brown bar identifies how many leaks have been found, and the blue bars represent the total amount of leaked memory. The Leaks instrument has been selected, and you can therefore see in the bottom panel the leaks that have been found.

Notice that not all leaks come from your own application. If you look at the *Responsible Library* column, you see that none of them are *SLQTSOR*—they are all Apple frameworks. Even Apple's code has leaks, and there is not much you can do about those. You'll also find that you get different libraries reporting leaks on the iPhone Simulator as you do on the iPhone. I have had instances where the iPhone Simulator reports no leaks, but the same testing on the iPhone does identify leaks.

Tip

Nothing beats testing your application on a real device. The iPhone Simulator is just that—a simulator (not an emulator). The performance on the iPhone Simulator is nothing like that on an actual iPhone. For best results, you really must test your application on different iPhone devices. Getting friends and family to beta test can help with this, and that's a topic we cover later in this chapter.

To demonstrate how a simple leak can be tracked down, open the project called `Leak`. This is a simple iPhone app that writes a couple of lines to the log file; nothing will be displayed in the iPhone Simulator apart from a grey screen.

In Xcode's menu, select *Run > Run With Performance Tool*, and then select the Leaks templates. The Leaks instrument appears, and the application starts to run on the iPhone. Figure 16.5 shows Instruments running the Leaks instrument.

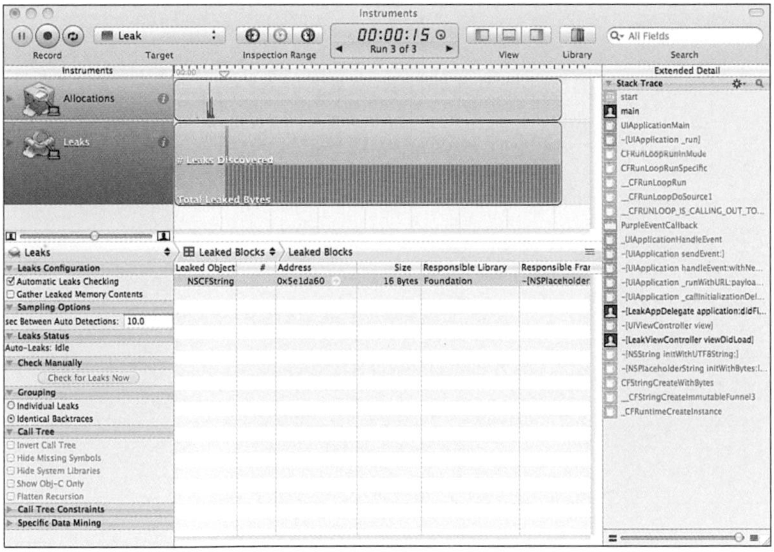

Figure 16.5   Instruments running the Leaks instrument.

You'll notice that, after a few seconds, the Leaks instrument shows that leaks have been discovered and the total leaked byte count. At this point, press the Stop button so you can start to track down the leak.

Make sure that the Leaks instrument is highlighted. This provides you with a list of leaked objects in the middle panel, as shown in Figure 16.5. Also, make sure that the extended detail view is enabled. Figure 16.6 shows the options that should be enabled at the top of the Instruments GUI.

Figure 16.6   Leaked block view and extended detail view enabled.

The extended detail view is really useful because this can show you where in your code the leak was detected. Select the leak, and on the right side in the extended detail view, you will see the stack trace to the point where the application leaked memory. Look for the last mention of the application; all stack entries related to your application will have the logo of a person to show they are entries from your app, not a framework or iOS.

The code where the leak was detected **will not** be shown in Instruments' center panel, as shown in Figure 16.7.

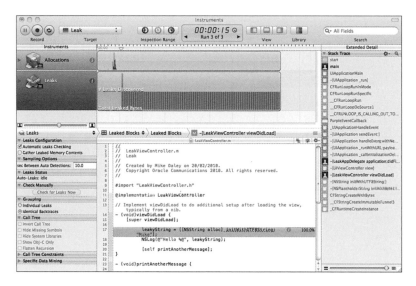

Figure 16.7   Code highlighted that has leaked.

You can see that the line in the `viewDidLoad:` that allocates a new string has been highlighted, along with the number of bytes that have leaked. Although Instruments has been able to tell you where it found a leak, it can't tell you why the leak is occurred. This requires some investigation on your part.

It should not be too hard to spot that we are allocating `leakyString` in the `viewDidLoad:` method and then again in the `printAnotherMessage:` method without releasing the already allocated string. This means the pointer to that first string is going to be lost—we can't release the memory, therefore creating a leak.

Add the following two lines of code in front of the string allocation in the `printAnotherString:` method:

```
if (leakyString)
    [leakyString release];
```

This simply releases `leakyString` before allocating it again if it has already been allocated.

Now recompile the application, run it in the iPhone Simulator, and then hit the Record button in Instruments. This time, no leak should be found and nothing should show up in Instruments' Leaks instrument.

Although Instruments could point to the leak, it probably won't tell you why it was leaking. This could be elsewhere in the code, and with a more complex application; it can take a while to track these down. A good approach to avoiding leaks is to identify where an object should be sent a `release` or `autorelease` message as soon as you have written the `alloc` for that object. This reduces the chances of forgetting that you have allocated an object and will need to release it later. It's also a good idea to run the Build and Analyze function within Xcode. This will point you to locations that the compiler thinks a leak will occur.

Using the OpenGL ES Instrument

The OpenGL ES instrument enables you to monitor the usage of the GPU as well as see the CPU usage. This is useful because you can monitor for drops in OpenGL ES frame rate and see if there is a corresponding spike in CPU usage. Although this instrument can't tell you what you may be doing wrong, it can at least point you in the right direction.

> **Note**
>
> The OpenGL ES instrument is available only when running your application on a real device; it can't be used when running in the iPhone Simulator.

Load the *SLQTSOR* project and then run the OpenGL ES instruments template. After *Sir Lamorak's Quest* is running on your iPhone, start playing a new game. Once in the game screen, move back to Instruments, as shown in Figure 16.8.

The top instrument provides details of what OpenGL ES is doing. Clicking the Inspector button (the one with the "i" on it) enables you to configure the information that each instrument is showing. If you don't see the same information shown in Figure 16.8, click the Inspector button again and select the information you want to see.

A detailed table view of this information can also be seen at the bottom of the window. I usually change the sort order of the sample number, which is the first column in the table. This keeps the latest sample at the top of the table while the game is running.

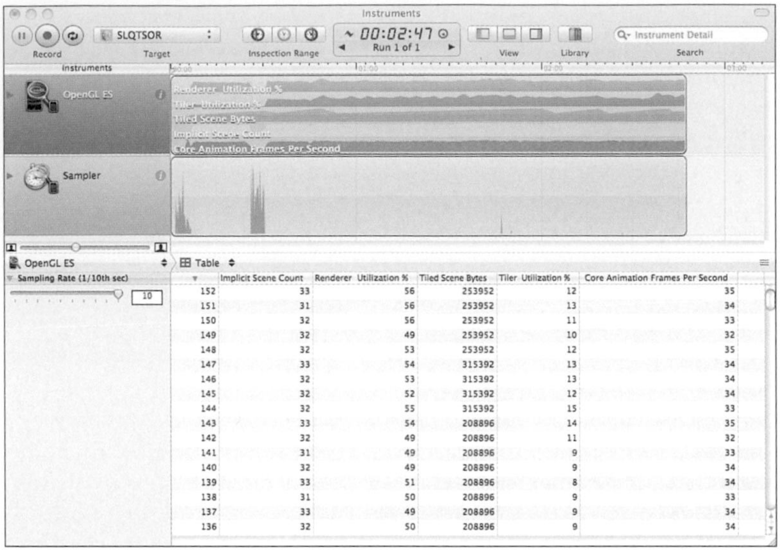

Figure 16.8   OpenGL ES instrument monitoring SLQTSOR running on an iPod 2G using iOS 4.

> **Note**
>
> The table lets you see the Implicit Scene Count, Renderer Utilization, Resource Bytes, Tiler Utilization and Core Animation Frames Per Second. It can take a while to get used to what you are looking at, but the ones I use most often are Renderer Utilization and Frames Per Second.

The table in Figure 16.8 shows that the OpenGL ES renderer is running at between 50 and 60 percent. This is a reasonable figure and means we have some headroom if a scene was to get busy with a lot of particle effects or a larger number of sprites being rendered. If you were constantly running at near to 100 percent then some optimization may be necessary if the game tends to slow down when things get busy with a lot of objects on the screen.

One area that can really push up the amount of work the GPU is doing is blending. Blending images into a scene using transparency puts a lot more load on the GPU. It's always a good idea to try to reduce the amount of blending e.g. transparency you have in a scene.

The second instrument in this template is a sampler. This records the CPU activity alongside OpenGL ES. This is useful if you spot a frame rate drop and a CPU spike at the same time. Identifying the code that is causing the CPU spike is relatively easy to track down.

Moving the tracking head along the time line at the top of the window enables you to select a spike on the CPU chart. Once selected, and with the sampler instrument highlighted, the sample associated with the spike is shown in the detail pane. With the Extended Detail View window visible, you can again see the stack track at that point in time.

If you double-click the first entry for the application in the stack trace, you will be taken to the code that was running, causing the high CPU usage. Figure 16.9 shows the code associated with a spike.

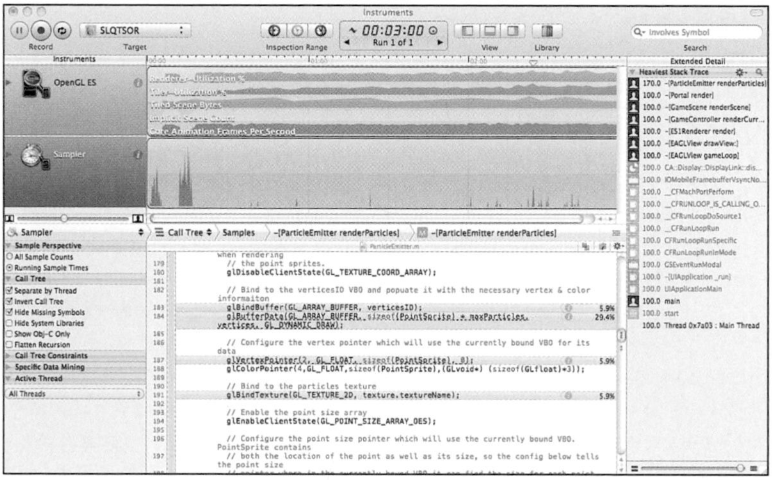

Figure 16.9   Code associated with a spike.

The great thing about this view is that it provides you with information on the amount of time, as a percentage, spent on commands within the code. In the example shown here, the `glBufferData` command is taking up 29.4 percent of the time in this class. Given that this command is copying the vertex information into a VBO before rendering, this would make sense.

Armed with this kind of information, you can start to track down code that is causing the spikes and work out strategies to improve performance. However, getting a spike does not mean that you need to fix something. As with *Sir Lamorak's Quest*, if the game is running fine with no noticeable slow downs, there is nothing to fix.

Compiling for Thumb

There is an easy way to gain a huge performance increase in your game without doing any work at all. The ARM processor used by the iPhone processes floating-point instructions natively. Therefore, you should make sure you use floating-point math whenever possible. By default, your project's build settings are set to compile using Thumb.[1] This stops the iPhone from using its native floating-point support.

---

[1] Learn more about Thumb and floating-point math as it pertains to the ARM architecture: **en. wikipedia.org/wiki/ARM_architecture#Thumb**.

Given that most games perform a *lot* of float-point math, this is bad thing. Disabling the Compile for Thumb option in the build settings of your project normally provides a significant performance increase.

Beta Testing

With the finishing touches added to the game, leaks tracked down, and acceptable performance, it's time to release your creation to a wider audience.

Beta testing an important part of your game's life cycle to the App Store. You may have been playing it for months during development and testing, and are now very familiar with all its features and functions. This can lead to a biased test plan, where you unknowingly don't press it too hard in areas that are a little weak.

Getting your application into the hands of others is a great way for the game to be tested by people who have no prior knowledge and will bash it into submission.

I wanted *Sir Lamorak's Quest* to be a polished game, not just a small example app to go with the book. This meant that when I was almost finished, I wanted to make sure there were no areas of weakness and also that the game itself played right.

Using my blog (**www.71squared.co.uk**), I put out a request for 10 people who would like to beta test *Sir Lamorak's Quest*. To my delight, I had all 10 within a matter of hours, which was fantastic. If you don't have a blog, you can use family and friends who have iPhone devices or even put a shout out on popular forums, such as iDevGames (**www.iDevGames.com**) or the **#iPhoneDev** IRC channel.

It's important to make sure the testers know what it is you want them to do and how to report back to you. It's also good to define a timeline when you would like the feedback to keep things moving forward.

You also want to make sure that the beta testers have a range of devices. If your game is designed to work on all devices, you really need to make sure it has been tested on *all* devices. This also means you don't need to own all the different devices yourself.

> **Tip**
>
> Although you can obtain the UDID of your device in Xcode, your beta testers might not have the developer tools installed or know how to obtain their device's UDID. There are a number of apps on the App Store that your would-be testers can use to collect and send their UDID to you via email. Just ask them to open iTunes, go to the App Store, and have them search on "UDID." They can then select one of the many free apps out there. It is also worth noting that these work on the iPad, too.

The UDID is a unique number that each iPhone, iPod Touch, or iPad has. With this, you can create an ad-hoc distribution profile and certificate that enables you to send the certificate and an ad-hoc build of your game directly to a tester, without going through the App Store.

At this point, it is worth noting that you cannot create these profiles or certificates unless you are a paid-up member of the developer program. More details about this can be found on the iPhone Development Center (**developer.apple.com/iphone**).

The process for creating provisioning profiles and certificates can be very daunting at first, but working through the wizards and documents available on the iPhone Dev Center will get you up to speed.

Multiple Device Types

One of the key benefits of using beta testers is that you can get your game tested across a number of different devices. This is important to make sure that performance and game play are consistent and that there are no specific device issues.

While beta testing *Sir Lamorak's Quest*, a tester (actually, my editor, Chuck) spotted an odd light anomaly appearing onscreen, like a white flash. He reported this via email, copying the other testers. After doing so, a couple more testers said they were seeing the same issue, whereas others reported no such anomaly.

After a little research, it became obvious that the people spotting the flashes were running *Sir Lamorak's Quest* on the iPhone 3GS. After more email exchanges to try to tie down the area where the flashes were being seen, the problem was traced back to the particle system. There were situations when the size of a point sprite fell below 0. This caused these flashes on the iPhone 3GS to render, while nothing happened on other iPod Touch or iPhone models. The fix was to simply make sure that point sizes were never smaller than 0 (that is, a negative number).

Without beta testing, I would never have spotted that because I didn't have an iPhone 3GS, and the flashes weren't showing up in the iPhone Simulator. Without proper testing, *Sir Lamorak's Quest* could have released with a nasty-looking bug.

It is also worth making sure that the final version of your game is working before compiling a release version and sending it up to the App Store. I had completed all the testing on *Sir Lamorak's Quest* and was ready to send it up for approval. I did, however, perform one more cleanup to remove old graphics assets I was not using. I compiled and ran the game it worked fine so I sent it up for approval.

The game was approved and appeared on the store about seven days later. Within hours, though, I had feedback that the game did not work, that the player was either stuck to the spot or there were not entities or objects in the map. I was really confused given all the testing that had been done.

I went back to the code and ran the project, again, everything was fine. So, I performed a clean on the project and ran it again, and—boom—I saw the exact problem the users were seeing. I spent a couple of hours tracking the problem that turned to be a missing graphics file that I had removed during my cleanup. The missing file was causing the code in the game to execute in an odd way due to a failure in loading this image. This in turn caused the issues the users were seeing with the game. I replaced the graphic, cleaned the project, and ran it again, and again and again, cleaning and running all the time until I was happy that it really was OK. I sent up this new version and, within a few days, version 1.1 was on the App Store and all was well.

This story really shows that you must test to make sure your final build really is stable and that nothing has changed.

Feedback

Beta testers can also provide great feedback around the actual game design itself. *Sir Lamorak's Quest* received great feedback on the look and style of the HUD in the game. The original, shown in Figure 16.10, was seen as being too big and taking up too much screen space.

Figure 16.10   *Sir Lamorak's Quest's* original HUD.

This can be a balance of personal preference. If a single person from a group of ten doesn't like something, it doesn't mean that it's wrong. I had over half of the testers mention that the HUD was too big. As a result, I decided that it needed to change.

Other feedback received was around the look of the fonts being used, difficulty in getting through doors, clipping of game characters under the door images, suspending the device was not pausing the game, and the list went on.

My overall feeling after the first round of beta testing had been completed was that the game was much more stable and polished, all because of the feedback from the beta testers. Without sharing the game with others, I don't feel the game would have been as solid as it is, even with all the testing I performed myself.

Summary

This brings us to the end of this book. We have been on a long journey, covering many different aspects of developing an OpenGL ES game on the iPhone, and I hope you've enjoyed it as much as I have creating the game and writing this book.

The concepts and technologies we have reviewed throughout this book should give you the foundations needed to create your own games and extend your knowledge further. The game engine that we have developed throughout this book that is being used for *Sir Lamorak's Quest* is only one approach. As with most things in software development, there are an almost infinite number of ways to solve the problems associated with writing a game.

Having looked at the details of implementing a complete game, you may now decide that you'll make use of third-party frameworks to develop your own game. There are open source frameworks, as follows:

- Cocos2D iPhone, a 2D Engine (**www.cocos2d-iPhone.org)**
- Oolong, a 3D Engine (**code.google.com/p/oolongengine)**
- Sio2Engine, a 3D Engine (**www.sio2interactive.com)**

There are also commercial engines:

- Torque, a 2D/3D Engine (**www.torquepowered.com**)
- Bork3D, a 3D Engine (**bork3d.com/engine**)
- ShiVa 3D, a 3D Engine (**www.stonetrip.com**)
- Unity3D, a 3D Engine (**www.unity3d.com**)

Having an understanding of what is going on "under the hood" helps make the best use of these game engines, especially the open source engines that you can open up and examine.

Creating my own engine for *Sir Lamorak's Quest* was both a frustrating and rewarding experience. I learned so much while tackling the problems encountered when creating my own game engine; I don't believe I would have learned as much by using someone else's framework. I can certainly see myself writing more game engines in the future, continuing to tweak them and improve them as I go.

So, all that is left is for me to wish you luck in your future game writing projects and that I hope what you have learned from this book will accelerate your learning and interest in game development on the iPhone platform. There is certainly more innovation happening on this platform than almost any other at the moment and now is a great time to be part of that revolution.

When you do create the next big thing, be sure to let me know, as I really enjoy playing other people's games.

Index

T

Essential Resources for
Mac, iPhone, and iPad Developers

Developer's Library

ESSENTIAL REFERENCES FOR PROGRAMMING PROFESSIONALS

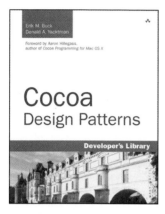

Cocoa Design Patterns

Erik M. Buck
Donald A. Yacktman

ISBN-13: 978-0-321-53502-3

The iPhone™ Developer's Cookbook, Second Edition

Erica Sadun

ISBN-13: 978-0-321-65957-6

Programming in Objective-C 2.0, Second Edition

Stephen G. Kochan

ISBN-13: 978-0-321-56615-7

Other Developer's Library Titles

TITLE	AUTHOR	ISBN-13
Android Wireless Application Development	Shane Conder / Lauren Darcey	978-0-321-62709-4
Cocoa® Programming Developer's Handbook	David Chisnall	978-0-321-63963-9
Developing Hybrid Applications for the iPhone	Lee S. Barney	978-0-321-60416-3
PHP and MySQL® Web Development, Fourth Edition	Luke Welling / Laura Thomson	978-0-672-32916-6

Developer's Library books are available at most retail and online bookstores. For more information or to order direct, visit our online bookstore at **informit.com/store**.

Online editions of all Developer's Library titles are available by subscription from Safari Books Online at **safari.informit.com**.

Addison
Wesley

Developer's Library

informit.com/devlibrary

FREE Online Edition

Your purchase of **Learning iOS Game Programming** includes access to a free online edition for 45 days through the Safari Books Online subscription service. Nearly every Addison-Wesley Professional book is available online through Safari Books Online, along with more than 5,000 other technical books and videos from publishers such as Cisco Press, Exam Cram, IBM Press, O'Reilly, Prentice Hall, Que, and Sams.

SAFARI BOOKS ONLINE allows you to search for a specific answer, cut and paste code, download chapters, and stay current with emerging technologies.

Activate your FREE Online Edition at www.informit.com/safarifree

> **STEP 1:** Enter the coupon code: USCQFDB.

> **STEP 2:** New Safari users, complete the brief registration form.
> Safari subscribers, just log in.

If you have difficulty registering on Safari or accessing the online edition, please e-mail customer-service@safaribooksonline.com